# City Voices

# CITY VOICES

## HONG KONG WRITING
## IN ENGLISH
## 1945 to the Present

Edited by Xu Xi and Mike Ingham
with a foreword by Louise Ho

香港大學出版社
HONG KONG UNIVERSITY PRESS

**Hong Kong University Press**
14/F Hing Wai Centre
7 Tin Wan Praya Road
Aberdeen
Hong Kong

© Hong Kong University Press 2003

ISBN 962 209 604 2 (Hardback)
ISBN 962 209 605 0 (Paperback)

British Library Cataloguing-in-Publication Data
A CIP catalogue record for this book is available from the British Library.

Secure On-line Ordering
http://www.hkupress.org

Printed and bound by Kings Time Printing Press, Hong Kong, China.

# Contents

# POETRY                                                          239

### Sixties

### Seventies

### Eighties

### Nineties

# Foreword

*Louise Ho*

At a literary conference held in Downing College, Cambridge, in 1999, Salman Rushdie held forth expansively on cosmpolitanism, speaking very much as a cosmopolitan himself. Following on from him spoke a well-respected Welsh poet who claimed 'the local' versus 'the global' as his fortified ground, saying, 'I am very conscious of being aboriginal.' Being Welsh, he would be so privileged! I felt very envious of his staunch avowal of his sense of belonging. Later on, I gave a mini-reading of my work and I was very conscious of speaking from Hong Kong; but, although I was sent there by the British Council as a Hong Kong delegate, I felt I could only represent my puny self.

Those of us writing in the English language in Hong Kong would know the feeling of isolation, perhaps of functioning in a void. There is no English-language literary community from which to draw some kind of affinity or against which to react. There is insufficient writing in English here for a critical mass to have formed. The literary traditions that do exist in Hong Kong are, obviously, those of the Chinese language. For us, it is a case of *chacun pour soi*, in that we each carry a culturally different baggage from the start; and presumably, we each work according to some implied tradition and critical standard of one's own adherence.

Thanks to Xu Xi and her entrepreneurial zest, here is a sampling of fiction, non-fiction and poetry put together between two covers, thus making what there exists accessible and tangible. There have been other anthologies; a few come to mind. *Images on Water,* edited by Joyce Hsia and T. C. Lai was an anthology of Hong Kong English poems that came out in the 1970s; and true to its title, it has disappeared with the water. Mimi Chan brought out *A Traveller's Literary Companion to South-east Asia* in the 1980s, and it included fiction and poetry. More recently, Andrew Parkin, who held poetry readings at the Chinese University of Hong Kong with offerings in Chinese and English, brought out *From the Bluest Part of the Harbour* in the 1990s; this was mainly a book of Chinese poems translated into English.

In the Introduction to *The Penguin Book of Contemporary British Poetry* (1982), the editors, Blake Morrison and Andrew Motion, locate themselves within the contemporary tradition of poetry anthologies in order to trace a line of continuity and development in British poetry. They go back to the first 'Georgian' anthology, edited by Edward Marsh (1912), to the 'Imagist' anthologies (1914, 1915), to Michael Roberts's 'New Signatures' (1932), to Robert Conquest's 'New Lines' (1956), and most importantly, to its immediate predecessor, A. Alvarez's 'The New Poetry' (1962). I quote from their introduction: 'The word "new" is conspicuous in all these titles, and making it new is the oldest of anthologists' arts.' With the present anthology, there is no need to make anything 'new'; it is new. Unhampered by any substantial predecessor, it has the field to itself; it can even afford to be experimental. Hopefully, this volume will do at least two things: become a node for future anthologies to grow from and a stimulus for the reading and writing of Hong Kong literature in English.

As Hong Kong Writers of English, we are loosely held together by the federation language of English: a multifarious tongue extending from old worlds to new worlds; from varieties of culture and language even within England itself; each speaking in its own way, the 'dialect of the tribe'. There will be echoes from Shakespeare, Donne, Eliot, Yeats; resonances from African and Indian writers; interesting inventiveness from Singaporean English; perhaps even a nascent kind of Hong Kong English. Now that we are using the English language, we would want to compete with the best users of that language among the living and the dead. To quote Pound, we might 'gather from the air a live tradition', and then ground it in our own soil? We begin with the global, then concentrate on the local.

Our land and space must mean very different things in Hong Kong from what they mean generally, as both are densely compacted into an international, cosmopolitan city. The wilderness is very much there, but Hong Kong is mainly known for its urban parts, a community that is constantly changing and endlessly varied. Hong Kong is also dense with history, from the pre-historic through the many changing Chinese dynasties, to its present position as a world financial centre where international routes interweave on a daily basis. What more can a writer ask for the stimulus of the new and the notable?

Xu Xi's selection of prose and poetry will serve Hong Kong well, presenting a wide spectrum of works, from the most established through to the least; from a voice of the canon, Edmund Blunden, to neophytes among students. Page upon page, turn upon turn, the prismatic colours and images build up our city, rising with and above the material one: they too give Hong Kong 'a local habitation and a name'.

Please allow me to quote at length from Derek Walcott in his Nobel Prize lecture of 1992: 'There is a force of exultation, a celebration of luck, when a writer finds himself a witness to the early morning of a culture that is defining itself, branch by branch, leaf by leaf, in that self-defining dawn, which is why, especially at the edge of the sea, it is good to make a ritual of the sunrise. Then the noun, the "Antilles" ripples like brightening water, and the sounds of leaves, palm fronds, and birds are the sounds of a fresh dialect, the native tongue. The personal vocabulary, the individual melody whose metre is one's biography, joins in that sound, with any luck, and the body moves like a walking, a waking island . . . This is the benediction that is celebrated, a fresh language and a fresh people, and this is the frightening duty owed.'

Isn't that an immense celebration of an 'aboriginality' that is of one's own making? Change the word 'Antilles' into Hong Kong, and we find ourselves a direction and a programme.

# Acknowledgements

During the three-and-a-half years it took to compile and complete this anthology, there were those who were generous in their early support, when this publication was only a delirium of my feverish imagination. I am grateful to Kingsley Bolton, Mimi Chan and Colin Day for their belief in the value of this effort. Without them, *City Voices* would never have existed.

Appreciative words are due to many who offered inspiration, discourse, source materials and contacts to authors, but especially the Asian American Writers Workshop and the Asian Canadian Writers Workshop, Martha Cheung, Eva Hung, Agnes Lam, Shirley Geok-Lin Lim, Leung Ping-kwan, David Parker, Bino Realuyo, Page Richards, Madeleine Marie Slavick, Elizabeth Walker and Shawn Wong.

Thank you to all the publishers and authors who granted permission in the spirit of this educational endeavour, especially Asia 2000 Ltd.; Chameleon Press; the estates of Edmund Blunden, Joyce Booth and Yang Yi Lung (John D. Young); Heinemann; C.Y. Lee, Liu Tai-Yi; Timothy Mo; Pegasus Books; Ronsdale Press and Ed Victor, Ltd. Thanks also to David Clarke and Colin Day who offered use of their photos for the cover.

All effort was made to contact and obtain permission from the known rights holders of the reprinted work included in this anthology, most of which first appeared in other published forms. We trust that the few who did not respond to our attempt to reach them will appreciate the spirit in which the Press has included their work.

Recognition is due to Clara Ho of Hong Kong University Press for her extraordinary calm and professionalism in the face of a massive production effort.

Finally, a debt of gratitude is owed to Mike Ingham, Mina Kumar and Louise Ho who aided and abetted in leading the delirium towards sanity.

Xu Xi
January 2003

Acknowledgements

# Writing on the Margin:
# Hong Kong English Poetry, Fiction and Creative Non-Fiction

*Mike Ingham*

## Background

As recently as the late 1980s the new Head of English at the University of Hong Kong, former Oxford linguist Roy Harris, infamously referred to Hong Kong English as 'the worst in the world' in his provocative inaugural lecture. Whether his more affectionately remembered predecessor, the prolific Oxford poet Edmund Blunden, would have subscribed to Harris's view is a matter of speculation. However, given Blunden's reputation for nurturing Hong Kong creative English writing at the university in the boom period of the 1950s and 1960s, it is highly unlikely he would have approved of Harris's cultural insensitivity. It is thus somewhat ironic that the decade that has passed since Harris delivered his scathing, and in retrospect influential, critique of local English standards has seen an impressive renaissance of Hong Kong creative writing in English, not only to match the seminal work of the Blunden era, but in some respects to surpass it, and lay the foundations for the resilient, albeit marginal, circle of present English-language writers in Hong Kong. It is also ironic, incidentally, that Harris should have co-edited a book on Asian Voices in English, the proceedings of a 1990 conference at the University of Hong Kong, which was characterized by the exclusion of Hong Kong English voices.[1]

Nevertheless, there remains the old nagging doubt about the viability of indigenous or expatriate English-language fiction, poetry and drama. In a community that is approximately 98 percent Cantonese speaking and one that is, in theory at least, post-colonial in consciousness, it is clear that for the population at large and for the burgeoning Chinese-language literary scene, local English writing must be seen at best as an irrelevance, at worst an irritating excrescence generated by the colonial era. Consequently it is curious and perhaps paradoxical that the first literary festival of Asian writers in English in May 2001 saw a resurgence of interest amid an eclectic audience coming to hear talks by a wide range of writers, including Hong Kong-born but UK-based literary heavyweight, Timothy Mo. The 2002 Festival was even more ambitiously conceived and was hailed as a big success by visiting and local participants. The work of local publishers Asia 2000, Chameleon and Hong Kong University Press, as well as the collective efforts of creative writing academics such as Shirley Geok-Lin Lim, Louise Ho, Dino Mahoney and Agnes Lam in promoting this new wave of English writing should not be underestimated. Nury Vittachi's now well-established literary magazine, *dimsum*, has played a vital part in promoting and publishing new material, both prose and poetry, and has a very enlightened approach to selection. Equally significant is the contribution of the Hong Kong Writers' Circle energetically championed by Lawrence Gray and Chinese Indonesian writer, Xu Xi, whose Hong Kong-oriented fiction is *sui generis* and

---

[1]  From the conference proceedings, *Asian Voices in English*, 1991, Hong Kong University Press, though not from the conference itself, which was co-organized by the British Council.

frequently challenging to more conservative Hong Kong attitudes and conventions regarding sexuality and femininity.

If the two halves of this literary puzzle do not quite fit together to make a coherent whole, it is scarcely surprising. It is difficult to assess literary movements and developments without the benefit of hindsight. When respected Hong Kong University academic Mimi Chan (whose semi-fictionalized memoir entitled *All the King's Women* is featured in this anthology) wrote her authoritative account of the Hong Kong literary scene in English for the *Routledge Encyclopedia of Post-colonial Fiction* and *Travellers' Literary Companion to South-east Asia* more than ten years ago, the majority of works represented in the present anthology had neither been written nor alluded to on grounds of their obscurity. The forerunners of the present crop of Hong Kong English writers such as Han Suyin (*A Many Spendored Thing*), Lin Tai-Yi (*Kampoon Street*) and others, as well as the already established Timothy Mo are featured together with an earlier generation of expatriate writers, of whom Blunden was the most pre-eminent. More space was allotted, however, to internationally-known popular authors such as James Clavell (*Taipan*), Richard Mason (*The World of Suzie Wong*) and John Le Carre (*The Honourable Schoolboy*), whose use of Hong Kong milieux for ambience and local colour in their work had inevitably presented limited and stereotypical facets of the territory's existence.

Based on the extracts and full pieces included in this first anthology of Hong Kong fiction and poetry in English and featuring around seventy authors, it would appear to be the case that a newer type of writing voice has been struggling to assert itself in the past decade or so. The contemporary boom in English writing can trace its roots back to Han Suyin and her successors, but ultimately it is more preoccupied with post-colonial and post-modern uncertainty and angst. In her insightful collection of stories, *History's Fiction*, Xu Xi has charted the changes over the past four decades in Hong Kong as they have affected the lives of ordinary people. The decade-by-decade structure of the collection gives a fascinating overview of Hong Kong life at various stages of development from the 1960s to the present, much as the films of Wong Kar-wai have done in a different medium. As is often the case with this type of writing, it is suffused with a deeply ingrained sense of autobiographical experience, beautifully transposed into the realms of imaginative fiction. Indeed, this strain of autobiographical writing has been evident in much Hong Kong English fiction from Han Suyin and Richard Mason onward, but it is important to make a distinction between this more imaginative semi-autobiographical work and the straight memoir form as popularized by Jung Chang, Adeline Yen Mah and others, which has found such a lucrative niche market in the West.

## Finding a Voice: Short Fiction or the Novel?

Thus, whilst it is true for Hong Kong English writers that we cannot expect to know who we are or where we are going, without knowing where we have come from, there is a clearly discernible focus on the here and now, which contrasts starkly with the orientation of Timothy Mo's *magnum opus* on Hong Kong's transformation into a colony, *An Insular Possession* (1986). Mo has of course been resident in Britain since the age of ten, and in much of his writing related to Hong Kong, particularly *The Monkey King* (1978) and *Renegade or Halo*[2] (2000), there is a sense of critical distance, almost alienation, somewhat akin to Kazuo Ishiguro's writing on Japan.

This question of genealogy also touches on issues of identity, which so-called 'ethnic writers' exiled or simply resident in the West are expected to agonize over at length in their works in the cliché-ridden climate of international book marketing. Interestingly, none of the longer or shorter fiction writers anthologized here indulge in such a deliberately restrictive approach to their creative work. Sexual identity and group identity, in contrast to ethnic identity, are explored as major themes in many of these works. Intercultural aspects of Hong Kong life, marginalization, isolation and the position of the social misfit or outsider are certainly significant themes in this literature. But the idea that a deliberate and crude strategy of exploitation of the hackneyed Asian memoir genre might also work commercially in the Hong Kong context would fortunately be anathema to these Hong Kong writers.

Hence there is a serious problem for these writers in being suitably promoted and reaching a wider audience. If the Hong Kong fiction-reading population is more than adequately served by Chinese-language fiction, not to mention the plethora of other fictions in or translated into English, and the overseas market is trained to appreciate no better than *Wild Swans* and other identikit sob-stories constructing a particular image of 'China', does this necessarily mean that Hong Kong English writers are doomed to a kind of literary twilight zone, struggling to get published and then remaining largely unread and ignored?

That they occupy an extremely marginal position on the periphery of the Hong Kong literary world is hardly surprising, but they may take comfort from the reflection that Hong Kong writing is itself pretty marginal, both in the context of classic and contemporary Chinese writing and of world literatures in English. Thus, if Hong Kong fiction were to achieve its moment of international recognition in the future, it will in all probability be English-language writers who reap the rewards. To come back down to earth again, however, the problem of finding a wider audience outside a narrow circle of intimates remains as acute as ever. Rather like Pirandello's six characters in search of an author in the eponymous play, Hong Kong English fiction is faced with a constant search for a stable readership. If Hong Kong writers are to retain their artistic integrity and avoid the awful fate of becoming Amy Tan clones, they need to write what they wish to, as opposed to what publishers believe the international English fiction-reading public wants.

Avoidance of cliché and essentializing narrative description and characterization must remain the self-appointed task of the Hong Kong English fiction writer, particularly in depicting the elusive and hybrid metropolis itself. The city is characterized by its modernity and Hydra-like multiplicity, but the attempt to fix its reality in representational terms can become as vainly quixotic as that of Calvino's Marco Polo seeking to evoke the melancholy invisible cities of that work's title. It often resists stable and tangible realistic depiction, no matter how well the writer knows the milieu, partly because of a cultural and linguistic divide, which may obstruct vision or more importantly aural perception. In other words, writers in English may see Hong Kong but they cannot always hear it in all its nuances of sound.

Novels by non-Chinese writers such as Christopher New, Martin Booth and Nury Vittachi have attempted to cross what is palpably a cultural divide by evoking a broader social spectrum and a specificity of milieu. Xu Xi's *The Unwalled City* and Simon Elegant's *A Chinese Wedding* also aim to present a more intercultural perspective on Hong Kong in their characterization and setting. By contrast, many ethnically Chinese novelists in English writing about the territory, including Lin Tai-Yi (*Kampoon Street*), Lee Ding Fai (*Running Dog*) and Lily Chan (*Struggles of a Hong Kong Girl*) have preferred to portray the predominant Chinese community and their vicissitudes, from post-war poverty and post-Cultural Revolution insecurity and hardship to greater social stability and economic independence. This sheer diversity of social and literary perspective according to individual authorial experience and point of view offers a rich mosaic of fictionalized Hong Kong life in the last half-century. It is tempting, therefore, to see Hong Kong novels in English as somehow complementary segments of a whole view, simply on account of their salient feature of East-West dichotomies. Such a view would, I believe, be an overly simplistic one. We should guard against the temptation to essentialize and read too much into the phenomenon of the Hong Kong English-language novel. Generically and stylistically they are rather like the short fiction examples we find here, heterogeneous in nature. In other words, they are not conducive to being grouped within the confines of a unifying literary movement.

Perhaps because critics tend to draw trite conclusions and make superficial analogies in order to pigeon-hole novels and place them within an existing framework for the sake of convenience, there is a greater tendency to assign the novel to preconceived categories than is the case with the short story. With novels the reader probably expects similarity, with the short story, difference. Hence, the most striking quality of the short stories anthologized here is their heterogeneity in theme, tone, style and ideology, their fundamental diversity and idiosyncrasy. The scope of authorial vision and expression does not seem to be encapsulated entirely within a framework of social realism. Milieu, characters, social background, temporal setting — all these relatively more concrete and painstaking elements of the Hong Kong English novel — give way to deft, quirky and lightly sketched vignettes, which are necessarily elliptical and evocative. It is not so much what the short story puts in as what it leaves out that makes it so effective. If this dictum is true for the form in general, it is doubly true of the relationship between Hong Kong shorter and longer fiction in English.

The literalism of realistic depiction in some, the laboured humour or repetitive lyricism in others, yields to a pithy, understated narrative, which paradoxically convinces us of its authenticity and virtuosity by not trying too hard. We can read the short fiction here as part of a greater Hong Kong narrative perhaps, but in stories like *Lau the Tailor, The Captain, Valediction, Lost River, Transcript t/23-098076/89, Conversion of a Village Ghost* and *Until the Next Century,* we find an allusive, frequently metaphysical quality that epitomizes short story writing at its best. It is, of course, unfair to expect Hong Kong English writing to produce its *Ulysses,* but judging by the diverse merits of its short fiction writers, it is not too far-fetched to compare the lightness in touch in many of these stories with that of other collections about a particular city like *Dubliners,* in which the 'unreal and teeming city', to refer to both Baudelaire and T.S. Eliot's evocations of other cities, is conjured up out of the existential angst of its miscellaneous inhabitants. No explicit novelistic description can match such narrative economy, in which the reader's imagination is wholly engaged with the latent spaces of the dream-like urban landscape. Baudelaire's prose poems say far more about mid-nineteenth-century Paris, for example, than all the more realistic descriptive passages of his realist contemporaries, with the possible exception of Hugo's *Les Miserables.*

The short story form is therefore better equipped, perhaps, to articulate the speed, restlessness, fragmentation and nervous transience of Hong Kong by virtue of the very compression and succinctness of its vignettes of city life. Longer and more leisurely oeuvres, tinged as they often are with more than a hint of imperial nostalgia and decline, such as Christopher New's *The Chinese Box* and *A Change of Flag* from his *China Coast Trilogy* for all his fine Greene-like authorial voice, cannot be seen as representative of Hong Kong English writing at the turn of the millennium. It is clearly not an easy task for the aspiring Hong Kong

English novelist to avoid the pitfalls of exoticizing stereotype and formulaic depiction of character and locale.

Few novels can support a predominantly Chinese cultural context, in which English is a natural medium. Unlike a work of Chinese fiction in translation, which functions as a cultural/ linguistic transposition on its own terms, the Hong Kong novel in English has frequently set itself the task of expressing a Chinese consciousness through the primary conduit of the English language. As a literary contrivance in the novel it tends to strike a false note with the reader, more readily than in the short story, perhaps for quantitative rather than qualitative reasons. Therefore, with a certain degree of healthy scepticism in mind regarding the viability of the extended novel, we should celebrate the more truncated forms of contemporary English expression in Hong Kong, not forgetting mixed-code theatre writing and especially the thriving creative poetry and short fiction scenes. There may be a novel in all of us, to echo the publicity for creative writing courses, but it is salutary to reflect that it is probably not a very good one, or at least a highly self-indulgent one. As the short fiction of David T. K. Wong, Xu Xi and the talented but under-published Rodney Davey testify, there are small gems to be unearthed in the English short fiction in Hong Kong. It is not necessarily, as a cynic might imply, the motivation of pecuniary awards for short fiction, which alone provide the powerful incentive for inspiration. Nevertheless, it is true that the *South China Morning Post* short story awards have in the past provided a useful platform for creative development. If there were to be a Hong Kong equivalent of the Booker Prize for extended fiction, it is more feasible that a new Timothy Mo will burst upon the scene.

## Historical Fiction, Memoirs and Newer Voices

It is also significant that the historical fiction (or 'faction', to use Truman Capote's clever appellation) genre, as exemplified by Mimi Chan's *All the King's Women* and Xu Xi's *History's Fiction* tends to be more engaging and persuasive in both the narrative voice and the loosely connected narrative structure than any of the more extended conventional novel extracts. There is a poignant and empathetic quality, tending to matter-of-factness, understatement, irony and implicit critique, as opposed to the sentimental excesses of the popular fictionalized memoir or chronicle of the best-seller variety that recommends both *History's Fiction* and *All the King's Women* to the reader, who wishes to transcend the formulaic clichés of that genre. *All the King's Women* stands out from much of the run-of-the-mill, Chinese female 'victim literature'. For one thing, it avoids the cheap sympathy syndrome for manipulating reader response so typical of the genre, by opting for a more lucid but at the same time empathetic portrait of female resilience in a patriarchal ex-Shanghai family in Hong Kong. As well as being a lively, semi-fictionalized version of events, it also constitutes a personal family history and a tribute to Chan's 'unsung heroines'.

Clearly, there is a thin line between this type of 'history' of Hong Kong and the non-fiction writing included in this anthology, a substantial portion of which offers the reader an insightful and diverse commentary on the 1997 Handover of the territory to China, from the expatriate whimsy of Charles Martin's 'Colonial Life and Times' piece to Jesse Wong's perceptive *Lives in Transition*. The latter captured the 1997 *zeitgeist* beautifully in all its tension and uncertainty, tinged with a spirit of pragmatic optimism, in his skilfully executed pen-pictures of a range of Hong Kong residents in the period leading up to the date with destiny. A refreshingly divergent perspective on Hong Kong's less recent past can be found in the selections from Austin Coates's fascinating 1968 account of his experiences as a colonial administrator and JP, *Myself a Mandarin*, and the tough and inspirational prose of Hong Kong doyenne, Elsie Elliott (Tu), in her 1981 retrospective, *Crusade for Justice*. The latter's frank exposé of her hard-fought battles with endemic graft, bureaucratic humbug and incompetence in establishing schools and improving the lot of the less fortunate in an often unforgiving social environment, is essential reading for anyone who is interested to know how Hong Kong made the painful journey from a third-world to more of a first-world infrastructure. The extract from Jackie Chan's 1998 autobiography also provides a fascinating glimpse of bygone Hong Kong days and an insight into the action star's early dedication to a hard profession. The rationale for English language as publication choice for Chan's memoir, as opposed to Chinese, is based on the actor's celebrity status and enormous popularity in the West. As a co-authored work, however, *I am Jackie Chan* cannot rank with Elliott's memoir for sheer gutsy readability.

To return to the fiction genre, one major development in Hong Kong English writing over the last decade has been a distinctive shift towards local writing with a stronger accent on the perspective of younger Chinese writers, both male and female. This trend is evident in the newer voices represented in the present anthology. Hark Yeung's work, for example, blends travelogue and social documentary with fictional narrative and dialogic conventions. Her travelogue idiom in stories such as *Walking on the Melting Ice*, an account of an almost transcendent experience on the ice floes of Greenland, as well as her perceptive and sympathetic exploration of her parents' generation in *Our Elders* (in collaboration with Fong So) offers a keen photographic vision to complement a deceptively straightforward narrative style.

Among the newer voices, the precocious talent of *South China Morning Post* short story contest winner, Divya Vaze, stands out. Her story, *Bid for Carpet Woven with Memories*, is the seamlessly interwoven narrative of past and present in the consciousness of a 62-year-old Indian man now resident in Hong Kong. It fuses his escape from Lahore in 1947 during the chaos of partition to safety in Hong Kong with his trip to an auction to recover a family heirloom, the carpet woven with memories of the title, a symbol of what he has lost and also of what he has gained. Other writers who have featured in university creative writing magazines *Writing in English* (the Chinese University of Hong Kong) and *Yuan Yang* (the University of Hong Kong) show considerable promise. Nancy Tsui Yuk Chun's *Addiction* underlines how far Hong Kong writing has come from the male expatriate world of Mason, Clavell, Davies, New et al. with their seductive but adoring Chinese sirens to Chan's marijuana-induced insight that 'the woman is 5 million light years from the man'. Much of this newer writing is steeped in post-modern scepticism and isolation, a recording of fragmentary experience rather than the more kaleidoscopic worlds of Suzie Wong or Han Suyin's Eurasian woman doctor in *A Many Splendored Thing*.

Lex Lao's email narrative 'Press Enter' provides a stimulating example of the possibilities of a fresh kind of epistolary fiction based on electronic communication, with its roller-coaster techniques for surprising, intriguing and thoroughly engaging the reader's interest and emotional response. His tale of a family divided by recent bereavement deals with the themes of generation gap, healing and reconciliation through the unlikely mediating force of information technology. Although no ICQ narrative writing is at present available for inclusion in this anthology, this medium seems an inevitable next step for Hong Kong young writing to take for the fundamental reason that it is such a vital and popular form of communication among the younger generation of Hong Kongers, and is, moreover, truly international in scope. Finally, Andy Barker's *The Monkey Trap* gives us a contemporary Hong Kong, in which the epicentre of activity is fittingly Lan Kwai Fong, playground of the *jeunesse dorée*. In its unsentimental portrait of a bunch of twenty- and thirty-somethings, it is brutally authentic, but observed with Mo-like critical distance. Barker's debut novel is clearly a work of promise, based partly on the author's personal experience, which is perhaps one of the reasons why it is highly entertaining.

## A Rich and Vibrant Voice: Hong Kong Poetry

The English poetry scene in Hong Kong is remarkably vibrant and diverse. One characteristic difference between the prose fiction and poetry selections in this anthology is that the fiction selections almost picked themselves, whereas for poetry there were harder choices to be made. Whilst English short story writing has established a strong presence and novel writing, despite some clearly talented contenders, is still an emergent discipline, the more performative mode of poetry and the popularity of poetry reading groups ensure a steady flow of fresh material and, arguably, a more immediate and democratic outlet for creativity and a more responsive audience.

The Outloud group, meeting variously at the Fringe Club, the John Batten Gallery and formerly at Visage Free in Central's 'Arts hub' around Soho, has provided a valuable seed-bed for new talent as well as an opportunity to hear more established poets. The introduction of a City Poetry event as part of the Fringe Club's annual City Festival during the 1990s also helped to promote the writing and appreciation of poetry and to identify an enthusiastic audience. Multilingual events, in which poems were read in their original language as well as in newly translated versions, have played an important part in communicating the idea that poetry is meant to be heard as much or even more than to be read. Another significant aspect of the Outloud group and other poetry reading and creative writing groups in university contexts has been the mutual support and synergy that such gregarious enterprises can generate. Collections of new original poetry, such as the 2002 Outloud anthology, and creative writing journals published by the university English departments, have stimulated enthusiasm and interest in poetry as a form of self-expression that crosses cultural borders. It is significant that two of Hong Kong's most reputed and prestigious Chinese-language poets, Leung Ping-kwan, whose *City at the End of Time* (1992) has to be one of the milestones of modern Hong Kong literature, and Laurence Wong Kwok-pun, a master of elegant lyricism, are both capable of the Beckettian feat of writing their poetry bilingually with equal facility. Remarkably Hong Kong's English-language poet laureate, Louise Ho, is only capable of writing in English, which she does with an unerring ear for the *mot juste* and an elegiac precision.

The poetry represented in this anthology spans the same period as the fiction and non-fiction, i.e. starting in the 1950s with Edmund Blunden's arrival to take up the Head of English Department post at the University of Hong Kong. As a published war poet (the First World War, rather than the then very recent Second World War), Blunden's name inevitably adds *gravitas* to this kind of anthology. However, it is clear from the three poems included here, as well as from his poems published in anthologies of war poetry, that Blunden was no Wilfred Owen or Ivor Gurney. Nonetheless, his mellow, reflective style in 'Hong Kong House', 'An Island Tragedy' and 'Lamma Island' conveys an awareness of the changes Hong Kong is embarking on, and is in its old-world way better poetry than the comparatively tame and to my taste over-sentimental war poems on which his reputation rests. In theme and tone, it would appear that Blunden's work pays tribute to a Chinese or Japanese poetic spirit, as did that of Pound and Brecht and other modernists who flirted with the elusive idea of Asian poetic and pictorial forms and nuances. 'And now a dove and now a dragonfly / Came to the garden; sometimes as we sat / Outdoors in twilight noiseless owl and bat / Flew shadowily by.' ('Hong Kong House')

Blunden's legacy as an inspirational role model and teacher for those who followed is echoed by the more recent success of Shirley Geok-lin Lim, who as Head of the English Department at the University of Hong Kong was instrumental in encouraging the recent renaissance in creative writing at the university. Her contributions to the publication of the *Yuan Yang* (tea-coffee) journal of creative writing and the groundbreaking Moving Poetry project, have also been extremely important. Moving Poetry has really fostered an air of exciting creativity among primary, secondary and tertiary students and helped to promote poetry as a communal and educationally valid form of communication. Shirley Lim's own impressive poetry is more oriented towards her homelands of Malaysia and the United States, but her influential role as a major Asian-American poet and academic is acknowledged by the inclusion of one of her Hong Kong-inspired poems, 'Passports', which evokes an Aberdeen waterfront scene strangely reminiscent of C. Y. Lee's 1960s' novel *The Virgin Market*.

Joyce Hsia's 1977 poem 'A Matter of Time' echoes Blunden's wistful lyricism with a pointedly intertextual, pastiche-like reference: 'Hong Kong House: A soon-to-be-relic / of a passing era of leisure and space / where sun pierces verandah windows / splaying a red carpet and acquiescent piano; / hibiscus blooms in an untended garden and / a vine's tendrils straddle a king palm.' Here there is a much deeper sense of imminent and profound change than in Blunden's poem, an ironic allusion to the inevitable passing of this tranquil, orientalist evocation surrendering its privileged air of time and space suspended to inevitable and encroaching modernization 'in an eclipsing case of glass and steel'. Other 1970s' poems such as Walter Sulke's tribute to Hong Kong, 'An Unfinished Symphony for Five Million Instruments' (population at the time of the present anthology being 6.7 million, with over 8 million projected for 2020), convey a more prescient sense of the geometric progression of infrastructure development over the following two decades. 'Symphony' is less pretentious than the title may suggest and its pivotal device of a five-movement musical suite with tempo markings such as *allegro* and *andante* is perfectly suited to the rapid variations and sharp contrasts of living in Hong Kong's hybrid environment. 'From the greatest population density in the world / To a lesser greatest population density in the world' stands in stark antithesis to Blunden's leisurely and contemplative pastorales. In his 'Western Approaches' of the same year, Peter Moss captures the city's fascinating blend of reality and chimera: 'The city is reality / and all our fickle day / a passing mirage / lulling us / momentarily / with its sweet conceit / of centuries retrieved.' Moss's Western modernist voice with his short lines and internal rhymes catches echoes, as we shall see, in the more extended and prolific poetic work of Louise Ho. Also in this period, Martin Booth's poems attest to his versatility as a writer of international talent, although his prose fiction is ultimately more developed. 'Those Not Swimming' and 'Dead Bones' reminisce and speculate eloquently about the bones of those who died in the Japanese occupation, while Booth's tribute to Blunden in 'On a Poet' ends with what may be a fitting epitaph to Blunden's achievement: 'I last saw you distantly / across a student distance / gowned and still / and I saw kindness / not knowledge.'

As we see from the anthology's irregular proportions, its poetic density expanded as its population swelled in the 1980s and 1990s. Thus, the thematic scope, diction and style of the poetry as represented here become more diverse, as we read on into the 1990s. The genteel and often elegiac, expatriate tones of earlier decades — the 'slow drawing down of blinds' on the Hong Kong House (to recontextualize Wilfred Owen) — gives way to a more local Hong Kong voice, as evidenced here by the selections from Ho Hon Leung, Jim Wong-Chu, Alex Kuo and Louise Ho. Their poetic worlds are intercultural spaces, occupied by real Heung Gong Yan (Hong Kong people), instead of plants and old colonial buildings. Ho Hon Leung's reflections on the impact of modernity on Chinese tradition in 'After the Three Characters' — 'Today speed is / as important as simplicity' — sees Hong Kong's increasingly frenetic lifestyle as 'a loose horse' with all the cross-linguistic resonances the character 'ma' evokes in the poem. 'I see a horse / run across a bar of my prison' begins the poem in a beautifully economical and graphic piece of imagery. Jim Wong-Chu articulates a sense of kinship with those who came from across the border, an increasingly common theme of the 1980s in all genres as the Sino-British Joint Declaration came and went. In 'the old country' and 'fourth uncle', we get a glimpse of a cultural schism and an aspiration to rediscover roots, as well as the growing awareness of the schizoid linguistic and cultural experience of Hong Kong's unique situation. The closing lines from 'fourth uncle' — 'At the end of my life / will I too have walked a full circle / and arrive like you / an old elephant / to his grave' — seek common ground between the Chinese émigré of an older, much less affluent generation and the newer type of overseas migrant.

The Chinese diaspora is important for an understanding of the writing of the period, as more and more people became 'astronauts', that is living in space between Hong Kong and elsewhere (usually Australia, the United States or Canada, rarely Britain!). This experience is also reflected in the poems of Alex Kuo, such as 'The Immigrant' (1986), and later more whimsically in the early 1990s in Andrew Parkin's 'Astronaut'. In these poems, the distances have become eclipsed in suitably post-modern fashion; it seems as though the poet's Hong Kong life is also that of an astronaut of a different kind, as 'Government House, Kowloon Clock Tower, harbour / narrow tub of bobbing toys / Legco Building, echoing with new voices / and Victoria, surrounded by penile monuments / well-oiled with wealth' all go rushing by.

Strangely enough, Parkin's more introspective or lyrical work such as 'In the Forum at the Chinese University' and 'On a Mountain above Tolo Harbour' or the beautifully minimalist 'Hong Kong Tanka' resonate with what could almost be described as Asian poetic sensibility, whilst his colleague at the Chinese University of Hong Kong, Louise Ho, writing in a pithily elegant, ironic and precise vein, has sometimes on her own admission been described as 'more British than the British'. This refers, however, to her style rather than her subject-matter, which is indomitably post-colonial and politically aware. 'New Year's Eve, 1989' is a masterpiece, the poetic counterpart perhaps to Xu Xi's short stories 'Manky's Tale' and 'Danny's Snake', but less oblique: 'Yes, I remember Marvell, Dryden / Yeats, men who had taken up the pen / While others the sword / To record the events of the sword. . . . The shadows of June the Fourth / Are the shadows of a gesture / They say, but how shall you and I / Name them, one by one? . . . As we near the end of an era / We have at last / Become ourselves / The catalyst / Was our neighbour's blood.' The echo of Yeats's 'Easter Rising' (on the brutal British suppression of the 1916 Irish rebellion) in 'we too have changed, if not "utterly", / And something beautiful was born' brings a literary consciousness and a perceptively allegorical mind to bear on a China-Hong Kong event that was difficult to write or even talk about with breadth of vision in the white heat of world reaction. Ho's poems I and II from her *New Ends Old Beginnings* collection in 1997, a publication year pregnant with meaning, about the 1967 Hong Kong riots against the Star Ferry fare increases specifically and British colonial repression aim at a different target: 'Stand your ground / even if for only / two foot square . . . the sentry stood / khaki shorts / rifle in hand / still as a statue / and held his ground / of two foot square. / This too is pomp and circumstance / without fanfare.' That 'pomp and circumstance' skewers the bombast of imperialism on the cold, keen knife of poetry. As we see from her poems and hear from her own readings, Louise Ho is a presence and a great Hong Kong voice.

By contrast, Leung Ping-kwan — perhaps the most distinctive and internationally representative of all Hong Kong poetic voices — writes, as he puts it, 'between Chinese and English'[2] and describes the two languages as becoming 'tangled' in his mind when writing some poems. His poems included here have been written in 'NICAM', with Chinese and English versions of the same poems. He doesn't blend the two languages in a single poem, but blends cultural feelings and flavours, rather like the concept *yuan yang* (tea-coffee) of which he writes in another poem entitled simply 'Yuan-yang'. This is both a bilingual and bicultural phenomenon. But unlike the work of Ho, which is steeped in a specific British literary consciousness, it speaks with a resonantly Hong Kong voice: 'The suns of our good old songs go out, one by one' ('At the North Point Car Ferry'); 'We'd rather not bend; / neither of us is in love with flags or fireworks' ('An Old Colonial Building'). This 'we' is aware of the eternal dialectic but knows where it stands, just like the protester and the sentry of Louise Ho's poem: 'Please don't make an imperial scene, or shout / anthems to the downpours; don't pretend, with the breezes, / to grant us our ditties. Have you ever noted a marginal leaf, / observed the veins converging like noisy streets, / that challenge your blueprints' rectangles?' ('The Leaf on the Edge'). These are poems redolent with pre- and post-colonial references and implicature, which seek to sing new their own (our) ditties rather than 'yours'. 'We need a fresh angle, / nothing added, nothing taken away / always at the edge of things and between places. / Write with a different colour for each voice', Leung avers in 'Images of Hong Kong'.

Without the crucial English-language channel of Leung's and Laurence Wong's culturally Chinese but exquisitely translated writing, it would be hard to cross between the separate currents of Chinese and English writing, and for each to interact. The cultural interflow that has emerged particularly from these two poets is invaluable for the English-language strand of Hong Kong's poetic consciousness. Wong writes with elegance and simplicity in 'I Fear I May Grow Old Before Frost Fall', 'The Great Bell of Yongle' and 'Rhapsody on a Rainy Night', in a limpid style that is somehow reminiscent of Arthur Waley's memorable translations of *The Book of Songs*. 'Rhapsody' in its very title makes a culturally resonant allusion to T. S. Eliot's *Cats*-inspiring poem of an almost identical title.

Another locally born poet whose voice has acquired increasing authority and timbre, both in her public readings and in her writing technique, is Agnes Lam. Lam grew up in Hong Kong and began to be published in Singapore, but the best of her work to date can probably be discerned most clearly in her recent collection, *Water Wood Pure Splendour*, which appeared in 2001. The poems from that collection represented here range from the lyrical and almost mystical ('Writing in the Middle of the Road', 'I Have Walked on Air') and the whimsy tinged

---

with melancholy of 'White Dust' to the historically reflective ('Water Wood Pure Splendour' — Over this land / of thousands of years / as earth becomes heaven / in water wood pure splendour / can the Chinese not forgive?) and the accusatory, politically aware ('You Say' — I could go on / but if I do / I shall sound / just like you). This is one of the most viscerally satisfying and acerbic responses to NATO/US arrogance and double standards in the wake of the infamous Belgrade Embassy bombing in 1999 that it has been my pleasure to read. Lam embraces the cultural symbiosis of the post-1997 era with 'a voice that comes from you and me' (to paraphrase a line from Don McLean's classic song.) 'Apology' is a particularly poignant example, as the poet explains to her mainland university counterpart that there is no need to apologize for the basic but homely hospitality, since 'I too am Chinese / This too is my country / If you must apologize/ Then should I? / For my navy Ferragamo shoes / My Max Mara suit a darker blue / My white blouse from Episode / . . . Ten years apart in time, / a few thousand miles in space / exchanging parents / I could have been you / and you, / me. / '.

Other more established poets regularly heard at Outloud, such as Madeleine Marie Slavick, Tim Kaiser, Jamila Ismail and Mani Rao, are also featured both in this anthology and in the Outloud anthology, published in March 2002. 'Let Us Move from Lonely to Alone', Mani Rao's abrasively solipsistic ode, hard-edged yet oddly wistful in its tone, could only come from Hong Kong, where 'the guard with no name . . . knows you by your floor.' The rhythms of this and other Mani Rao poems — 'home is where the heart is, and the heart is full of habit' — leaps off the page and demands to be spoken aloud or Outloud! Slavick's 'Mid-Levels Front Door' also illustrates the point that a very short poem, rather like a haiku, can be beautifully compact and complete in its succinct imagery. Ismail's work, such as 'translit' and 'country-'n-chinese', explores more esoteric formal and tonal effects than most Hong Kong English poets. Her diction is jazzy, often quirky but always thought-provoking, seemingly full of free association, but in fact carefully articulated and laid out on the page. Memory, word-play, intercultural mosaic and sensual pleasure of language — all of these are conveyed in her poems, particularly 'translit-'. Of the new voices contained here, Ted Mathys's 'Hong Kong Nocturne' shows him to be a writer of tremendous promise with a precociously Rimbaud-like gift for the felicitous phrase and the *mot juste*, despite being a transitory Hong Kong poet. 'Rave on Hong Kong', he writes. Rave on, Ted, wherever you are! Ted's imagery is nothing short of seductively visual and tactile, a rare quality in a poet. Other exciting new voices talk of a Hong Kong experienced in childhood and evoke the smells and touch of Hong Kong street life, as in Michelle Fok's moving 'Fried Chestnuts': 'You bought me fried chestnuts / and the yellow mist in your eyes thickened. / . . . I won't buy fried chestnuts again / as, soaked with tears, / they are bitter.' In many cases the new voices in English are local tertiary or postgraduate students from the Chinese University of Hong Kong, the University of Hong Kong, City University of Hong Kong and Lingnan University. Sharon Sung Sau Fun's 'The Tear Collector', for example, reflects in its three short stanzas the frustrations of life and the tears that are shed and collected by the masochistic Tear Collector, who torments all of us eventually: ' "What do you want them for?" I ask. "To chain them together and put them around your neck one day." '

## Pedagogical Applications

In this introductory piece, there have been frequent references to the strong connection between university creative writing teachers and courses and the development of Hong Kong's English literary ethos. Not surprisingly, then, this anthology was envisaged partly, but not exclusively, as a teaching and learning tool. An increasing number of schools and universities are showing interest in indigenous literature and culture, which is to some extent a manifestation of post-colonial consciousness and a sign of validation of local English (and Chinese) writing. Of course, there have been reactionary attitudes shown by cultural snobs from a number of quarters, who would like to resist this tendency in Hong Kong education, but increasingly local writers are collaborating with schools and universities on critical and creative programmes designed to teach literature and culture from a Hong Kong cultural perspective.

Nowadays in many countries students' interest in learning history is captured by learning about local history on the grounds that it is more immediate and meaningful to them. This paradigm can also be applied to the study of local literature and culture. The perennial debates about the standard of Hong Kong English fail to take into account that the way English is taught and learned in Hong Kong can often be described as vapid. Frequently it is a subject without an authentic, or indeed remotely interesting, content, except in those contexts where English is the medium for the learning of real content, such as in EMI secondary schools (i.e., the schools using English as the medium of instruction), English for academic purposes and, of course, in culture and literature courses. There are a number of university Asian Voices courses, which teach films and novels by Asian writers, and authors writing about Hong Kong are beginning to appear on these syllabuses. The Advanced Level English literature syllabus also has an Asian Voices section.

It is to be hoped that the teaching and learning of literature and cultural studies in English will not be sacrificed in the curriculum reforms, which are projected for the second half of this decade by the Education Department. The contributions of the Moving Poetry project and the efforts of a small but dedicated group of literature-in-English teachers in secondary schools, as well as other school-based initiatives have been crucial in maintaining students' awareness that English can be used to express ideas, experiences and feelings, rather than existing solely for the purpose of making reports and writing memos.

So how can the extracts in this anthology be used to develop students' linguistic and aesthetic awareness and appreciation of their own cultural milieu? The following are simply a few suggestions. Possibilities for exploiting the texts are legion and limited only to the imagination:

**Reading**:    vocabulary work; exploring synonyms; identifying keywords and lexical and syntactic repetition; analysing discourse features, e.g. changing tenses or deictic pronouns to see what effect this has; exploring subtext (reading between the lines); predicting what will happen next (in the case of the novel extracts/short stories); highlighting the use of slang or bad language in the text; highlighting the use of metaphor; deciding why specifically literary words and phrases are used by the writer as opposed to more common alternatives; try the alternatives.

**Writing**:    summarizing; writing reports/reviews for an online book club; setting up a website to review stories, poems, films etc; simplifying the text for a younger reader; writing speeches/letters/emails etc. in the

|                          | character of one of the protagonists of the story; writing a biography of the author; writing an invitation to the author to speak at the school/university. |
|--------------------------|---|
| **Speaking**:            | reading aloud (particularly poetry), recording, reciting, performing poetry; dramatizing scenes; holding debates on the issues and moral conflicts of the texts studied; role-playing characters and asking them questions to explain their actions. |
| **Creative adaptation**: | turning a poem into a story; writing a poem based on a story; writing a poem based on another poem (poem into poem); writing a story/ poem from another character's or persona's viewpoint; writing a reply to a critical essay; writing a film treatment for a favourite story. |

These are some of the approaches that teachers of language and literature use. In my own experience of teaching Asian Voices in English courses, I find that students can relate to many of the writers and contexts, including those of the diaspora. These courses are popular and motivating on account of the content, which is closer to students' personal experience and awareness of the world and of their immediate environment. Although at the outset of the course students often lack a sense of how the past is contained in the present, they become more conscious of this relationship, especially *vis-à-vis* Hong Kong, as the course progresses.

The older liberal arts tradition encouraged the use of literary texts in learning language, since it sensitized the learner to the effects that language can create. This is exactly how and why an older generation of fluent English speakers in Hong Kong became so proficient. To teach only Anglo-American literature would clearly be inappropriate now, but the lesson provided by those who fell in love with English through reading *Pride and Prejudice* in Secondary Four (or perhaps Secondary Two in the so-called 'brand-name' schools) remains as true today as in the 1950s. The reading of local writers (and perhaps later international writers) together with the creative responses such reading can generate offers a meaningful strategy for motivating Hong Kong students to engage with the English language. One only has to look at the popularity of Japanese cultural products among our students to see the attraction of an engaging content that does not alienate.

## Language Issues and Concluding Observations

The use of romanized transliteration of both Cantonese and Mandarin terms is common to virtually all of the writers in this anthology. Whilst the device is advantageous in its ability to convey the plural language and culture of a hybrid city with strong cross-cultural currents, it can easily degenerate into literary shorthand as well as empty signifier. One axiom for original writing in any language is that the writer can impart new meanings to old words. Therefore, such mixed code and code-switching vernacular in Hong Kong English-language writing needs to be expressive of semantic invention and ambivalence as opposed to convention, stability of meaning and *idée reçue*. Language in works of art, as the formalists and the post-structuralists coming after them recognized, should defamiliarize the reader in order to counter-balance the staleness of official and everyday discourses. Thus, the choice of Chinese transliterations, or of any other extraneous codes needs to be weighed up carefully by the writer at any given point in the text. There is, furthermore, a qualitative difference between the frequent use of Chinese-language expressions in direct and reported speech as opposed to omniscient authorial narrative. In the latter, it can have a jarring effect where it is used seriously. By contrast, Nury Vittachi often achieves his whimsical-cum-farcical effects in his idiosyncratic, comic sub-genre precisely through the use of these linguistic accretions.

There is, therefore, no reason *per se* why contemporary Hong Kong literature in general, and fiction in particular, should not be represented in some small part by English-language voices. The post-colonial critique of the language of the colonizer, as defined so incisively by Fanon, Memmi, Said and others, is rapidly becoming superseded by the cultural and linguistic depredations of global imperialism and monoculture, as well as a Western geopolitical hegemony, in which English is the language of power and capital. Such empires are often most effectively critiqued from within, as Fanon recognized. There is a need for the kind of critical fictional discourse that English can provide, albeit in a minor key. Much, though not all, of the fiction anthologized here offers critical insights to complement the wider scope and representativeness of indigenous Chinese fiction. In this connection, it is equally important to nurture and value non-English or Chinese literature coming out of Hong Kong for reasons of its very difference, as non-official languages. Those further margins are capable of affording critical and aesthetic perceptions of the city and its inhabitants that both the Chinese centre and English inner margin are unable to express. The Japanese, Pakistani, Filipino and French voices, to name but a few, have their Hong Kong stories too.

In conclusion, it is important that this collection of poems, novel extracts and self-sufficient shorter pieces should be seen as a representative sample of the creative work of disparate Hong Kong voices, rather than as a definitive canon. The literature of a small minority cannot constitute a canon, which is probably a distinct advantage for newer, younger writers, since there are fewer burdens of tradition on their shoulders. The irregular output and lack of continuity reflects the historical limitations and marginality of this medium of writing. However, as tertiary institutions encourage greater emphasis on creative writing in English as opposed to the merely functional and mechanical modes of writing, English writing appears to have a robust future in the territory. Given the choice of medium and language, perhaps young bilingual writers will prefer to express their thoughts and experiences and work out their narrative ideas in English because they feel greater freedom from precedent or a degree of impersonality or anonymity. Authors like Martin Booth, Christopher New, Jane Camens, Louise Ho and Xu Xi probably do not have much choice as to their writing code, whilst for others like Han Suyin, David T. K. Wong, Agnes Lam, Lily Chan, Lee Ding Fai and Yang Yi Lung, the use of English was probably a conscious choice from two options. The Irish writer Samuel Beckett consciously chose to write in his adopted tongue, French, before translating his work back into an English-language version, because he thought that the French language endowed his writing with greater rigour, discipline and exactitude than would be the case if he wrote initially in English. Likewise, a small but significant group of Hong Kong indigenous creative writers are sensitive to the qualities of English as a medium of expression. The language belongs to them as much as it does to expatriate writers. They no longer need to sound more British than the British, as Timothy Mo sometimes does, since the language has become common property. Now that we talk of 'world Englishes', it is entirely conceivable for a novel, short story or poem to be written in Chinglish, just as Singaporean and Malaysian writers have used mixed code or local patois forms.

Whatever the developments in the next ten years in Hong Kong English poetry and fiction, the creative surge of the mid-to-late 1990s will be seen as a watershed. Some of the newer voices will almost certainly produce formally exploratory work, such as Simon Elegant's 'Transcript', Jamila Ismail's 'translit' and Alex Kuo's 'The Catholic All-Star Chess Team'. The influence of overseas writers will also probably result in more elliptical, discontinuous and less coherently organized fiction and poetry, reflecting more *avant-garde* tendencies. The sentimentality and earnestness of tone, which we detect in earlier writers, such as Lily Chan, together with the lyricism of a Han Suyin, is unlikely to be replicated in the harsh climate of the twenty-first century. I think, however, that English poetry and fiction writing in one form or another will survive and even prosper in Hong Kong, just as English-language theatre has done.[3] If English creative writing does, it will owe something of a debt to its creative precursors, to Richard Mason, as well as Han Suyin and Timothy Mo. It will also be one of life's great and somehow satisfying ironies if post-Handover Hong Kong proves more prolific in producing new writing in English than prior to the 'Change of Flag'. Nobody would have anticipated such an outcome, but then truth is often stranger than fiction.

---

[3]   The forthcoming anthology of Hong Kong playwriting in English will focus mainly on the 1990s because it was only in this decade that original new voices emerged writing plays on local issues and themes.

# From and of the City of Hong Kong

## Xu Xi

When I first proposed compiling this *dungsai,*[1] it was partly because disparate voices were squawking — like so many surly teenagers — in an unruly and chaotic chorus. Was it the 'great' or 'meagre' Hong Kong story we were telling in our various genres? We were all accidents that happened upon this former British colony on whom the Muse, or some lesser goddess, foisted her imperative, *in English* to boot, and made us what we are.

Yet as we hover at the top of the twenty-first century, I look back at my own writings, and those of others, that emerged out of what was once an extremely narrow sphere, and realize that a body of work now exists, which, while hardly a cornucopia, represents the beginnings of adult, as opposed to adolescent, squawking. Over the last decade, especially, the volume has risen steadily, and shows little sign of softening.

This anthology was born of necessity: no other volume like it exists. In the last twenty-five years, there have been a few anthologies of only poetry in English, although Chinese-language poets in translation are included in most.[2] One recent anthology takes an historical look at Hong Kong writing, primarily in English. Given its focus, the majority of the authors are English, and the selections articulate a colonial sensibility which is unrepresentative of contemporary writing and culture.[3] However, it is very Hong Kong-entrepreneurial to invent our existence, and hence, history, and this anthology lives because city voices in English have existed and continue to do so.

It is time we were heard in tandem, from our novels, short stories, essays, memoirs and poetry. This current era is an appropriate one — the 'borrowed time' of fifty 'special' years as the 'SAR'[4] — the ideal construct for our accidental, but hardly 'barren' culture.

In compiling this anthology, the goal was to provide as *representative* — if not as comprehensive — a selection as possible to reflect the voices over time. Selections are from previously published work, although a small number of unpublished pieces is included. There is also a final section of new voices, chosen from the work of creative writing students and other emerging writers.

---

[1] Cantonese. Literally, 'east-west', meaning 'thing' (in Putonghua, *dongxi*).

[2] *Hong Kong: Images on Shifting Waters,* ed. Joyce Hsia and T. C. Lai (Hong Kong: Kelly & Walsh, 1977); *Vs,* (Hong Kong: Big Weather Press, 1993); *From The Bluest Part of the Harbour* Hong Kong, Oxford and New York: Oxford University Press, 1995); *Tolo Lights: A Collection of Chinese and English Poems,* compiled by Andrew Parkin and Wu Ningkun (Hong Kong: Shaw College, The Chinese University of Hong Kong, 1995); *A Collection of Poems: Hong Kong in the Decimal System and HK 1997,* publication of the first Hong Kong International Poetry Festival (Hong Kong: The Hong Kong Arts Centre and The Provisional Regional Council, 1997); *Outloud: An Anthology of Contemporary Poetry from Outloud Readings* (Hong Kong: Xtraloud Press, 2002).

[3] *Hong Kong: Somewhere Between Heaven and Earth* (Hong Kong, Oxford, New York: Oxford University Press, 1996).

[4] Special Administrative Region — Hong Kong's official designation by the Chinese government.

What this volume offers is an introduction to literature from and of Hong Kong in English, one of our two official languages, from post-Second World War until the present day. A point on language in this bilingual culture: we did include a few local Chinese poets — meaning those who are bilingual but publish primarily in Chinese — whose selected poems *originate in English* or are *self-translated*. However, the bulk of selections originate in English, regardless of the authors' mother tongue.

As one of the authors in this anthology, I believe I speak for my fellow authors by saying that our texts speak for themselves. As an editor, however, I feel somewhat responsible to make a few remarks on two fronts. First, by offering a brief autobiographical note of the evolution of my own voice, I hope readers will find a useful introduction to understanding how marginal literatures like ours can and do emerge, survive and thrive. Second, the process of selecting and whittling down the final contents of this anthology was instructive, consoling and delightful to me as reader. I therefore wish to share a little of that experience in the hopes that others will be instructed, consoled and delighted as I was by these voices that echo my city, Hong Kong, this place I sometimes call home.

## Evolution of One Hong Kong Voice

> While everyone is scrambling to tell the great Hong Kong story, many artists and writers in Hong Kong don't seem to be keen to take part in the race.
>
> from 'The Story of Hong Kong' by Leung Ping-kwan (Ye Si)
> translated by Martha Cheung (1997)

> When both ideas and reality are foreign to his audience, the writer has an added burden — that of making accepted and universal what is strange and esoteric, that of making accepted and familiar what is repulsive and rejected. By converting into starkness, realism, what his audience regarded as unthreatening exoticism, the writer disturbs, profanes, *foists a new nakedness upon those piteously clad in the phantasms of conformity.*
>
> from the Plenary Lecture by Han Suyin
> *Asian Voices in English* (1991)[5]

I became one of Hong Kong's 'voices in English' by accident, which is pretty much the history of my home city — an accident, that is, a city that, like some surly teenager still cries, 'but I never *asked* to be born,' to whom the thinking parent replies, 'but you were, so live.'

We in Hong Kong exist in such a perpetually tense present of frenzy that the idea of 'racing' to tell any kind of Hong Kong story, *especially* in English, seems like an unnecessary effort. It isn't profitable, which our culture instinctively abhors, and does not seem to suit the international buyer's market that prefers the musings of those who write 'real' English, an added burden indeed for the hapless writer.

In reflecting on the shaping of my own voice, my earliest encounter with 'Hong Kong writing' was almost entirely fiction by Western residents and visitors for whom English was

---

[5] *Asian Voices in English* ed. Mimi Chan and Roy Harris (Hong Kong: Hong Kong University Press, 1991).

a native tongue, both linguistically and culturally. Their perspective was frequently that of an outside observer — often romanticized or orientalized — with little, if any, of what could be described as a local aesthetic or sensibility. In 1981, the American writer James Clavell[6] had this to say in the epigraph to his novel, *Noble House*:

> Of course this is a novel. It is peopled with imaginary persons and companies and no reference to any person or company that was, or is, part of Hong Kong or Asia is intended.
>
> I would like to apologize at once to all Hong Kong *yan* — all Hong Kong *persons* — for rearranging their beautiful city, for taking incidents out of context, for inventing people and places and streets and companies and incidents that, hopefully, may appear to have existed but have never existed, for this, truly, is a story . . .

His 'apology' is not unlike that of a parent who says, 'I *am* sorry I gave birth to you, but there you are, it happened.' In Clavell's case, that apology is only due for profiting at the expense of literature, which, unfortunately, is not a crime.

There was nonetheless *some* fiction, within what was an otherwise barren culture that spoke to me about my city. *The World of Suzie Wong* (1957) by Richard Mason did, because, unlike *Noble House,* it truly *is* a story that, in its day, defined Hong Kong in fiction, even if it did eventually become what is expected by the West of novels about Hong Kong. An even earlier book, *A Many Splendored Thing* (1952) by the Eurasian author Han Suyin, was courageous in its frank handling of cross-cultural passions, an unspeakable theme in the very Confucian, polite society world of her day. Her ethnicity was important as well because she was the only role model of a part-Chinese writer who voiced a Hong Kong story in English. To be sure, these were solos from the margins, sounding empathy for 'unsavoury' characters and situations.

But by writing in English, wasn't I also part of this 'mongrel' margin?

Growing up in Hong Kong, my contemporaries chattered, as did I, in Cantonese, Cantolish, Eng-ese, and English. Chinese friends recited dynasties and were children of legal concubines; I was spared those 'trials' thanks to being the offspring of *wah kiu*[7] Chinese-Indonesian immigrants. My parents' native tongues were Javanese, and in my father's case, Mandarin as well. English was their second or third language, Cantonese their least fluent, acquired purely for survival in their borrowed land, Hong Kong, in which they separately arrived after the war. They met and married in the city which is where I was born and raised. Despite half a century's residence, neither one of my parents ever sounded like a Hong Konger in either of the city's 'native' tongues. My private language at home was English, but really, like that of my parents, ESL (English as a second language). The public one was often Cantonese, but more accurately, CSL.

Today, I am more fluent in English than Chinese, and rarely read in Chinese. When I do, it is limited to contemporary fiction or newspapers, with the aid of a well-thumbed pocket

---

6    Clavell lived in Hong Kong for a number of years and wrote several novels about Asia (*Shogun, Tai Pan, King Rat, Gaijin*) that were commercially successful.

7    This refers to 'Overseas' Chinese. In Hong Kong, the term (in Putonghua, *huaqiao*) was mostly applied to those from Southeast Asia.

dictionary. I hardly ever write Chinese. When I speak English, I have been told I sound like a New Yorker — or slightly British — depending on the listener's acculturation. Somehow, I still manage to sound Hong Kongese, or so I'm told, when speaking my reasonably competent Cantonese or far less fluent Putonghua. A mongrel's voice, indeed.

However, English was the *only* 'official' language of Hong Kong until the mid-1970s. My writing language proved a weird brand of power under colonial rule.

Determining when I first saw myself as part of a 'voice' of Hong Kong isn't easy, mostly because I kept leaving the city and returning. No one wrote in English, or so I believed, because I did not meet writers who did. During the mid-1970s, the only 'local' novelist I could find was Derek Maitland, a long-time resident and author of *The Only War We've Got,* an acclaimed novel about Vietnam.

As late as 1991, Leon Comber, formerly the managing director of Heinemann Asia and also publisher of Hong Kong University Press, wrote in his introduction to *Prizewinning Asian Fiction:* [8]

> It will be noticed that no *indigenous* writers from Hong Kong are included in this collection of stories. While, of course, writers in Chinese abound, it would seem that creative writers in English are not yet ready to emerge, although there is no shortage of skilled speakers of the language. There is perhaps a further reason for their present 'writing block', apart from the language not being their own. It is that Hong Kong is reverting to Chinese suzerainty in 1997 and there is a move towards learning *Putonghua,* the national language of China.

Heinemann did publish one Hong Kong writer, Lee Ding Fai (pen name) whose novel *Running Dog* (1980) is excerpted in this anthology. While Comber was right that few writers emerged, I believe the lack of a culture that supported, encouraged or published creative work in English was more the cause than a question of readiness. Certainly, a 'writing block' was never an issue for me and the language was one I considered my own.

But I should begin at the beginning because, as fiction demands, there must be a beginning, middle and end, with the ascent to a climax somewhere near to, but not at, the end, followed by a denouement. This is the classic dramatic arc, and, after all, Aristotle *said so,* and who are we to argue?

As a graduate student at an American MFA programme,[9] I could not exclusively buy that premise.

Chinese fiction evoked timelessness without such seemingly rigid formulas. The classic novel, *A Dream of Red Mansions* sent me floating endlessly through red dust. The works of early twentieth-century writer Eileen Chang (Cheung Oi-ling), such as *The Golden Cangue,* invoked and sustained an emotional mood to tell its inner story. These were at least *artistically* relevant to a Chinese writer — albeit of a Hong Kong Chinese culture — inasmuch as classic, modern and contemporary novels by English-language writers were. Similarly, the study of

---

[8]  This was an anthology of short stories published between 1981 to 1988 by the Hong Kong-based regional magazine *Asiaweek.*

[9]  Master of Fine Arts. A 'terminal' degree, generally in the graduate English departments of many American universities, in the area of creative writing. At present, only a handful of universities offer doctorates in this field.

Putonghua in the 1980s ought to have been *required* of any Hong Kong writer who wished to observe the cultural and linguistic shifts in her society. However, those arguments fell flat at my American university, resulting in the loss of my fellowship, which was reinstated only because my advisor, the novelist Tamas Aczel, strenuously argued my case. He wrote in English and Hungarian, having fled Hungary in 1956.

The first time I left Hong Kong was in 1971. I spent the next three years completing my BA in English in the United States and *never* wanted to go home. I called myself Indonesian-Chinese, rather than the reverse, touting passport over culture. At the time, I had not even been to Indonesia. But my family maintained our Indonesian citizenship, even transforming our Chinese surname into a pseudo-Indonesian one in the late 1960s, partly because of my father's business dealings in Indonesia where any hint of our Chinese cultural heritage was anathema to Suharto's regime. Another less pragmatic but perhaps more significant reason was that my parents did not see a long-term future as 'Hong Kong British' subjects (the other passport available to us), especially since 1997 hung over our city like Damocles' sword.

I had begun writing as a child, at first because it came naturally, but later to articulate the frustrations of living 'my Hong Kong' as a 'minority' *wah kiu* who spoke English too well to be truly 'local' or Chinese. On top of that, I was ethnically mixed with two Asian bloods, as locals were quick to comment of my appearance. This often made me feel that I did not belong in Hong Kong, even though it was, at that time, the only place I considered 'home'.

An idyllic life as a college student in America of the liberated (and liberal) post-1960s era, where classification as a minority 'Asian' was straightforward (although not without its own issues) coupled with my immersion in literature and creative writing — without question *in English* — was as close to heaven on earth imaginable. Had the possibility of living in the US after graduation been an option, I probably would never have returned.

Speaking as the writer I have become, I am eternally grateful for that lack of choice.

Colonial life during the 1970s bred in me a fondness for the work of Anthony Powell. His twelve-volume comic opus about upper-class English society, *Dance to the Music of Time,* echoed the world I lived and worked in with one exception: Hong Kong was 98 percent Chinese.

In my bilingual world, this detail could almost be overlooked. The 'noble house' at which I earned my daily noodle bowl hired only 'Oxbridge' and Hong Kong University graduates — apart from a few odd exceptions, myself being one — and perpetuated a two-tiered management track, for expatriate British and 'locals', meaning anyone Asian regardless of nationality or country of origin. Locals got fewer vacation days, benefits and opportunities than expatriates. My Australian-Chinese colleague, who never lived here until he came to work for the company, was deemed 'local', and received only partial 'expat' benefits. This was similar to the civil service, universities and other spheres of the ruling elite. English was still the 'power language', and, other than the rich Chinese, expatriates ruled. Less than thirty years later, many middle-class 'local' Chinese professionals run the noble houses of this city where English still has currency. But it is Cantonese, Hong Kong-style, that has become the 'power language' of the SAR — this linguistic outpost that does not yet chatter comfortably in *Putonghua.*

Back then, however, Chinese Hong Kong — meaning the majority local culture with limited or no access to the English-speaking world — perpetuated its own path, regardless. As a colony, we did not pretend to be a democracy. The ruling elite, both Chinese and expatriate, could forget about the majority as long as the natives were not restless. As a middle class took root, local culture and literature in Chinese naturally evolved, chronicling voices from society at large, restless or otherwise. Whether or not these writers had access to the bilingual world is immaterial; all Hong Kong Chinese learned English, even if they would not choose to write in that language.

To write in English therefore meant one of two things. Either I was a part of that Chinese bilingual elite or I belonged to the non-Chinese and/or mongrel caste who might or might not be 'elite'. In any event, it was the language more widely used around the world than Chinese.

This seeming privilege had a downside. Like any writer, I naturally wrote of what I saw and knew of my society, just as a Chinese-language writer would. Thus in 1981, I left home for a second time, because, despite my local, bilingual life, I was too 'mongrel' to fit among the local elite and therefore had nothing to lose. More importantly, however, I had to do something about all that background noise. It was deafening.

Distance provides a useful, almost necessary perspective for any writer. Squatting in America as a more mature, and hence, less surly being, I was able to ignore the day-to-day milieu of my home city. Consequently I was able to 'hear' clearly for the first time, what and why I needed to write of Hong Kong.

It is a universal truth that a woman writer, having acquired a room of her own, will eventually emerge with *something* to say. I was finally able to heed the siren call of my 'city village' and write about it from both heart and mind, and ultimately return to Hong Kong to draw from its soul for my work.

Today, I live somewhere between New York and Hong Kong. Both cities play a role in my sense of home and identity. However, the search for voice transcends place, race and even language. Hong Kong is in my blood no matter what I may choose to write about, and 'heart's blood', this rather useful Chinese term, is what any writer pours into her work.

## Voices for the City

It is not my intent, in these few pages, to comment on all the selections. However, I would like to detail my response as a writer and editor in reading and selecting some of the more important voices in this anthology as well as those that foisted 'a new nakedness' on my consciousness.

What was surprising and heartening was just how much literature existed, although much of the earlier work is out of print and ignored, and more importantly, how good some of it was, not all of which could be included in this anthology. Until I began the search backwards in time, it was unclear how academic neglect, or perhaps, fear of the unknown, prevented the exposure of this body of work. This seeming timidity might have been due in part to the sheer volume of popular work, especially in fiction, that appropriated the city.

My earliest encounters with the city's voices were in novels. A literary education ensured I would distinguish Blake from Dickinson and Shelley from Whitman, but a writer's life *demanded* I learn from those who did what I wanted to do. Since the age of 11, I knew I wrote fiction ahead of any other form, and that Hong Kong figured in it somehow.

During my teenage years, it was easy to read *The World of Suzie Wong* (1957) and *A Many Splendored Thing* (1952). Both novels were readily available in the 1960s and their movie versions dominated the popular imagination. I devoured these books, feasting on this literature which I did not think of as 'marginal' at the time. What was startling to me, when I returned for a third time from the West in 1992 to live and work in Hong Kong, was the absence of these two books from public view even as a host of sensationalist new work featuring the city, of a far inferior quality, continued to appear. In revisiting these texts for this anthology, I was refreshed anew by both authors' candid and honest vision of life in this city, some of which feels remarkably contemporary. Of the two, I preferred Mason's novel as a teenager (due no doubt to my own youthful romantic notions). Its narrative retains a vibrancy on the re-reading although the setting and plot lock it into a specific time and place. Han Suyin's novel, however, holds greater appeal for a more mature and inquisitive reader and has a resonance in the voices that followed.

Likewise, the shock of recognition on first reading Timothy Mo's *Sour Sweet* (1982) was personally important in understanding my peculiar Chinese perspective. Here was an aesthetic sensibility and language extremely unlike my own (so British, I thought, since this was in the 1980s and I was by then 'so American'). Yet, there was a familiarity about his treatment of Hong Kong culture that I hadn't experienced in reading Chinese-American or other Chinese diasporic writers. Mo brought an insider's voice to the experience that I was struggling to articulate.

Mo is, of course, the most widely recognized voice for Hong Kong in contemporary literature. It is his irreverence I like best, coupled with his wickedly comic perspective, that makes his voice such a liberating force. Both these qualities characterize the particular selections of Mo's novels in this anthology. As well, the 'Asian expatriate' protagonist in *Renegade or Halo*[2] (2000) is a departure from the more typically Western expatriate character in much English-language fiction of Hong Kong.

The process of uncovering texts from the two earliest works of the 1950s through to the present day yielded a mini avalanche of emotional responses. In retrospect, those responses can all be described as the consolation of shock.

Reading Edmund Blunden for the first time was rather like being sent back to secondary school again. In my ignorance, I had barely heard of him except in passing. Despite his stature as a poet in England and Hong Kong, we did not read his work in school (and certainly not in American universities), nor did his 'Hong Kong House' exist except, perhaps, in the privileged world of ivy-covered walls. Yet the ambivalence, even fear, expressed in 'On Lamma Island' (1962) gave me pause. Although Blunden's colonial world has all but vanished, songlines remain to remind us of what we once were, inasmuch as we may wish to bury that past.

Similarly, the music of Chinese poetry and language colours the work of Laurence Wong Kwok-pun and Leung Ping-kwan. This is English poetry that moves beyond the traditional canon. Hong Kong is a natural birthplace for such work, especially by poets who are fully bilingual and bicultural, as both Wong and Leung are, and reading their work was, for me, an adventure and discovery of how Chinese poets could enrich English when they take on the language and make it their own.

The encounter with Louise Ho's poetry was the shock of delight and rigour. Here was a voice for the city's culture and history that recorded and commented on our uncertain and confused identity. 'Home to Hong Kong' (1994) and 'Well-spoken Cantonese' are poems that establish a call and response of 'right on!' On a more serious note, 'New Year's Eve, 1989' (1995), the pair of 'Hong Kong Riots' poems (1997) and 'Island' (1997), among others, force me to confront the issues of history and language in my own work. Ho's approach is always rigorous, demanding of the reader an appreciation of the literary canon she alludes to as well as a local historical knowledge and sensitivity. It conjures up being whipped for pleasure. As the first Hong Kong Chinese poet in English to win critical recognition, Ho stands out as a 'must read' for anyone engaging in the subjects, verbs and objects of this city.

But it is Agnes Lam's voice that provides me with poetic consolation, for in her work resides the 'unheard melodies' yet to come of this literature. It was a shock of recognition, not unlike reading Mo, except this time, the familiarity was in *language* as well as perspective. Lam's poetry captures the diction and rhythm of contemporary Hong Kong. 'Writing in the Middle of the Road' (2001) is one of my favourite examples of this, because it sounds the way Hong Kong people speak English — frenetic, almost but not quite naïve, profound at unexpected moments — transformed into art by the poet. Lam calls her own poetry 'pedestrian' and tells students and young writers that anyone can write poetry. This seems unduly self-deprecating and overly generous. If, however, by 'pedestrian' she means the second language English voice of Hong Kong Chinese people, then yes, this is it, and thank heaven for it too. Lam, a linguistics scholar, instructs teachers of English and is fluent in Chinese, although she writes poetry only in English. This might account for her special sensitivity to the language of the people.

It was also intriguing to see parallels in the intensely personal work of Brent Ambacher and Agnes Lam. Ambacher's 'One Perfect Kiss' (1995) and Lam's 'First Draft' (1997) validated the kind of artistic 'confession' that colours some of my earlier work. This quality is hardly exclusive to Hong Kong writing, but that such literature does emerge from the pens of two indigenous poets, whose obsessions dovetail at times with mine, offers solace to one without a native literary tradition.

Turning back to the prose, a strain that intrigued me was the appearance of 'localized' non-Chinese characters in several of the novels, by which I mean the atypical expatriate who interacts closely with the Chinese community. Hong Kong's image in numerous popular novels gives the illusion that the only books from and of this city must include *tai pans,* triads and tricks of the trade, preferably slant-eyed and devious. Above all, East and West are twain, unmet. Small wonder it is the Eurasian Han Suyin who leads the 'empire' in writing back, with Simon Elegant not far behind.

Coming upon Elegant's *A Chinese Wedding* (1994) was like receiving an invitation to a feast. In the novel, a young American woman marries into a Hong Kong family, and lives and eats her past through the courses of the wedding banquet. No visitor to this city can fail to be overwhelmed by the sheer number of restaurants per square foot. Somehow food references are bound to appear in the literature, as in Elegant's novel and Mo's *Sour Sweet,* as well as in several others.

Almost thirty years before Elegant, however, C. Y. Lee featured an American priest in *The Virgin Market* (1965), a remarkable novel about Pigtail, a red-haired Eurasian orphan raised among the boat people. This Eurasian, unlike the Dentons in Christopher New's novels, speaks no English and can only wonder at her supposed American father, the closest image of whom she can imagine being the priest who works among the fishing community of Aberdeen. Lee's novel startled the most, because it chronicled the world of the boat people and their day-to-day travails, employing a main character who is almost 'profane' (as Han Suyin might say) yet far from unrealistic in this city. Lee is also the author of *The Flower Drum Song,* better known through its Broadway and Hollywood incarnations.

Another priest appears in *An Iron Tree* (1993) by Martin Booth, a British author who, like the American Ambacher, grew up in Hong Kong. The world Booth details is the underbelly of Western expatriate life, a sharp contrast to the privileged existence in noble houses, government, media and universities of much popular fiction, where the *lingua franca* is English.

Mimi Chan's first novel *All The King's Women* (2002) was the only one included where the author acknowledges the roots in family history. The personal tone of the narrative was a delight, and the lives of the concubines she details were fascinating because of her matter-of-fact tone, without the disturbances of 'exotica' or the memoir *des misérables.*

Among the short stories, the one that 'shocked' like a shower of red dust was Alex Kuo's 'The Catholic All-Star Chess Team' from *Lipstick,* a collection that won the American Book Award. I first read the story in manuscript in 1998, and was so struck by the brilliant collision of fact and fiction — one that could almost *only* happen in Hong Kong — that I foisted it upon the editors of *dimsum* where it was first published in 2000. For me, this is the brilliant diamond among a selection of gems, the kind of short story that re-invents the form (as well as time, place and circumstance), allowing layers of meaning to settle and reside and is truly fiction at its most challenging.

An interesting contrast in terms of language and perspective is in the stories of three Chinese writers, David T. K. Wong, Yang Yi Lung and Hark Yeung. The first publishes only in English while the other two also write and publish in Chinese.

Wong's story 'Lost River' (1990) has a poignancy and yearning that characterizes a number of his short stories, even while providing a commentary on Hong Kong society, which he does directly in 'The Cocktail Party' (1996) and other tales. Wong is to date the most prolific short story writer among us.

Yang Yi Lung's (John D. Young) stories were an unexpected find. A noted historian, he had begun to write short fiction in the 1990s, but sadly, was killed in an accident. He would have been a welcome addition to our literary scene. We are fortunate to be able to include one of his unpublished stories and an essay that appeared in the now defunct *Asia Magazine.*

Hark Yeung (pen name) is a Chinese-language journalist with a background in translation. Her first book of essays *Our Elders* (2000) signalled the presence of a distinctly Hong Kong English voice in prose, just as Agnes Lam's is for poetry. Her extremely spare prose and almost deliberately unsentimental perspective has a kind of defiance that feels, to me, very much like our contemporary culture. In reading the work of new and emerging young writers, I often heard echoes of Yeung.

Lest readers think that our city never laughs at itself, I must remark on the comic work selected. The most notable writer in this area is indubitably the Sri Lankan author and journalist Nury Vittachi, a long-time resident of Hong Kong who is also the editor of *dimsum,* the first journal of Asian English-language fiction. A few excerpts from his numerous books which satirize the foibles peculiar to Hong Kong life appear in this anthology. Vittachi also has a talent for seizing on examples of the grammatically and syntactically unusual English in Asia and turning it on its head.

What surprised me was the number of authors who have written in English satirizing Hong Kong. Most of the work contains overtones of the colonial master laughing at the natives, with little or no understanding of local culture, and celebrates, or at least posits, an 'us and them' comic vision. Vittachi is unique in his ability to adopt the 'native's' point of view in a deliberately farcical manner as in the piece 'Why Compromise? Get Divorced Instead' (1993). Likewise, the American author Charles Philip Martin, reaches across a broad range of perspectives, as in 'Colonial Life and Times' (1997), one of his many amusing columns from the *South China Morning Post,* as well as in his rather darkly comic short story 'Lau the Tailor' (1998).

Although we did not include journalistic reportage, the one exception was Jesse Wong's piece 'Uneasy Riders' from his book *Lives in Transition* (1997), a close-up look at ordinary lives around the time of the Handover. The historical event coloured much of the contemporary literature, and Wong's writings, which first appeared in *The Asian Wall Street Journal,* captured the uncertainty and confusion by personalizing the voice of the masses. Unlike many of the English-language journalists in Hong Kong, particularly of Wong's generation and earlier, he has the advantage of Cantonese fluency and access to local society in a way others do not.

There were few autobiographies of notable citizens, which are the memoirs I most enjoy. Reading Elsie Elliott's (Elsie Tu) *Crusade for Justice* was an education in local history where her place is unquestionably assured, just as, for completely different reasons, Jackie Chan's place is. His book is also excerpted in the anthology.

A few words on the new voices. There was a remarkable wealth of talent to choose from, a heartening experience for this reader. In fact, I would like to think that it will not be too long before an anthology of contemporary writers in English in all the genres will follow this one.

Nicole Wong Chun Chi's story 'Back Street' (2000) foisted that 'new nakedness' both by its tightly-wound language and immersion in a completely local world. In the latter respect, it was reminiscent of Lin Tai-Yi's 1964 novel *Kampoon Street*, which is excerpted. Lin authored several critically acclaimed novels in her day about Chinese life, but all have disappeared from view. Perhaps she was ahead of her time, by writing in English, just as C. Y. Lee did, whose books are also almost all out of print. The emergence of writers like Nicole Wong Chun Chi, Nancy Tsui Yuk Chun, W. H. Y. Wong Ho Yin and others among the new voices may create a resurgence of interest in earlier work.

There was even more poetry than fiction to select from, which is not surprising, since poetry seems to be the preferred form for many fledgling writers in Hong Kong. Among my personal favourites are 'Coming Through' by Canti Lui and 'She asked "Who is Franz Kafka?"' by Raslo Layton. Both voices embrace a courageousness that rings through loud and clear; they tackle challenging subjects, the way Louise Ho and Agnes Lam do. Call me mongrel if you will — marginal to suit academe — but at heart, I believe first and foremost in words for the soul, the only charge of the writer in her time.

It is courage and creativity, as Han Suyin implies, that will ensure the continuation of a literature in English or indeed, any literature. It is up to us to disturb, even to *profane,* in order to get at the truth of what we have to tell.

Yet remarkably, English, this 'borrowed' tongue, may serve us well in this city that manages to thrive in survival. It is interesting that Leung Ping-kwan, a Chinese poet who never wrote in English except for critical work, has begun, in recent years, to write poetry in English, some of which appears in this volume. His thought-provoking essay on writing in both languages (from *Hong Kong English: Autonomy and Creativity)*[10] is a useful study for any cross-cultural writer or indeed any creative writer who cares about the nature of language.

In the end, this English language is merely an instrument to voice human passions.

So it need not be a 'great' story we have to tell, but it is a Hong Kong story-in-progress, occasionally nostalgic for a British or Chinese world that was and was not ours, perhaps irreverent and a little defiant because of its tenuous beginnings, but above all engaged in this city — real or imagined; as emigrant, immigrant or native; defining or liberating — the place, people and spirit transformed by our words. The city has given birth to this mongrel crew, comprised of 'running dogs' who attempt to outrun their 'masters'. If our 'gamble' pays off, our story is one that will continue into a future, where time and place are owned, not borrowed.

---

[10] *Hong Kong English: Autonomy and Creativity,* ed. Kingsley Bolton (Hong Kong: Hong Kong University Press, 2002).

# PROSE

# NOVEL EXCERPTS

## A Many Splendored Thing

### 1952

*Han Suyin*

*Born in Chengdu, Sichuan to a Chinese father and Belgian mother, Han Suyin (pen name) came to Hong Kong in 1948 where she worked as a medical doctor. Her second novel A Many Splendored Thing (excerpted here), written in Hong Kong, established her international reputation as a writer; the story was based on an actual love affair between the author and a British foreign correspondent. Other books include numerous novels and books on China and the Chinese, including two on Mao Zedong and the Chinese Revolution. She currently lives in Switzerland.*

———

Seldom is there such close proximity of squalor and wealth, misery and ostentation. Here, within sight, sound and smell of each other, rich man and poor man live, intimate neighbors and brother refugees.

There are two kinds of street in Hong Kong. The smooth level main streets parallel to the shore, lined with shops, crowded with the newest cars; and the narrow, staircased climbing streets which cut across them. In the large level streets can be found all the world's finished goods in profusion, for everything comes to or goes through Hong Kong, and the harbor is full of ships unloading more. "You can buy anything here," is the Colony's motto. Anything from a fighter airplane to the latest perfume. There are no restrictions. And now that the rich have come from Shanghai there is plenty of free capital floating about, and there is a boom on.

There is a boom on. Hong Kong is dazzling with prosperity. The rich have brought their money, and they build and banquet and buy. The shops are crammed full with everything that the rich can desire, and what do the rich like best but American things, slick and streamlined and colorful? Cameras, bathing suits, lipsticks, perfumes, watches, shoes, nylons, silks and brocades, perfumes and stockings, all in great heaps on the shop counters. Hong Kong is a shopping paradise.

Like battalions of sea gulls, the idle rich Chinese women walk from shop to shop, their voices raised above the din of the street, their bracelets tinkling on their wrists. Their scarlet-taloned hands dig into the silks and velvets, the brocades and the satins. Cantonese shopgirls and Indian salesmen unfold roll after roll of iridescent satin, drape shimmering silks round themselves for the inspection of their clients. The rich women crowd into the jade and gold shops, congregate at beauty counters, eddy among the lipsticks glistening in their gold cases, the strapless bathing suits, the Chanel perfumes, the "falsies" spread on the counters. They buy and buy, noisy, rapacious, and bored.

Around the Hong Kong Hotel, in the English business section of the city, American sailors amble, hail taxis, have their shoes shined by little boys. On their arms hang shrill Chinese prostitutes. Tourist women in off-the-shoulder dresses gaze at embroidered silk underwear and ornate Chinese coats. Shanghai bankers and businessmen in twos and threes, all in natty sharkskin suits, flamboyant American ties, with fountain pens in their coat pockets, talk business in earnest sibilant tones. Wounded lost soldiers of the Kuomintang, dirty and ragged, some on crutches, stand against the walls of the shops, and watch the street with an angry scowl on their dark faces. Under the covered archways of the sidewalk glide, flow, rattle and clatter the anonymous common men of Hong Kong. Each man, despite his air of belonging, a transient, claiming as his origin a village back in South China, refusing to belong to the Colony, maintaining his status of passer-by even when he works here all his life, even when his children are born here, sometimes even when he is born here. This is the most permanent fact about the Colony: with few exceptions, those who come regard themselves as on the way to somewhere else.

In the narrow, vertical, staircased streets of the Chinese district abide the poor, and few go to look at them. The streets are dirty, the houses smell. The tenements are four-storied. Their insecure rotting wood balconies are draped with washing. These structures have no bathrooms, no latrines, no courtyards, and only one communal kitchen for anything up to twenty families. The floors are divided into cubicles. Each cubicle is eight by eight feet and houses a family of five or upwards. The beds in these cubicles are in tiers. At night the pails of human excreta are placed outside the door for collection. Up and down the staircase of the street the innumerable children of the poor play in the dust. Here are the street sleepers, the human scavengers that live off refuse from the hotels. Here a family spreads a mat between a cobbler's stall and a congee man's table and calls it a home. Here between the feet of the passer-by the offal of the markets — two rotting tomatoes, a handful of beans, one broken egg — is offered for sale by the poor to those poorer than they.

As beings from different planets, invisible to each other, unconscious and indifferent, these people move, walk side by side, jostle each other, sidle to avoid contact. Their glances skid over each other and rest nowhere. Absorbed in their preoccupation, aware only of their own perils and opportunities, riveted to their individual search for safety and survival, each is filled with the illusion of entireness, moves in his world and denies the others, for to acknowledge others would breach his own tenacity in the struggle for existence.

And here on the pavement, I run into my friend Anne Richards, American free-lance writer, met in Chungking ten years ago, met in London at a cocktail party five years ago, and met here again, in Hong Kong where I was to meet so many people; she is lost, as I am, in contemplation of the streets.

"Come to the Immigration Office with me. I must renew my permit for staying in Hong Kong," says Anne.

The Immigration Office is housed in an old baroque building on the Praya, the broad avenue which runs along the waterfront. The walls have not been painted for years, and the ceiling drops flakes of plaster quietly on our waiting heads.

"It is one of the lovable things about the English," says Anne. "Unlike us Americans, their important administrative offices are not lodged in steel and reinforced concrete, furnished with imposing desks and comfortable chairs, guarded by soundproof doors, connected with the outside world by a battery of modern telephones. Their government departments function, as this one does, in two or three dim, shabby rooms, with worn floors, doors that cannot shut properly, with one antiquated telephone inconveniently placed, just out of hand's reach, on the desk of the Head of the Department." We laugh as we note the one single wooden bench for the waiting crowds, and along the wall at its back the oily gray band where sitters have rested their heads. Files marked *Urgent* and *Not to be Removed* lie in careless heaps on the marble top of the chimney mantelpiece. Chinese clerks in shirt sleeves tap meditatively on archaic typewriters. Two unruffled young men in police uniforms talk in low voices to the visitors.

This is self-reliant security, authority without pomp to make it bullying and inefficient; this is how government should govern, it seems to me — casual, good-tempered, human among its ramshackle desks and rickety chairs and insecure file boxes with broken bottoms. Anne and I are delighted with the Immigration Office.

The blond young policeman comes back with Anne's passport between his fingers and a large stamp dangling from his left hand. "You're not a missionary, are you," he half states.

"No, I'm a writer," says Anne.

"That's all right then. We'll renew you for six months. We only give three to the missionaries, there are so many of them. Seven hundred on our books."

"Come to Church Guest House and meet a few of the seven hundred," I say to Anne.

The evening in gray and gold strides across the sky as Anne and I walk to Church Guest House. In the hall Mabel Chow grins feebly at me. Her face is tired-looking. "I have a pain in my back, I think maybe Baby is coming," she says to me. "Good luck," I answer. "Hope it's another boy." Lucy Koo and the children are back from the cinema. Mei says to me: "It was all about love again. Aunt Lucy likes love. Love, always love." The dinner gong sounds, and we file into the dining room with the first lot of diners. There is great excitement, and Helen Parrish rushes up to us.

"Dr. Han, meet my husband, he's come this afternoon on the train from Hankow."

I shake hands with Alf, tall and fair and very quiet. Back in China, Hankow fell today. Mr. Parrish left a week ago, just in time. He has brought some news from Mary Fairfield's husband. Mr. Fairfield is not going away, he has decided to stay, and so Mary Fairfield is going back to China, just as God told her some time ago. Her face is beautiful with serenity, and as I look at her I am a little awed, because I never thought that she was beautiful at all. "Well," she says in the New England drawl that used to irritate me, and which now has dignity and resonance for me, "I think we'll stick it till we're thrown out. Perhaps we'll understand what it's all about when we go back to China. I only feel at home there, and I think, yes, I believe, that we must have faith in the Chinese people."

After dinner Anne, Lucy and I sit in the common room and look at Hong Kong, where we are, and then beyond the hills at the darkness that is China, unseen, but always felt, the China which is the reason why we are here.

We are all here, bankers, businessmen, rich women, missionaries and squatters. Those that take off half a hill to build themselves a home and those that crowd on a mat on the sidewalk to sleep. Wanderers against our will, we are the refugees. And to me, a transient among so many transients, that is Hong Kong in April 1949: a refugee camp. Harbor of many ships, haven of people out from China, squatters' colony, fun fair, bazaar and boom town. Hong Kong, where people come and go and know themselves more impermanent than anywhere else on earth. Beautiful island of many worlds in the arms of the sea. Hong Kong.

And China just beyond the hills.

\*     \*     \*     \*

## Hong Kong Profiles

*October 1949*

"Oh, Mark, a butterfly is perching on your shoulder. Turquoise and ebony. Such a good omen for us. Please do not move."

"Is it still there?" said Mark, very pleased and careful not to turn his head. "I hope it settles on you too."

The butterfly circled away, lazily volplaning above the long, seeded grass, leaving our hearts as light as its touch upon Mark.

"So I wish my love, if it be love that I bear you, to rest upon you no heavier than a butterfly."

"Darling, no one will say these nice things to her lover in your New Democracy," said Mark. "Everyone will be so busy with work, self-criticism and dialectics."

"Politics don't stop love. He will say to her: 'You are as beautiful as our new hydroelectric plant.' And she will reply: 'Comrade, how progressive of you.'"

It was hot on the hill slope. The sun slid into each corner of our bodies, palpable like hands, deft and loving, so much like love that I could scarcely bear it. Merged into the earth, the green tea scent of the grass, and the tobacco smell of Mark's pipe. His eyes very near and wide open. "You and the sun," I said to him. "I never knew that blue eyes could be so attractive."

"Look," said Mark, who had decided to be purely intellectual, and had brought papers and magazines and *The Times* crossword puzzle to help him: "Paragraph 7 of the Marriage Constitution of the New People's Government of China: 'Widows may now remarry.' Isn't that good? Your family won't lose face with their neighbors now, because of you."

"Widows have been remarrying, 'unvirtuous' ones; and divorce by mutual consent we've had for years. But we, like your people, are more bound by custom than by law, and old customs die hard. China is such a hodgepodge of things new and old. Anyone who tried to write a book about the Chinese of today would contradict himself at every step."

Mark said: "Anglo-Saxons are muddled with wishful thinking about your country. To us it is still a wonder land of hidden wealth and subtle wisdom. We say: 'How awful of you to give up those dear old customs, that wonderful family system we admire so much (since we did not have to live under its yoke). It's not you we want, but your traditions, your culture, your civilization.' We are collectors of a glass-incased past labeled: *Do not touch.* But some of us, I think, do understand the present."

I said: "Foreigners have such rigorous ideas of how Chinese should behave, speak, display at all times fatalism, inscrutability, serenity, figments of Western imagination so wrongly attributed to an earthy, extrovert race. They don't want the uncomfortable truths about China, its enormous and collective hunger, its exorbitant poverty, its violence, its urge towards assertion, and the inevitability of its revolution. The civilization they admire, who but they destroyed it? Who but they broke down the dikes of institution and tradition which used to contain our exuberant and vital spirit?"

Mark said: "You ought to write something about the soul in torment of the Chinese today, since you are one about whom lingers fragments of the past, yet who wants to fit into the new and yet unknown pattern that your country is shaping. I predict great suffering for you, my dear."

"If I should write anything, my critics will say: 'This is not Chinese. There is no inscrutability, serenity, fatalism, and mighty little philosophy. This is savage and violent and perverse and decadent all at once.' People will read politics into my nonpolitical statements, and dispute the meanings of my words, because all meanings are distorted. The independent mind is a dangerous thing, for it belongs to no party, and is suspect to all. No, I'll go to China and stick to my medicine. They are my people, and what does it matter to me that they may be blue, red, or dark green? For, like all Chinese, I am spellbound by my own country."

Mark said: "In two months your year in Hong Kong is ended; and go you will. I shall try to follow you, for I, like many foreigners, cannot get away from China. I too am spellbound. Like you, I have faith in the common sense of your people. But I think it will be difficult for you to fit into the new pattern. I still think you ought to go back, but I am afraid you are already too mellow to participate in your country's brash adolescence without cutting out great pieces of yourself. You are too detached and undeluded, in spite of your love for it, to be possessed by those burning faiths, and those fierce angers; you are too balanced, the multiple *yous* holding delicate equipoise in courteous harmony, to undergo again the abrupt divided mind, and the appeal of a simple mystic to hungry idealism. Truly, you will have to be born again.

"The West is old, the East is new. Our roles are reversed. It is only too clear that China is young, agonizingly so; with its aspiration after human perfection and social brotherhood, its belief in machinery and achievement, its intolerance, its black and white universe, and its slogans."

"You make it sound too simple," I replied. "There are all kinds of people in China, all as complicated because they are as alive as you and I. The early Christian Chinese, with their confessions, their repentance, their conscience searching; the patriotic Chinese, that hard core of strength in all Asiatic communism which is ardent nationalism: my country, right or wrong, but mine. The historic-minded Chinese, haunted by the past and memories of the Great White Injustice; the Chinese *émigrés* who go away, hoping that one day they will return. Those who are here, in Hong Kong, waiting to let the dust settle, to see clearly what is going to happen before they make up their minds. And the many fence-sitters, who will go with the victor. And who can blame them, after all? For very few people have the physical means at their disposal to choose what is called *Freedom*. A word I do not understand in Asia, where hunger is absolute and freedom so relative."

Mark said, a little sadly: "Shall we be able to choose?"

"I don't know," I replied. "At the moment we are, like so many others, subjects of destiny. We want to go to Peking, you for your paper, I to do medicine. It does not depend on us whether we can go together. It depends on politicians, and economics, and markets, on all these things which I do not understand."

"Do you think that your new regime will allow newspapermen like myself to come in?" asked Mark.

I replied, "Wait till the dust settles. You are such a nice person, Mark, everyone will like you. I bet, though, that if you write anything in favor of New China, people in London clubs will frown over their paper and say: 'Is that chap going Red?' And if I say anything good about England (for I learned freedom of speech there), they will say: 'She is corrupted in her thoughts by that British imperialist newspaperman.'"

Mark was silent for a while, then he turned to me, and we laughed, pleased with the sun and each other, and in this pleasure thinking that we had hope in this life, hope for life together.

Around us lay Hong Kong, basking in the sun — Hong Kong, tiny excrescence of the Chinese mainland, rock of exile to so many — poised, expectant, waiting for the future, just as we were.

\*　　\*　　\*　　\*

## Amour Profane

*October, November 1949*

Nothing so delights a lover as the loved one's pleasure. For Mark I would have ramsacked the world of beauty.

"Look," my eyes said, "look, is he not beautiful, this man? I sit under the Tree of Love we planted together, watching him, as one watches a bird on a high branch, a hovering butterfly — content with sight and sound, and knowledge of him on earth. And let me not want more, for more is murder." One thing vexed me, the fear that he might deny himself because of me. I did not wish him narrowed in any way.

"A European woman would find it difficult to understand that because you love me, you urge me to be unfaithful to you, Suyin."

"But it is so unfair to restrict, to hem you within the boundaries of myself. Your pleasure is my delight, and that you might miss or regret a particle of your life would sorrow me."

"*Elle ne fait rien pour exciter mon amour,*" said Mark, "*car elle a l'insouciance des grands enchantements.*"

"Did you read a book called *A Floating Life*? It is the story of Shenfu and his wife Yun; lovers of beauty, they also loved each other with delicate and moving tenderness. Yun tried to purchase a girl as a concubine for her husband. 'But our passion is so full,' said Shenfu to her, 'need we add to it?' Yun replied: 'She is beautiful and lovable. Let me arrange it.' Like ourselves, Shenfu and Yun looked at the moon, collected books, recited and wrote poetry, arranged flowers, drank wine and had many friends. As we do, they propitiated Heaven with sacrifice, strove for good omen, and went in fear of wrath from above, for great happiness displeases the gods. And theirs was short-lived, alas — only twenty-three years of married love together."

"Only twenty-three years," said Mark.

"It seemed so short to them. Shenfu says of his wife: I do believe Yun's sensitive nature never recovered from the grief she felt when this girl was sold to a boorish trader instead of joining our household, and this was the cause of her short life.' Shenfu and Yun lived in China nearly five centuries ago."

"I wonder what your pet missionaries, and Father Low, would say if they heard you," pondered Mark.

"They would moralize. But moralists have no place in an art gallery. Shenfu and Yun were moral for their own times. Yun's unselfishness and wifely generosity would be highly praised by the family and her husband's friends. 'A truly loving and unjealous wife,' they would have said. Love and jealousy do not abide together. How can one be jealous, when one loves?"

"I, like Shenfu, do not want anything else; it would be adding feet to a snake," Mark quoted the Chinese proverb. "Our passion fills me, and please notice," he said with the slight solemnity he employed to tease me, "that I use the word not in the narrow sense to which our uncouth and barbarous age has whittled it down, but to indicate that mixture of the elements converging towards one aim, *le transport total de mon âme envers vous.*"

Yet I was afraid that he would clip the wings of his imagination to my stature. I feared him diminished by wordless compact, as others are by that frightening apparatus of possessiveness and habit which established couples form between them. He was born free and I would keep him so. And by so doing, I bound him to myself with a tenfold chain.

"One of my first memories of hair," said Mark, "is of my amah in Peking. I remember her long pigtail, a thick vigorous braid depending from her glossy head to the back of her knees, and tied with black string. Alive and vibrant the strong coil I grasped in my six-year-old hands, twisting it once round my wrist as I pulled. I can still feel the many strands of that heavy rope between my palms, and like to think that my Victorian passion has its roots in that first sensuous recollection. All my life, until you, I have wanted, unavowed, a woman with long black hair streaming down her back."

"You continue for me the tradition under which I lived during my marriage," I replied, "perhaps because you were born in Peking, although you are so English. My husband being Chinese loved long hair. He would not let me curl, cut or show mine. I kept it in a tight knot, as now. He deemed it bad taste for a woman to flaunt, blunting the fine point of beauty in herself."

"I did not know yours was long until the night you combed it out . . . do you remember?" said Mark.

"You must see my sister Suchen," I replied, cheeks hot with violent recollection. "She wears hers spread out as a mantle of grace upon her shoulders. It will give you pleasure."

Suchen had arrived in Hong Kong two weeks before, and lived on the Kowloon side in a room rented from a Portuguese family, awaiting her visa for the United States. Sitting in the Parisian Grill, waiting for her, and for Mark, I saw Suchen push open the glass door; she wore pink linen, her face rounder and happier than when we were in Chungking.

Then Mark came in, slightly unsubstantial, and walked in the opposite direction. "That is Mark," I said to Suchen, and felt turned to water. Suchen scanned him efficiently, beginning with his back, and when he turned and came towards us in his soft, unhurried way, from the thick hair through the old careless clothes to the shoes and up again. "Of course, you choose all your beaux the same type, don't you?"

I protested indignantly. "This one's English."

Suchen shook her head. "Ever since your University days, all the beaux that took you out, and your husband also — all were the same type as this Englishman."

Mark stood in front of us, waiting to be introduced. I stared at him as if I had never seen him. He gave us both a disarming smile; his eyes, friendly, went to my sister's face framed in a close crop of curls.

Deeply miserable, I too gazed at Suchen's shorn head. She noticed it and smiled, exhibiting once more our inherited enamel:

"Yes, I am glad I can look nice again. All that awful hair. I could not wait a moment longer to get it cut and have a perm."

# The World of Suzie Wong

## 1957

### Richard Mason

*The author of several novels and screenplays, Richard Mason came to Hong Kong from England in 1956 where he wrote* The World of Suzie Wong *(excerpted here), his most successful book. Born in Hale, Cheshire, he began writing as a young man and published two thrillers under the pen name John Lakin; his last novel was published in 1962. He travelled widely, continued to write and eventually made his home in Rome where he died in 1997 at the age of 78.*

I had no idea, when I first discovered it, that there was anything odd about the Nam Kok.

It was my fifth week in Hong Kong, and I had been to call at a house on the escarpment behind Wanchai, following up an advertisement for a room to let. The advertiser had been a Mrs Ma, and I had found her flat on the second floor, but the moment she had opened the door, and I had glimpsed behind her, in the small living-room, the usual abundance of children, grandparents, cousins, aunts — they must have numbered nearly a dozen souls — I had known that it would be no use, that there would be no privacy for me to paint; and I had been relieved when Mrs Ma had told me that the room had already been taken by a Chinese. She had been sorry, she had wished she had known I was coming, for she would have liked an English guest so that she and her husband could have improved their English. She had insisted, anyhow, on rewarding my wasted journey with a cup of tea, which I had drunk whilst sitting stiffly on a hard, straight-backed chair, my presence scarcely noticed by the relatives seated about the room.

"Well, perhaps I can get something down in Wanchai," I said. "It's one of the few districts I haven't tried yet."

Mrs Ma, who was very neat and bird-like, tittered with merriment as if I had made a joke. "You wouldn't like Wanchai," she said.

"Why not?"

"It's very noisy . . . . No Europeans live in Wanchai — only Chinese."

"That's what I want," I said. "The trouble with my present place is that there are only English." I told her about Sunset Lodge, which was at the lowest contour of the Peak at which a European could respectably live, and where I had been living until now — not for respectability, but because I had not been able to find anywhere cheaper. And I told her about the other residents: about the bridge-players whose sessions began at eleven o'clock every morning in the lounge and continued all day; about the sad wistful wives who said "Of course we're spoilt out here" but really wished themselves back in Sutton; about the feuding middle-aged ladies, and about the garrulous ladies who lay in wait for you, trapped you, and then turned their flow of talk on you like a hose; and about how I had taken to entering by the kitchens to reach my room without being caught. It sounded quite funny when I told it, but really wasn't. I had become almost desperate; for by now a whole month of my year had gone by and I had still not settled to work, I had done nothing. At first Hong Kong with its teeming, jostling populace, its atmosphere tingling with activity and excitement, had been too stimulating, too confusing; the impressions had whirled in my head too swiftly to record. "I must let it take shape," I had thought. "I'll be all right in a week or two." But nothing had taken shape; I had been able to find no centre of interest, no point of beginning; and I had begun to wonder in dismay if I should have chucked up rubber-planting at all. Then I had begun to understand. My work had always depended on sympathetic feeling, on a sense of identity with the people I sketched or drew; and here I was a mere spectator in the streets, making my occasional sorties from another world. A great wall divided me from the Chinese — how could it be otherwise, living in Sunset Lodge? And thus I had begun another room hunt — for I had given up once in despair — and again taken trams from district to district, trudged from street to street, only to be reminded again everywhere, by the swarming pedestrians, by the quantities of washing hung out overhead, that this was the most over-crowded city in the world. Only a few years ago, at the end of the war, the population had numbered barely half a million; but since the revolution in China, from which the refugees had come flocking across the border in their hordes, it had swollen to two and a half million, and some thought to three million by now — who could tell? And when the firstcomers had packed themselves into every available room — each divided into ten, fifteen, twenty "bed-spaces" — there had been nothing left for the remainder but the empty sites and the hillsides, and such shanties as they could build from threadbare sacking, flattened tins, and treasured gleanings of wood. And if indeed any room did become vacant now it would be let at an inflated rental that no legislation could restrain. And so for a second time I had found nothing within my means, and dispirited and footsore had once more given up; and it was only Mrs Ma's advertisement that had brought me out again this afternoon.

I put down the little decorated cup and said, "It was delicious tea. You were very kind."

"Not at all, not at all," she tittered politely. "The tea was very poor."

"No, it was delicious." I rose to go.

"I hope you are not really going down to Wanchai?" she said anxiously, coming to the door. "It is too noisy — too dirty. The people in Wanchai are so poor, you will get such a bad impression of the Chinese. You won't go?"

"Well, perhaps not."

But I did go nevertheless — descending the escarpment by the long steep flights of steps that dropped straight down into the oldest part of Wanchai: into the teeming alleyways with the litter-filled gutters, the pavement vendors, the street-stalls, the excitement and bustle. The sun slanted brilliantly down, making deeply contrasting patterns of light and shade and giving the overhead washing the gaiety of bunting. I saw a post-office and went in, thinking the clerk would speak English; but when I asked him about rooms he shook his head and said, "No, sorry. No sell."

"I don't want to buy anything," I said. "I'm just looking for a room."

"Sorry. Only sell stamp."

I crossed Hennessy Road, with its clattering trams and its two huge modernesque cinemas showing American films, and came out on the waterfront by the Mission to Seamen. Next to the Mission was a big hotel called the Luk Kwok, famous for Chinese wedding receptions and obviously too expensive for me even to try. Further along the quay shirtless, bare-foot coolies were unloading junks, filing back and forth along the gangplanks like trails of ants. Sampans tied up amongst the junks tossed sickeningly in the wash of passing boats. Across the road from the quay were narrow open-fronted shops, between which dark staircases led up to crowded tenement rooms; and along the pavement children played hopscotch whilst shovelling rice into their mouths from bowls, for all Chinese children seemed to eat on the move.

I sat at the top of a flight of steps leading down to the water. A month gone, I thought. A whole month gone, and I've done nothing. I must take myself in hand. I must bully myself.

But no, that's no use, I thought. I've already been bullying myself and it doesn't work. You can't bully yourself to paint. It's like bullying yourself not to hear a ticking clock. The harder you try, the more the sound fastens itself into your ears.

Sometimes will-power is its own enemy, I thought. You can't paint by will-power.

Yes, relax, I thought. It's only when you relax, when you're not trying to grab what you want, that you suddenly find it's there. . . .

I leant on the sun-warmed stone. A rickshaw went by, the coolie's broad grimy feet making a slapping sound on the road. Then my eyes fell on an illuminated sign amongst the shops. The blue neon tubes were twisted into the complicated, decorative shapes of Chinese characters. I recognised the last two. They meant hotel.

Well, that looks more my cup of tea, I thought. And right on the waterfront. Of course it would be perfect. So perfect that there must be a snag. Still there's no harm in trying.

I got up and crossed the quay, and turned into the entrance under the blue neon. And still not a suspicion passed my mind. Indeed the hall gave the impression of such solid respectability, with the middle-aged clerk behind the reception counter, the old-fashioned rope-operated lift, the potted palms at the foot of the stairs, that I was reminded of some old family hotel in Bloomsbury, and felt discouraged. It was all wrong for the waterfront of Wanchai — and anyhow would probably be too expensive after all.

I approached the desk and asked the clerk, "How much are rooms by the month?"

"Month?"

The clerk's fingers paused over the beads of his abacus: he had been making calculations from figures in his ledger, as though playing some musical instrument from a score. His Chinese gown, like a grey priest's cassock, gave him an old-fashioned appearance in keeping with the potted palm, the antiquated lift. His head was shaven, and he had several silver teeth.

"Month?" he repeated.

"Yes, don't you have monthly terms?"

"How long you want to stay?"

"Well, it would be a month at least . . ."

He gave me an odd look, then dubiously began a new calculation on the abacus. The beads clicked up and down under his fingertips.

"Two hundred and seventy dollars," he announced at last.

"A month?"

"Yes — month."

The Hong Kong dollar was worth one shilling and three pence, so that was about seventeen pounds — a little dearer than Sunset Lodge, but with cheap meals I could just afford it. I asked to see a room, and the clerk called one of the floorboys on the telephone while I went to the lift. The liftman lounged inside against the mirror reading a Chinese newspaper. He folded the newspaper, crashed the gate shut, yanked on the rope, and we rumbled upwards, our passage punctuated at each landing by a loud metallic clank. On the third and topmost landing, where I alighted, a miniature radio on the floorboy's desk was emitting the falsetto screeches of Cantonese opera. The floorboy, a smiling fresh-faced youth of about twenty, dressed in a white jacket, wide-legged cotton trousers and felt slippers, led me down the corridor and unlocked the door of the end room.

"Very pretty room, sir," he grinned.

It was not pretty, but it was clean and perfectly adequate, with a wide hard bed, a cheap dressing-table and wardrobe, and the inevitable enamel spittoon on the floor. There was also a telephone and a padded basket for a tea-pot: I remembered hearing that in Chinese hotels a constant supply of green tea was provided free of charge. I could almost live on tea; it would be a great saving.

"And a pretty view, sir."

He opened the doors on to the balcony, which was roofed over but beautifully light: a perfect studio. And the view was indeed superb, for the balcony was on a corner and commanded an immense panorama. On one side it looked out over the rooftops of Wanchai, behind which rose the skyscrapers of Hong Kong and the Peak, whilst in front was the harbour scattered with ships of every shape and size: cargo boats, liners, warships, ferryboats, tramps, junks, sampans, walla-wallas, and numberless comic, graceless rusting mongrels — some lying at anchor, some in ponderous movement, some bustling about busily, criss-crossing the harbour with their wakes. And across the harbour, so close that I could count the windows of the Peninsula Hotel, was the waterfront of Kowloon, with a backdrop of tall bare hills stretching away into China.

I said, "This'll do fine."

"My name is Tong Kwok-tai, sir," the floorboy grinned deferentially. "Will you please correct my bad English?"

"There's nothing to correct, Ah Tong."

"You are too kind, sir." And as we turned back into the room he said, "You have a girl here, sir?"

"A girl? No."

I supposed that by "here" he meant Hong Kong and still did not realise. I went down again in the rumbling lift, and paid the clerk a deposit to make sure of the room. He wrote out a receipt in Chinese. I could hear the muffled sound of dance music coming from a swing door leading off the hall. I nodded to the door, asking the clerk, "What's in there?"

"Bar."

"Good, I'll have a beer."

I turned away across the hall, and just then the door swung open and a Royal Navy matelot came out. He was small, wiry, and darkly tanned by the sun. He wore a hat with *H.M.S. Pallas* in gold letters round the brim.

He cocked his head at me in casual salutation.

"Good lord, the Navy!" I laughed. "The last thing I expected to meet here!"

He gave me an odd look like the clerk. "Well, you won't meet much else here, mate," he said. "Not at the Nam Kok."

"No? You mean there aren't any Chinese here?"

"Only the girls," he said. "The girls are all Chinese."

# Kampoon Street

## 1964

*Lin Tai-Yi*

*Born in Beijing, Lin Tai-Yi (a.k.a. Anor Lin) is the daughter of the prominent Chinese writer Lin Yutang. The author of several critically acclaimed novels in English, she is also a translator and wrote a Chinese-language version of her novel* Kampoon Street *(excerpted here). She married a Hong Kong civil servant and lived in the city for many years where she wrote several of her books. She now lives in the United States.*

——

*Kampoon Street is the fictitious name of a fictitious street. All the characters, companies, establishments, and their names mentioned in this novel are fictitious. Any similarity between them and actual persons, companies, establishments, and their names is purely coincidental.*

His mother was sitting beside him in her neat dark clothes, her hair uniquely confined in that fine hair net of hers, which gave her an appearance of tidiness which belied the nature of the mother Lam knew was underneath. She was a small-boned, pretty woman with a fine, sharp-featured face, which she would abuse by screwing up into an ugly scowl but, just as quickly, could smooth out again like a piece of silk.

It came to Lam that his father was only pretending to be sick, and his mother pretending to be sewing, and that one day something devastating would happen to them, and they would begin to live their real lives.

Then his mother, Eling, saw him, and putting down her sewing, came to him and seized him by the wrist. "Lam! I've been waiting for you! Read this! Your father doesn't believe it, but they wouldn't print it in the paper if it wasn't true!" She picked up the newspaper on the table.

Lam glanced at his sister, who was lying on the veranda reading a magazine, but Riri did not move so Lam guessed that this was probably just another of their mother's false alarms. He should be used to her pouncing at him when he came home . . . to tell him the discoveries she'd made in the day's wash — a hole in a vest, a stain which wouldn't come out, or a piece of material which shrank — or to announce to him that she'd bought four mangoes for twenty cents. Her days were crowded with a hundred surprises and disappointments in a constant struggle to keep up with the demands of their lives, but each time she seized him like this Lam half expected to hear that they had just won the lottery.

"Read it!" she cried. Then, unable to wait, she told him the news. "They're going to tear down these buildings and the landlord is going to give the tenants ten thousand dollars each to get out!"

He looked at her, wondering if the moment had indeed come.

"The only question is when they're going to get to us," she said. "On Monday I want you to find out from your school when they're going to get to Number 31, Kampoon Street."

His mother had had a wild misunderstanding ever since he had passed the Primary Six Examination and was admitted to a Government Grammar School that he had access to a direct source of information about all that was going to happen in the colony. He was the Grammar School bird.

He went out to the bedspace and said to his sister, "Is it true?"

Riri was lying flat on her back with her feet propped against the veranda railing. "In life nothing is impossible," she said without looking away from her magazine or changing her position.

"Read it! See if it doesn't say Kampoon Street!" his mother said.

Duck Face, who occupied the bedspace to the right, said, "What about Kampoon Street?"

"They are going to tear down the buildings on this street and give the tenants ten thousand dollars each compensation," Riri said from behind her magazine.

Up and down the length of the veranda the people looked up. Ah Sook's eldest daughter, Michu, said, "I don't believe it."

"Why don't you believe it?" Eling cried. "Read it out loud, Lam!"

Everybody except Riri looked at him while he read the item out loud.

"What do you make of that?" Eling cried.

Duck Face got up from his cot and came to the wire net.

"Well, in the first place, they probably won't get to Kampoon Street for years," he said. "But when they do, what makes you think the landlord is going to give you ten thousand dollars, hey?"

"Why not *me?*" Eling said, her eyes very round.

"Think about it," Duck Face said. "The owner of the building might give the person who holds a long lease to each floor ten thousand dollars. But what makes you think he is going to give the subtenants ten thousand dollars each? If he did that, he'd have to give away forty hundred thousand dollars on this floor alone!"

Everyone laughed, and Duck Face grinned, pulling his wide lips back. He glanced at Riri but she did not appear to be aware that anything was going on.

"Oh! For a minute I thought I was going to get my three-room flat!" Eling said, sitting down on the cot and joining in the laughter at herself — and taking the loss of ten thousand dollars rather lightly, Lam thought. "A nice three-room flat, with kitchen and bathroom and running water. That's what I would get the first thing if I had ten thousand dollars. Nothing elaborate. Just a three-room flat, nice and clean, easy to keep. What would you do if you had that much money, Duck Face?"

The barber, whom everyone called Duck Face, pressed his naked body against the wire net. "I'd buy my boss out of his business."

"*Chi!*" Michu said. "Ten thousand dollars won't buy you that barbershop on Des Voeux Road!"

"I'd buy myself a share of it at first," Duck Face amended.

"Go into partnership with him. Then, I'd buy him out."

"That's not bad," Eling said, and turned to the bedspace to the left of theirs, where Michu's younger sisters and brothers sat on a double-decker bunk. "What about you? What would you do, if you had ten thousand dollars each?"

The children looked at each other and tittered.

"Don't you hear her asking?" Michu goaded. "Go on, tell her."

They were silent and embarrassed. Beyond them, the Thin Woman sat in her bedspace assembling the petals of plastic flowers and fitting them into their stems. "It'll never happen," she murmured, sitting waist-high in bluebells, gladioli, and chrysanthemums.

Eling looked at her sharply. "Why not?" she snapped. "You don't think that a person who is born poor has to stay that way forever, do you? Good fortune rotates among people in turn, according to how much merit a person has accumulated. That is the law of the Wheel."

There was silence.

Eling looked at them all angrily. "Don't tell me you don't believe in the Wheel?" she said. "The Buddha said, 'The spokes of the Wheel are the rules of good conduct, justice is the uniformity of their length, wisdom the tire, and compassion is the hub in which the axle of truth is fixed!'"

"*Omitofu!*" Michu said, rolling her eyes and smiling.

"I believe it," Riri said, sitting up at last. "The Wheel shall turn."

"Of course you do," Eling said.

"The Wheel shall turn," Riri said, her lean face without expression, so that Lam could not decide for a moment whether she meant it. "I shall see to its turning."

"Oh, Riri," he said.

"I mean it," she said.

"Stop it."

"I'm not joking."

Abruptly, their mother put her hands to her face and began to weep.

"How's Papa?" Lam whispered, knowing suddenly that his father's illness was the cause of all this.

"About the same," Riri said.

"Take any food?"

"No food."

"Maybe we should get him a doctor."

Eling pulled her hands quickly away from her face. "No, no doctor," she said. "If we had a doctor every time your father gets sick, we'd be out on the streets by now. All he has is a bad cold. You remember how he came back in the pouring rain that day. I said to him, 'You take a little time off, do you hear? You're not used to doing all this heavy muscle work. Tell them you're used to making a living by your brain, and not the muscles of your back! You're paid to set type, and not to be a porter. Let them hire regular porters to move their books and paper!' But you know what your father always says. 'Stop fussing, Eling!' Whenever I say anything he says I'm fussing. Well, somebody has to fuss. It's being cooped up in that dark shop all day with all that lead. It gets into a person's blood. I said to him, 'Tell them you'll quit if they don't stop making you do a porter's work!' But he never opens his mouth, and he never will. Well, it isn't his nature to put up a fight, that's all. He'll just work there until he cannot work any more. That's what he's like."

He might be listening inside, Lam thought. How can she talk about him like this? Maybe he is better, and she is getting it off her chest. Yet maybe he is worse, and it is too much for her to bear.

"Don't say any more, Mama," he said.

"No, let me talk. I must talk!" Eling said. "I can't help talking any more than he can help keeping quiet! It's *my* nature. You can't force a person to be what he isn't. Your father's an educated man. Otherwise how do you suppose he knows how each character is classified? And that's why I can't forgive him. I can't forgive him for all this. I tried. I kept Riri in school for as long as I could, pinching pennies the best I knew how. We're slipping and slipping, and there's only the two of you who can even understand what I'm talking about, because *you're* my own flesh and blood, and it's just as though we were a different kind of plant — poppy, or cockscomb — and the Tsois were another kind — yellowwort — and you can't force a cockscomb to be like a yellowwort no matter how hard you try."

She began to weep again — out of weariness from trying to be like a yellowwort when she wasn't one, Lam supposed. But he couldn't help seeing her a little through his father's eyes, too — because wasn't he a mixture of them both? the combination of their mismatch? — and knowing that she was a little on the hysterical side.

In the silence, he heard his father calling. Had he been listening and waiting for the right moment to call? His mother did not stir, so Lam went inside.

"A drink of water, Papa?"

He poured a cup from the thermos, and his father lifted himself on one elbow, drank it, and sank back on the bunk. He could tell that his father had been awake for a little while, and probably had heard everything, but he did not say anything. Unlike his mother, his father was a person who fought all his battles deep inside.

"Can I get you anything else?" Lam asked.

Ati shook his head and closed his eyes.

Lam stood watching him for a few moments, and then returned guiltily to the bedspace. His mother had begun to talk again, but more softly.

"Poor's poor, but it wasn't like this in China. We were never lacking for space. We always sat outdoors in the evenings after a day's work, and the country smelled so good. You could smell the tangerines on the trees in the winter, and the pomelos in the autumn. And when you looked up, there was a big stretch of sky, and not just a slice of it. You could walk for miles and not bump into anything — no car, no houses — you could walk for as far as your legs could carry you sometimes and not even see people. When I was a girl I used to tear about, along with the boys. We used to steal up to a rich man's orchard and scramble up the fruit trees. You could eat as much as you wanted, but you couldn't carry any away. That was the rule, and everybody abided by it. But that's because everybody had enough to eat and work to do, and there was none of this wire net and padlocking everything, bars on the windows and grills across doors, and everybody thinking everybody else is a thief. Oh, the good times we used to have! Every family who had a pig killed one on new year's, and there were so many different ways to cure the meat. It took days! Some of it would be salted, and some cut up and made into sausages. The head, liver, and tail were rubbed with salt and saltpeter and hung high on the eaves to be wind-dried. The trotters were pickled in vinegar. But the kidneys we always ate right away. There's nothing like a pair of fresh kidneys, sliced very thin and thrown into boiling water for a second. I was a good cook. There's lots of things I could make for you if I had the time and the space, and the money."

"When was all this, Mama?" Lam said. "After the World War and before we came to Hong Kong, or are you talking about when you were a child?"

"What?" she asked, resenting the interruption.

"I mean did they kill the pigs when you were a girl scampering up the fruit trees, or was it later?"

"Oh, I was talking about before the World War," she said. "No, there wasn't much slaughtering of pigs after the Japanese left, I can tell you! And now there is even less. All that is gone now. Well, I suppose we should be thankful to be here and not there. All the same, I can't help longing. When you graduate from school, Lam, you'll get a nice job and get your Mama that three-room flat, won't you?"

She had written their father out of her life. She seemed more composed now. It was as if she had reverted to the cockscomb she once had been, blooming in her memories in the hot, humid night. She was content to be silent now. When Ati called, she rose with the strength that this gave her, and went in to him.

"What? Water again? Lam just gave you a cup. My, your forehead is burning! Shall I warm up some of that soup? All right, I won't mention it again! I asked only out of my concern for you. If you don't mind being sick, I don't mind!"

"Riri, I'm worried," Lam said.

"Do not worry," she said. "All things resolve themselves."

"Stop talking in that way," he said.

"I'm not talking in any way," she said.

"Why don't we get him a doctor?" he said.

"If he's not better tomorrow morning we'll get a doctor," she said.

She got up and went inside also.

Lam washed his hands and face and feet in the quarter-bucket of water on the veranda and stretched out on his cot.

The half-moon bathed the street in an eerie luminescence and gilded the roof tops. It was nice to think that his mother had run in the fields and had had as much fruit as she liked when she was a girl, and that she still remembered. It also proved that change was possible. He closed his eyes, and dreamed of a phantom land of cockscombs behind the blue mountains which separated the peninsula of Kowloon from China, and saw a three-room flat in the middle of it. He was standing under some fruit trees and wondering which one he should clamber up first when he was snatched awake by Riri's voice.

"Wake up! Lam! Wake up!"

The light was shining directly into his eyes from the cubicle. Sookmo and his mother looked unreal in it, as though they were getting ready to be photographed while the rest of the city slept, drenched in midnight black.

Going inside, he found his father writhing on his bunk and gasping for air. He seemed to be choking. Beside him, his mother stood frozen in disbelief.

"Ah Sook's gone to call 999," Riri said.

"It shouldn't take them very long," Sookmo said. Her mass of tangled hair was spread about her shoulders like a lion's mane. "There's nothing to do except wait."

Riri crouched, put her arm under her father's back, and raised him a little to help him breathe. But it did not help very much, and they stood listening to his choking and gasping noises until an ambulance wailed into the street.

Lights came on everywhere. People leaned over the verandas to see what was happening. A white-clad man came out of the ambulance. Ah Sook was waiting below. They came in together and soon materialized in the cubicle, the man in white like an intruder in the night, bringing with him an alien smell of antiseptic.

The intern bent over Ati, felt his pulse, and listened to his chest. He quickly walked to the veranda and called down for the stretcher to be brought up.

"Pneumonia," he said. "In both lungs. Why didn't he receive any medical attention sooner?"

"Pneumonia!" Eling gasped. "We thought he had a bad case of flu!"

"Why didn't you take him to the clinic to see the doctor?" the intern said. "It's free."

"There's always such a long queue," Eling murmured.

The intern shook his head and chuckled to himself.

"My mother said we didn't know it was pneumonia," Riri said.

"Well, the clinic is the place to find out, isn't it?" said the young man.

"You're right," Riri said. "Bully for you."

"Who's coming to the hospital with him?"

"Stay here, Mama. I'll go to the hospital with this brilliant young man."

The stretcher came. The men set it on the floor, carried Ati from the bunk to it, and marched out briskly.

The intern went after them, and Ah Sook and Riri followed.

Lam's heart hammered. He recognized that "something devastating" was happening. It's a mistake, he thought. It should have been getting ten thousand dollars for moving out of Kampoon Street, not this.

Confused, he hurried after the little party which was already going down the stairs.

# The Virgin Market

## 1965

### C.Y. Lee

*Born in Hunan in 1917, C. Y. Lee went to the US in 1943 where he obtained an MFA in playwriting from Yale University. He authored several contemporary and historical novels about Chinese life, the best known being* The Flower Drum Song, *which was adapted into a Broadway musical and film.* The Virgin Market *(excerpted here) is his only book set in Hong Kong. Other published work includes stories and journalism in English and Chinese, which appeared in* The New Yorker, Writer's Digest, Ellery Queen's Mystery Magazine, Chinese World, *among others. He lives and writes in California.*

The wedding dinner had not been meager. It consisted of a pork dish besides fish and vegetables. Lum Sin had a desire to clean the bowls of the gravy, but it was not proper, as a bit of food left in the bowls would indicate future prosperity for the newlyweds. He put his chopsticks down on the deck and belched properly to show his appreciation, and then proceeded to pick his teeth; the other six male guests had also begun this ritual.

The junk was rocking slightly on the undulating dark water; the large red sun was sinking behind one of the barren isles in the Hong Kong Bay. It had been a successful wedding. The bride was big-boned and strong, with plump rosy cheeks; but according to Lum Sin's calculation, she was not quite worth the two thousand dollars' "engagement money." He believed his brother-in-law could have gotten her for less if the matchmaker had bargained a little harder. She was not exactly pretty; she needed at least a few gold teeth to compensate for this weakness.

He cast a glance at the stern where his wife had been eating with the female relatives. The bride and the groom had just finished serving the after-dinner tea, and were ready to retire to the stern cabin to sit out the wedding night properly chaperoned by an aunt. Lum Sin remembered his own wedding night well. He had spent the whole night restraining himself from choking the chaperone and tossing her into the sea. But he had observed the custom so as not to offend the water god.

As he glanced at his wife he felt a faint glow in his heart. Mae, at thirty-five, was the only woman who looked younger than her age. If the other fishermen owned mechanized junks, at least he owned the prettiest wife in Aberdeen. "*Ai*, brother-in-law," he said to the host, who was sitting on the deck beside him sipping the hot tea, "a good dinner. You have a good cook for a wife. Hope your new daughter-in-law can cook as well."

"She is strong," the brother-in-law said modestly, smacking his oily lips.

"She is well worth the two thousand engagement money," Lum Sin said. "She will be a good hand at the oar."

"No oars for her. I'm installing an engine. Her first duty is to give me grandsons."

The thought of an engine depressed Lum Sin. Everybody seemed to make enough to buy an engine these days but him. And those who had already installed one had elevated themselves to a different class of water people, almost equal to the land people. They brought in more fish and could afford Western clothes and more gold teeth. This brother-in-law, at forty, only three years older than he, already had everything. Lum Sin decided it was about time to leave.

When he got up from the deck, Mae, his wife, also rose. That was Mae, amiable and obedient, always doing the right thing. She gave him much face by following his example so promptly. They thanked the host and stepped onto their own sampan. Mae untied the little boat and started to row.

Squatting on the bow Lum Sin took a half-smoked cigarette from his pocket, smoothed it and lighted it with a match. "*Ai*, my son's mother," he said, blowing out the smoke heavily. "How old is Pigtail?"

"Seventeen," Mae said. "She was three when we found her on the street in Wan Chai."

The memory came back vividly. It was a New Year's Day fourteen years ago. They were returning to the junk after their annual visit to the flower mart. He was carrying a heavy pot of peach blossoms, and wanted a rest. As he was putting the pot down he heard a weak whine. Mae rushed to a doorway and peeked into a heap of rags. It was a red-haired, skinny little girl, with a note pinned on the rags saying that the mother wished some kindhearted lady would take her in and feed her, and that she did not eat much. It was bad luck to bring home a sick girl, let alone a half-breed. But Mae had insisted. It was one of the few times she had been stubborn. Now he was glad that he had consented. The girl had been a help, and now at seventeen she was quite pretty, except for her red-colored hair. If his brother-in-law had paid two thousand for that broad-faced wench, he could at least marry Pigtail off for the same amount. Perhaps he should visit Blinking Mama Woo, the matchmaker, and find out the possibilities. "*Ai*, my son's mother," he said, tossing the cigarette butt away and rising. "I'm going to visit a friend. I'm taking the sampan."

"Shall I go with you?" Mae asked.

"No."

He took over the oar and sculled vigorously. Aberdeen was full of noise and sampans, in which peddlers were selling hot food, fishermen were returning to their junks and tourists were visiting the floating restaurants. Lum Sin was ashamed; no other sampan was as shabby as his. He skillfully maneuvered the little boat till he reached his thirty-foot shabby junk anchored between his hateful neighbors — a big mechanized boat and a gaudy sail junk owned by a quarrelsome old goat. As soon as Mae had climbed on their own junk he was off again. "I shall not be long," he said.

He did not look at the floating restaurants as he passed by them. Their bright lights, ostentatious carvings and decorations seemed to belittle him, making him feel more wretched. He quickly rowed his boat out of the crowded area and headed for the Dragon Palace, which loomed darkly in the distance. Soon the heavy smell of hot food and fish diminished; there was only the smell of the sea, carried in the eastward wind. He looked at the small, full moon and knew that Blinking Mama Woo would be telling fortunes at the Dragon Palace now; he could see her in his mind's eye, blinking habitually, smiling and scowling alternately as she studied horoscopes, consulted the lunar calendar, and glanced at the moon with narrowed eyes for mysterious information.

When he reached the large, dilapidated barnlike floating house he grabbed the short ladder, tied his sampan, and climbed aboard. The Dragon Palace was full of activities under those bright bare lights. In one section four groups of fishermen were playing mahjong, slamming their tiles loudly and crying out their ecstasy and anguish. In the other section people were sipping tea, eating hot noodles and steamed buns. A few plump, heavily painted water harlots roamed about, trying to flirt with disinterested fishermen.

Lum Sin saw a few acquaintances but avoided them. They all wore Western shirts and khaki trousers, a symbol of prosperity, a glaring sign to tell the world that they had mechanized their junks. He hated that smug look; even worse, their forced modesty. He dreamed that one day he would go up to them in the best Western clothes, slam a stack of bank notes on their mahjong table, and challenge them to a game at a dollar a point. That would show them that Lum Sin was not an ordinary water bug who always scampered around for food.

He saw Blinking Mama Woo telling fortunes in her usual corner beside the cracked window, through which she glanced at the moon for consultation. She was talking to a customer and scowling. It was safe to scowl at a fisherman who did not wear Western clothes. He was obviously not doing too well. Lum Sin had sworn that he would never have his fortune told until he had gotten rid of his patched sails and his shabby coolie blouse. But Blinking Mama Woo was a good matchmaker, knowing the conditions of every family in Aberdeen. "Hmm, I see a star, however," she was saying to the customer after pursing her lips for a moment as if the moon god had just dispatched some good tidings. "Your wife is bearing a baby in her belly. Four months. If the baby is born before noon, in the eighth moon, he will have a great future."

Lum Sin waited for Blinking Mama Woo to finish. He thought it was quite safe to say that an unborn baby would have a great future, for Blinking Mama, at seventy, was not going to wait that long to see her predictions come true. Nevertheless she knew everything and everybody in Aberdeen.

Presently the satisfied customer was leaving. After he had paid and promised to come back for details of his unborn baby's future, Lum Sin came to the old red-lacquered desk and took the vacated bench.

"A detailed fortune told year by year, Lum Sin?" Blinking Mama asked, blinking and smiling her toothless smile, doubling the thousand wrinkles on her narrow face. "Or do you want a simple prediction told by the sacred turtle shell?"

Lum Sin glanced at the ancient turtle shell which Blinking Mama Woo was smoothing with her dried-up bony hand. It would cost a dollar to ask his immediate future. Why should he spend the dollar? If he could find a husband for Pigtail, he would be two thousand dollars richer. That would be his immediate future. "How is the matchmaking business?" he asked.

Blinking Mama Woo's smile disappeared. For a brief moment she almost stopped blinking. She stared at Lum Sin, her thin lips tightly pursed. She had now switched to the role of a shrewd matchmaker. "Who do you wish to marry off?" she asked. "Pigtail or your own daughter?"

"My own daughter is only six."

"That does not mean nobody will have her. She will not bring good engagement money, but there are men who will take a suckling pig for their sons."

"Little Jade is too young. I'm speaking of Pigtail."

"But she is not even your own daughter."

"I raised her."

"It is hard. She has no parents."

"Will you try?"

"If the engagement money is not too high."

"How much is not too high?"

"It depends. Decent fishermen don't take wives who have no real parents."

"One of her parents was a foreigner. She is better off without them."

Blinking Mama leaned back in her rattan chair, looking shocked. "I didn't know that! You mean her father was a foreign devil?"

"You have seen her."

"No, I never saw her. No, I cannot find a husband for a half-breed."

Lum Sin quickly glanced around to see if anyone had overheard her. Luckily the room was full of noise and nobody was paying them any attention. He leaned forward and said loudly, "I want a decent man to marry her, a man with a mechanized junk!"

Mama Woo threw her head back and laughed. Lum Sin stared at her, embarrassed. When he was leaving he felt anger rise in him. The old witch would have been more polite if he had come in Western clothes. He was going to install a motor. He would show her!

When he was walking toward his sampan and mumbling angrily to himself, a man at the nearest mahjong table hailed him, "*Wei*, Lum Sin, just had your fortune told?"

Lum Sin did not have to look. It was the omnipresent Hop Fong, the tourist guide. Lum Sin recognized his cracked voice. His first reaction was to ignore Hop Fong, who was a gossip and a busybody; he probably supplied Blinking Mama Woo all the information in Aberdeen, such as who was sick, who had painted his junk, and what women were pregnant, probably all seeded by him. Now Lum Sin was sure he was going to spread the rumor that Pigtail couldn't find a husband. The man was also a show-off, always wearing neat black Western clothes and pointed leather shoes, which he often dusted with his white handkerchief on busy occasions. Whenever he played mahjong he always pulled the sleeve up high so that nobody would miss seeing his gold watch. Lum Sin just could not bring himself to believe that this man could make so much money without a boat or hard labor. He was ugly, and according to physiognomy, a man with such a rat face was destined for poverty and misery. But here he was, the most prosperous-looking man on the Dragon Palace.

"*Wei*, Lum Sin," Hop Fong was calling again, "if you have good fortune coming, play a game of mahjong for me. I need a little luck."

Lum Sin halted. The itch to play a game suddenly became overpowering. The players had just finished a hand; they were mixing the tiles now by pushing, stirring and moving them around with the palms of their hands. He came to the table. "What did Blinking Mama say about your luck?" Hop Fong asked, a cigarette dangling between his lips.

"She sees a star," Lum Sin said casually. "I'm going to have another son."

"Did she say a son?"

"Yes, a son."

"Here, play a game for me," Hop Fong said, rising quickly. "I need some of your luck."

Lum Sin sat down on the warm bench and started gathering the tiles. He had never played mahjong with somebody else's money before. Now he might even enjoy losing a little. It was Hop Fong's money.

The first game, to his surprise, was so lucky that Hop Fong, standing behind him, watching, secretly knocked him with his fingers. By changing only five tiles he completed a good set and won the game with doubled points. When the other three players paid him two dollars each he wished he were playing his own game with his own money. "What did I say, eh?" Hop Fong was laughing with delight. "A man with a pregnant wife always brings luck. *Wei*, Lum Sin, let me name your son. How many months now?"

Lum Sin changed the subject. "How about some tea and a cigarette?"

"Sure, sure!" Hop Fong promptly offered him a cigarette and lighted it for him. "*Wei*, waiter, bring a fresh cup of tea! And wash the cup!"

The second game was even luckier. He made the set after seven changes of tiles and won the game with tripled points. Everybody paid three dollars. Hop Fong offered him another cigarette and ordered hot buns for everybody at the table. "I should play for myself tonight," Lum Sin said as he started mixing the tiles.

"Why not?" the man at his left said. "Five can play. We can play shift mahjong. A change of number and seat might change my stinking luck."

"Play five more hands for me," Hop Fong said. "Five more hands. After that you can fight your own battle."

"I'm short of money tonight," Lum Sin said.

"After five more hands I'll loan you twenty. I can loan you two hundred. You have a boat. I don't worry."

During the following five games Lum Sin won two. By this time he had completely warmed up, and knew that he could not tear himself away from the table now. He borrowed twenty dollars from Hop Fong and started the shift game with gusto, coughing and blowing on his hands for luck . . .

# The Chinese Box

## 1975

*Christopher New*

*The former head of the Department of Philosophy at the University of Hong Kong, Christopher New has written several novels set in Asia, where he lived for many years. He is best known as the author of the novel* Shanghai *which, along with his two Hong Kong-based novels (excerpted here), form a trilogy about the British Empire on the China coast. Originally from England, he now writes full-time and lives in Malta.*

———

'Have you ever been here before, Mila?'

She shakes her head. 'I usually pass through the border at Lowu.'

'I mean to the New Territories.'

She shrugs. 'I do not come. It is not my home.'

'A true Chinese.' He smiles. 'Some of my students have lived in Hong Kong all their lives and never even been to one of the outlying islands. Let alone Macau.'

'Nor have I.'

'I'll take you.'

'We are not as restless as you foreign devils.'

'Yet you have lived in London.'

'To study, yes. That is different. We are not tourists.'

A sudden flurry of quacking comes from the unseen ducks. Some dogs start barking wildly.

'What are you going to do about it?' Mila looks at him for the first time.

'How did you know that was on my mind?'

A faint shrug. 'What are you going to do about it?'

'There's only one thing *to* do, isn't there?' They are speaking in English, but their voices are lowered as if they are afraid the Hakka women might overhear and understand.

She is gazing at the heat-hazed mountains distantly bounding the Chinese plain. 'You will report it to someone?'

'To the police.'

She frowns slightly. Otherwise her face is still. 'But it was the police who did it.'

'So?'

But she does not follow her protest through. Instead, she comes closer to what is behind her doubtfulness. 'What will you tell them?'

'What we saw. What we saw and heard.' His voice is touched with impatience. He has felt all the time she will pull back. That is why at first he has delayed speaking about it, why now he is bristling already at her indirect reluctance.

'Do not say what *we* saw and heard. Say what *you* saw and heard.'

'Why?'

She ignores the sharpness in his tone. 'Because I cannot afford to be involved.'

'Oh? What do you mean by that?'

'I mean that it will make a lot of trouble for me and it will not do any good. So it is . . . stupid.' Her voice too is hardening.

He looks at her, but she gazes unblinkingly away at the mountains, refusing to meet his eyes. One of the Hakka women behind them hawks loudly several times, then spits.

'Won't it do some good if someone is tried and found guilty, and everyone knows it?'

'It would, perhaps. But it will not happen.'

'Why not?' He cannot keep the coldness out of his voice.

'Because we are in Hong Kong . . . And the communists and the riots . . . There would only be much trouble and nothing happens.'

'In the first place,' he says cuttingly, 'you don't know that nothing will happen. And in the second place, the only trouble will be making a statement to the police. Is that bothering you too much?'

She is silent for some time, but seeing the pulse throb in her throat, he knows she is not calm. 'How will you explain to Helen how I came to be in your car?'

'As a matter of fact I've told her already.' He smiles with a certain malicious triumph. 'I told her I saw you at a bus-stop on the way home from the library and gave you a lift.'

'Ah.' She smiles too. 'You have protected yourself very well . . . The trouble is, I cannot protect myself. If I went to the police with you, I would never get a visa for England.'

'Hong Kong's not as corrupt as that, Mila.' He laughs. 'That's ridiculous.'

'For you it is not as corrupt, because you are British.'

'I simply don't believe that anyone could prevent you from getting a visa if you got a work permit from London.'

'You have lived in Hong Kong a long time,' she speaks with a quiet scornfulness, 'and of course you have visited the New Territories and the islands. But still perhaps you do not know Hong Kong very well. Why should I sacrifice myself for someone I do not know, especially when it will do no good?'

Dimitri's eyes are set on two Gurkha soldiers oiling their machine-gun fifty yards beneath them. "The thing I can't stand about you Chinese, you traditional Chinese, is your total callousness about everyone except your own family or your own clan. If that's what they're trying to get rid of over there' — nodding across the river — 'Well, good luck to them, that's all.'

'It is not callous. And what do you know about "over there"? Do you think you can understand us because you have learnt a bit of our language?'

'I've heard all that cultural chauvinism before. *Ad nauseam.*'

Her face has become rigid. 'I will never get a visa if I am mixed up in this.'

'How do you know?'

'Because I am Chinese. And I have lived here a long time too. I will never get a visa. And how will it help the man, anyway? Do his family want you to meddle? You do not trouble to ask.' She falls into Cantonese, despite the Hakka women watching and listening. And instead of frigid exactness, she speaks now with a rush of fierce heat. 'You and your foreign justice! It's easy for you because all you're going to get out of it either way is a nice smug conscience. You're safe anyway because you're British. But for me it's different. Don't you know how your great British colony works yet? If you really care so much about it, why don't you give his family some money — something that's worth something?'

Dimitri has never seen her angry before. Her face is flushed under her fine, pale skin and her lips are set tight. He looks away at the border fence again. The Gurkhas beneath them are laughing quietly, the ducks quacking in the farm and the red flags of China fluttering still in the vast fields.

'Once, when I was in the internment camp, at Stanley . . . in the war . . .' he begins almost musingly, 'I saw them beat a man . . . He'd been caught trying to escape . . . The guards had these long bamboo clubs . . . I can still hear the sound of them swishing and thudding . . . They took it in turns. And one of them kept hissing through his teeth when he hit him. A sort of whistle of enjoyment . . .'

He feels her looking at him while his own eyes dwell inwardly upon the pulped body that had lain like a sack in the afternoon sun.

'What happened to the man, Dimitri?'

He shrugs. 'He died too.'

She is still for a long time, only her eyes moving as she looks from the Gurkhas to the red flags and back at the unmade road to Shum Chun. At last she too shrugs, speaking in English again. 'I am sorry. I can't.'

# The Monkey King

## 1978

*Timothy Mo*

*Timothy Mo is the most well-known contemporary novelist from Hong Kong. His novels have won numerous international literary prizes and were shortlisted twice for the Booker. Born in Hong Kong, the Eurasian author grew up in both Hong Kong and England. He is author of six novels, three of which are excerpted here; his most recent work* Renegade or Halo[2] *(2000) won the James Tait Black Memorial Prize. He is now based in Southeast Asia after more than twenty years in London.*

Mr Poon had plans for Wallace. And the moment had come to introduce his son-in-law into the design. Wallace had not worked out quite as he had expected but he was used to making the best of imperfect material; it was the story of his business success. Moreover, time (usually a great ally of Mr Poon's) did not in this instance seem to be on his side. He did not see Wallace's behaviour improving; indeed, in the long term, he saw it deteriorating. He might have felt more comfortable if his son-in-law had taken the dowry or some portion of it. However, he was determined not to offer money unless actually asked: he placed economic priorities higher than political.

Although a wealthy man, Mr Poon was dissatisfied. Using the dowry Mrs Poon had brought him, he had by craft, thrift, and daring accumulated a substantial fortune. His thriving network of businesses and investments was sufficiently diversified for him to be unconcerned about fluctuations in a particular commodity or service. Above all, the war in Korea had brought unexampled prosperity to black marketeers and smugglers. But for some time now he had wished to establish the foundations of this wealth on a sounder dynastic basis.

He had no illusions about Ah Lung. He had long abandoned the idea of his son as a business successor. He disciplined Ah Lung for appearances' sake. The little demonstration with the golf club at New Year, sabotaged by Wallace, had been so intended. The issue which really exercised Mr Poon was how to proof his estate for survival, more or less intact, until his grandsons came of age. None of the males in his family for the past five generations had lived beyond their middle sixties and he was nearing that dangerous age.

The commercial empire he administered could be controlled only by himself; only he understood its complex interrelations and dependencies. With his own death it would break up under the kinds of strains and pressures only he had been able to moderate. He was looking now to simplicity and security rather than the speed and size of returns. This was a complete contradiction of all his practice to date. The major portion of Mr Poon's capital had come from playing the stock market with a gambler's intuition and disdain for risks. He now wished to leave some tangible memorial behind himself. Some artefact. It wouldn't matter that his name might not actually be linked with anything he built. It would be in the nature of a tribute to an unknown soldier.

After long thought he had decided to enter the construction industry; specifically the building of highways, jetties, roads, tunnels and bridges. He saw opportunities here, especially in the rural hinterland of the New Territories. There was a certain logic to the growth of communications. One began at a point and measurably worked to another. It was discernible. He would begin a road. His grandsons would finish it. And if he entered the field quickly enough he would be able to capture enough to be consolidated after his death.

But how to get into the industry? It was not technicalities which worried Mr Poon. He could employ others to master these. He would be the financier, the one occupied with the grand view, while others were bogged down in the petty details. It was getting the work that was difficult. And it was here, in the area of contracts, that Wallace could be useful.

Mr Poon found Wallace and flung an expansive arm around his narrow shoulders. Wallace started. He had been comfortably digesting his ration of morning congee. Now he felt it curdle in his stomach.

"Just borrowing your newspapers for a while, Uncle."

"Any time OK, son. What was mine was also yours."

Suspicion displaced apprehension in Wallace's mind.

"Come to my office for a while. More private. I got some good news for you." Wallace understood Mr Poon to mean his desk in the corridor.

"It was a bit early in the day for good news to arrive already?"

"Sit, sit." Mr Poon beamed. His manner was reminiscent of the days before the marriage when he used to visit the Nolascos in Macau. "Now, Wallace, I could see you were getting unhappy just lying about with nothings to do. It was demoralising for the young fellow like you."

"Demoralising?"

"Yes, demoralising mean . . ."

"OK, OK."

Mr Poon's smile lost none of its blandness. "The sweet, Wallace?" They were sour plums. "Put one in your pocket. I knew you like them." He chuckled indulgently, then with unexpected bluntness said: "I got a job for you."

Wallace dropped the preserve he had been holding. He regarded Mr Poon with deep suspicion.

"Please or not please, Wallace?" Mr Poon left Wallace in no doubt which answer was expected of him.

"You would have to tell me more about it first."

Mr Poon ostentatiously hid his wounded feelings. He gave vent to a sigh, which suddenly turned into a belch. "That congee always gave me hiccup."

"No, that was burping you did."

Mr Poon frowned. "I didn't like how that word sound. We Chinese, as you knew, have no word like that. Our culture was too refine."

The sisters arrived with glasses of steaming tea, quartered oranges, and perfumed flannels.

Wallace sensed he was in a position to barter something, what he was not exactly sure, but he was correspondingly emboldened. "Where was this job?"

"Government job. You work in department for building and that kind of thing."

"PWD, hah?" Wallace looked forward to the challenge of employing some of his engineer's training.

"No. Not the same as PWD but doing same sort of things. It was good job. Your pay not too much but you could help your friend and family to make money, then you all got rich together."

Wallace grasped the general idea. "But that was corruption!"

"Wallace! Wallace!" Mr Poon raised his hands in horror. "You didn't understand."

"I sure did. You want me going to Stanley Prison? Anyway it was bad thing to do."

Mr Poon wiped his lips with a fragrant blue flannel. "Wallace, Wallace. This was the Chinese way. It was our custom, it go on thousand and thousand of year. You help your friend, you help your family. What was so bad about that, hah?" He wheedled, his voice soft and silky. He filled Wallace's tea-cup. "You got a chance to make new friend for yourself, too. Beside, when you staying here a little longer, you found you knew everyone else here. It was small place. So how you stop from giving your friend business, hah? And I tell you something else. It was so expensive for the English to make a government here. It cost money to pay for these civil servant in their suit and tie. When they got a commission it was just like a tax so they could keep going."

Wallace fiddled with his orange segments.

Mr Poon tried another tack. "You know Chinese people like to be doing their business this way. You didn't ask for tip: they wanted to give it to you. It wasn't like you were in the police or something, Wallace. It wasn't like going around showing your gun and asking for tea-money from street-hawker."

Wallace could not disagree with this. He peeled the ends of the rind away from his piece of orange.

Mr Poon pursued his advantage with a pragmatic argument. "How you thought everyone here getting so rich? How you thought we all got the work done quick-quick, not like in England, hah? I tell you why: you gave commission, it made more work and it got it done fast. No one going to help you for nothing, Wallace."

"You know, Uncle, I never thought of it like that before."

Mr Poon shrugged modestly.

"And I got some tip out of it, hah? Like you said, no one did nothing for nothing."

"Of course, son, of course. You wouldn't have to do anything wrong. Just helping with some entertainment."

"And it help our family, Uncle?"

"It helping us. Also helping Mabel. You like that, hah?"

This was a pleasant surprise to Wallace. It confirmed his decision. He fitted the quartered orange to his teeth and stripped it efficiently from the peel, sending the juice trickling out of the corners of his full mouth. Mr Poon passed a flannel to him.

"Good, son. I knew I could depend on you."

# Running Dog

## 1980

*Lee Ding Fai*

*Lee Ding Fai is a pen name of the author who wrote* Running Dog, *excerpted here. This is her only known published work.*

———

In the all quiet of pre-dawn, Yau Man, two rubber balls strapped on to his back to increase his buoyancy, drifted semi-consciously towards the shore. He felt the muddy bottom caressing his belly and wallowed in it with exhausted abandonment. Through the flapping sound of the waves he sensed the enthralling silence and his aloneness. He lay there motionless for a while, savouring this aloneness like a gourmet sampling his wine. Had he really made it across the border, he wondered. The twelfth of April 1962 dawned as he surveyed his surroundings. Through the pale light he saw stretched in front of him a patch of uncultivated paddy fields. Not far away to the left stood a small structure that looked vaguely like an outhouse in the dim light. Not a soul was in sight, not even the faint murmurs of insects were heard. Yau Man felt his strength slowly return and pulled himself up. He walked stealthily towards the hut to investigate. It was a dilapidated wooden structure that must once have been a farmer's rest house. Except for a broken bench the place was bare. Yau Man went in, took off his clothes and wrung them dry. He judged that there must be a couple of hours before most people would stir. Fatigue weighed like lead in his bones, and he curled down in a corner for a quick nap.

It was cold. Oh heavens above, it was so cold! He stroked frantically to keep the blood circulating and to help forget the cold. A sharp noise. A gun shot! He woke up with a start. It was broad daylight. The door of the hut was banging in the breeze, which produced the noise that woke him. His clothes, almost dry now, were strewn on the floor. Quickly he put them on, and from the inside of his Mao jacket he unplucked a few threads to disengage a sealed plastic bag, which contained some paper money, two diamond rings and a couple of letters. Having decided to discard his jacket for fear of its conspicuousness he tucked the bag under his belt. In undershirt and a crumpled pair of trousers, with damp shoes that squelched as he moved, he felt self-conscious and uncomfortable. However, having survived the swim and crossed the border, nothing was going to be too terrible to face. He committed to memory the address he had to find, and started off from the hut.

Yau Man, a man of fine, delicate features, was one of the first of thousands of refugees who flooded into the colony and attracted world attention in 1962. In other clothes, found under other circumstances, he could easily be taken as an intellectual capable of reaching the higher realms of fancy and sensitivity. Indeed, if brought up in a society of a different structure, there was no telling of what he might have become. As it was, he was a refugee who had gone through two sharply contrasting social and educational patterns. At twenty-four, he was faced with the prospect of being sent to work in the coal mines in the north. This bleak outlook, together with the romantic notions he had developed from novels he read and vaguely remembered when he was a child, prompted him to act. His plan had the full blessings of his parents who were educated middle-class people before the Communists took over. They had accepted their spartan way of life meekly, but grieved over their only son's lack of future. The painful part of it all was that they did not even dare to whisper their worries to Yau Man as they were not sure of his political conviction. How they had cried with relief when one night Yau Man came home, right after he got news of his imminent despatch to the north, to say that he was leaving that night.

Striding along the path that he hoped would lead to a main road, Yau Man regretted the little time he had had with his parents. There were always meetings to attend after work at the factory, and they had been taciturn with him, unlike the days of old when they were cheerful and indulgent. He could not tell exactly when it was that the change took place, but looking back he could clearly remember a life that was different, with his parents behaving differently towards him. In later years he had the feeling that they regarded him almost with suspicion, as if he was a stranger coming into their house to spy on them. Their show of emotion on the night he left shocked him into the past, back to the days of family chit-chat and unguarded outburst of affection. In tears his mother handed him the diamond rings and a thin roll of Hong Kong dollars.

"We have hidden these hoping they would be of use to you one day, Yau Man," Mr. Yau said, patting his back.

"The Gods of Heaven willing, when you reach Hong Kong, go to Uncle Chen. He's your father's old friend," Mrs. Yau instructed, sewing the plastic bag onto the inside of his jacket.

Yes, the Gods of Heaven had been merciful, he thought. He was now approaching a high road. A van painted yellow and red went by. A farmer with a bamboo pole on his shoulders and two basketfuls of vegetables swinging on each end sidled up to him.

"Can you tell me how I can get to the city?" Yau Man asked. The farmer stopped, scrutinized him silently, then pointed his finger to where the yellow van had disappeared. He stood watching Yau Man as he moved away, which unnerved him a little.

There was more traffic on the road now. A few cyclists pedalled their wares along and more yellow vans drove by. One driver stopped to ask if he wanted to go to Yuen Long Market. While he was hesitating a police jeep cruised by and the two men in their khaki uniforms glanced cursorily at him. Hastily he boarded the van.

In Yuen Long, a fast expanding town where farmers were found selling live chickens right in front of bank buildings and tall modern apartment blocks loomed over squatter huts in the fields, Yau Man bought a shirt and asked for directions.

"That's in Kowloon, Mister, a long way from here," the shopkeeper said, eyeing him curiously.

"I know," he replied brazenly. "I just wondered if you knew which part of Kowloon."

The shopkeeper told him where to board the New Territories bus bound for Kowloon and how much it would cost. He silently accepted the large crisp Hong Kong bill that Yau Man handed him and gave him back the change.

"You may use the cubicle at the back if you like. Perhaps you'd like to buy a new pair of trousers too. You would feel more comfortable and appear more of a local person that way," the shopkeeper said, his face immobile and his eyes expressionless.

Yau Man took his advice and refreshed himself at the tiny washroom at the back of the shop. He was touched by the shopkeeper's subtle way of hinting at his identity. Before boarding the bus for Kowloon he had a bowl of noodles at a roadside foodstall.

With new clothes on and food in his stomach he felt restored, like a patient finding his strength again. The fields and distant hills were studded with the new green of spring. The vegetable beds looked succulent and wavy. Two girls sitting in front of him chatted non-stop on the way. One of them was wearing a T shirt and trousers so tight-fitting that they made her body protrude as smoothly as a clay figurine, while the other's short skirt showed off her legs in a way no less seductive to Yau Man. In one corner a farm woman was baring her bosom to feed the baby, while somewhere at the back of the bus three men loudly discussed a movie which they had seen. Their smut talk contained references that teased a young man's imagination, especially that of Yau Man who had had little opportunity or leisure to brood on the subject of sex. His crush on a female worker in the factory had been brief, abruptly terminated when a comrade from the management extended his friendship to her, long before his virginal worship could mature to any speculation of intimacy. This first encounter with eroticism on the bus excited him because it gave added impact to his realization that he was at last in a different world of experience.

The bus pulled into the city at noon. While it converged with other cars and buses in a sea of traffic Yau Man felt safe and anonymous among the crowds. All the shops on the thoroughfare were open for business. There was an intentness on people's faces that he found reassuring. He was sure nobody would pay any attention to him even if he were to mutter something anti-revolutionary. This sense of freedom so exhilarated him that after disembarking he stood in the middle of the pavement and laughed. The little girl helping her mother at the news-stand stared at him with some interest, otherwise he was taken no notice of.

He was fascinated by the bustle around him and the abundance of merchandise in the shops that was available to everyone with money. There was a vitality about the place that quickened his heart beat, galvanized his urge to participate, and stirred up hidden desires for things that had so far been denied him.

He stepped into a small cafe to have lunch and to chart, if he could, his course of action for the near future. He had with him the address of his father's friend from the old days, a Mr. Chen Wan See, and a letter of introduction in which his father said Yau Man would be grateful for his teachings and assistance. Yau Man was not sure what kind of assistance he could expect from Mr. Chen, in any case he decided to get himself temporarily settled so that he wouldn't have to thrust himself on a stranger like a sick dog landing on his lap. There were more than five hundred dollars in the plastic bag, a sum he surmised would be enough for him to live on frugally for a month. The two rings contained big stones which looked valuable even to his inexperienced eyes. He wrapped them up carefully, determined not to sell them unless it was absolutely necessary. The newspaper he bought had one full page devoted to advertisements for rooms and flats to let. As he looked them over he found it impossible to decide on a location as he didn't know anything about the place. It might be a better idea to look up Mr. Chen first after all. He could say he had got himself a place to stay if the reception did not turn out to be as warm and fruitful as his father had predicted.

# Sour Sweet

## 1982

*Timothy Mo*

Lily had never met the wives of Chen's colleagues; she knew of the staff only by report, having seen Lo just once for the time it took him to drink a glass of her scalding tea. She liked what Husband told her of Mr Lo and warmed to him at their first short meeting. At secondhand she conceived an intense dislike of Roman Fok; although when Husband complained about him, she tried to suggest extenuating circumstances or good aspects of Fok's character. She felt it was her duty to do this.

As Chen had no family of his own who might celebrate birthdays, lunar New Year, hold impromptu *mah jeuk* parties or christenings (there were a few Catholics and Baptists in the restaurant, the Baptists hilariously preponderant amongst the dishwashers), Lily moved in a restricted circle: herself, Mui, Man Kee. There were the English neighbours, the Polish doctor, but these were hardly more than nodding acquaintances. Husband, of course, didn't count.

It came, then, as a nice surprise when during a shopping expedition to the Brent supermarket she came across two Chinese women at the rice shelf, both a lot older than herself or Mui. One was plainly mistress, the other obviously *amah*. The latter was dressed in the maid-servant's classic uniform: black trousers, white tunic, her thin grey hair cut short and plastered close to the scalp, coming just below the ears, in the lobes of which she wore tiny earrings of jade. She had a bracelet of the same, flecked inferior stone around her bony wrist and was pushing the wire shopping trolley. It was crammed with food. At the moment when Lily came round the corner with her steel basket on her arm and Mui wheeling Man Kee in the rear, the *amah's* employer was comparing two bags of rice. Lily squeezed past to pick up her own packet. The older woman politely made way for her, then noticed that Lily was an oriental. She nodded and smiled. Then Man Kee arrived, waving a rattle and banging his stockinged heels. Both the strange women melted. Man Kee closed his eye in a huge, lugubrious wink and kept it shut while Mui tried to lift his eyelid with her thumb and scolded him without much conviction. Man Kee hit her on the head with his toy and laughed at his appreciative audience.

'Handsome boy,' the strange woman complimented Lily in Cantonese. As Lily merely smiled without saying anything, she repeated her remark in English: 'The boy good-looking.'

'No. Not at all. He's a very plain child.'

'Ah, so you are Chinese. I thought you might be Filipino.' The woman used the idiom 'Person of Tang', a peculiar southern idiom.

'But not from Hong Kong. Singapore, maybe?'

'Kwangsi.' Lily smiled.

'I thought your accent was strange. Yes, you don't have the appearance of a Hong Kong person. Too independent-looking.' She laughed at her own joke. She was, Lily estimated, in her late forties and later discovered she had been over ten years out in her guess. Mrs Law was over sixty at their time of meeting. She was dressed in sober but expensive clothes and had a pleasant, homely face which was rather at variance with her elegant outfit.

'You must let me buy him something.'

'No, no. You will spoil him.'

They left together. At the check-out Lily finally allowed Mrs Law to present her son with a chocolate mouse bought at the rack of confectionery near the till. At this point Man Kee had an attack of shyness, burying his chin in his chest and moving his big head slowly from side to side, which further endeared him to his new admirers. He was persuaded to purse his lips and applied them in a kind of red trumpet to Mrs Law's cheek. Mrs Law insisted on taking their address and a fortnight later Lily received an invitation to 'drink tea', personally delivered by the servant Ah Jik who had brought a musical spinning-top for Man Kee.

Mrs Law was the widow of a wealthy ship-owner, twenty years older than his wife, who had died in Hong Kong. They had married in Swatow where he had been a lighterman and she the third daughter of a *yamen* clerk who had been forced to become a public letter-writer after the 1911 revolution. They had worked their way up in the world together until he had collected a fleet of fourteen rusty coastal tramps. At one point there had been eighteen but four, heavily insured, had foundered in mysterious circumstances. Greatly mourned by his wife but without children, Law had died in a private hospital of the nasopharyngeal cancer so prevalent on the southern coast, caused by a lifetime's inordinate consumption of the dried salt fish he had loved so much.

Bored and unhappy in Hong Kong, Mrs Law emigrated a year after her husband's death, starting a new life in England at the age of fifty-five. The country was her second choice: Canada had rejected her because of TB scars on the lungs.

Lily was over-awed on her first visit to the big flat. 'Tea drinking' turned out to be a sumptuous affair of delicacies she hadn't seen for years: sweet black gelatine rolls, formed of layers of transparent film thinner than tissue paper, which gleamed and shivered tantalisingly; cakes of crushed lotus seed paste with fiery, salty egg yolks inside; cold cuts of abalone, chicken, ham, smoked fish, fungus strips, mushrooms so thick and succulent they tasted like meat; English strawberry tarts and fragrant jasmine tea of the kind Lily adored. The girls seriously disappointed Mrs Law on their first visit when they were too shy to do more than pick at this magnificent buffet, but Man Kee more than compensated. He laid on a star's performance, turning somersaults on the carpet, playing hide-and-seek behind curtains and under furniture, turning on both taps in the bath, a thunderous cacophony heard in time in the sitting room so that disaster was averted. He fell asleep on the top deck of the bus on their way home but didn't cry when Lily woke him at their destination.

When Chen came home the girls didn't tell him about the visit; there was unspoken agreement on this.

The visit to Golders Green became a weekly event. Man Kee found a new present every time he went, which was added to the growing collection in Mrs Law's airing cupboard. The adults sat on Mrs Law's emerald silk sofas and were waited on by Ah Jik who watched from the kitchen door.

Mrs Law was a good listener. She even drew Mui out. Perched on the sofa with a cup of tea she became quite garrulous, much to Lily's surprise. Mrs Law found she had something in common with the girls' background, and she warmed to them. Her own father's fall hadn't been such a blow as the orphaning of the girls but she could sympathise.

'So father was a *sifu*, was he?' she said, 'How noble!'

The girls tittered, politely.

'Did he teach you or just Elder Brother?'

Mui answered her: 'We have no brother. But Father taught Lily as much as he could before he was killed. Quite unsuitable, really, for a girl.'

Hearing of their father's violent death, Mrs Law didn't make the jokes she had intended about them being a deadly pair. Instead she filled their cups for them in a respectful silence. Fearing Mrs Law's exterior of well-bred calm concealed embarrassment, Lily tried to put her at ease. 'If you look at my knuckles here you can still see how they are larger than the others although the callus went away years ago.' Mrs Law politely inspected the hand which seemed quite normal to her. 'And I'm still supple,' Lily kicked off her flat shoes and proceeded to do the splits on Mrs Law's fine carpet to the private alarm and consternation of the owner. Even with the last inches Lily needed no help.

'How truly remarkable,' Mrs Law complimented her, and for once the comment was not formulaic good manners. Then she changed the subject skilfully. Lily, only slightly abashed, felt old reflexes awaking. That night, in the locked bathroom, she went through some of the old suppling movements she remembered; did a half-hearted shadow set. For a few days she repeated the exercises, then grew bored and abandoned them.

# Struggle of a Hong Kong Girl

## 1986

*Lily Chan*

*Lily Chan is the author of* Struggle of a Hong Kong Girl, *excerpted here.*

———

Not long after the Japanese surrender, Mo-ying disposed of all her personal effects and paid a high price to get transportation to Canton. Things were not yet back to normal. Only those who could afford exorbitant charges could get passage to Hong Kong from Canton. Mo-ying bought an expensive ticket for a deck bunk on a boat to Hong Kong.

During the Japanese occupation, people had suffered from hunger and cold. They looked gaunt, pale, and weak. In order to provide firewood for the winter and cooking, deserted houses and buildings had been stripped of doors, doorposts, flooring, stairways, and woodwork. Most of the houses, buildings, and shops stood in ruins.

Just after the Japanese surrender on 30 August 1945, the Colony was sparsely populated. Many houses, shops, and flats were empty and needed repairs.

After settling down in a flat in Causeway Bay, Mo-ying informed Yat-sing of her return by sending him a letter, asking him to call on her at her address.

A few days later, Mo-ying was roused by the ringing of a doorbell when she was reading. When she opened the door, she beamed radiantly and said, "Please come in."

Yat-sing stepped into the house, wearing the same smile.

"Sit down please. I'll get you a drink." Mo-ying headed for the kitchen and returned a few minutes later with a glass of brandy. She could not stop herself smiling long enough to speak. Here's your favourite drink."

"You haven't forgotten me." He took the drink and looked at her, trying to see whether she had changed.

"No, how could I forget you? I hope I don't have to leave Hong Kong again. At least you can come to see me sometimes."

"How about your university studies, Mo-ying? Have you graduated?"

"I haven't done any studying or entered any university," answered Mo-ying.

"What! You haven't been doing any studies? What a shocking thing to hear. What were you doing in Chungking then?"

"I was busy making money."

"Who asked you to make money? Haven't you got enough money to spend? Why didn't you continue to study, Mo-ying? All the time I thought you were studying in Chungking. I had great hopes in you, but now you've failed me. I told you that if you didn't have enough money you should let me know." He sounded angry and annoyed.

Mo-ying was frightened. She had never seen him angry.

He got up, then sank into a chair again, lit a cigarette, and smoked, but did not say anything more.

Timidly, she settled herself on the floor near him and gently took his hand and said in a very soft and low voice, "Please forgive me if I've made you angry. I promise you I'll study hard again if you want me to."

"It made me so mad because you'd wasted three precious years. If you had continued to study in a university, you could have continued your studies in Hong Kong University for a year or two and then you could go abroad to get a master's degree. You see, I've planned it well for you. How can you go to Hong Kong University; you don't even have a School Leaving Certificate or reached matriculation level. During the war, Hong Kong students had a priority to join a university in China even if they did not have matriculation standard provided they had a good knowledge of English. You'd thrown away that opportunity, my dear."

"I didn't know that."

"You didn't know anything because your mind was obsessed in making money. Tell me, what do you want so much money for?"

"You don't understand. Hong Kong currency was of no use in China because it was very difficult to change it into Chinese currency, and I could not pay for my passage with Hong Kong dollars to go further. So I came back to Hong Kong to spend the money to buy goods and take them back to China to sell. I made a lot of money by doing this trade."

"Now, you've become rich. What good are riches to you? Those years were more precious and important to you."

"I wanted to make a lot of money to repay you."

"Who asked you to pay me back?"

"I did."

"I'll never take a cent from a woman. Do you understand? I'm a man."

"I guess I was wrong."

"Now what are you going to do? Make more money again?"

"I don't know. I thought I would make you happy, but I've angered you. Can I make it up to you?"

"How can you make up for those three precious years. I'm really very angry with you. I am not going to come here again. I mean it. You know my address and telephone number. If you are ever in need of money, let me know. I've promised to help you; I'll keep my word."

Those words pained her more than anything which had happened before. He was not going to see her any more. All her hopes were shattered. All her life she had not wanted anything or anyone but him. Now he did not want her, not even to be a friend; he would never have dinner with her or talk to her again. Her tears choked her. He let her hold his hand, but he did not look at her. He usually comforted her, but now he did not. Silence was even worse.

He freed his hand from hers, got up, walked to the door, and left without saying a word. He had never been like that.

She could not bear it any more and burst into tears. Without him, life seemed to turn into nothingness. She shut herself inside the flat without eating or drinking, but tortured herself with pain and misery. Lying in bed, staring into emptiness with an aching heart, she spent sleepless nights in despair, thinking that she had lost him forever.

On the third day, the doorbell rang. She did not stir or get up to open it, but lay in bed letting it ring, ring, and ring.

Yat-sing became afraid that something might be wrong. He went to call a locksmith to open the door. When the door was opened, he went inside. She was not in the sitting room or kitchen. At last he found her in the bedroom. Her haggard and pale appearance hurt him.

Mo-ying was not aware of his presence. She was still lying in bed with her eyes staring at the ceiling.

He sat down on the edge of the bed, took her hand, and stroked it gently. His heart was full of compassion and regret, letting her suffer so much. He then called her name. "Oh, Mo-ying, my dearest girl, what's happened to you? Please turn and look at me. I'm here, I'm Yat-sing. Don't you remember me? Please look at me. I'll not leave you again, my darling. Let me take care of you and nurse you back to your health."

She sat up, turned to him and said, "It's really you. I thought I would never see you again." Big drops of tears fell onto her cheeks.

"Please don't cry, my darling." His tenderness touched her.

"Are you still angry with me?" she asked sobbingly.

"No, I am not angry with you. You're very sick, my poor darling. Don't cry. I'm going to call a doctor, and I'll be back soon."

"No, you aren't going to leave me again. I can't bear it. Please don't leave me alone here. I'm afraid; I'm afraid."

"I am not leaving you. I'm just going to call a doctor. You need medical care and attention."

She came to her senses again. "I don't need any doctor or medicine. I need you. If you just stay here, I'll be all right. Don't ever stop seeing me; if you do; I'll die. I thought you didn't care for me any more and wouldn't ever come. My hope was gone and my life became meaningless. I wept and wept and felt terrible because I thought I would never see you again."

"Oh, my poor darling. It pains me to see you so unhappy. You must not destroy your health, your youth, and beauty. It is my fault in making you suffer. I must help you to restore your health and your happiness." He then kissed her tenderly. "If you don't want to see a doctor, you must eat something. You just rest here. Let me fix you something to eat." He went out to get some food and returned quickly to cook her a bowl of chicken soup and boiled some eggs. About an hour later he brought her a tray of food. "Take the soup and eat the boiled eggs."

She obediently ate the food and then said, "Oh, how wonderful you are! How can I live without you? You're ever so sweet, so tender to me. Can you promise me something?"

"It depends on what you want me to do."

"I never ask for anything which you can't do."

"Well, tell me then."

"Will you come to see me every day?"

"Is this what you want me to promise you?"

"Yes."

"Can we talk about this later?"

"Is there anything wrong with sharing your love with me for an hour a day?"

"How can I make such a promise? How do I know whether I can sneak out every day? Don't forget, I have a family."

"I haven't forgotten your family. That's why I ask you only to spend an hour a day with me. There is nothing wrong in being with me for a little while every day. I'll make you very happy in that hour."

"I know you'll make me very happy. It isn't that I don't want to. It's just circumstances won't allow me."

"You're such a good man. Many men keep mistresses outside but you aren't that kind of man."

"I am not used to telling lies. Even when I slip out of here, I'm afraid that I may meet somebody I know. Let's not talk about anything beforehand."

"All right."

Yat-sing continued to come to see her every day. She devoted her time to serving him, to making the place pleasant and cosy. For a while, she imagined that she had already possessed him because he never failed to return to her house. She regained her health again and was full of life and vitality and youthfulness. They would sit talking endlessly and enjoying each other's company. These few hours of happiness a day lasted for only two months.

# A Change of Flag

## 1990

*Christopher New*

## A mite glum

There were so many people at the Dentons' on New Year's Eve that they had to have three large round tables, each laid for ten. Grace placed Rachel next to San San on the middle table — 'To talk about America,' she said vaguely. But Alex Johnston was on San San's other side, so Rachel was able to watch and listen to Patrick — who was sitting opposite her — almost uninterruptedly. In any case his ringing voice dominated the table as usual. 'When the British government sells Hong Kong down the river,' he declaimed to Stella and John in particular, 'as sell it in the end they presumably will, will anyone stand up in Parliament to point out that it will be the first time in history that a non-communist people twice as numerous as Denmark have been handed over to the very communist regime that half of them escaped from a few years before? And all without so much as a by-your-leave? Just for the sake of some squalid commercial deals, a sordid nuclear reactor or two! Did you see that pretty lord from the Foreign Office on the box the other night, positively smirking just because China had said something moderately friendly at last? My dear! What a tatty way to end an empire. Not with a bang, but a simper!'

The man in government, on Michael's table, looked up, gave a sheepish smile, then looked away in relief when Stella spoke.

'You make it sound like a disaster,' Stella said in her fluent icy voice, as if reading from a prepared text. 'Whereas it may only be a Change of Flag. In Beijing we met some of the Top Officials, and they assured us they meant to apply the One Country Two Systems Policy. They really Want it to Work. I don't see why we should worry, provided —'

'My dear Stella, it may be necessary to shine one's future patrons' shoes in order to continue making a living here, but one doesn't have to polish their kneecaps as well. Really, how far are you prepared to go? All the way up? One's mind positively boggles!'

But it wasn't what he said that Rachel noticed so much as the tones, the inflections of his voice, the changing, laughing expressions in his eyes, his high-spirited gestures, his rising exhilaration as the evening went on. She'd never observed anyone before with that kind of interest, with that sense of warmth and, yes, pride. She could almost imagine he was performing for her, especially when his eye caught hers. Some hope! Oh God, it would have to be him of all people! She'd never expected to feel like this in the whole of her life, and now she felt it for a gay. How ridiculous could you get? How absurd?

She was glad she hadn't put any of it in her diary yet. It would have committed her too clearly if she'd written it all down, stamped her too definitely as a pathetic natural spinster who'd simply lost her head. So long as she didn't form the words, it wasn't acknowledged yet, it wasn't quite real. So she hadn't opened her diary for weeks — longer than she'd ever left it before.

Paul, sitting as a treat beside Patrick, choked on some soup he was slurping up and knocked Patrick's glass over as he coughed and spluttered. Patrick led him serenely away without a trace of embarrassment or annoyance, while Ah Mui clucked apologetically beside him.

How was she going to bring him the stuff she'd written, and sit there next week, listening to his comments as if nothing had happened, as if everything was just the same as before? How was she going to write it, for that matter? *You schoolgirl dolt*, she scolded herself. As if he'd care. He wouldn't even notice. And, if he did, he'd only laugh. Heartlessly, too.

Promptly at quarter to midnight their glasses were filled with champagne, and they filed out through the french windows on to the lawn. The cold winds from northern China had died down a few days before, and the air was mild, as though the old year wanted a mellow ending. The sky was clear, the stars glistened moistly, the ships in the harbour were lit up from bow to stern, and all their lights had misty haloes round them. 'See, there's not a single ship in the harbour approaches,' someone said. 'They all want to stay in port tonight.' And it was true: the sea was empty, dark except for the desolate flashing of buoys and the lighthouse on the Lamma rocks. Rachel moved to the edge of the lawn, and saw below her that bluish necklace of lights she'd noticed on her first night in Hong Kong.

A minute or two before midnight they all stopped talking, one after another, the last voice — querulous Alison's — fading in mid-sentence. The man in government started counting the seconds off self-importantly on his watch. When he stopped there was a moment of stillness, as though the whole city were holding its breath. Then the sirens started hooting in the harbour — a wild chorus of blasting, whooping, shrieking and screaming from the hundreds of lonely anchored ships. To Rachel it sounded more like a dirge for the old year than a welcome to the new.

'Happy New Year,' Michael said gravely, raising his glass. 'A prosperous 1984.'

'At least not an Orwellian one,' Dimitri murmured.

They drank self-consciously.

'I always feel sad on New Year's Eve,' Rachel said, approaching Patrick despite herself. 'I can't see why everyone else is happy.'

'Who wouldn't be sad, dear girl, listening to that simply monstrous cacophony of ships' hooters? It sounds like an orchestra of out-of-tune French horns conducted by a raving anarchist.'

Elena's friend Tom said he guessed Hong Kong's fate would be settled by the next new year. 'It'll be a Chinese colony from then on, instead of a British one.'

'Oh, hold on tight,' the man in government protested mildly. 'Might be all right in the end.'

'Hong Kong as we know it is finished,' Tom declared in a level certain voice. 'Even if you don't.'

The ships' sirens were giving up now, frayed and tired, as if they knew it, too.

'I spent New Year's Eve on a boat once,' Dimitri said, looking down at the harbour. 'Years and years ago, when people travelled by P & O. It was at Port Swettenham, in Malaysia, and an English rubber-planter came on board just at midnight. He was retiring, going back to England. The thing was, he'd spent thirty years there, it was his whole life he was saying goodbye to, drinking toasts with his friends at the bottom of the gangway. He'd been through the Japanese occupation and the communist rebellion, and everything, just living out there in his jungle bungalow with its verandas and sundowners and parties at the Club on Saturday evenings.'

'It sounds insufferably tedious,' Patrick said. 'I trust there was the consolation of seducing the other planters' wives at least, in authentic Maugham fashion?'

'Or the other planters,' Elena suggested brightly.

'I don't know. But the thing I noticed was that the last person he said goodbye to, while they were all cheering and bawling out "Auld Lang Syne" and throwing those paper streamer things across to the boat, the last person was a Malay girl — well, woman — who'd been standing on the edge of the group all the time in the shadows. And just from the way he turned to her last and the way he took her hands, both of them in his, I thought: That's the one he's going to miss; that's the one that'll give him a wrench when he goes up the gangway —'

'Dimitri dear boy —'

'And I was right, too. You know what Port Swettenham's like, going down the coast at midnight with the silhouettes of palm trees against the sky? Well, he watched her and she watched him without a word or even a wave, till long after they must have been out of sight. I don't know if she was his servant or his mistress or what, but it had meant something to both of them, whatever she was.'

'Dimitri dear boy, I never realized you were a romantic at heart.'

'Only when I'm drunk.' He glanced down at his glass. It was empty, but he raised it to his lips anyway, as though drinking a silent toast to that distant man or that distant year. 'A whole life,' he said. 'Thirty years. And now they fly in for two or three, and stay in identical rooms in identical flats, and work in identical offices on identical contracts with identical brief-cases and identical suits, trying to make the place identical to all the identical places they came from. And never really live here at all.'

'Mila dear girl, he's positively inspired! Did you know he had such depths in him? He should be drunk all the time.'

'Oh, yes,' Mila said, eyeing Dimitri as if there was more she could say if she chose, 'I've always known. He isn't really what he seems at all.'

'I spent New Year's Eve in Mandalay once,' Michael said abruptly.

'Who's next?' Tom asked in his dazed deadly monotone. 'I spent it in Vietnam once, having my ass shot at.'

*There was a cripple outside the hotel,* Michael nearly said, but didn't. *A young boy who didn't have any legs at all; he just dragged himself along on his hands. He used to whistle birdsongs for a living. He could go on and on for half an hour and never do the same one twice. I used to throw him money, he wouldn't come nearer, he was afraid you'd hit him — sometimes children used to chase him or chuck stones at him for fun. I often used to think: That's Asia; that's what I'm afraid of.*

The words went through his mind, but all he said was 'It was hot and sticky.'

'What on earth were you doing in Mandalay on New Year's Eve?' Elena asked.

'Trying to buy some teak. Nothing romantic, I'm afraid.'

'I think you're holding out on us,' Elena said. 'Something terribly exciting happened, and you're not telling us.'

But Michael was moving away, hunching his shoulders as if somehow dimly ashamed.

'I'm beginning to feel a trifle dullish,' Patrick murmured. 'I think I'll get another drink.'

'So you were in Vietnam?' Mr. Ma from Taiwan said to Tom, holding his glass in both hands as though about to drink another toast. 'A pity the wrong side won.'

'Did it?'

Mr. Ma blinked uneasily behind his thick lenses, as if Tom had told a joke in questionable taste. 'You were reporting the war?' he asked cautiously.

'I didn't know enough about it. I was only fighting it.'

'Ah, on active service,' Mr. Ma said, seeking the restoration of harmony with a polite respectful laugh. His lips didn't quite cover his teeth when the laugh was over. He raised his glass again in salute.

'I was just glad to get my ass out in one piece. More or less.'

'He's got some lovely scars,' Elena assured Mr. Ma. 'You ought to see.'

Mr. Ma laughed again, backing off with a little bow. He touched Michael's arm and went indoors with him, nearly colliding with Alison, who was just coming out, holding a brim-full glass, with intense concentration, in both hands.

'You'd think they'd know better than to drown your gin in tonic,' she said to nobody in particular. 'After all these years. Can't stand champagne; it makes me depressed.' She raised the glass very deliberately towards her lips as though not at all confident she could actually get it there. 'Anyone seen Peter?'

'Not recently,' Elena said. 'Has he slipped his lead again?'

Alison's eyes slewed slowly round towards her, and were followed more slowly still by her head and body. 'Why? You on heat again?'

She walked off with careful swaying steps, then suddenly slumped down on the bench beneath the bauhinia tree and started blubbering silently, her mouth slack and wet.

'Oh Jesus,' Elena said. Rachel had never seen her put down before, and never expected to, either, but now two pink spots had appeared on her cheeks and her lower lip quivered slightly. Was it shame, humiliation, or anger?

'I think Peter's over there,' she said, going across to Alison. Alison nodded, sniffed, drank and lurched off with an old woman's sigh. Rachel sat where Alison had sat and watched the groups dispersing on the lawn, couple by couple, going indoors together to say goodbye, even Alison and Peter. Car doors slammed, engines growled, voices called out, headlights slipped like bright shadows over the trees. Soon she would be the only one left. She felt she could have cried like Alison.

Then Patrick drifted across the lawn towards her, Paul trustfully clutching his wrist. 'The dear child's been showing me his paintings,' he said. 'And unless I'm mistaken Alison has made a scene.'

'I guess she was provoked. But she was witty, too.'

'Oh?' He cocked his head, asking for more.

But Rachel wouldn't give. 'Paul's paintings are good, aren't they?' she said. Paul was gazing at her with those disturbingly attentive yet absent eyes of his. Sometimes she thought maybe he understood everything people said, but just discarded most of it like so much junk at the door of his mind. And wouldn't he have been right?

'Wasn't the grey-haired man sitting next to Michael at dinner the head of that communist publishing company?' she asked when Patrick didn't answer.

'Yes. Most of the authors he publishes have spent so many years on pig-farms during the Cultural Revolution you'd think they'd all write pastoral poetry now. Or pig-breeding manuals. The man on his other side was a luminary of the Taiwan government, by the way. The one with a laugh like English gravy, thick and greasy.'

'Yes. I met him. How does Michael manage to get on with both of them?'

'In Hong Kong one learns to keep all one's options open, dear girl. Particularly in the present dismal situation. Besides, they've probably all known each other half their lives anyway. They're all from Shanghai. You never know which one you might need help from next. Or sometimes you do know.'

Ah Mui came shuffling across the lawn, calling Paul by his Chinese name.

# The Iron Tree*

## 1993

*Martin Booth*

*Born and educated in Hong Kong, Martin Booth is the acclaimed author of several novels, children's books, historical and other work, many of which are associated with Asia. He has also written poetry as well as for cinema and television, and received a number of international awards for his wildlife documentary work. An excerpt of his novel* The Iron Tree *and several poems are included in this anthology. He lives and writes in England.*

---

As happens these days with increasing frequency, I am startled by a voice on the stairs.

Sometimes the voice may be one I recognise but that still does not reduce the level of surprise. I find I am becoming susceptible to sudden noises, that they increasingly catch me off my guard. There is no explanation: I have never suffered from shell shock or tinnitus and loud noises have never made me jump.

'*San foo*, my old friend. How you doing?'

I remove the key from my door and turn to find Mr Wu standing a few steps up from the landing. Quite often, the startling voice is his. I sometimes wonder if he does not lurk on the stairway waiting to pounce on me although I know this to be nonsense.

In the flat glow cast by the light over the lift door his face looks as if it is covered in parchment stretched across a frame of angled bones. Upon his nose is balanced a pair of circular spectacles with thin, black frames. They are not positioned squarely but askew, the right lens a good half an inch lower than the left.

'I'm doing okay,' I reply. I slip my key into my trouser pocket, placing my handkerchief over it as a defence against the light-fingered street operators one may encounter in the evenings. 'And you?'

Mr Wu has not been well for several months. He does not confide in me exactly what is wrong, but he drops occasional hints so I might be in a better position to sympathise. He thinks that as I am old like him I will offer him a greater sympathy than he might get from a younger man. He may be right and he may be wrong. I have never considered the matter.

'Better, better,' he responds.

When we meet, he likes to talk in English. This is not a pretension for his command of the language is good. He does it because he thinks it makes me feel at home. I have told him, over and over, it is not necessary. My home is here, I tell him, in Hong Kong. In China. He smiles benignly and nods his head but I can tell he only half believes me. Like many Chinese, he hopes to return to some distant nook or cranny in Kwangtung or Kwansi provinces to die with his ancestors and he mistakenly assumes Europeans will ultimately do likewise, going back to a leafy village churchyard in the shires of England to let their bodies rot in the mother soil whence they sprang.

---

\* Copyright © Martin Booth, 1993.

'I been to see my doctor,' he continues. 'He has given me a prescription.'

He holds up a piece of flimsy paper on which I can make out printed red lines and a dense passage of characters in black ink. The paper has a similar texture to his skin.

'What is it?' I enquire, pressing the button for the lift.

'Herbs, spices. Deer's tail . . .' Mr Wu squints over his spectacles. 'You know, *san foo*, I can't see so well these days.'

I reach over and straighten the old man's glasses.

'That will not improve it. But thank you.'

'You need new glasses,' I say, not for the first time. 'You've had these for eight years at least.'

Mr Wu calculates time in his head.

'Now is 1961. I bought them in 1952. But they do me, my old friend. I need no more. New eyes, perhaps.' He holds the piece of paper out. 'See if you can read it.'

'Deer's tail is there,' I confirm, surveying the characters written with a calligraphic brush. 'And anis, ginseng, some other things I don't know the English for.'

'Do you think it will do me good?' Mr Wu enquires.

'I'm sure it will.'

'This is strange,' Mr Wu remarks, smiling at me. 'I am Chinese and you are a *gweilo* and I have to ask you to read my own language and then I ask you if you think the medicine will be good. You who do not believe . . .'

'I believe,' I interrupt him. 'I have seen Chinese medicine working many times. Do not assume, because I am a *gweilo*, I take only aspirin.'

A tinny bell pings to announce the arrival of the lift and the doors rattle open. A metal grating sound can be heard: the lift is never serviced. I put my hand against the safety bar to prevent the door closing, signalling Mr Wu to go in first and we step into the lift.

'I should do that for you, my old friend. By your standards, I am a youngster. Why! When you first came to China, I could have been your pupil. Learned my English speaking from you.'

'You could not,' I answer, pressing the ground-floor button. 'You are the wrong sex. I taught only girls.'

I look up in silence at the numbers flicking slowly on and off. It is not my custom to discuss my affairs, even with those whom I know well, unless I choose to do so. There has to be a proper time and place for such intercourse and a lift is not one of them. A man must keep himself to himself unless he wishes his life to become public property. Not that I think Mr Wu would start blabbering about me. We have a certain secret in common which ensures we neither of us spill the other's beans. It is just that lift shafts carry sound, especially in an old tenement, with the efficacy of a tannoy.

'What were you doing on the roof?' I ask. 'In the daytime.'

'Nothing,' Mr Wu replies defensively. 'Nothing at all.'

He stares at the door as if willing it to open. I look at his profile and consider how much more quickly Chinese age than Europeans. Mr Wu is much my junior at seventy-three yet we look quite similar, racial physiognomy apart.

The old Chinese lives alone in Flat 36, third floor, one of the less salubrious quarters of the building for it looks out not on to the busy street crowded for eighteen hours a day with pedestrians and traffic but on to an alleyway at the rear in which dubious characters meet to carry on their suspect business and which, when there is no human presence, is the domain of some particularly large rats. Sometimes he curses these rodents and sometimes he feeds them. It all depends upon his mood or whether or not he wants to earn a credit in the account books of the gods. He has the idea that, if he shows compassion for his enemies, the gods might treat him kindly when he comes into their company. The rats being enemies, he sees feeding them as a good opportunity to be charitable.

The lift stops abruptly, my legs momentarily giving way then regaining their strength.

'Where are you going, *san foo*?' Mr Wu asks.

'You know,' I say, 'I am not a *san foo* any longer. That was a long time ago. I do wish you would call me something else.'

'What do I call you?' Mr Wu rejoins. 'There is nothing else. I am always a tailor, Tsoi will always be a cook, you will always be a *san foo*.'

Deciding not to follow this line of conversation, for it is one we have at least once a week without resolution, I say nothing. Mr Wu chuckles, a soft gurgling laugh I have grown to know well. At the street door, we part company. Mr Wu waves as we set off in different directions.

'I shall see you later?' he asks me.

'Later?' I consider his words. 'No, I think not.'

'You should come,' Mr Wu calls after me. 'Need to relax. You are too busy for an old man.'

Yet I have made up my mind, wave and walk away.

There are times when I do not want Mr Wu's company, and others when I need it. Tonight is one of the former. I seek only my own company in the presence of strangers, wish to be alone in the crowds, just another European wandering the streets.

Now it is evening, the tourists are out in force in Tsim Sha Tsui: their day excursions are over, they have had their hotel dinners and their guides have gone home. Left to their own devices, they have embarked upon a shopping spree in the brightly lit streets, pausing in front of camera and jewellery shops, being accosted by touts wanting to sell them silk ties and leather wallets. I mingle with them, watch and listen as they are persuaded, beguiled and cheated. One American, his tropical shirt decorated with palm trees and hula-hula girls hanging down over his belt, a Leica camera suspended around his neck, enquires into the price of a pair of binoculars.

'Six hund'ed eighty dollar,' the shopkeeper tells him. 'Good price. For you, first customer tonight, I say six hund'ed fifty. You wan' buy?'

'Six hundred,' the American bargains.

He has been told no one pays the asking price. It is the done thing, the guidebooks instruct him, to dicker with vendors, ignore the marked price on the label and go for the deal.

'Six forty,' the shopkeeper suggests. 'I make little p'ofit.'

'Six twenty,' the American demands.

'You hard man. Strike good bargain,' the shopkeeper congratulates him, smiling sheepishly. 'Okay! Six twenty.'

He grimaces, pretending to be a loser. The American grins and winks at his wife who is standing behind him clutching her handbag. He starts to remove traveller's cheques from his wallet, laying them out on the glass counter next to his purchase.

'Honey, give me a pen.'

'Okay. I got a pen,' says the shopkeeper and takes one out of his pocket.

The American's wife looks relieved. She does not want to open her handbag: she has read the Orient is awash with thieves.

'Say,' the American asks, 'is that US or Hong Kong dollars?'

'US dollar,' the shopkeeper says.

So the American signs six hundred and twenty US dollars' worth of cheques for an item he could have purchased for six hundred Hong Kong. I glance across the street at a money-changer's shop: the rate is four Hong Kong dollars and ten cents to the American buck. It occurs to me there should be another beatitude: blessed are the fleeced and suckered for they shall remain in blissful ignorance of their own stupidity.

In the side-streets, others are looking for a different deal. These would-be customers carry no cameras and are not accompanied by their wives. They walk in twos and threes, comrades-in-arms facing the thrill of the Oriental night. Some are visiting businessmen but most are sailors from the cruise ships, stewards from the airliners or soldiers posted to Whitfield Barracks in Nathan Road or Kowloon Tong.

Here, where the streets are narrower and the traffic slow moving, pimps are out in force. They are less strident than the silk tie hawkers but no less insistent.

'You want girl?' they enquire, walking beside a potential client for a few steps. 'Good girl. Young girl. Speak goo' English. Free beer for you.'

Some accept and are hustled down alleys: some refuse and are left alone for a few yards before another pimp confronts them. Only a few make it to the end of the street undecided or unmolested.

I am not accosted. I do not look right and am therefore left alone by both touts and pimps. There is something about me these canny operators can sense. Perhaps, in their eyes, I am too old. They think I am past it, have purchased all the silk ties a man can require in one lifetime and am too decrepit to lie with a woman young enough to be my great-granddaughter.

My perambulation is not to strike a hard bargain or to rent young flesh for an hour or two. I do not look upwards at the neon signs advertising the *Bayside Night-club* and *Eddie Shiu*: *Tailors*, *Rolex* and *Longines*, *Zeiss Ikon* and the *Opal Factory*. I am not here to swim vicariously in the wake of the more adventurous or foolhardy but simply to watch, to be with my fellow man as he makes an ass of himself, degrades himself, surrenders himself to base instincts. I do not criticise him nor try to prevent him going along the course he has set: I am not a judge or a jury, merely a lone spectator sharing in the quandaries of human existence, looking for truths which I know, deep within myself, I have never owned nor shall ever find.

# A Chinese Wedding

## 1994

*Simon Elegant*

*Born in Hong Kong, Simon Elegant has lived and written in Asia for more than half his life. A journalist and author of two novels, the Eurasian writer studied Chinese history at the University of Pennsylvania and at Cambridge. An excerpt of his first novel* A Chinese Wedding *and one of his short stories are included here. He currently lives and writes in Malaysia.*

For as long as Amy could remember, Chinese had meant food: spring rolls, fried rice, mushu pork; one from Column A and two from Column B; the Ho Sai Gai on Race Street in Chinatown, its name spelt out in spiky, bamboo letters on the garish violet and vermilion neon sign that flashed all night above its red doors.

And now — sitting in the midst of the wedding banquet watching hundreds of Cantonese apply themselves to a heaped platter of food the menu calls 'Four seasons starter' — now that she has spent several months in Hong Kong, living with a Chinese family the whole time; now, in fact, that she has just married a Chinese man (here she looks across the table to where he is leaning over to talk to her mother, his shoulders square under the hired tuxedo jacket and his stiff black hair swept back, held in place by gel, his face already brick red from the brandy) — now she knows that in one respect she was absolutely right: the Chinese, at least the six million who live in Hong Kong, are totally absorbed by the getting, the preparation, the presentation and, most important of all, the consumption of food.

Do other people make eating such a central part of their culture? she wonders, smoothing the heavy brocaded red silk of the wedding dress over her thighs. Not the Irish, that's for sure: Uncle Mike would eat his own shoes if you sat him down at the table and served them to him covered with ketchup. And if you gave him a few beers to wash them down with, he'd probably smack his lips and ask for more.

The Italians maybe: pasta, pasta, pasta, though, and cheese or tomato on everything, at least in South Philadelphia. People always claimed to know the best places — little family-run restaurants, tucked away in a side-street. But it would always prove impossible to find, you'd be wandering around looking for the place — a little nervous, it'd be dusk and people would seem to be staring, it was a tough neighbourhood. Finally, you'd come to a dusty glass door that looked as though it had been sealed shut since Christmas and realize with a sinking heart and a twinge of hunger that the place was closed.

Here, she admits to herself, she is thinking of Richard: he always said he knew the best restaurant, the latest place, be it Italian or Ethiopian, always swore it was the only one to go to, then could never find it, or it would be shut. 'Sorry, sorry,' he'd say in that blurry, nasal rush, 'too bad, too bad, ah, ah, unfortunately they're not open.'

Irritating man, she thinks. Thank God he faded away, or thank God I faded him away, turned off the set and watched him dwindle into a tiny spot like one of the old black and whites we had when I was a kid.

Amy shifts her backside and tugs surreptitiously at the sides of the dress, a *kuah* it is called, she has been told repeatedly. The heavy silk is smotheringly warm and she can feel a sheen of sweat on her thighs, popping through the pores of the unfamiliar stockings. She pulls too hard and feels herself starting to slide, the silk *kuah* slipping easily over the vinyl of the seat. She clutches the sides of the chair and digs the stiletto heels into the carpet to check herself, then slides carefully back into an upright position.

She looks around but nobody has noticed; most of the people on the other tables seem to be too busy eating. Anyway, even if she had disappeared under the table, all the Chinese would just assume she was drunk. All *gwei-los*, foreign devils, are drunks, it seems, even the women; so her prospective sisters-in-law had told her, the two eldest, the nasty ones, the ugly sisters.

Amy glances to her left. Winston's second eldest sister, Mei Yoke, is sitting one place away from her. Their eyes meet and Mei Yoke stares back unblinking so that Amy finally looks away from that pockmarked, heavily powdered mask, thinking: She really doesn't like me. What did I ever do to her?

Composing herself, she picks up her glass of hot tea and takes a deliberate, dainty sip.

A fine omen that would be, anyway, the bride disappearing under the table during the first course. From the evidence of the elaborate preparations to ensure good luck for the wedding — the consultations with the astrologer, the peculiar rituals, the endless worries about auspicious timing — the Lees would cancel the whole thing. They would probably pack her back to Philadelphia in one of the crates they use at the factory, the box simply marked in huge red Chinese characters, 'unlucky bride'.

A giggle building up inside, slightly hysterical, threatens to burst out, chasing her racing thoughts upward. She smothers it with a cough and something catches at the back of her throat so that she has to hack a few times to get it out. She feels a heavy hand clap her on the back and turns with a smile, nodding her thanks to Win's mother; to her new mother-in-law, she should say. They haven't really been married, not in a church, but who's counting? Only *my* mother, Amy thinks ruefully.

She smiles again, nodding her head foolishly, muttering '*M'goi, m'goi*', 'thank you, thank, you', under her breath, the only Cantonese words with which she feels safe. Win's mother smiles back, nodding her head, flashing her gold tooth. As always she looks a little alarmed when Amy addresses her in Cantonese, as though afraid that she won't understand a word her new daughter-in-law is saying and will be forced to sit there smiling mutely like a fool until someone breaks in to help.

'Is everything all right?' Win asks from across the table, looking up from his conversation with Amy's mother, an expression of concern on his face that causes something down in the region of Amy's stomach to flop over with happiness.

'No, no,' she says, waving her hand in the air, almost toppling over the glass of tea with the long sleeve of the *kuah*. 'I'm fine. It's just a frog in the throat.'

'A frog?' says Win slowly. He looks stunned by the brandy.

'You know,' everyone else at the table is listening to their conversation, 'a catch, a rasp, a burr: a frog in the throat.' She gestures vaguely at her own neck, this time wary of the swinging sleeve.

'Yes, I see.' Win purses his lips. 'It's probably heatiness. Take a drink, some tea, that will help.'

He speaks rapidly to his mother who immediately pushes her own glass of tea towards Amy, rucking the tablecloth up in her haste, nodding again and smiling. Amy shakes her head, smiling back: they must look like a couple of those stupid dogs that sit in the back of cars and wag their heads.

'No, thanks, I'm fine now, really. *M'oi, m'oi. Yi ga ho.*'

Mrs Lee looks dubious, obviously finding the attempt at Cantonese indecipherable as usual, so Amy carefully takes a sip of her own tea, smiling again and patting herself on the sternum to show she has recovered, pushing the proffered glass back across the table.

Apparently mollified, Mrs Lee turns back to her plate.

What am I supposed to call her anyway? Amy wonders. Mom? Mrs Lee? I don't even know her Christian name; not that she has one, of course, not being Christian. She probably doesn't even have a real first name either. The Chinese put their personal names after the family name, that Amy had realized before. Fair enough. But to complicate things, they usually also have two personal names, which are sometimes used together, sometimes separately, sometimes not at all, as in the case of close relatives who often call each other by their rank in the family: third uncle on mother's side, or whatever, which sounds clumsy in English but manages to fit into one word in Cantonese. Take Mei Yoke. Her family name is Lee, of course, like Win, and her personal name, Mei Yoke, comes after that, though family and friends usually drop the first part and just call her 'Yoke'. Her younger brothers though call her 'Jie' for elder sister.

All of which leaves Amy, blessed with only her paltry single, cropped little American name, feeling rather inadequate. And, to make things worse, all the Lees call her 'A-mee', which she was told by a giggling Mei Mei, the youngest daughter, sounds something like 'noodlina'.*

Amy remembers the first time Win tried to teach her to say his name, early on; the first time they really talked, in fact, over a cup of coffee in Hardees. She had asked what exactly he did in Hong Kong and he had fumbled in his wallet and produced a business card with his name on it: Winston G.F. Lee, Senior Executive, Tong Fatt Electrical and Toys Manufacturer, then an address in Hong Kong.

'What does the G.F. stand for?'

'Winston Gah Fatt Lee,' he'd said. It was a grey winter afternoon, all the lamps on already though it was only three o'clock, the light bleeding out of the day outside.

'That's my full name. My Chinese name and my western name.'

'Say it again. The Chinese part in the middle.' She had called him Win until then.

'Gah Fatt.'

'Um . . . gay fat,' she repeated after him.

'You are teasing me.'

'No, no, I'm just trying to say it right.'

'Not "Gay". It's "gah", like g with "ah" after it. Like what you say at the doctor's office: ahhhhh. And it's not "fat" like Buddha either, it sounds like "father". The beginning of "father".'

'Gaah Faat.'

'That's better, yes. Try once more.'

'Gaahhhh Faaaaat.' She rolls out the sounds, gurgling a little.

'Now you are teasing again. You sound like you are a dog.'

---

* 'noodlina' — 'little noodle' (*a-mien*) in Cantonese.

'Who are you calling a dog, buster?' She pokes him in the arm lightly. 'That's not a nice thing to say to a lady in this country, you know.'

'I wanted to say that you sound like you are calling a dog.'

'Sound like a dog? Look like a dog. You really know how to compliment a girl. Woof, woof!'

He had given her a baffled smile and picked up his coffee cup. After a while, she had held the card up in the air again and said: 'What's this toy company?'

'My family's business.'

'So you're rich? That's good.'

'No, we have no money, business is very bad. The recession here in America means no one is buying toys.'

'Just toys? It says electrical, too.'

'Electrical things too, yes.'

'Oh.'

She'd looked at the card again. The flip side was covered with Chinese writing, three large characters in the middle, the rest smaller, strung in scratchy columns down the right-hand side.

'If it wasn't for the characters, no one would ever know you were Chinese. Do you always write your name Winston G.F. Lee, or is that just for America?'

'No, that is how I always write it on the card.'

'Winston G.F. Lee,' she repeats. 'You could be a second hand car salesman from Atlanta or someplace, you know: "Winston Lee, pleased to meetcha an take a lookee rite heer at this lil beauty, not a scratch on her, only two thousand on the clock and a fresh set of whitewalls I put on myself just yesterday." '

He had smiled at her again with a puzzled but, she noticed then for the first time, affectionate look: after that he always smiled at her jokes; sometimes he even laughed.

'Then you'd tell them,' she had continued, 'if you were this Winston Gaylord Farmington (his mama's name, of course) Lee, you'd tell 'em: "The owner was a preacher, ya see, never used the car, bicycled around town. It was his second car, anyway, his wife's car, and she never drove either on account she was confined to a wheelchair, wasting disease, couldn't drive, a terrible tragedy. Only five-ninety-nine to you." '

She flourished the empty plastic cup.

'And then you'd have made a sale. Maybe you should think about taking up that line of work. It's a lot easier than beating your brains out to get an MBA, isn't it?'

Oh, no, he'd replied, seriously, the degree was very important. He couldn't drop it now, he'd already spent so much family money on it. And anyway, there was no money in second hand car sales in Hong Kong. Most people rode motorcycles. There was only one car per ten thousand people. He'd read the figure in the *Far Eastern Economic Review* just last week.

One per ten thousand, she'd replied, shocked, that's amazing. But hadn't she read somewhere that there were more Rolls-Royces per head there than anywhere in the world? How could that be if there were only, what one hundred cars per . . .

That's the trouble with Hong Kong, he interrupted quickly, seeing a glimmer of comprehension in her eyes. It's Rolls-Royces or nothing. People throw the Mercedes off the docks, just like your Boston Tea Party.

But she hadn't been listening, had continued talking.

'. . . million people and there are only a few million there, so there are only a couple of hundred cars in the whole place? That can't be right.'

And then she saw him smiling broadly and was flabbergasted to realize that he'd made a joke, suckered her completely, sucked her right in. She'd pretended to be outraged, of course, if only to give him the pleasure of his coup, but underneath she had been intrigued, it was something she hadn't expected in him at all; it made him a real person instead of a curiosity to be examined over a cup of coffee and then dismissed. It was after that joke that she began to like him.

Amy gazes fondly across the table at Win for a second, then starts, looking at the chopsticks stabbing from all sides towards the dish at the centre of the table, realizing she hasn't eaten yet. There are only a few pieces of food left on the plate, most not immediately identifiable. She picks up her chopsticks and, playing safe, spears one of the slices of thousand year old egg. The taste is rich and musty, the consistency solid but almost slimy, just on the edge of being disgusting.

Amy considers reaching for a piece of the pickled ginger that comes with the eggs, but before she can move a pair of meaty arms reaches from behind her and unceremoniously whisks away the serving dish so that she is left waving her chopsticks in empty air.

# Asian Values

## 1996

*Nury Vittachi*

*Nury Vittachi is a prolific comic author, editor and journalist. The Sri Lankan writer is the author of numerous books of fiction and non-fiction, and has also published children's books. A long-time resident of Hong Kong, he edits* Dimsum, *the first journal devoted to publishing new pan-Asian English-language fiction, and is also an organizer and founder of the city's international literary festival. An excerpt of a novel, one of his stories from* The Feng Shui Detective *and several of his essays are in the anthology. He lives and writes in Hong Kong.*

----

## 4.05 PM

This was not a family gathering, thought Licia, with deepening gloom. It was a trial. A court martial. A sentencing. She and Davis were placed in chairs in the middle of the room, while the older male members of the families, plus one very elderly woman, sat on an array of chairs, facing them.

They were in the Sajbalani family's main Hong Kong island home, a cavernous flat in an old building in Robinson Road. They had been taken there in a convoy of limousines. The atmosphere in the car had been silent and grim, like a company picnic for Mafia employees. The only word spoken on the journey was by the chauffeur, who had said: 'Congratulations,' as they had got into the vehicle. Licia had replied with a short, scornful laugh. No one else had reacted at all, and the Filipino had ventured no further comments.

The apartment had been expensively decorated in Indian style, with beaten copper trimmings around the doors, and tapestries hanging from ceiling to floor. The thick, spongey carpet was beige, and so deep Licia found it difficult to walk on. The walls were dark red, and metallic gold drapes blocked out all sunlight from the windows. A statue with eight arms stood by the door, and several young brown faces gazed into the room from a doorway. Despite the size of the room, it felt oppressive, because a low false ceiling had been fitted, inlaid with ugly brass lights. The room smelt of incense and curry, and she suddenly remembered that she had had no lunch.

Anjali sat on one side with her mother and several female friends. At first, Licia thought they would direct their fury against her, but she noticed that their murderous glare was fixed firmly on Davis.

Sweating servants appeared from nowhere carrying a grand, old-fashioned desk, and set it in front of Anjali's father. Another servant carefully placed some thick, legal-looking volumes on it. These seemed to be present only for effect, as Licia noticed that one was actually a children's encyclopedia and another was an index of import-export companies in Kowloon.

Looking at the way the people were arranged in the room reminded her of her days as a cub reporter, covering labour tribunals. She and Davis, set apart on two chairs, too far away from table to lean on, were like prisoners in a dock — a visual analogy strengthened by the handcuffs binding them together. A young woman called Sarvinri — she looked like she may be a cousin or older sister of Anjali's — had been asked to sit on one side and take notes, just like a court reporter.

It was clear that Anjali's father, Dippitha 'Dippy' Sajbalani, fancied himself as a judge. He placed a cap on his head, and looked curiously happy, as if being in charge of this meeting was partly compensating him for the money and face he had lost this afternoon. Suleman Das, an unpleasant, sneering individual in his mid-40s who Anjali referred to as Uncle Sully, sat on Dippy's left, and whispered regularly into the patriarch's ear.

The old man spoke: 'First, we must be establishing the facts, gentlemen. Now let us take my daughter's point of view first. Mr Davis Lee, you agreed to marry Anjali Sajbalani at 3 pm on this day, today, is this correct? This was to be a, a, completely normal wedding? You were not saying to her beforehand anything about bringing a friend or anything? She was expecting you to be turning up entirely by yourself, is this correct?'

'Yes, of course, I —'

'Simple yes or no answers will be doing just fine at this stage. We are only trying to establish the facts, and thus establish your guilt.'

'Or innocence.'

'What? Oh. Yes, that's technically true.' Sajbalani frowned slightly at what he seemed to perceive as an irrelevant point.

Suleman Das, who had scraggy, white facial hair and red skin, interjected a comment in a raspy, unpleasant voice: 'Well, there seems to be little question of innocence, Dippy, since a large lump of evidence against him is attached to his right wrist for all the world and his neighbour to see.'

'Large lump?' squealed Licia.

Davis burst in. 'Yes, but the whole point is that it wasn't my fault in the least, I —'

Sajbalani tried to sound reassuring: 'Nobody is trying to find fault with you, Mr Davis Lee, at the moment, anyway. That will be coming later. Please be quiet for a moment while I am establishing all the relevant facts. Now did you hint in any way that you may be turning up at this wedding with a young, er, Western woman handcuffed to your wrist?'

'Well, obviously I didn't say to her that I would —'

Suleman looked suddenly very happy: 'So he lied to her.'

He picked at the hairs on his chin and nodded at Sarvinri to make a note.

'Aiyeeah! I did not lie to her. Of course, neither of us had the slightest idea that this would happen, so we never discussed it. I think you have got entirely the wrong —'

'Please just answer the questions with a simple affirmative or positive, prisoner, er, defendant,' continued Sajbalani, tucking his legs under him so that he was sitting cross-legged on the chair. 'What you are saying is that Ms Sajbalani never asked directly whether you would be turning up with someone attached to your wrist. Is that true?'

'Well . . . It's sort of true —'

'I think it is very clear that Ms Sajbalani was led, by you, to believe that you would be turning up to this wedding by yourself, solo. Please make sure you are noting that down, Sarvinri. Okay, now I would like to ask you a few questions, Ms Manley. May I be calling you Ms Manley?'

The young English woman looked up and turned a cool smile to the old man: 'Well, it is my name.'

'Thank you. In that case I will. Now what can you tell me about bondage?'

'Bondage? Look, I am not some sort of pervert.'

'Please just answer the —'

'I'm not a pervert. You've got this all wrong —'

Sajbalani widened his mouth, flashing brown and yellow teeth in what he seemed to believe was a friendly smile: 'No one is calling you a pervert, Ms Manley. No one has said anything like that. Have you heard me or anyone in this room call you a pervert?'

'No,' she whispered, the strangled inaudibility of her voice expressing the depth of her anger.

'Okay. Let us establish that fact. No one has called you a pervert. So please calm down. There is no need for anyone to be raising the voice.' He showed his bad teeth again.

Sajbalani relaxed in his uncomfortable chair and became slightly effusive. 'These days, a wide spectrum of sexual preferences is considered acceptable, and many people are interested in bondage and other activities which once upon a time would have been considered perverted. To you, these things may be interesting, and other people are having no right to pass judgment on them.'

'But I'm NOT interested in —'

'Nobody said you were, Ms Manley. Please try and be less excitable. Now just answer the question. What can you be telling me about bondage practices?'

'I — I — this is so ridiculous. I refuse to answer.'

Suleman Das hammered his fist onto the table in triumph: 'Ah ha!' He expressed his excitement by rubbing his hairy cheeks furiously. The old lady on the other side of Sajbalani picked up a fork and started picking her teeth with it. The women observing from the sides of the room started whispering and shaking their heads.

The patriarch leaned back in his chair and looked down at her with barely contained horror as if she had just owned up to mass murder. 'Your silence may be interpreted as an admittance that you are guiltily hiding something. I would advise you to answer the questions, Ms Manley.'

Licia had had enough. Her eyes blazed fury. She stood up and tried to move away, struggling to find her balance on the over-sprung carpet. 'I am not going to. I am not going to say anything at all about anything. I want to leave. Let's go, Davis. Let's go find another blasted locksmith. Come on.'

Her companion resisted. 'No, I'm afraid I have to stay.'

# Hong Kong Rose

## 1997

*Xu Xi*

*A Hong Kong native from a Chinese-Indonesian family, Xu Xi is the author of several novels and fiction collections. She has lived most of her life in Hong Kong and publishes under her Chinese name; earlier work was published under her current and former English names, S. Komala and Chaoko, respectively. Literary awards include a New York State Arts Foundation fiction fellowship, several international writers' residencies and other awards. She has an MFA in fiction from the University of Massachusetts at Amherst. Excerpts of novels and short stories appear here, including her most recent novel,* The Unwalled City *(2001). She currently lives and writes somewhere between Hong Kong and New York.*

"It's Paul." My mother handed me the phone, her face beaming with complicity.

Although he had called me every day since I returned, he had tactfully waited a week before asking to see me, knowing it was what my parents expected. When he came by that evening to take me out, I wished I hadn't agreed to the date. But with Paul, it wasn't like "dating" anymore.

"You're still so beautiful, Rose," he said, as soon as we were alone in the lift. "I've missed you." He put his arm around my shoulders.

Unaccountably, I tensed up.

He pulled his arm away. "What's the matter?" His voice was concerned, kind.

"Nothing. Just not used to being back, I guess." I managed a smile.

"Of course."

But his solicitude strangely irritated me.

We went to the Scene, the disco at the Peninsula which had been our hangout. I had expected it to be different, changed. But it was much the same as before. "*Wai!* Rose Kho!" I kept hearing people from our old crowd call out, surprised as they were to see me back in Hong Kong so soon.

All night long, I felt the tension of being around Paul. On the surface, things seemed just the way they used to be. We chatted with friends who were happy to see me back home. We gossiped about the ones who had hung on in America, joking that they would turn into ABCs. I found out there was a club of American college graduates from Hong Kong who met regularly, although it was dominated by West Coast graduates. Still, I agreed to go to one of their functions in a couple of weeks, and Paul was game enough to say he'd come along.

On the dance floor, I relaxed, knowing that conversation was impossible. Paul had already taught me the steps to the hustle, the latest dance craze. I was happy. Dancing meant an easy oblivion. We were once again the most popular and admired couple. Paul always shone when he danced. He was handsome and taller than the average Hong Kong guy, and had an elegance and grace that made him the most sought after dance partner. But what delighted me most was that he was mine again, to the obvious envy of several of the girls in our circle who, in my absence, had probably made an unsuccessful play for Paul. This, I knew, was why I had come back. Paul had waited, true to his promise. He smiled at me across the space that separated us, and my earlier nervousness disappeared. He wasn't just a teenage Prince Charming anymore, but my Paul, my fiancé.

That night, when he took me home, we stopped at the park. As I sat down on a bench, I tugged at my skirt, which was short.

I caught Paul staring at my thighs for just a second before he sat down. "You really don't have to worry, Rose. There'll be plenty of jobs. What about government?"

I wondered why he was being so serious. On the ride back in the taxi, he had barely touched me except to hold my hand. Still a bit high from the alcohol and dancing, I edged closer to him. "I can't see myself as a civil servant, can you Paul?"

His body wouldn't relent. "Hey Paul, it isn't that late yet." Unbuttoning my blouse so that the top of my bra showed, I whispered, "I'm not that civil, am I?" I wanted him to touch me, to be as hot and bothered as I was.

"Rose, please."

My hand slid onto his thigh. I felt the bulge in his pants. "Rose, let's not take any more chances." He removed my hand.

"Paul," I put both arms around his neck, pushing my body closer to his. "Don't you want to? You did the first night."

"That was different. I couldn't help myself. Besides, you're not in America anymore."

"But I feel the same, don't I? Isn't this what you wanted?"

He stood up. "You're just over-excited from seeing everyone tonight. I'm taking you home before we get into trouble."

My body remained a mass of nervous energy in bed that night. But he was right, of course he was right. Things were different here. For a moment, I wished I were back in my own place in America, away from the restrictions of living at home. It seemed absurd that we should have to neck in a park, as if we were still teenagers, as if we were still virgins, especially when we had known each other as long as we had.

The first time Paul had called to take me out, I was sixteen.

"Do you remember me?" he asked.

I hadn't thought about anything else after we met. That he thought I could possibly forget who he was astounded me. "Yes," was all I could manage. Mum was watching me from the dining table where she was sewing. I turned my face towards the veranda and tried to keep my voice low. Even with my back to her, I knew she was straining to hear every word. Paul asked me out to a party the following week. I mumbled thanks and hung up as quickly as possible.

"Who was that?" She stopped the escape to my bedroom.

"Just a friend."

"It was a boy."

"I know." I wanted to add that she did too since she answered the phone, but thought better of it.

"Did he ask you for a date?"

Regina would have told her it was none of her business, and had in fact been telling Mum to mind her own business since the first time a boy asked her out at thirteen. Paul was the first boy ever to call me. I didn't reply right away.

"Rose, look at me when I'm talking to you."

I turned around. "Yes, he did."

"I hope it's not to a tea dance?" The afternoon tea dances at dimly lit nightclubs where "boys and girls cuddle each other" were, to Mum, the epitome of the sordid. Regina had been going since she was fourteen without Mum's knowledge.

"No, to a party."

"Whose?"

"One of his classmates at La Salle."

"Oh, so he attends La Salle. That's good. Catholic?"

I nodded, wishing the inquisition would end.

"Is he Chinese?" She had been warming up to this all-important question.

"Yes." I omitted the fact of his Eurasian heritage, because Paul looked almost completely Chinese. Since she didn't ask, I also didn't tell her that the classmate having the party was Portuguese.

"Well I hope he comes to the house to pick you up. You know I prefer boys to do that."

I breathed a sigh of relief and rushed back into the bedroom.

The week flew by.

"Auntie, Uncle, I'm very pleased to meet you."

From Mum's face, I knew she was delighted with Paul at first sight. She gushed over him, asking him all about his future study plans, until I wanted to hide from embarrassment.

Dad was far more reasonable. "Don't keep these two with all your chatter. They want to go out."

Paul smiled. "That's quite all right, Uncle. I arrived early because I wanted to meet you and not rush out straight away. It seems so rude to be at a friend's house, and not even have the courtesy to speak to their parents."

Dad's right eyebrow rose slightly, unimpressed by Paul's speech. Mum beamed a huge smile at him.

"That's very true, Paul," Mum began. "It is important for young people to have manners. Rose, you can learn something from Paul."

I cringed, and glimpsed Dad's amusement at the situation. He caught my eye and his smile reassured me. It let me know that nothing mattered more than my own mastery of the situation.

I found my tongue. "We should go now Paul, shouldn't we?" The authority in my voice surprised me.

"Yes." He answered with a rapid smile. "We should."

That first date resides in my memory with a startling clarity. Paul told me then that when we met, which was at a barbecue Regina dragged me along to, he knew he wanted to be with me. I wondered how he knew, but all of me fluttered with a strange nervousness that night, and I never asked. I felt adult with Paul. And then, when he brought me home, he kissed me very lightly on the lips, and I knew, with absolute certainty, that I would see him again.

Mum, and even Regina, didn't believe Paul would continue to see me. But I knew. Somehow, he made me know, right from the beginning, that I was special. By simply being with me, from the very first time, he made me feel loved.

So what infuriated me most of all now was that Paul could, and wanted to, maintain such control, that he accepted the absurdity of our situation, even though he claimed to love and want me. He hadn't even suggested a motel. Yet I knew he just wanted the best for me, so I forgave him. He understood something about me, the way his mother did, and helped me to grow up, although I wouldn't admit that to him. And perhaps, after all was said and done, I remained in love with Paul because he reassured me over and over and over again that he thought me the most attractive girl in the world, and because of my mother's parting words as I packed for college, "Don't worry, maybe one of the Chinese boys will ask you out over there if the American boys won't, because there won't be many Chinese girls and they can't be choosy," words for which Paul said she deserved to be forever condemned.

# All the King's Women

## 2000

*Mimi Chan*

*An English literature professor for over thirty years at the University of Hong Kong, Mimi Chan has written on Hong Kong literature, Asian writers, bilingualism, images of Chinese women in Anglo-American literature, translation and stylistics. She was educated in China, New York and Hong Kong.* All The King's Women *(excerpted here) is her first novel. She currently teaches at the School of Professional and Contining Education, the University of Hong Kong.*

———

*Ah Hing lamented years later, 'People nowadays are not like that anymore. My Ma told me the custom was for betrothals to take place when babies were still unborn. They wouldn't meet until they were seventeen, and then, just like that, they would be married. Didn't matter if the man or woman had scars or was pockmarked or was as ugly as sin. Like it or lump it, we had no choices.'*

As things turned out the baby Ah Hing was betrothed to was also a girl. There was nothing to be done. Then some years later the Heshan couple's oldest son lost his wife, who died of a tumour. The man came to Cheung Chung with a proposition, saying. 'I still think it is a good thing for our families to be united. Why don't we wait until your daughter is grown. Then she can marry my oldest son. He needs a wife very badly because he has a little girl who is blind in one eye and needs a mother's care.' Cheung Chung agreed.

Meanwhile Ah Hing grew up at home. The Cheungs were farmers. The men tilled the fields and worked very hard. Two crops were grown every year. In the summer they harvested and then sowed the crops that would be harvested in the autumn. There were years of plenty and years of famine. The women in the family were weavers and wove cloth at home. Ah Hing also helped with whatever work she could. She became used to working as soon as she opened her eyes in the morning until she closed them at night. But there were also opportunities to have fun, too, although they were so poor. They didn't need any store-bought toys. On summer evenings, they would catch fireflies and put them in bottles and set them up like electric lights. They played cat's cradle with bits of string. But in general life was hard. An incident that took place when she was about seven or eight had a defining effect on the way she perceived life and death, the human world and the nether world of spirits. Ever afterwards she was to see the two worlds as having little demarcation.

Hing's mother was a woman of great energy and determination, but worn out by hard work and childbearing, she succumbed to what was described as 'an ill wind'. I think she had a stroke. She died after a short illness. Her family and friends tried everything, used every herb and oil to try to help her but to no avail — they could not make her recover consciousness. There were no splendid funeral parlours in the poor villages of Panyu in those days, and even if there had been, the ordinary tenant farmers would not have been able to afford the services of professionals. Things in Ah Hing's village were done at home. All the relatives and friends were deeply distraught because the whole household had depended on Ma Cheung. Her body had been cleaned up and laid out in the house. All the mourners sat around according to the custom. Neighbours, relatives and friends came from all over to pay their last respects. One cousin who was particularly attached to her came in weeping shockingly. When she saw the dead body, she kept shouting in a loud voice, 'Come back, come back. Your husband needs you. Your children need you. We all need you.' I suppose there are any number of scientific or medical explanations for what happened subsequently. But why is it always necessary to 'unweave the rainbow'? The cousin's wails pierced the heavens and caused the Lord of the Underworld to release Ma Cheung. To the great shock of those gathered around, her fingers began to twitch and her eyelids to flutter. Her eyes struggled to open, and then closed again. Finally they heard a creaking sound and Ma Cheung, still wearing her white *shouyi* ('longevity robes' worn by the dead) managed with difficulty to lean on one elbow and ask, 'Where am I?'

*Years later, Ah Hing explained matter-of-factly, 'You see, it wasn't time for Ma to leave yet. We all have set times for coming into the world and for leaving it. After Ma came back, she lived for a great many more years. The Jade Yellow Emperor of the Underworld still hadn't admitted her through the gates. That's why she was able to come back. I know of one other person who has come back — my second granduncle, but I suspect he had already entered the gates because ever afterwards he seemed to be shrouded by a deathly pallor. When my Ma came back, her voice had changed. It had become very deep and gravelly. A man's voice. That was only to be expected since she had been exposed to the sulphur in the Yellow Springs. What was more, she had entered halfway into another body for her next life — a man's body.*

*'Have I told you that I have* yin yang *eyes? I can see things happening in the human world — the* yang *regions, but I can also see things in the supernatural* yin *regions, the regions of the dead. Since I saw my Ma coming back to life, I see there is very little that separates the living and the dead. I am not afraid of ghosts; I've lived with them all my life. They can be very friendly.'*

After her mother returned from the dead, Ah Hing continued to live at home, waiting to be married. When she was seventeen, she was married to the widower son of the Lam family in Heshan, as was agreed so many years ago. Lam was a good man, twenty years older than Cheung Hing. He had received some education and worked as secretary for a weaving factory. Ah Heung, his daughter, was eight when Ah Hing entered the door. By that time his father had died and his mother was an invalid. Ah Hing took very good care of her. Because she was so frail, Ah Hing had to do everything for her, including clip her fingernails and toenails once a month.

*'The skies above only know why her toenails were so tough. I had to use gardening scissors. Poor lady! She was only in her sixties, but illness aged her very quickly. I used to cut her nostril hair every so often, and lo and behold, it was all snow white!' recounted Ah Hing years later.*

\*    \*    \*    \*

### Like Niobe, All Tears:
### Fifth Concubine Surnamed Poon
### (1900–1992)

When the Heshan couple, surnamed Poon, had offered Leung their little girl, she was at first not the least bit interested. The girl was squat and square. Everything about her seemed square. She had a square face, a square chin and a square, chunky body. Her nose was broad and her lips were thin. She had a square-cut China Doll hairstyle. Her eyes were her one saving grace: they were set far apart, small, but dark, twinkling and suggesting candour and honesty. Leung had a preference for beautiful little girls, who would fetch a much better price later. The Poons pleaded. 'We have had a very bad year. We cannot live through another famine, and we have other children to feed. Hoi Sum will do you good service. She is always cheerful. That is why we call her Hoi Sum (happy). She is a really hard worker; she is as strong as an ox, never complains . . .' The mother had one arm around her daughter and her eyes were filled with tears.

Leung looked carefully at the child, and the child, instead of lowering her head, gazed straight into Leung's eyes, and, although tears were brimming from her eyes, she smiled bravely, in order to endorse her parents' claims about her. Leung was touched and decided that perhaps she could keep Hoi Sum as her own *muitsai* to do heavy work around the house. She also saw that Hoi Sum had ample hips, and this augured well for her future as a childbearer. Perhaps she could sell her eventually to some peasant . . .

Leung was not a cruel woman, but matter-of-fact and business-like. She treated her *muitsai* fairly. Hoi Sum did a great deal of work in the kitchen, helping out with the cleaning and the washing. She also helped the cook *amah* cut and clean and prepare food for cooking. Her routine was tedious and back-breaking: up with the lark, take out the 'horse-buckets', boil water, fill the thermos bottles, make the tea, sweep the floor, clean the latrine, bring in the 'horse-buckets', mop the skywell, help with lunch in the kitchen, wash the dishes, clean up the kitchen, help with the washing and the ironing, help with dinner — in a never-ending cycle of a lot of work and very little sleep. But, to be fair, nobody was deliberately cruel or malicious. Hoi Sum did not ask for much, and as long as she had a warm bed and sufficient food, she was content. This life was to last for seven years. She grew up but did not grow much taller. She remained a squat little figure with merry eyes. Leung did not see much potential in her and was prepared to let her spend some more time in her house when one day she received an unusual request. A Guangzhou man was in the market for a concubine for his younger brother. This in itself was not unusual. What made it unusual was that the man insisted on a very plain but very pleasant and honest young woman.

Apparently the man's family was an extremely wealthy one: the Ho brothers were known far and wide for their business success. The younger Ho was a notorious womanizer, and, though only in his early thirties, had six concubines together with innumerable mistresses. His older brother was a direct contrast to him. A man of strict morality, he had only one wife, and she was not a raving beauty. He heartily disapproved of his brother's way of life. Naively he thought up a scheme: for his younger brother's birthday he would present him with the gift of a 'good but plain' woman to show him that women need not be beautiful to be worthy. I must reiterate that this scheme was naive in the extreme. Leung introduced Hoi Sum to the older Ho and, after talking to her for fifteen or so minutes, he found her to be down-to-earth, simple and honest. He agreed to buy her.

Hoi Sum was duly sent to the younger Ho on his birthday. The younger Ho had been surprised at his moralistic brother's choice of a gift, but when he saw Hoi Sum he was aghast at what he supposed to be his brother's bad taste. He didn't dare reject his brother's gift outright but made a mealy-mouth pronouncement about his decision not to take any more concubines. A few days later, he thought of a plan: 'My old buddy, Lee (the King), is such a garbage man that he will take in anybody to be a conclubine. I shall give this Hoi Sum to him as a gift. I warrant he won't reject her. Ha! Ha! Everybody knows he is not very discriminating.' And so Hoi Sum became installed as the King's fifth consort.

In spite of having been passed on like some undesired Christmas present, Hoi Sum settled quite happily in the Lee household. A rise in fortunes affects people in different ways. For some, the Chinese expression, 'like a water ghost who becomes a king' is applicable, and the new status and power go to their heads. For others, they so marvel at their own good fortune that they ask for nothing more and are quietly content. Hoi Sum's difficult beginnings as a bondslave had toughened her up physically and emotionally. She was overwhelmed by the grandeur of her surroundings and by the kindness of the King. She was able to repay him by bearing his first son. By 1918, the King was waxing pretty desperate. He was thirty-three years old and still without a male heir. The fifth concubine had the gods on her side, or so it seemed, when she gave birth to a healthy, well-formed — a perfect — son called Tak Yan or 'Virtuous Benevolence'.

# Renegade or Halo²

## 2000

*Timothy Mo*

The Smiths weren't exactly what you'd call Old China Hands but they were by no means greenhorns. After leaving the navy, Commander Smith had bought a practice in Surrey, then, when that had failed to live up to expectations, gone to Singapore. They'd stayed there nearly three years. From what I could piece together the island republic had been more to Mrs Smith's taste than either her husband's or daughters'. They'd lived near Tanglin Road with another Filipina, called Mary-Anne, to wait on them but no chauffeur. Apparently the vehicular tax was already so high a driver as added expense was uncontemplatable. This perhaps saved me embarrassment as my performance could not be compared with any predecessor's. Mary-Anne, whose name still figured frequently, usually in piercing whispers when Babyjane was around, had clearly been a much more satisfactory maid than Babyjane who was always cack-handed (as Fr. Paul would have put it) except when she was thieving. Commander Smith had retained their flat in Singapore as an investment and rented in Hong Kong (when as the subsequent graphical comparisons of Jenny showed, he should have done the very opposite). He had also left their Lexus there, a far superior model of automobile to the Civic I drove round Hong Kong at the Smith beck and call. I was provided with a pager on my belt — the cheapest form of cellular communication — which to avoid antisocial disturbance vibrated instead of sounding. Then I'd look at the messages running across the tiny screen: Pick us up at Dragon Seed Dept Store at 4:11 p.m. Return home to take Nicky to the tennis-club. Go to the surgery and get my Number 5 wood.

After Manila, driving in Hong Kong was a cinch, once I'd adjusted to travelling on the left-hand side of the road. The granny-ish approach for which Noy Demosthenes had chided me suited the Smiths just fine. They had no desire to travel at the speed of fright, *di ba*?

The three years they had spent in Singapore meant that they, and thus I, knew a disproportionate number of Singaporeans in Hong Kong. These included Commander Smith's receptionist and dental nurse whom he'd brought with him to the Crown Colony, so impressed had he been with them, as well as these young women's set of compatriots. It was easy for Westerners to befriend Singaporeans. In fact, when I think about it, no other folk in the whole world who lived at the equator were quite so befriendable by Caucasians as Singaporeans. It was as if they'd been put down by Divine oversight in quite the wrong latitude, their true situation belonging many degrees North, like Britain, or South, like New Zealand. In the hot spots of the world physical danger and the language barrier are what usually prevent intercourse between native and foreigner, *di ba*? Neither of these fences circumvallated Singaporeans and Westerners and the latter certainly were in no danger of being eaten by the former. Singaporeans were as close as Asians can get to being small Caucasians with straight hair and slanty eyes. Of course, I mean that it was easy for Hong Kong expatriates like the Smiths to get close to Singaporeans, not for members of the expat underclass like me.

Singaporeans had a low opinion of the *pinoy* even if many of us spoke English as well as they did. We were like wasps without the sting, *di ba*?

Jenny was the Smith most enamoured of the notion of possessing Asian friends, while Nicky was the one who actually had them, a little *barkada* of multi-national teeny-boppers. However, Jenny did have a Malaysian-Chinese admirer. It would have been too much to call him a boyfriend.

Nicola still teased her older sister about Jerome, eliciting a conspiratorial grin from Jenny which inclined me to think she had been trifling with him. In Singapore he'd, apparently, taken her to Newton Circus and the Satay Club a few times; they'd been to Chinese-language cinema, Jerome taking advantage of the opportunity to translate in whispers into Jenny's ear, and they'd eaten curried giant prawns off banana leaves at an Indian Club which was the only memorable thing about poor Jerome for Jenny. She'd enjoyed that, but he'd baulked at *pan* afterwards. She'd had his as well. He still phoned a lot. One thing I knew from the Smiths' tut-tuttings over their HK Telecom bill and the rueful comparisons they drew with their ones in Singapore, was that Singapore had the cheapest phone rates in the world. (Their bill would have been a great deal smaller if Babyjane hadn't been in the habit of phoning the Philippines when they were out, unbeknownst to them as calls were not yet itemised). All the same it must have been costing Jerome a bundle of ringgit and Sing dollars to court Jenny down the wire and, unless his job was bringing him regularly to Hong Kong, even more on the airfare. They'd have long, desultory conversations about nothing much. Jenny would rest the receiver on her shoulder and file her nails or signal to Nicky for the bottle of varnish. Sometimes she'd pick up one of Nicky's teen-zines off the phone-table and flick through it in preference to Jerome's monologue.

He was, I think, too nervous to ask her a direct question. Not, "Will you marry me?" or "Will you sleep with me?" but even, "Do you like me?" in case he met with a direct rebuff. This would have been unlikely as Jenny, whatever the uneasy stage of life she presently discovered herself in, was essentially a kind and gracious girl. She was far more likely to accept a date against her own inclinations than to manufacture some tactful excuse. She'd have done this even for an English boy, but was additionally at pains to cater at all times to the oriental concept of "face". Sometimes when everyone was out I'd be the one to field Jerome's increasingly plaintive calls. I tried to speak kindly and reassuringly to him but don't think I got through; he adopted a distant and impersonal tone when he heard my male voice. Once, I heard him get very short shrift from Babyjane. "No, go out already a long time," she snapped. "Why you always da one to be calling, hah?" He'd made his excuses and hung up before I could get to the receiver. Atheism and boys on the phone, the cocktail of depravity for Babyjane. But Jerome was by no means a typical name for a Malaysian or even a Singaporean. Most of them wore their consonant-heavy monickers like emblems of Chinkiness: Ng Chok Bing, Lim Teck Por. The romanisation of the Chinese ideograms tended not to correspond with the two conventional academic systems Fr. Paul had explained to us during a discussion of Ezra Pound, one of his favourite writers; so the names of quite conventional human beings often seemed outlandish to me. Had Babyjane been capable of two-step logical thought as well as rapid mental arithmetic she might have deduced there was a high probability of Jerome being a Roman Catholic. In which case Jerome would have found a fifth columnist in Jenny's household: a co-conspirator, willing to advance his suit at every opportunity and relay intelligence about his prospects and any possible rivals. But Jerome languished.

Months later, I was driving Jenny, Nicky, Mrs Smith, and two American currency-traders younger than Jenny, from the "country" club.

"Yeah, the Hong Kong guys are wimps," one of the American boys said *á propos* the perennial topic of discussion amongst expatriates, the shortcomings of the host country and its population. He himself had the anaemic pallor that comes from looking intently into a fourteen-inch monitor ten hours a day. "The guys are kinda lacking in *cojones*. Same with the Penang Chinese and the Singapore fellers. But the Singapore gals are the ones wearing the pants. Go-getters, right, Al?"

"*Aggressive* go-getters," Al corroborated. "Yeah, the guys are mostly wimps."

"Jenny would know about that," Nicky said slyly. Jenny pretended to throttle her younger sister. I drew up at a red light. "That's not really fair, Al," Mrs Smith said, "Their culture is different."

"They're wimps," Nicky said, with tired fifteen-year-old's conviction, as if knowing the score adults would rather not. "Jerome was a wimp. Nice but a wimp. A wimp but nice."

"Would that have been Jerome Chow, the analyst from the Hongkers and Chancres?" asked Al with a lack of concern that certainly didn't fool me. "I thought he was from Hong Kong?"

"No," said Jenny. "This Jerome's a Flight Captain with Goldair. He was in the Air Force before. He was a fighter pilot. He flew F-whatever they are. He's fifth dan at Tae Kwan Do."

At that moment the light changed to green.

"Goodness me, Rey!" exclaimed Mrs Smith as horns sounded behind us. "It's not like you to stall the car."

\*　　\*　　\*　　\*

I'd been celibate myself for longer than I cared to calculate. Counting the months made me wince, worse than the dull ache of the deprivation itself. I stopped trying to work it out.

There did exist a couple of streets in Kowloon in a run-down area called Mong Kok where commercial sex could be had, commercial sex that was cheap by Hong Kong standards but way over the Visayan odds, of course. I'd found out about it from the exposé and thundering denunciation in the local newspaper, which thoughtfully laid out the tariff as well. Most of the action took place in Portland Street, which marked an ancient boundary between Chinese and British territory. I couldn't read Chinese but all you had to do was look for a yellow sign. The working girls weren't Hong Kongers. They were mostly mainland Chinese girls, though there were Thais, Indonesians, and, needless to say, Filipinas among them. Mostly they were illegals: sneak-ins like myself, overstayers, and those engaging in acts a tourist visa was never designed to encompass. The local girls, Chinese teeny-boppers moonlighting from school for the money for designer-brands, preferred to work in karaoke boxes.

The narrow stone stair-cases in Portland Street were clean and litter-free but with iron-gates blocking the way on every flight. You rang a buzzer to summon hard-faced mamasans or sharp-faced Chinese kids with gang written all over them. The whole street was a Triad-monopoly, 14-K mostly. Man, what a purgatory. It was a joyless and, yes, sordid place, squalid in a way Subic, Olongapo, Angeles, Ermita, and Lapu-lapu back home weren't. The guys walked furtively on the way there, by themselves rather than in groups; no one smiled, no one dared to be drunk. Suddenly, I thought of Danton and the other seminarians in Amsterdam and

I burst out laughing. I guess Danton would have liked that. After I'd investigated a few staircases and had the Cantonese for nigger reinforced in my memory bank, I gave up.

It was very difficult for me to go with a working girl, to use her like a urinal. Nothing particularly exemplary about me, just a matter of what I'd come from. Anyhow, I'd succeeded in dampening the urge and emerged with a laugh on my lips and money still in my pocket. I decided to regard that as a victory.

After those mean lanes, the mall seemed a place of mirth and innocence, an urban Garden of Eden where discrimination between good and evil was unknown, not that Atty Caladong had failed to drum into us the elementary legal principle around which all systems were predicated: ignorance of the law is no excuse. Gossip, the electricity which ran the machinery of Philippine social life, crackled in the air. The *pinays* giggled together; the *pinoys*, caps back to front, just hung out, some with their arms round a *pinay*. Not as great a feat of courtship as you might think: Filipina workers outnumbered Filipino workers. Of course, the last thing I looked was Filipino. Nigerian shoplifter, Caribbean syphilitic, take your pick. The dwarfish crowd washed around me, as if I was a creosoted pier leg at low water. I smiled at a pair of *pinays*. They were talking in rapid Tagalog about the cost of flights with a particular Travel Club, direct to Manila and Cebu or via Kota Kinabalu. One of them, the older, blanked me out; the pretty one made a grimace at the companion I wasn't interested in. Language was the key that unlocked doors. Some Tagalog from me would have done wonders, but I'd still be working up from lost ground. I looked for *pinays* in pairs, that was the combination that was up for naughtiness. Anything larger than that, even a trio, was fruitless. *Hiya* and *ulaw* — in Fr. Paul's classical lexicon, *pudor* — got the better of them. Sinning didn't perturb the Filipina, being found out by her friends did. And a Filipina on her ownsome on Sunday had something sad, unbalanced, and risky about her, like a rogue elephant or a lioness with a thorn in her paw.

Like a gift from the gods, there was a promising-looking pair of fun-lovers by a trash can. Their jeans were the new kind with very narrow bottoms. In Manila they still wore bell-bottoms with pride, even at rich-girl colleges. These two were also sporting lace-up shoes and tinselly socks, which glittered under the street lighting. It was a propitious moment for fishing; twilight, *di ba*? The girls had to say yes or no quickly, for all of us lackeys had to be home soon. I sidled up to the girls. In life, as on a basketball-court, the most fruitful scoring point was from the flank. *Pilipino ka ba*, I would inquire.

"Good evening, serr. Where you are going?"

"Hah?"

Two strange Filipinas had come out of nowhere, like the way Cheech Chong had once stolen a pass out of my hands.

"Where you are going, serr? Who's your *kasama*?" They half-sang it in our friendly way. And our in-born courtesy to the stranger, our reluctance to snub, inclined me to reply, "Stroll, *na lang*," though I wanted nothing more than to shake off these two plain Janes and get to the chicks in the shiny socks. It was always easy for me to look over the heads in a crowd but as I searched for the girls I wanted to pick up, the two new chicks caught my crafty glance. "You meet your friend here, serr?"

"Ay, no," I said, "*Iring², di ba?*" *Iring* just meant cat. Saying it twice, as I've told you more than once, made it familiar, watered it down, and making water was what this cat was bent on. Perhaps Fr. Paul would have come up with the translation of "Tom-catting." You can see I wanted to shake the young ladies off by being a bit naughty but not wholly obnoxious. Unfortunately, they took it in their stride. "Oh, serr, better you have friend, good friends, than

*Iring-Iring.* We can be your friends, serr." Not once had they asked if I was a Filipino, or expressed surprise at the obvious fact that I was one of them from the forms my politeness and my salaciousness had both taken. I looked harder at them. They smiled back with a confidence that was pleasant for its openness. Neither overweight, elderly, nor hideous, just the common or garden *pinay* abroad, they were still, in all honesty, unglamorous girls. I looked for the glittery-socked pair, but the few seconds had been enough to lose them. They were wiped from the face of the earth. Don't know how many times that's happened to girls I've been following. It was physically impossible for them to be more than a block away but it might as well have been Mars.

"*Sama,* serr," the dumpier of the two urged, giving the series of spaced half-inch nods that constitute our girls' sincerest encouragement. "OK, *lang*," I said, doing my best not to sound too resigned, and failing. Even then I knew this: you were much better off having sex with someone ugly but friendly than someone beautiful but hostile.

I looked at the short-legged one's ass. Her figure wasn't as conventionally good as her (slightly) slimmer friend's, but I found the way the seat of her jeans twitched from side to side somewhat more alluring than the friend's staccato steps in her high-heeled clogs. I was now in the process of discovering something else: settling for the silver, or maybe it was even gonna have to be the bronze medal, while thinking all the time of the golden opportunity lost, that also made you low gear horny.

I was prepared to walk a good distance. None of us liked to waste our change on even public transport. Wages were, of course, much better than home — that's why Filipinos were there. But the higher cost of living ate into the bigger wage-packet. It was like treading water to stay afloat. Only the margin which contract workers could scrimp and save to remit home got magically compounded in its buying power.

My companions stayed quiet. I didn't need to be told why. I thought I understood; communication being by *pinoy* telepathy. They'd been forward, they'd been friendly, in the way of the *pinay*. Now, every action having a reaction, in the way of the *pinay* they were being modest and reticent. Silence was a necessary part in getting to know someone. Who knew? It was not impossible that they, too, were looking forward to a jump.

Our walk turned out much shorter than I expected. Back home this would have had alarm bells ringing in my head. Only full-time hunting-girls or robbers' accomplices would have had a pad so conveniently near. But this was Hong Kong. No one had guns, no one in their right mind would choose me as a mark they had to overpower with their bare hands, or even a blade. And I was sure as hell too smart to drug in a Coke or a soya-dip.

Up steps we went. "We are here," said the taller girl. "Fraise da Lord."

The door flew open, as if someone had been watching through the spy-hole. Dumpy, the one with the swishing-ass, pushed me with surprising force and in I tripped.

"Welcome," intoned a deep male voice, before a jubilant female choir broke into a religious refrain — I wouldn't dignify it with the name of hymn — the burden of which seemed to be the unoriginal notion that Jesus dearly loved a sinner. Even as I stood rooted, aghast — for sure I'd have been cooler if four Ukrainians had pounced on me with clubs — I felt embarrassment for how easy it had been to lure me and indignation at the deception, for such it truly was. And being a *pinoy* through and through, saturated in our ancient tribal values like a wick of cotton-wool in blood and lymph, I fought with every fibre in my body to repress my anger, or at least not to show it. Knowing, and even despising, what has shaped you doesn't stop you being its slave. It just adds helpless self-consciousness to your woes.

They'd seen it a hundred times before, of course: the sickly smile on my face, the wish for a hole in the ground to open and swallow me. You know, I've never liked group singing; it's aggressive and excluding, especially when Filipinos do it. I guess the Born-Agains had good intent but it was still the gang laying it on the outnumbered victim and the worst, most transparent, of them wore the same quiet triumphal smirks that the creeps in the Frat wore at an initiation hazing, or rites of a still greater evil. It was the look the galley-boy had worn. It was the Runt's Smile.

"Come," said the preacher. "You are among friends."

With friends like you, I thought, I prefer my enemies. But what I said was, "I think, a-huh, I have made a mistake, I'm in the wrong place."

"No, you are in the right flace."

"O," corroborated half a hundred female voices. They still had one arm outstretched to heaven, the open palms either reflecting God's glory or telling me to halt just there. The girls who'd brought me nodded to the preacher and departed. I really didn't like that. No time to waste; they might still be able to fetch another convert if they were quick about it. Shit, it was as impersonal as being a fly in a spider's web. "Who are you people?" I asked.

"We are Pentecostals."

"Well, I am a Roman Catholic. In fact," I decided Fr. Paul and Fr. Boy wouldn't mind if I stretched a point, "I nearly had a vocation."

"No froblem," the preacher said. "Plenty of us Catholic until we're seeing the light."

"I'll just go, *na lang*," I said

"No, please, friend. Outside, it's the world, the darkling world, a bad flace, full of temptation for a young man. In here you are with brothers and sisters. Please. Here is a hymn-sheet. I'm the one composed it myself. Please sing with us."

"*Sige. Pero* . . . for a moment, hah? I'll be the one to phone home first. ET phone home, ha, ha. *Balik ko*. I'll be back."

"*Balik*, hah? Be sure to come back." He didn't look too disappointed. Filipinos never did with that response, even if everyone knew it was always a lie. It was probably a better reaction than he was used to. Any guilt I might have had about hurting decent folks' feelings vanished when I saw the looks of mild amusement or frank distaste on the faces of his choir.

As I reached the bottom of the stairs, they were starting on *All things bright and beautiful*.

# The Unwalled City

## 2001

*Xu Xi*

It was half-past midnight at Visage. Saturday night overflow from nearby Lan Kwai Fong spilled into the club. A young Chinese crowd and a few Western faces peppered the scene. Wall-to-wall bodies. Even the space behind the bar was filled; the barber chairs were both occupied, one by a Chinese painter visiting from Shanghai, the other by the Cuban-American correspondent for *Businessweek*. Vague improvisations had begun to emerge from the cluster of musicians and would-be musicians in the corner opposite the bar.

The proprietor unlocked the door marked "private party," letting in Clio and Andanna.

"Ugh, it's so crowded in here," Clio remarked as they maneuvered their way through the crowd. "Besides, why d'you want to hang out at a hairdresser's?"

Andanna peered around, looking for Michael. He wasn't there. "I've told you, it's a club on Saturday nights. They only cut hair during the day."

"Let's not stay." Clio tugged her friend's arm. "Let's go meet my friends down in Causeway Bay for karaoke instead."

"Oh, don't be a spoilsport. It's still early." She surged forward. The music rose in volume. "Come on," she dragged Clio behind her.

"There's someone I need to talk to."

Andanna pressed towards a man with a round, youthful face and a neat-shaggy haircut. He stood apart, surveying the crowd with detached interest. Occasionally, people greeted him and he would acknowledge them with a nod and veiled smile. He seemed impervious to the smoky, inebriated talk surrounding him. Studiously dressed down in ironed jeans and a long, loose white shirt, he was contained in his own private aura.

"It's Albert Ho," Clio uttered in hushed tones to Andanna, her eyes widening at the presence of the society figure.

"I know," Andanna replied. "Albert," she called out without raising her voice. "You look lost."

The veil lifted from his smile, and his lips twitched into the mockery of a grin. *"Wei, Lei You Fun, gammaaaaaahn dim a?"* He drew out the "night" in a Cantonese opera drawl.

"Same as usual." Andanna looked him straight in the face. "You didn't call me."

He sipped his Perrier. "Drink? For you and your friend?"

Andanna knew her friend was about to shy away and say oh no, thank you very much, and rapidly nudged a discreet elbow into Clio's ribs. "But of course, we're thirsty. We'd like a bottle of red, please."

Eyes narrowed to a feline stretch, he signaled the bartender. A bottle of something other than the house red appeared. *"Leng leui, leng jau."* Beautiful girl beautiful wine. Handing them each a wineglass, he poured the silky Shiraz. "Cheers," he said in English.

She and Albert made a dramatic pair, and Andanna knew it. People said he was gay, and possibly he was, but no rumors of liaisons circulated. Clio had stepped outside the circle they created around them. More than one of the patrons at Visage exchanged words with each other about their joint presence. Andanna drunk half her wine, and placed the glass carefully on the island counter behind Albert.

"Must be running along. Keep your promise and call me, okay?"

He gave her a deliberate, lazy smile. "Okay, *leng leui*."

She took Clio by the arm and led her out of Visage.

As they climbed up the cobblestone path outside the club towards Lyndhurst Terrace, Clio stopped them in their tracks. "Will you please explain what all that was about?"

Andanna kept moving uphill. "Nothing."

"I'm not moving till you tell me."

She stopped. "You're being a big silly."

"And you're going all mysterious on me. Are you going out with him or something?"

"Michael's my boyfriend. You know that."

"Are you going to tell me or not?"

Andanna sighed, exasperated. "It's nothing. I want him to pay for a music video or a CD for me."

"You asked him for money?"

Clio's astonished look cracked her up. "Stop being so in awe of all this. He's rich, everyone knows that. And he loves to hang around the young, arty crowd so that he can be everyone's benefactor. I'm just trying to get my slice of the pie."

"But how did you meet him? At Visage?"

She hesitated, wondering whether or not to tell the truth. Albert was more or less her *tohnggo*, an "elder brother cousin" from her father's family. His mother was a sister of her aunt, Sylvie's mother, the wife of her father's eldest brother. When Andanna was growing up, Albert sometimes attended the larger family functions on special occasions. He was much older than her, the same generation as some of her younger uncles and aunts, so she had never paid attention to him although he teased her a lot when she was a girl. The family connection didn't hurt, but she didn't want Clio to get the wrong idea.

But her friend had already guessed. "You're related, aren't you?"

"It's not what you think."

"Oh sure. You're always crying poverty but you know perfectly well that's not true."

"Don't start. Come on, let's go over to *Luhksei*." She ran up to Lyndhurst Terrace and began walking east in the direction of Club 64.

Clio followed and stopped when she reached the road. "You go to *Luhksei*. I'm going to Causeway Bay to meet my friends."

Before Andanna could prevent her, Clio had hailed a taxi and hopped in. She watched the taxi drive away, not sure if she were annoyed. Her friend's idea of night life was boring, limited to karaoke and disco. But she knew Clio was impatient with her these days, although she wasn't sure why.

Well, what to do now? She glanced west towards Hollywood Road. Home was a short walk away. Perhaps she should call it quits, since the encounter with Albert had strained her theatrical energies for the night. Then, she caught sight of Tai Jai across the road, probably headed to Lan Kwai Fong. She ran after him, hoping he would know where Michael was.

At three in the morning, Tai Jai walk-dragged Andanna home.

"You shouldn't drink so much," he said as he deposited her at the doorstep.

"I'm not drunk," she declared. She fumbled with the lock and pushed open the door. The flat was empty. "Where the fuck's Michael?"

"Quit swearing. It's not ladylike. He's probably lost track of time, rehearsing. You know how he is."

Swaying slightly, she collapsed forward onto the sofa. Tai Jai nudged her towards the bedroom. "C'mon, off. I gotta sleep there."

"Fuck you," she said, "why don't you go home for a change?" The insides of her head swung like a wrecking ball, anticipating the crash. But as she tried to rise, she was suddenly overcome by dizziness. A sickening surge soured her esophagus. "Oh fuck," she heard Tai Jai say, "you're going to puke, aren't you?" And she felt herself hoisted off the sofa, his voice urging, "hold on just a little longer, can you do that?"

Andanna brought her hand to her mouth and nodded. He moved her towards the bathroom where she threw up into the sink. She pushed the hair out of her face. Her makeup felt like a layer of dirt. Looking down at herself, she saw that her sweater and slacks were also covered with vomit. Tai Jai had his arm around her waist and was rubbing her back. "You'll feel better," he kept saying, and she leaned forward again, the night's poison erupting out of her body like some exorcised alien invader. "I've got to clean this," she groaned, after it was all over. "Never mind that," Tai Jai said. "I'll clean up. C'mon, you need sleep."

He dragged her across the flat towards the bedroom where she tried, unsuccessfully, to pull off her clothes. His hands raised the sweater over her head, and then, she was aware that he had begun unbuckling her belt, unzipping her jeans and forcing her legs out of them. A protest began but subsided. Down to only her underwear, Andanna felt Tai Jai lifting her, placing on the bed and drawing the covers over her. A damp towel landed against her face and he cleaned her mouth and cheeks with it.

She did feel better, although the nauseous odor on her person disgusted her. "I want to take a shower," she declared.

"Get some sleep. You're still drunk."

"I am not." She tried to sit up, but her body wouldn't budge. He left the room, closing the door quietly behind him. Turning over, she shut her eyes and tried to sleep, but the thought of Michael finding her like this irritated her. He would be bound to deliver a lecture in the morning, and they'd end up quarreling again. She had to shower.

She sat up on her elbows, her head still a mess. What had possessed her to drink so much? She hated to admit it, but Tai Jai was a little bit right when he had said that she cared way too much what Michael thought, and that she should stop trying to impress him. Well, it wasn't that she cared, but she couldn't help admiring Michael because he was ambitious and knew what he wanted, and worked hard to get it. He wasn't like Tai Jai who drifted from job to job, borrowing money. Michael only helped him out because he didn't want to see his friend head back among the triads, but she figured Tai Jai was a lost cause anyway.

Forcing herself out of bed, she opened the bedroom door. Tai Jai was sleeping on the couch, fully dressed. Andanna crept past into the bathroom. It had been cleaned. She climbed into the shower. The lukewarm trickle had its effect as the soapy stream eradicated the evening's stink. What was that Tai Jai called her earlier? Oh yeah, "astronomical dark matter." It sounded awful, like human waste. When asked to explain, he replied that she was like a dense galactic mass masquerading as a lightweight universe, hiding her light in the distance. Definitely weird. The thin spray glided down her back, along her legs. The cracked drain sucked down all remaining odors. She turned off the tap. At the front door, Michael's key clicked.

# The Thrush and the Snail

## 1980

*Rodney Davey*

*A former professor of comparative literature at the University of Hong Kong, Rodney Davey writes drama and short fiction. Two of his stories are included in this anthology. A long-time resident of Hong Kong, he now lives in England.*

"I shall eat you," declared the thrush to the snail. "I shall take you in my beak to the nearest stone and there I shall smash your shell and swallow you whole, saving just a little for my children, perhaps. But that depends on whether you are fat enough. My children shall have what I do not want. Afterwards I shall fly to the top-most branch of that ashtree and sing. I sing all the better on a full stomach, you must understand. And because singing is very important to me I shall not spare you. You are doomed, snail."

The snail unplugged its mouth from a feast of tiny fungi and sighed.

"But," the thrush went on, "you may console yourself with the thought that my song's beauty will owe itself entirely to you. Had you not fed so well on that wall and grown so big you would not be able to satisfy my appetite. I should have had to go in search of another snail and that would have made me tired, angry even, and my song would have suffered. Console yourself with the thought that your death is to be the source of great artistry. You are to be metamorphosed from a slimy, ugly mollusc into music. That is a fate whose glory very few can hope to share."

The snail wiped its lips slowly against a dry brick.

"Off we go!" shouted the thrush without attempting to hide the pleasure it felt in anticipation of a good meal. It plucked the snail from the wall and flew up into the air. "In the meantime," it continued, a little muffled because its beak was clamped tightly against the tip of the snail's shell, "enjoy the view. Splendid scenery, don't you think? The sun is about to set behind those hills. The air is full of dessert," it added somewhat arbitrarily, eying a cloud of gnats enjoying themselves in the shade of an elm. "Evening is a time for singing. It is the time when one *has* to sing. That is the way we are made. Nothing is my fault and everything is designed for my enjoyment."

The snail scarcely listened. It was contemplating salvation. It did not like flight. It was troubled by the imminence of death. It felt a growing home-sickness for walls. "Walls," it murmured to itself as the thrush circled what looked like an outcrop of rocks.

Slowly an idea formed itself in the snail's head. Not so much an idea as a picture. It saw itself glued to a magnificent green pillar which stretched high into the clouds. It saw an absence of thrushes. The charm of this picture so overwhelmed the snail that it could think of nothing but returning as quickly as possible to the ground. Although it had been eating continuously ever since it could remember, it felt hungry. "If only, if only," lamented the snail, "thrush would open his beak and let me crawl down to earth again. I don't care if his song is good or bad," it added in a fit of resentment.

"Thrush," said the snail at last, "let me go."

"Never!" replied the thrush. The outcrop of rocks proved to be a fallen haystack. "On!" it cried enthusiastically.

"But I am ill," the snail said without much conviction.

"Then thank heaven that your life is coming to an end."

"Ill and wasted away."

"Nonsense. I can tell by your weight. You are so fat that your shell is almost too small for you."

"Ill and full of poisons from which you will certainly die."

"Wonderful! The greatest songs have been sung on a full stomach with the mind possessed by the certainty of one's own death."

"Poisons so venomous," said the snail desperately, "that you will die before uttering a note."

The thrush flew a little higher. "Listen, snail," it said after a pause, "do you want me to open my beak . . . ?"

"Oh, yes, I do, I do . . . !" said the snail very convincingly.

"And allow you to fall back to the ground where you belong?"

"Yes, yes, oh yes, dear thrush! Nothing would please me more!"

"Would you be grateful to me, snail, if I fulfilled your wish?"

"Oh, thrush," said the snail, tearfully, "oh thrush, I should never cease to thank you. Every day I should say a prayer for you. Every day I should wish you the fattest snails — only not me — to make your songs the noblest in the world. Oh, thrush, I should be more than grateful!"

"Then I shall let you go," said the thrush opening its beak at once.

The snail fell in an ecstasy of gratitude. On the road beneath, it smashed into a thousand pieces. A moment later the thrush alighted beside the mess and swallowed it.

The song the thrush sang that evening was the most beautiful it had ever sung, supported as it was by a full stomach and the satisfaction of having shown kindness to a doomed snail.

# The Captain

## 1980

*Rodney Davey*

There are cities one remembers because, like the face of a person one has loved, their recollection brings happiness. Then there are cities, many cities, whose casual ugliness so appalls the mind that they can be remembered only with fear and sadness. But it is with something more than fear and sadness that I recall the city of X. It evokes in me, even after so long a time, a feeling of such intolerable loneliness that afterwards, when I have recovered my good spirits, I am amazed at myself and at the enduring vividness of my memory. Perhaps it is on account of the freshness with which the affair comes to mind each time that I have finally decided to set it down. I believed until now — and still do believe, in a way — that what happened then should go unrecorded. Its true significance lies in silence, in forgetfulness. But I cannot forget, and there are times when we can no longer resist the urge to speak.

I had gone to the city of X on business. Due to my straitened circumstances, I put up at a small hotel in a certain Pedlar Street. It was a poor area, grey, treeless, where the unending monotony of door and window immediately depressed the spirits. Late summer though it was when I arrived, the dampness of so many winters lingered between the walls that summer made no impression. Of the small number of guests that patronized the hotel while I was there, I remember only the Captain.

He was Polish by nationality. No one knew where he had come from. He had simply appeared one afternoon, taken a room in the hotel and remained ever since. Yet in the thirty or more years he had lived there he had made no friends, had spoken voluntarily to no one except insofar as his occasional needs made this unavoidable. Scrupulously polite, a characteristic which served only to make him the more unapproachable, he quickly became an object of impenetrable mystery. Rumours of one kind or another circulated for a time, but their confusedness and incompatibility finally reduced everyone to an aggrieved indifference.

A like attitude was shown by the proprietor of the hotel. It was only modified by his never wholly obliterated fear that the Captain would one day depart as strangely as he had arrived, and that with him would go his regular, if not very large, source of income. Consequently, an aura of respect was created by the exactness and expedition with which the Captain's routine was attended to. He had his breakfast at . . . a.m., his lunch and dinner at . . . p.m. His paper was brought to his room the moment it arrived. His bell was always the first to be answered, if it ever happened that another guest required attention at the same time. In fact, it would be true to say that the life of the hotel arranged itself around the habits of its most permanent guest.

A stay of several months was, however, a rare enough event for me to pass from the role of intruder — a part inflicted on all the hotel's more ephemeral visitors — to that of a guest in my own right. Of course, there was no question of my bell being answered in preference to the Captain's. But one or two of my personal idiosyncrasies were accepted as natural additions to the routine. I progressed from 'Sir' to 'Mr . . . .' But the crowning event which marked my acceptance was the morning the Captain greeted me as I was about to leave rather earlier than usual. From that moment onwards, I was indisputably a member of the household. My table was always the same and no one sat at it but I. It was only less sacred than that of the Captain.

Yet one could not regard Pedlar Street as home. It was part of the proprietor's peculiar genius to retain just sufficient formality for it never to be forgotten that one lived in a hotel. Indeed, the routine itself, for all that it devolved from the Captain, was a means of maintaining the requisite distance. It was inviolable, as sacred as a religious service.

My reasons for staying in X exhausted themselves at the end of November. But as I had no immediate plans and nowhere to go, I decided to stay on for a time. It was already bitterly cold. Some snow had fallen and lay in dirty patches at the side of the streets. Often the clouds were so low that the top of the roofs could scarcely be seen. What little summer light had penetrated Pedlar Street was now almost totally lost. In the hotel a single bulb burned all day in the hall to light the stairs. A deep stillness filled the house.

In the weak electric light and the dark mornings and evenings our routine continued undisturbed. Guests were even less frequent. Day after day the two of us breakfasted, lunched and dined alone, each with a lamp on the table before us and darkness between, in which the waitress moved. One's morning or evening greetings were discarded. One did not disturb the figure sitting within his own circle of light.

At the beginning of December the Captain fell sick. He kept exclusively to his room, eating the same meals, reading the same newspaper. The only noticeable change was that his table was unlaid and his lamp out. After a week I inquired about him and was told he was better. But the next morning a doctor came and returned the same evening. I learned shortly afterwards that the Captain was dying.

It was not only curiosity that prompted me to ask if I could see him. There had grown up a relationship between us which made me feel sad at the thought of his lying alone. No one but the doctor, the proprietor and the waitress visited his room. It was impossible to imagine that he had any thing to say to them, or they to him.

His room was a replica of my own. The gas fire burned, lighting the ceiling and the bed where he lay. The curtains were drawn. There was no light. I had been announced and he lay looking at me for a moment as I stood inside the door before asking me to sit near the fire. His face did not appear to have changed. In the glow from the stove it was even somewhat red and his eyes were a little more animated. For a long time, perhaps as much as a quarter of an hour, we did not speak. I wondered if he had forgotten I was in the room.

Eventually he turned his head a little on the pillow and said without looking at me: "You see how impressive silence can be. It has infinite volume, like sleep." I said nothing. He continued: "I have waited . . ." he assessed time, "for thirty years. More." He thought for a while. Then he went on: "Well, have you come here to be my confessor? Come here, then, put your chair beside my bed, incline your head and listen with the compassionate, earnest curiosity of a priest." I did not hesitate to do as he asked. "There, now, for all but the cassock and the cross you are like the young priest called to my mother's bedside. There she held him all night until she lost consciousness and he could go home and sleep. That was the dutifulness of inexperienced youth. The old ones know how to ease out the last little sin as easily as a milk-tooth. But my mother, she clawed his hands and bit his sleeves and clutched his head to her lips. That was an agonizing purgation. Those sins were wrenched, bleeding, from her soul and laid bare and twitching before the trembling young priest's eyes. Not because they were great sins. But because they were constantly lived and relived until they had assumed dimensions and meanings far beyond their moral value. The smallest lapse had struck roots of immense complexity and cast sinewy branches with little black, putrid buds throughout the lives of those who were most dear to her. We heard it all. We watched the struggle to step from antecedent to antecedent back into the remotest galleries of her memory. And then the despair, the tears, the long dumb plea for understanding and absolution from the priest who sat there with downcast face and quivering lips. He did not dare ask her if she had anything further to confess until it was evident that she could no longer find the strength to speak. His cowardice was plain even to himself. As soon as she closed her eyes, he hastily took our hands and fled." The Captain was quiet for a time. "We sat in silence until she died. I was sunk in the deepest misery. I had watched my father die and two of my sisters; death was nothing new to me. I even thought I understood it in some impersonal way. But this death was monstrous. The will to remain alive did not spring from any love of life itself, but from a passionate longing for time. I had the feeling, more, I was convinced, that if she had had to suffer extreme physical pain for a few more hours, days, she would unhesitatingly have done so. Time for what? Time to make amends for the revelations which had come to her so late. Time to nip other little buds before they bloomed into black lilies. Yet, if ever she sinned, not consciously, but all the same grossly sinned, against us, it was on her deathbed. I hope God spared her any knowledge of what she had done. For instead of death heightening in us our awareness of being alive, she made life impossible. When we left the room, at last, and walked downstairs into the garden, life had become intolerable for us.

I looked at his face expecting to find some sign of emotion. It had not altered. We sat on in silence. At length I asked him if that was why he had come to X.

"What small changes have taken place here, either in this hotel or in the city itself have done nothing to erode its more durable characteristics. Dirt, ugliness, soullessness, indifference to its inhabitants. You know them yourself. It is a hateful city. That is, it is hateful to you, no doubt. To me, no, it is perfect. I owed it nothing when I came. I never wanted to give it anything, and anything I had given it would have made not the slightest difference. It could give me nothing and it did not want to. I could come and I could go without leaving any significant impression. I owe no debts and no one owes me anything. It will be as if I had never existed and that will be my dearest, my only, wish fulfilled." He waved his hand. "Now go, please."

He died a few days later without my seeing him again. In his will his desire to be cremated and then scattered within the city limits was clearly expressed. I said that I would see to these last details myself. This was made all the easier since he had himself set aside sufficient money for the funeral costs.

And so it was done. It was raining and a cold, hard wind was blowing as I opened the casket and scattered the contents in a small, muddy park I had earlier discovered. The ashes vanished at once.

# Lost River

## 1990

*David T. K. Wong*

*Born in Hong Kong, David Wong was educated in six countries spanning four continents. The author of three collections of short fiction in English, he won recognition for an early story 'The Cocktail Party' (included here). He worked as a journalist in London, Singapore and Hong Kong, and later joined the Hong Kong government, retiring as one of its most senior Chinese officers. To encourage Asian voices in English, he founded the David T. K. Wong writing fellowship at the University of East Anglia. He now writes and lives in London.*

It was one of those glorious July days that came all too infrequently during the English summer, and Jasmine took it as a special welcome to mark her return to London after more than thirty years. She luxuriated in the brilliant sunshine as she strolled from the Savoy, past the crowds on the Strand and down towards the Embankment.

A few heads turned upon her passing. The fact that she could still produce such an effect at the age of fifty gave her a momentary glow of satisfaction. Her smooth skin and her black hair, gathered in a stylish chignon, certainly disguised her age, while the designer dress from Harrods showed to advantage her small, trim figure. A necklace of Mikimoto pearls conferred an additional touch of elegance. But it was really her deportment that was arresting. There was a certain majesty in her carriage, with every movement feline and supple and a joy to behold. That kind of grace could only have come from long training as a ballet dancer.

On reaching the Embankment, Jasmine followed the walkway alongside the Thames. The placid river was shimmering with sunlight and a light river breeze brushed her like a whispering caress. It was a day in which a person ought to be bursting with the joy of being alive. And yet she was being bothered by an unsettling ambivalence. It was as if she had some pressing task to complete and yet dreaded getting down to it. Thus her stroll seemed an evasion.

She had taken that same aimless walk for the past three days, ever since Pong went home to leave her to that extra week in London she wanted. If she did not sort herself out quickly, she would go out of her mind.

After a while Jasmine stopped, as she had done on previous days, and leaned her arms against the thick stone wall bordering the river. The fingers of one hand played with her string of pearls. Her tilted, Oriental eyes gazed for a long while at nothing in particular, hardly taking in the luminous sky, the traffic plying the river or the slight river haze rendering indistinct the buildings on the far bank.

When her dark eyes rested upon the graceful arches of Waterloo Bridge in the middle distance, they took on a preoccupied look and her mind zoomed back to the distant past. Her generous mouth broke into an ironical smile. How much water must have flowed beneath that bridge since her last visit, she thought. She had been right to stay away. London contained too many memories, too many ghosts. After more than thirty years they still had the power to unsettle her and to play havoc with her emotions.

No one in her circle of friends quite understood her reluctance to visit London. She had refused all explanation, leaving them to their own surmises. Some had ascribed to her a dislike for the fog and the damp, others an aversion to English food. Still others put it down to her dismal student days. She allowed them their speculations and kept her own counsel.

Even Pong, before flying back to Hong Kong, chided her by saying: "Ever since I have known you, you have refused to visit London. You did not want to come as part of our honeymoon, you did not want to come to put the children in school and university, you did not want to make it any part of our holidays in Europe. One would have thought the Black Death was still stalking its streets.

"And now, when we've finally persuaded you to come for Charity's graduation, you suddenly want to extend your stay without explanation. If you had told me earlier, I could have rearranged my schedule. Now I have to leave you on your own. I'll never understand women."

"It'll only be for a week," she had replied. "I'll be home soon enough. Don't worry."

Standing there beside the Thames, Jasmine pondered again her restlessness over the last three days. Why had she given way so suddenly to the impulse to remain? She had no friends to see, no unfinished shopping to attend to. And yet the urge to remain had been so compelling that she was impatient for Pong to be gone. What was she hoping to experience or discover or achieve? She did not know. If she could not find an answer for herself, how could she explain to others?

London, of course, was the most beloved of all the cities she had known. She had gone there at the fervent age of sixteen to enroll at Sadler's Wells, as the Royal Ballet was then called. For three years it had been an enchanted place where dreams of artistic success, happiness and love had blossomed like flowers, where on a certain enchanted evening she had attained that status known as womanhood. But it was the bittersweet memories of what happened thereafter that now held her to the city.

For more than three decades she had guarded those memories against all comers, relegating them to the level of the subconscious. But now they were intruding upon her willy-nilly, completely out of control.

Perhaps the old sights and sounds of London were responsible. Charity's graduation and her departure for a European holiday with her fiancé were also to blame. They suddenly made her realize the best part of her life was over and done with and left her wondering what it had amounted to.

She had been a dutiful daughter, a faithful wife and a loving mother. Had that been enough to counterbalance the evasions and surrenders pressing so uncomfortably upon her conscience? If so, why that bitter nostalgia for what Arnold called the "youth-time" of her life? If not, then what else must a woman do to find peace?

Ever since she could remember, the only thing she desired was to dance. Soon after the war, when she was nine, her parents had enrolled her for ballet lessons in the belief that ballet was good for a girl's posture.

She soon found she could express herself in a dance in a way she never could with words. Her progress had been so exceptional that Mrs. Rubinovich, her Russian teacher, persuaded her parents to send her to Sadler's Wells for further training.

Mrs. Rubinovich also arranged as her guardian a woman of ancient vintage, Eastern European origins and formidable proportions. But apart from settling her into a boarding-house, which suited her modest circumstances and inviting her to an occasional meal, the guardian rarely intruded into her life. She was thus left to fend largely for herself in an alien city, which had taken a month by boat to reach.

Her first weeks in London were a period of utter misery. She could not get used to boarding-house food nor the necessity of sharing a communal bathroom. Her fellow boarders were for the most part students but there was not a ballet dancer among them. They were too boisterous to suit her disposition and their horseplay and shrill laughter got on her nerves. She felt utterly wretched until Arnold Beresford made friends with her and introduced her to the endless delights of London.

She had met Arnold by chance, when they both turned up late for dinner at the boarding-house one evening. They were the sole occupants of the dining room and sat across from each other as plates of cold sausages and mashed potatoes were dumped before them. Then their eyes met and they both burst out laughing at their common misery. From that moment onwards, Arnold assumed the role of guide, advisor and friend.

Arnold was two years her senior and was one of the few non-students living in the boarding-house. He had sandy-coloured hair, ardent blue eyes and a resolute jaw with an attractive cleft at the bottom of his chin. There was an air of purpose about him, which set him apart from the other boarders.

He was from Doncaster and was the son of a coal miner. He seemed to have tried his hand at an incredible number of jobs. He had started by delivering milk in a horse-drawn cart. Then, because he developed an interest in horses, he became a stable boy for a year. At the time they met, he was working as a sales assistant at Bennington, that venerable firm which had provided sensible footwear for British gentlefolk for more than a hundred years.

But he indicated his real mission in life was to become a writer and regarded everything he had done or was doing as a preparation for his chosen calling. His clear ambition and determination to succeed filled her with admiration.

Arnold saw to it that she savoured everything London had to offer. He made a point of showing her the paintings and sculptures by Degas. She took to them immediately, for they seemed to express the essence of the life she sought. She could easily imagine herself posing for each of the works, in a basic position, exercising at the barre or simply lacing up a ballet shoe.

Arnold, as if reading her thoughts, had then said in his low, earnest voice: "You could be better than any of them. You could be a Chinese Pavlova or Ulanova. All you have to do is to want it desperately enough."

"Oh, I have never aimed so high," she had replied. "I just want to dance. I should be quite happy dancing in an ensemble."

"You must not short-change yourself. You must have ambition. When you set out to do something you must aim to be the best. There is nothing sadder than to see talent going to waste, since so few of us are really talented. You are talented. You have been endowed with a gift and, as its possessor, you have a duty to perfect it and bring some beauty into this dismal world of ours."

No one had spoken to her in such a way before. Hitherto, her sheltered existence as the only daughter of a small textile manufacturer had led her to believe that dancing was just a passing indulgence. It was something to be enjoyed before assuming the burdens of adulthood, of helping in the family business, and of finding a husband and raising children.

Arnold's exposition had given her a fresh point of reference. Thereafter she did her barre exercises with heightened enthusiasm, conscious that every perfectly executed pirouette or entrechat quatre had the power to brighten the world. That new awareness was the first of many that Arnold was to bring into her life.

Her association with him soon settled into a pattern. From Monday to Saturday, they would have dinner together. After dinner, he invariably retired to his room, to follow a strict regime of reading and writing. He advised her to devise a similar schedule for herself.

Sunday was the day for fun. They would spend it together, wandering around London or visiting nearby places like Greenwich, Windsor and Bath. They would make their plans over dinner during the previous week and their obvious contentment in each other's company soon caused them to be dubbed "the turtle-doves".

Such teasing by other boarders drove her to the verge of tears on more than one occasion, for it carried the implication that her relationship with Arnold was less than innocent. Since she was thirteen, her mother had impressed upon her the need for a girl to be chaste and those exhortations had been emphasized more forcefully prior to her departure for England. Her mother kept repeating the lines from the Odes:
"A man may do a wrong, and Time
Will fling its cloak to hide his crime:
A woman who has lost her name
Is doomed to everlasting shame."

She had often trembled at the thought that her feelings towards Arnold might contain more than friendship. She could neither explain those feelings nor give them a name. All she knew was that she felt comfortable and safe in his company and derived a peculiar pleasure if he so much as allowed her to sew a button or darn a sock for him. When he failed to turn up for dinner, she would become unaccountably lost and she would tingle with curiosity whenever she thought of what he might be doing each evening locked up in his room.

Once she asked to see some of his writing but Arnold replied: "You'll read them soon enough, when the world is ready for me. But if I don't make it, why bother with the scribblings of a failure?"

On the contrary, she wanted to share everything with Arnold. It pleased her enormously when Arnold took an interest in different aspects of her development. He would correct her faulty pronunciations or her wrong usage of idioms. He would recommend books for her to read, music for her to enjoy and ideas for her to ponder. He took particular interest in her progress as a dancer and sometimes asked her to improvise outrageous dances like "a radio suffering from static interference" or "the metamorphosis of a character out of Kafka or Dostoyevsky".

"Dancing is more than just mastering sets of steps. Every mother's child knows how to dance like sylphs or dying swans," he once told her. "For it to become real art you need to find a unique way of expressing what people have been struggling to express. Nothing else is worth a damn."

In order to live up to his expectations, she redoubled her efforts to perfect her dancing. Then, one day, he suddenly began addressing her as "Dancer" and she knew her progress had met with his approval.

Jasmine smiled to herself in recalling those days. Wonderful things never seemed to last, she thought. One day you were young and innocent and in no time at all you were old. It was so unfair.

She turned away from the river and crossed over to the small park on the other side of the road. She walked the length of the park and back again. When she came to an unoccupied bench in the shade, she sat down and felt refreshed by the subtle coolness of the shade.

Trying to re-live the past was a stupid exercise, she told herself. If she continued on her present tack, all she would find were nothing but memories of pain, of lost opportunities, of surrenders and regrets. Yet, somehow, she knew she had to press on, to confront her past and come to terms with it. If purging the past was necessary, what better place was there than the very city where the most traumatic events took place?

Jasmine took herself back again to her final year at Sadler's Wells. She remembered how attached to Arnold she had become by that time. It seemed that so long as she could dance and enjoy his company that would be the acme of happiness.

She recalled her apprehension on the approach of graduation. Unless a miracle happened, that would mean the end of her stay in London. That prospect filled her with desperation. She knew it was possible for students doing well to enter the school's ballet company after graduation. Without so much as pausing for thought, she applied for a position.

"You've done very well, my dear, and I'm exceptionally pleased with your progress," her teacher said. "You're a superb little dancer but I'm afraid it's going to be difficult to find you a place."

"Am I not as good as the others?" Jasmine asked.

"Oh, no, no! Quite the contrary. You're better than most. But you see, my dear, it is not only dancing that counts. You also have to fit in."

"I don't understand."

"Well, my dear, try to imagine yourself in an ensemble or a chorus. Can't you see that you will not blend well? You're smaller than the other girls. And then there is your Asiatic face. One dark face among all those pale ones. It just won't work, don't you see?"

"I only want to continue dancing."

"Why not go home and join one of the companies there?"

"There are no ballet companies in Hong Kong."

"Well, there's your chance to start one."

She had returned to the boarding-house devastated. When she recounted the episode to Arnold amidst a flood of tears, he was indignant.

"What do those old fogies know?" Arnold demanded. "That's the trouble with us British. We cling to a constipated life. We stick with what our grandfathers are accustomed to. We don't realize the world is changing. Hell! In America all kinds of new dance forms are evolving. Size and colour don't matter two hoots. Don't worry, we can shake the dust off this place. We'll go to New York and show the world what can be done."

That evening, because of her distress, Arnold allowed her into his room and as he comforted her the inevitable happened. Arnold declared his love, causing all the pent-up affection she felt for him to burst forth. She forgot about her mother's admonitions, about the Odes, and surrendered herself.

Thereafter, staying at the boarding-house and sneaking into each other's room became intolerable. Arnold urged her to move into a place of their own. But she was hesitant.

"Look, this is the youth-time of our lives," Arnold argued. "It is a time for following the dictates of our hearts. Life will force us into retreats and surrenders soon enough. But in the youth-time of our lives we can defy the world and make of life what we will."

Shortly thereafter, they moved into a small flat and the two or three months that followed were the happiest in her life.

But news had a way of travelling thousands of miles, especially when one did not particularly want it to spread. Before she knew it her father was in London, demanding that she pack her bags for home. Those terrible three-cornered scenes, with the two men she loved shouting incomprehensibly at each other, remained as vividly as if they had happened yesterday. No effort by her could soften the sharp edges in their exchanges.

"Have you no shame?" her father demanded, in a voice filled with both sorrow and anger. "How can you take up with a common salesman?"

"He's not a salesman, Father," she tried to explain through her tears. "He aims to be a writer. He's still trying to learn about life."

"Then let him learn with someone else's daughter! Your mother has been sick with worrying since she heard what you've been up to."

"I'm sorry Mother had to learn of it that way. But we love each other."

"Love? What do you know about love? You're just in your teens."

"What's going on?" Arnold interjected, catching the anger and frustration in the voices. "Tell him we want to get married."

After she had interpreted, her father replied: "You think marriage will solve everything? How will you live? You're our only child. Are you going to remain ten thousand miles away? What would be the difference then between having a child and having none?"

"We could come to live in Hong Kong," she suggested, desperately.

"And what would this man do in Hong Kong? Sell shoes? He does not speak our language. He does not know our customs. He may not even like our food. Will he just sit there when relatives gather on festive days? And when you have children, am I supposed to take them to the park and explain to all and sundry why my grandchildren have blue eyes and fair hair? If you have any consideration at all for your mother or for myself you will pack your things this instant."

As her tears tumbled down in torrents, Arnold kept demanding: "What's he saying? What's he saying?"

She avoided interpreting the worst of her father's outburst and simply said: "I have to go home. My mother is sick and is asking for me. I owe her a duty to go back."

"I'm sorry to learn of your mother's illness," Arnold said. "But let us get married first. Then we can both go to see her."

"No, you don't understand. I am Chinese. Chinese girls have to get their parents' permission before getting married. My father is upset now. But when I get home I can explain things to him and to my mother. Please be patient and trust me. I will come back to you very soon."

"How soon?"

"A few months. A year at the most."

"No! If you leave I know I'll lose you. I love you and don't want to lose you. Can't you see we have our own lives to live? We can't be governed by what parents want. Confucius has been dead for twenty-four centuries. It's time we buried him. Let us just go and get married. Things can sort themselves out afterwards."

"That's impossible. You just don't understand."

"Yes, I do understand! I understand better than you. Listen to me, Dancer. What you decide today will seal both our fates forever. So listen very carefully. Your parents mean well but they cannot live your life for you. Only you can do that. You must know that if you go back, your parents will never let you return here. And I haven't got the money to come to you. It will mean the end of both your dancing and our love.

"Don't you realize what we are both facing today is our Rubicon, our river of no return? You see, there is something very peculiar about rivers. A river never remains the same because fresh waters are flowing into it all the time. Therefore no on can cross the same river twice. We are now on the edge of our special river. We either cross it together or we lose it forever."

"If we fail to cross, then that something which makes you want to dance and makes me want to write will die. If that happens, then we might as well be dead too. We may go on breathing and eating and talking but for all intents and purposes we will be dead. So let's cross our river together now."

"I can't! I can't!" she wailed.

Jasmine looked up at the sunlight filtering through the tracery of leaves and suddenly realized that she had been crying. She took out a handkerchief of fine Irish line and dabbed her eyes.

Yes, Arnold had been right, she thought. Something died that day and everything thereafter turned colourless and flat. She wrote numerous letters to declare her love and to plead for patience but Arnold never replied. After more than a year she stopped writing.

Then relatives introduced her to Pong, an architect at the start of his career. Pong never enthused about any mission in life the way Arnold did. He just had a knack for desiging buildings, which maximized plot ratios and squeezed out every last bit of useable space. Developers loved him. She eventually married him for want of anything better to do. Although Pong provided her with all the luxuries she could possibly want, their years of marriage passed like grey shadows, one indistinguishable from another.

Now her parents were dead and her children had grown up. Her son had become an architect and had acquired his father's designing talents. Charity had just graduated from the University of Manchester with a dentistry degree. She would happily spend the rest of her days straightening teeth and filling cavities. It was strange that both her children had opted for careers that were safe and practical. They would never be troubled by yearnings of the spirit or lose sleep over intractable human issues.

Jasmine speculated momentarily whether she would have made anything of her dancing if she had gone to New York with Arnold. She had a failure of nerve at the crucial time and now she would never know.

But what of Arnold? Did he remain true to his destiny or did his divine spark die as well? If he had carried on writing she would feel less guilty about her own failure. Through the years she had kept an eye out for books bearing his name but found none. She comforted herself with the thought he might have used a pseudonym.

All of a sudden she felt an overwhelming need to know. She realized at once that was the real purpose of her extended stay. But how could one go about locating someone after more than thirty years? Well, Bennington had been in existence for over a hundred years and that was as good a place as any to start. So thinking, she got up from the bench to make her way back to the Savoy.

It took her half an hour of telephoning to discover that old staff records were kept at Bennington's headquarters in Birmingham. Several calls later she got through to the Personnel Manager.

"I'm terribly sorry to trouble you," Jasmine told the woman at the other end of the line, "but I'm wondering if you could help me with a personal matter. I'm from abroad and I'm anxious to locate an old friend who used to work for Bennington thirty years ago. I know this is a long shot but I thought you might have a forwarding address or something to help me pick up the trail."

"We do keep records for a fair while but thirty years is a very long time. I'll see what I can do. What is your friend's name and where did he work?"

"When I knew him he was a sales clerk at the Piccadilly branch of Bennington. His name was Arnold Beresford."

"Oh, goodness gracious me!" the voice at the other end exclaimed with a laugh. "Mr. Beresford is still with us! He's now our Sales Director. I'm sure he will be delighted to hear from an old friend. Unfortunately, he's out of the country at the moment. Summer vacation, you know. He'll be back in a fortnight. If you would leave a message I'll see that Mr. Beresford gets it."

An image of Arnold flashed across Jasmine's mind. It was an image of a stout, greying businessman with a gold watch chain strung across his waistcoat, leaving a house in suburbia to catch the 8.15, absorbed with the weekly sales figures and the schedule for the stores promotion. Her heart felt like a stone within her breast.

"No, there's no message," Jasmine said to the telephone. "Now that I know where he is I can get hold of him when he returns. Thank you very much."

Jasmine heard the receiver being replaced at the other end. She lowered her own instrument onto her lap and sat holding the dead telephone for a very long time.

# Red, Amber, Green

## 1990

*David T. K. Wong*

"Your mother's . . . !" the young man sitting next to Old Mak cursed.

Old Mak did not pay any attention. His face, lined and weather-beaten like the bark of old oak, remained lifted towards the small barred window set high up in the wall of the underground cell, while his timid brown eyes, drooping at the corners, continued to stare at the grey November skies outside. His whole being was absorbed in the marvel going on, in the subtle changes in colour accompanying the slow unravelling of the dawn.

The sight brought back with nostalgic vividness the days of his childhood and early youth in a village in Kwangtung Province. It brought back the Pearl River, flowing sluggishly and silent, the lonely monastery on a distant hillock, the friendly noises of farm animals, the comforting warmth of fresh congee and the pervading fragrance of the country air. It also brought back the fields, friendly and eternal, the source of all life.

"Your mother's . . . !" the young man cursed again. A distracted mop of black hair reached over his forehead and clawed at his bright, aggressive eyes, whilst some unruly strands sprung up at the back of his head like the sickle feathers of an agitated young cock. "It's just my luck to get arrested the very day I stock up. Now my oranges and pears are going to be confiscated again. Your mother's . . . ! "

The other occupants of the police cell, some fifteen or sixteen in number, began to stir, awakened by the cursing of the young man. One or two of them stood up and stretched themselves. The cell was small. Its air, already stale with human odours, was made worse by the smell from a wooden toilet bucket standing in a wet patch in one corner. The inmates tried to steer clear of it while sitting and dozing on the cement floor, with their backs against the walls or against the steel bars which made up one side of the cell. Consequently a chaos of limbs covered the centre of the floor. Old Mak's were gnarled and covered with varicose veins.

It had been a long, long time since he witnessed the breaking of the dawn, Old Mak thought, as he watched the sky turning a light translucent blue. The cubicle in the lodging-house, where he had occupied for years one layer of three three-tier bunks, was windowless. Day and night were distinguishable only through the comings and goings of the other eight occupants as they went about their shifts as coolies, street sweepers, night watchmen or whatever. In the police cell there was at least sunlight.

"They squeeze you till there's no way out, those lackeys of foreign devils," the young man said, with a note of righteous complaint in his voice. "If you cannot afford to line their pockets, you cannot get a licence. If you sell without a licence, you're breaking the law. Then they put you in gaol and confiscate your goods. How is a man to live?"

Old Mak turned towards the young man. He noticed that he had long ears, with large fleshy lobes, just like his own. To the Chinese long ears were supposed to mean longevity, and he wondered if the young man ever found any pleasure in the thought. He himself had once.

But that was forty years ago, when he first came to Hong Kong, when he was filled with hope of crossing the seas to the Golden Mountain to earn enough money to buy back the family land. Now, worn out, kinless and without hope, a long life seemed a cruel and unnecessary burden.

Old Mak sighed, shut his eyes and rested his head against the wall. His close-cropped hair, cut almost like that of a bonze, contained a liberal scattering of grey. Although he had spent so many years in the city he had not yet learned to mask his feelings. His simple peasant face displayed bewilderment for all the world to see. His sad drooping eyes, his broad flat nose and his apologetic mouth all confessed his helplessness and despair.

He reflected upon the woes that had befallen him one after another and the circumstances that had brought him to Hong Kong. It seemed his whole life had been one long chronicle of woes. They began in the year of the great drought, when his two sisters had to be sold to a fate he had never quite discovered. A couple of years later a typhoon had devastated the village and had killed many people, including his father. The funeral expenses, coupled with the loss of the crops, had forced the sale of the small family plot. Thereafter he and his mother had had to work as casual farm hands. When he was eighteen his mother also died and nothing remained thereafter to bind him to the village.

It was around that time that he heard stories about the fortunes being made in the new land across the seas, through building railroads or panning for gold. He decided to head for Hong Kong to earn his passage to the Golden Mountain. But once in Hong Kong he found making a living hard for someone without connections or education. Since his only advantage was his peasant strength, he became a rickshaw puller.

For six years he pounded the hard city streets between the shafts of his red rickshaw, with his feet protected only by sandals cut out of old rubber tyres and held together with strips of cloth. But in spite of the exhausting work, the years had not been altogether unsatisfactory. There was little in the way of motorized transport in those days and the rules of the road were simple. The sudden spring and summer showers always generated plenty of business and when there was no business there was never want of other rickshaw pullers with whom to pass the time of day.

At the end of that period he had saved enough for his passage. One of his fellow lodgers offered to arrange a discount on his fare with an American shipping company. He handed over the money in hope but he never saw that lodger again.

So it was back to pounding the streets, to dreams of opportunities in a distant land. As the days merged into years, life gradually became harder. More motor vehicles appeared and their mean horns berated anyone not getting smartly out of their way. The rules of the road also increased and became more strict. It became more essential to carry passengers only along the left side of the street and to first extend his arm before making a turn. Although the number of rickshaws plying for hire progressively declined, so too did patronage. It simply became more and more difficult to put away those hard-earned copper coins.

He became troubled by the thought he was not meant for life in the city. The city seemed to suck vitality out of him like a leech. The dead asphalt jarred his bones, sapped his energy and gave nothing in return. It was not like the good, brown earth back on the farm. There he had been in touch with the very substance of life itself, with the vital currents of the earth which replenished and rewarded him for his labours. He had been able to feel communion with something eternal in the soft ooze of mud between his toes and to find pride when the fields rippled with golden grain. In the city the only return he got was the dull clink-clink of copper coins.

More years drifted by before he managed to accumulate sufficient passage money again. But by then his longing to return to the land had become intense. The prospect of further years of exile in a foreign country was more than he could bear. So during a moment of dark desperation he took his entire savings to a gaming-house. He would leave his future in the hands of the gods. He would either win enough to buy back his land or reconcile himself to being trapped in the city for the rest of his days.

He lost. And from that moment hope began ebbing from him like blood seeping from a troublesome wound. The seasons came and went and he lugged his rickshaw with indifference, like some docile beast, without purpose and without dreams. He no longer kept track of the years, except that with each passing year the streets became more congested and traffic regulations multiplied. Licences had to be renewed by a certain date, rickshaws had to be inspected annually for road worthiness, right of way had to be granted to pedestrians at zebra crossings, and so on.

He submitted to such impositions with resignation. Nothing seemed to bother him any more, not the pointlessness of his life nor even the rumblings of a spreading war.

When the war did come and the Japanese occupied the city, life became harder still. Not only did the enemy soldiers take rides without paying but, as often as not, they handed out beatings for good measure. As the occupation wore on, food became scarce. He felt half-starved most of the time and it was then that he developed a cough and a pain in his chest. By the time the city was liberated, he had become a pale shadow of his former self.

His appearance no longer inspired confidence and his stamina deserted him. If he were lucky enough to win a fare, he would find difficulty maintaining a steady trot. Every breath he drew seemed to light a fire in his chest and every exertion triggered a spasm of coughing.

Nothing prepared him, however, for the even crueller world that awaited him after the war. The whole tempo of life suddenly quickened and speed became of the essence. Motor vehicles crowded the streets and pushed into obsolescence the more sedate forms of transportation. More traffic regulations were proclaimed. Streets became designated only for one-way traffic and he had to learn new routings to get to old destinations. Familiar places where rickshaw pullers used to congregate to wait for fares suddenly became no-parking zones and no-stopping zones. The drivers of motor vehicles showed little tolerance when he got in their way.

Worst of all, traffic lights began appearing at street corners like ugly mechanical monsters, with eyes forever blinking red, amber and green. He had to learn to stop or run on the command of those lights. If he were tardy in obeying, horns would scream at him or else he would receive a tongue-lashing from some uniformed guardian of the law.

He became bewildered by all the new tensions and restrictions and watched helplessly as fellow rickshaw pullers abandoned the trade one by one. He could not afford that luxury, however, because he knew of no other way of making a living. During moments of despair he often wished he could simply go to sleep and never wake up. But the gods obviously had a worse fate in store for him, for here he was locked up in a police dungeon! Perhaps he was destined to die in the company of common criminals. His heart chilled at the thought.

A fresh torrent of abuse from the young man shook Old Mak out of his reverie. All the inmates of the cell were now awake but none paid any attention to the young man's recital of his grievances. Each seemed to have troubles enough of his own.

Old Mak felt sorry for the young man. So, as a gesture of sympathy, he asked: "Will you have the capital to start again?"

"That can be found," the young man said, "but the whole vicious cycle will just repeat itself. We hawkers try to help one another by organizing ourselves. That is the only way we stand a chance. A man can no longer live alone in this world. Every time they raid us, a few stay behind. We block the way while others escape with their carts and goods. They can arrest us and confiscate our goods, but those who got away will help us pay the fines and make another start. That is the only way to survive." The young man's voice lost some of its anger as he spoke.

A sudden spasm of coughing seized Old Mak. When it had subsided, he said: "That is good. At least you can start over again."

"And you, old uncle, what are you in for?"

"I am not sure. For smoking, I think."

"You mean smoking opium?"

Old Mak nodded.

"Oh! How can you allow yourself to fall into such a trap? They are cunning, these foreigners. Before the war, they encouraged everybody to smoke. They sold opium at government depots. Then, when people have caught the habit, they changed the law and imposed fines for smoking. It is just their way of squeezing money from you. One day all this will change. We will throw them out. Anyway, you should not smoke opium, old uncle. It is not good for you."

Old Mak caught the subtle note of reproof in the young man's voice and he felt ashamed. He wanted to explain that he was not just an old idler living on pipe dreams. He wanted to tell him about the forty years of pounding the streets, about his unbearable longing for his land, his endless struggles and his desire merely to ease the pain in his chest. But he knew that explanations would be pointless, just as his whole life had become pointless. So he accepted the reproof and remained silent.

Just then the early morning sun suddenly emerged from behind some clouds and shot a ray of sunshine through the small barred window. It stamped a golden oblong upon the wall above Old Mak. The sight of the sunlight stirred Old Mak in a way that he could not explain. He rose unsteadily to his feet, a pathetic figure in a grey cotton jacket which had grown too large for his shrunken body and a pair of baggy black shorts which exposed his grotesque legs. He stood so that the sunlight fell upon his weather-beaten face and his bony frame. As he soaked in the warmth he felt comforted for the first time since his arrest.

Presently, some wardens came, read out the names of selected inmates and took them from the cell. When Old Mak's turn came, the young man called out: "Don't be afraid of them, old uncle. Don't let them bully you."

"Thank you for your concern," Old Mak replied, as he was being led away.

After Old Mak had been taken from the cell, he was made to join a small group of detainees from other cells. They were marched along a long corridor until they arrived at the bottom of a narrow flight of stairs. There, attended by a number of warders, they waited.

Every now and then one or more people would come down from the stairs and be led away by wardens. Then an equal number of detainees would be selected from the group and sent up the stairs. Old Mak observed the proceedings with a degree of nervousness and that make him cough more than usual. He could sense that the warders and the detainees were conducting themselves in accordance with rules he was totally ignorant about. He wondered whether the rules might be as uncompromising as the lights which went red, amber and green.

When Old Mak's turn came, he proceeded up the stairs with trepidation. At the top of the stairs he found a surly warder standing in an enclosure filled with people, huddling like animals in an overcrowded sty. All around him, there was the hum of voices, some speaking loudly and others in whispers.

"Squat down!" the warder ordered, and Old Mak struggled to find a space in the congested enclosure. Eventually a sickly-looking man with a bandaged left hand moved over to find space for him.

The enclosure was in fact the dock located in the centre of a large courtroom of archaic design. It was a small square affair, with a forty-inch high wall made of sturdy hardwood panels affixed to stout posts at each corner of the square. The panels were topped by sets of polished brass grilles with perpendicular bars set six inches apart. The curtain of brass bars added another ten inches to the height of the enclosure, making a happy compromise between appearance and security of inmates.

Immediately in front of the dock was a long mahogany table for the use of prosecutors and defending counsels. Beyond the table, on a dais, an imposing magistrate's bench stood beneath a wooden canopy fashioned as a large replica of the St. Edward's Crown. To the left of the bench was the witness box whilst to the right a similar structure provided accommodation for the court interpreter. Behind the dock was the public gallery crammed with a mixture of human fare.

By raising himself slightly from his squatting position Old Mak could survey the court from behind the gleaming bars. The strange environment, with its peculiar sights and sounds, left him agape with awe. The blue-eyed foreigner with fair hair sitting beneath the wooden crown reassured him a little, for he appeared to have a kindly face. He looked just like one of those young tourists who would ask to have his picture taken sitting in his rickshaw and then reward him exhorbitantly for the privilege.

But the other solitary foreigner sitting at the long table with his back towards him intimidated Old Mak by his sheer bulk. He had a very broad back and was dressed in a police inspector's uniform. His neck was short and thick like a bull's and his hair was red. When he stood up to address the young man on the bench he towered over everything like a giant and he spoke with a deep booming voice. From these observations Old Mak imagined that his face must be something fearsome to behold.

"Squat down!" the warder snapped, and Old Mak almost jumped with fright. He sat down on the floor with a thud and broke out in a spasm of coughing. That only earned him another stern look from the warder.

"There are rules here, old uncle," the man with the bandaged hand whispered. "You have to squat down until your case comes up. There is no change in getting people upset with you."

"I'm sorry. I didn't know," Old Mak whispered in return.

Old Mak settled down to follow the proceedings as best he could. He noted that names would be called out from time to time and then someone would stand up from within the dock or else come forward from the public gallery to present himself or herself. Thereafter the court interpreter would read out the charge, the defendant involved would plead guilty, an exchange of conversation in a foreign language would take place between the inspector with the booming voice and the young foreigner on the bench, and finally the interpreter would convey the court's decision of a fine or a term of imprisonment.

What baffled Old Mak as he listened to the proceedings was the variety of offences that people could be charged with. He had never heard of most of them. Nor could he figure out why some of the activities should be considered crimes at all. For example, people were pleading guilty to loitering. Yet he himself had often loitered, especially among the food stalls when he could not decide on the kind of meal he wanted. Had he, unwittingly, been committing a crime as well?

Again, there appeared to be a crime known as larceny by finding and another of possessing an instrument fit for an unlawful purpose. How could finding something be a crime? And surely, any instrument could be used for an unlawful purpose if its owner were so minded. He thought of the spanner and the screwdriver which he kept under the seat of his rickshaw for emergency repairs. Would they constitute instruments fit for an unlawful purpose? If so, could he be held responsible for two more crimes? It all seemed beyond him. Most puzzling of all was the fact that all defendants appeared to admit their guilt and accepted their punishments without ado. They must know something he did not. They must be bound by a set of rules which operated like the lights which went red, amber and green.

Finally, Old Mak's case came up. "Case number one-six-seven-one-three," the interpreter intoned in a bored voice. "The Crown versus Mak Wai. Who is Mak Wai? Mak Wai, come forward."

Old Mak stood up uncertainly. He rested his arms on top of the brass grille for support.

"Stand up straight!" the warder snapped. "Put your hands to your side!"

Old Mak complied and looked from the magistrate to the interpreter. The interpreter was a thin, bird-like man with a partially bald head and a pair of steel-rimmed spectacles perched low over his small, pointed nose.

"Are you Mak Wai?" the interpreter asked, shooting Old Mak the barest of glances over the top of his spectacles.

Old Mak nodded.

"You are 59 years of age, a native of Kwangtung Province and a rickshaw puller by profession?" the interpreter continued.

Old Mak nodded again.

"It is charged that you, Mak Wai, on the twenty-eighth day of November, 1952, in an unnumbered hut on a hillside at West Point, in the Crown Colony of Hong Kong, did have in your possession an opium pipe fit for smoking, such possession being contrary to Section 8, Subsection 4 of Ordinance No.127 of 1946. Do you plead guilty or not guilty?"

Old Mak struggled to grasp the meaning behind the charge. He perceived dimly that he was being accused of possessing an opium pipe instead of smoking opium. Perhaps under the rules of the strange world in which he now found himself, the two amounted to the same thing, for it stood to reason that a man could not smoke opium without an opium pipe. However others might put it, to him the truth was the truth, and he wanted to tell the truth to the young foreigner sitting in judgement over him.

"I went there for a smoke," he began. "It was late in the afternoon and my chest was hurting something terrible. I know . . . ."

The interpreter cut him short by a wave of his bony hand. The movement was as listless as his voice, but it had the effect of reducing Old Mak to silence.

"Do you plead guilty or not guilty?"

"I want to explain. I only wanted a smoke . . . ." Again the interpreter motioned him to silence. Then, turning to the magistrate, he said: "Your Worship, the defendant is trying to make a statement."

"Explain to the defendant that he will be given a chance to speak in his own defence later. Right now we are only interested in his plea," the magistrate said.

"You can tell your story later. For now, just plead guilty or not guilty," the interpreter said.

"I want to tell the truth. I only went there for a smoke."

"The defendant persists in making a statement, Your Worship. He said he went there for a smoke."

"All right," the magistrate said, evenly. "I'll take that as a denial of guilt. Inspector, please call evidence."

A police sergeant was called to the witness box and he testified that, acting on information, he led a raiding party to an unnumbered hut on the hillside at West Point. On entering the premises, he found the defendant sitting on a bed clasping an opium pipe to his chest with both hands. There was a strong smell of opium in the air which suggested that opium smoking had recently taken place. No other person except the defendant was found. The defendant appeared somewhat dazed and, when asked if the opium pipe belonged to him, he replied in the affirmative. A total of three opium pipes, three opium lamps, still warm, and a quantity of opium dross were seized.

The sergeant then identified the opium pipe found in the possession of the defendant from among the court exhibits.

"The defendant may now cross-examine the witness," the magistrate said.

"Do you have any question to put to the witness?" the interpreter said.

"I only went there for a smoke. I rented a pipe from the owner of the hut and he told me I would be held responsible for it," Old Mak said, still anxious to relate everything that had happened.

"The defendant said he went there for a smoke and hired the pipe from the owner of the hut," the interpreter said.

"Tell the defendant that he must cross-examine the witness only on material points in his testimony. The witness cannot give evidence on what transpired before the witness arrived on the scene. The defendant can tell his side of the story later and call evidence in his own defence if he wishes," the magistrate said.

"You can tell you story later. Do not waste time now. Just ask the witness questions on what he has said. He does not know what happened before his arrival," the interpreter said.

Old Mak broke out in another spasm of coughing. The whole proceeding was incomprehensible to him. He could not understand why no one wanted to hear the truth. If no one heard the truth, how could justice be done? He merely wanted to tell them about the terrible pain in his chest which led him to seek a smoke. He wanted to explain that when the alarm was raised by the look-out, the owner of the hut and the other smokers ran away. But he did not know what to do. He had rented the pipe and had been made responsible for it. If he ran away with it, the owner might accuse him of theft. If he abandoned it, the owner would hold him responsible for its loss. What the sergeant said was true but it was not the whole truth. He thought that the young foreigner with the kindly face would give him a fair hearing but it seemed that he too was not interested in his explanations. Had he violated some rule or other by trying to explain? Had he condemned himself already by failing to plead guilty like all the others?

"Do you have any question to put to the witness?" the interpreter repeated wearily.

Old Mak shook his head, convinced of the futility of attempting to explain further.

"That is the case for the prosecution, Your Worship," the inspector said.

The magistrate told the police sergeant to step down from the witness box and then addressed the interpreter: "Tell the defendant that he may now speak in his own defence.

Explain to him that he may give evidence under oath in the witness box or he may make a statement from the dock. If he testifies under oath, his words will carry more weight with the court, but he will also have to submit to cross-examination by the prosecution. If he elects to make a statement from the dock, his words will carry less weight, but he will not be subjected to cross-examination. Of course, he may also remain silent."

"You can speak now," the interpreter said. "You can speak from where you are or you can speak from the witness box. If you speak from the witness box, the inspector can ask you questions. If you speak from where you are, no one will ask you questions. If you speak from the witness box, your words will be more believable. If you speak from where you are, your words will be less believable. You can also say nothing, if you like. What do you wish to do?"

The instructions from the interpreter filled Old Mak with confusion bordering on panic. Speak now, speak later! Speak from here, speak from there! Speaking from one place more believable, speaking from another place less believable! The rigmarole made no sense. The truth was the truth. How could it be more believable when uttered from one place as opposed to another? All the restrictions he had endured in the city over the years had been irksome enough but the rigmarole of the court seemed far more terrible.

Life might be hard on the land but at least a man was free to live according to his own rhythm. If he walked about his village at night to admire the brilliance of the moon or to enjoy the song of the cicadas he would not be accused of committing a crime. Why should the city be different? In so thinking he suddenly realized how much his life had been diminished by the city. It had taken away his hopes and his dreams, his health and his strength. It had made him submitted to rules he could not understand and forced him to follow the dictates of lights which changed from one colour to another. And now, it was requiring him to squat or stand or speak at the command of others. Something deep down inside him rebelled against such an imposition. He would not be reduced further, to the level of a circus animal performing to the cracks of a whip. No, enough of the oppression of the city! He would free himself from its clutch and return to the life-giving land, even if it were the last thing he ever did.

"Speak up," the interpreter said. "What have you decided?"

"I want to go home!" Old Mak cried. There was a desperate and heart-rending quality in his cry, like that of a lost child or a wounded beast. But mingled with the bewilderment and the hurt there was also a note of defiance.

The cry so startled those in the room that a great hush descended upon the court. The inspector turned around in surprise and Old Mak saw that he had bulging eyes, flaring nostrils and a red, bristling moustache. He looked like one of those fierce images which guarded the wings of temples back home. But Old Mak was no longer afraid of anything.

"It is now your turn to speak. Do you not wish to tell your side of the story?" the interpreter asked, a note of incredulity livening his voice for the first time.

Old Mak shook his head. "I want to go home," he repeated.

"The defendant does not wish to make any statement, Your Worship," the interpreter said. "He states that he wishes to go home."

"If the defendant does not wish to enter a defence then, on the evidence as presented, I have to find him guilty as charged," the magistrate said. "Is there anything known about the defendant?"

"The defendant has no previous conviction, Your Worship," the inspector said. "But if I may make an observation, Your Worship. The defendant does not appear to be a well man. It may be a kindness for Your Worship to consider banishing him from the Colony since he appears anxious to go back to where he came from."

"Yes," the magistrate said. He scribbled his findings into the court records and then announced: "In consideration of his clean record, the defendant is sentenced to two months' simple imprisonment. At the end of that time he is to be banished from the Colony. The opium pipes and implements are confiscated for destruction."

"You go to gaol for two months and then you will be banished from Hong Kong," the interpreter said.

"Does that mean I can go home?"

"Yes, you'll be sent back to Kwangtung," the interpreter said.

"Thank you, thank you," Old Mak said.

As the warder ushered him down the stairs back to the cells below, Old Mak felt as if he had regained something that had been lost to him. Two months, he thought, and he would be free of the city forever. By then it would be spring.

# The Cocktail Party

## 1996

*David T.K. Wong*

The cocktail party is an all-purpose rite in darkest Hong Kong. It can be used to celebrate a betrothal, an anniversary or a national day, to gain face or to give face, to launch a business, to seal a contract or to reassure a creditor. It can be employed just as easily to turn a heart, to slight an enemy or to forestall a social death. Chinese Communist cadres adapt to it in no time at all. Sometimes even the underworld flouts the success of its criminal undertakings with such parties.

No-one is more familiar with the multifarious uses of the cocktail party than K. B. Woo, that billionaire entrepreneur known to admirers and foes alike simply as "K. B.". As the most famous tycoon in a city replete with taipans and captains of industry, he is the darling of the cocktail cult. His name figures on the invitation lists of virtually everybody pretending to the upper crust. It is not unusual, therefore, for him to attend three or four cocktail parties in a single day. He attends them grudgingly, however, as a concession to his shareholders, his financial backers and the legion of photographers, financial journalists and social reporters who keep his name in the public eye. He knows that unexplained absence would provide grist for the rumour mills.

In truth K. B. finds cocktail parties an interminable bore. He had thought otherwise when he was just the impecunious son of a roadside hawker of fish balls and noodles. Then he had hankered after the untasted glamour of such occasions. But now, as chairman of Trans Universal Enterprises, that famous international conglomerate he has built up from scratch, such parties have become an imposition, deflecting him from the serious business of exploiting the greed of others.

Indeed, he wishes nothing more than to be relieved of the rituals of the cocktail cult. He resents their artificiality and their pretences. Mixing with mediocrities is bad enough, but the charade of smiling at dowagers with vanities as outrageous as their over-rouged faces, of humouring commercial parasites wheedling for crumbs of insider information, or of posing for photographs with treacherous rivals coveting various bits of his empire seems beneath a person who has already paid his way to the top.

Such are K. B.'s thoughts as he prepares to leave for Lulu's cocktail party to launch the high-fashion boutique he has agreed to finance. As he tidies his papers he feels a vague distress and, being in the privacy of his office, he gives rein to his discomfort. He allows his penetrating brown eyes to mist over behind his gold-rimmed glasses and his high, intelligent forehead to knit into a frown. He compresses his mouth into a severe line and in the process his jowl quivers with unfamiliar tension. All of a sudden a certain crudity or want of refinement returns to his features so that neither his immaculate Savile Row suit nor his expensive accoutrements prove sufficient to disguise his humble origins.

He knows deep down he is going to lose Lulu, no matter what he does. She has told him as much. But he still refuses to reconcile himself to that prospect. She remains the only pleasant thing that has happened to him through a cocktail party. That was more than five years back, when he was 45, and nothing quite as pleasant has happened to him since.

The remembered thrill of that meeting still quickens his blood. He had just acquired his first bank and had hosted a small cocktail reception at a leading hotel for the lawyers, accountants, merchant bankers and others involved in the deal. At the end of the function, Lulu had come up to him with a leather folio containing the bill.

Perhaps he had been unduly elated by his acquisition or perhaps he had had too much to drink, but the sight of Lulu simply stopped him in his tracks. She must have been fresh out of school for she could have been no more than 20. Her face, then as now, had been at once childlike in its innocence and mysterious with oriental complexities. Her eyes had a bright, trusting quality, her nose was dainty and her mouth, pleasingly large against the other features of her face, hinted at unawakened passion. Her long, silky hair, black as a raven's sheen, swung sensually against her crimson Chinese long gown. Although the gown was no more than a uniform for hotel staff, on her it had looked provocative, for it hugged the agreeable contours of her body and revealed two tantalizing slivers of thigh between its tall side slits. She had looked so unspoilt, so vulnerable, so in need of protection, that his bowels had churned and he had felt a surge of libido inappropriate for his years.

"I hope everything has been satisfactory, sir," Lulu had said in a cheerful voice, as a prelude to presenting the bill. At the same time she had flashed a smile that melted into dimples on her cheeks.

He had peered at the identification tag pinned on her gown, noting that it read: "Lulu. Trainee. Customer Relations." He had never felt so powerful and irresistible as he did then. So, waving aside the proffered folio, he had declared: "Lulu, you're being wasted. Have dinner with me in Paris next Saturday and I'll give you the world."

"Oh, Mr. Woo, you are teasing me! Why would an important man like you want to have dinner with somebody like me? I must seem a mere child to you because I'm no older than some of your children."

"Do you know my children?"

"No, but I've seen them in the hotel restaurants."

"I'll introduce you to them one day. I have a great interest in the young. After all, the future belongs to them. Hence my interest in you. The bit about giving you the world may be a slight exaggeration, though Paris in springtime is close to being the world. And I am dead serious about dinner."

"How am I to get to Paris? I have never even been out of Hong Kong!"

"Why don't you just say 'yes' and see what happens?"

"Do you always extend such extraordinary invitations?"

"No, because you're the very first to deserve one."

"I can't believe that! But it sounds so fantastic that I must find out what happens next. So all right, let's have dinner in Paris."

By noon the following day he had arranged for airline tickets, hotel reservation vouchers and a bouquet of roses to be delivered to Lulu and that was how their relationship began.

After three days of the magic of Paris their separate suites had become superfluous. He had meant to win her in the same way he would acquire a hotel chain or order a new supertanker, but a strange emotion that went beyond the mere joy of possession soon invaded his person. An arrangement had been swiftly arrived at. He would provide for Lulu's financial security and creature comforts in return for her favours. The arrangement could last for as long as both parties wanted it and it would be kept perfectly private and discreet. If it were to end, then it would be in a civilized manner, without recriminations and unreasonable demands.

Since all that had already been foreseen and agreed to, why should he now feel that strange ache inside, that unbearable sense of impending loss?

His thoughts drift between Lulu and his wife. There simply is no comparison. His wife is an old-fashioned woman, barely literate, someone selected for him by his father. She hardly fits into the circles in which he now moves. But she has been a marvellous mother to his children and from the very beginning she had accepted all his transgressions without complaint, as if his status as husband gave him an unqualified right to behave as he chose. Lulu, on the other hand, is full of life and adventure. She stirs something in his blood. He looks forward to their regular Friday evenings together like a child waiting for a weekend treat. Often he would make a terrible tangle of his business schedule just to steal an hour or two with her. In his heart of hearts he knows that the relationship has no future and can only result in unhappiness for both of them. And yet future pain seems so abstract compared with his present pleasure. In another age the solution would be simple; he would take Lulu as his concubine.

But the British had closed off that possibility by outlawing that perfectly sensible institution. Damn their smugness and their missionary zeal! Why do they have to foist their prejudices on others? A man has diverse needs. How can a solitary woman satisfy all of them? All the ancient cultures used to recognize this. The Hindus used to think nothing of having one woman to bear children, another to discourse on philosophy and a third to provide the delights of song. The Muslims have long been used to multiple wives and the Chinese their concubines. But everywhere they went the British had to spread their obsession with monogamy like a contagion!

K. B. straightens his tie and makes his way to Lulu's reception. During the short walk from his office he recalls the discussion he had with Lulu a few weeks ago, during one of their assignations.

"You have been so good to me, darling," Lulu had said. "You have been the soul of generosity. How can I ever repay your kindness?"

"By loving me. Or at least by pretending to love me," he had replied with a teasing chuckle.

"I do care for you a lot. You must know that. We have had some wonderful times together. I've seen so much of the world going around with you, posing as your Executive Assistant! But I'm not getting any younger. A time has to come when a girl has to think about her future."

"Your future is quite secure. I've already arranged for money to be set aside for you."

"It's not just about money, K. B. It's about career and making something of myself. It's about my own place in society. I don't want to have to sneak around all the time to avoid being seen together. It's about marriage and raising a family."

"But we agreed at the outset that there would be no question of marriage. It is not that I don't want to marry you but I can't. My wife has been a good wife and mother and she has shared all my ups and downs without a single harsh word. I cannot abandon her."

"I am not asking you to abandon her. But I want something better than just spending every Friday evening with you."

"I have always tried my best to spend more time with you. We go on trips and the rest of the time you've always been free to do whatever you want. You can see your own friends, play mahjong, go shopping or whatever."

"That's part of the trouble. My friends all have regular jobs and are getting married. They are beginning to think there is something wrong with me because I don't work and I don't go out with young men."

"If you want something to occupy your time I can set up a small business for you to run."

"That is very kind of you but I think our time is up, K. B. You've taught me many things. You've taught me that in life, as in business, there is a time for fighting and a time for letting go. You have also taught me that a person should always honour a contract even if it is against his interests to do so, because if he does not, nobody will ever trust him again. Well, we have a contract. We agreed to part in a civilized manner when the time came. So why don't we do so and part as friends?"

"I wish I had not taught you so many damn things. But I'm glad you haven't learnt the wrong things. Most women would become greedy and devious in a situation like this. Talking things over so calmly is to your credit. You're right, of course, about us. You're young and you have your whole life ahead of you. I am just trying to be selfish. What are your plans afterwards?"

"Well, I thought I might start a boutique. I have enough money put aside. You've spoilt me, exposing me to Paris fashions."

"Why don't you let me do that for you, as a parting gift. Fit it out and stock it up any way you want and send me the bill. When it is ready for business we can say goodbye."

"You are very sweet and understanding. Thank you, darling."

As K. B. approaches the venue for the party, he feels the taste of ashes in his mouth. The boutique is ready and after the party a relationship that had brought him so much joy will have to end. He nevertheless puts on his best cocktail party expression and walks in briskly.

After he has been formally greeted by Lulu, he surveys the room and his heart sinks. Apart from some popular personages from the entertainment world there is hardly a familiar face to be seen. The whole room seems filled with people only half his age. He circles the room disconsolately with his drink, in the best traditions of the cocktail circuit.

Suddenly he spots Wilson Chang, a real-estate magnate of his own generation, standing alone in a corner. He manoeuvres himself in that direction and greets Chang warmly.

"What are you doing here, K. B.?" Chang asks. "This isn't your kind of scene."

"Lulu and my children are close friends," K. B. replies without hesitation. "I'm supposed to meet them here before going off to dinner. What about you? You're not hunting for a Paris gown for some sweet young thing, are you? It has been almost three years since your wife passed away, hasn't it? It's not healthy for a man to live alone, you know." K. B. winks and gives Chang a gentle dig with his elbow.

Chang laughs good-naturedly. He leans over and lowers his voice. "I'll let you into a secret, K. B. Lulu and I are planning to get married. We've been seeing each other every Wednesday night for the last two years. I know she's young enough to be my daughter but what the hell! You've always held that the only women worth getting involved with are those young enough to be your daughter! So I'm just following your advice. But please keep the news under your hat till it is announced."

K. B. blanches. "Congratulations!" he exclaims, in as enthusiastic a voice as he can muster. As he does so the ache inside him sharpens suddenly into pain. He excuses himself after a few more pleasantries on the pretext that he has seen someone he has to talk to. He escapes the reception through a side door. He fears losing his self-control if he had to bid Lulu a formal farewell.

As he makes his way to his next engagement, he digests the implications of Chang's news with a slow brew of jealousy and outrage. But in spite of his inner turmoil, he sees also the irony in the situation. Lulu had merely seized the initiative and exercised that entrepreneurial spirit that successful businessmen like himself are forever pontificating about to the young. One can hardly complain when one is taken at one's word, he observes wryly. Well, one lives and learns, and what he has just learnt is that there is no limit to the usefulness of cocktail parties.

# Valediction

## 1996

*Xu Xi*

*"So let us melt, and make no noise*
*No tear-floods, nor sigh-tempests move,*
*'Twere profanation of our joys*
*To tell the laity our love."*

from "Valediction: Forbidding Mourning" — John Donne

London, 1989. Winter. Note in my *ga je's* hotel room.
Dear *muihmuih*,
Until we meet again.
Love.

Hong Kong, 1995. Fall. My fortieth birthday. Letter to my elder sister.
Dear *ga je*,

Do you remember that day, twenty or so years ago, in your *appartement* in Rouen, that modern if sterile place in a tower in the town you were going to leave once your husband got a job back in Paris . . . do you remember how you designed my sanctuary, the one I would some day have as a published, income earning novelist (yes I can hear you breathing an enormous sigh of relief — at last, about time)? You sketched every room for me — the monk's cell for my rough wooden writing desk; a cushioned reading space where the dumbwaiter led "downstairs" to an invisible kitchen and a cook who would cater to my every appetite; the library filled with shelves of books . . . and you promised you would one day commission an architect to build what you had drawn. When I saw Elvis' Graceland two years ago, and all those special rooms he designed, I remembered. But I don't want a Graceland; the imagined sanctuary of your charcoal sketches is all I need to survive my writing life.

And now, after the years have disappeared, vanished with my *gwailo* foreign devil husbands and insignificant others who no longer employ my life (thank god for US laws and alimony, however meager and late the payments), I finally found that space, albeit smaller and less grand than you originally imagined, and not a stone house in some coastal town along the eastern seaboard of the United States as you promised. It's taken me, oh a lifetime, or at least a few decades, moving and looking and striking out on new paths with such regularity that I am no longer surprising to any member of our internationally over-extended *wah kiu* family. When my first novel appeared in 1990, the Vancouver branch disowned me, you know, so there goes the last of the inheritance aspiration; the Singapore-singers-of-karaoke cousins refuse to keep my books at home as they consider them poison to the minds of their children; the clan in Java, that fried-in-peanut-oil-seriously-overcholesterolized horde of doctors, lawyers and pussy-whipped chiefs have told me I will never have the services of any of their chauffeured vehicles ever again (twice I was driven from Jakarta to Bandung and back to visit grandma's grave — for this I should be prostrate with gratitude); and the ones in Hong Kong are hugely thankful I write under a name that cannot be linked to theirs, since they must suffer me here in their city.

But what would amuse you most is our grandfather's reaction, issued edict-like from his haven in Perth — he said that what literary talents I had came from his branch of the family, but that it was a shame I chose to prostitute my talents in novels with "too much sex" instead of marrying a nice Chinese man (meaning Jen-Wei, his partner's grandson, who has more mistresses than condoms, but will inherit the fortune his father has amassed) the way he always told me I ought to, which would then free me to write about his life and the heritage of our family, a much "nobler" subject. Shades of Red Chamber nightmares! I must descend from a different lineage.

Dear *ga je* – Just what is family anyway? Bloodlines tie us. And for me, marriage and relationships created even more "families" which I couldn't avoid or disavow, unless, like Mission Impossible, a disintegrating tape could disavow all knowledge once each episodic week — How I used to love that show; how you used to tease me about it.

Family aside, it's also this "overseas Chinese" *wah kiu* business that gets in the way. Grandpop never fails to remind us of our heritage as he updates the genealogical chart each year for the family and all its branches. (His latest thing, you know, is proving the purity of our Chinese blood, despite the Indonesian, Caucasian and even Latino bloods that have seeped their infectious way into the generations). What kind of *dongxi* are we? How English fails me, despite all my English language novels! And *ga je*, how the Western World fails us for our most intimate expressions, our sense of family, our understanding of love.

Yet *c'est la vie*, isn't it, for this daughter of Hui.

*Ga je*, you'd probably like this flat I found back home in Hong Kong. Even by Paris standards, it's very large, over 1,500 square feet — 150 square meters to you. (I remember how you taught me that easy, approximate conversion. Helpful, as your teachings always turn out to be, because Hong Kong will be going more than merely metric in 1997). But large it is, larger than your Paris apartment and a lot more expensive, though not a walk up of six flights (how did you endure it with baby Jean-Pierre on your hip, the shopping in your bag, and your briefcase of work . . . I always admired your energy, your stamina to get a Ph.D. and married both in the same year while I struggled to finish my Bachelor's over six years, and then still didn't, during which time you kept me going by the example of your life) — so my flat is enormous compared to our old home, and, well, luxurious. Yes, I hear you chiding me — *Muihmuih!* Ever my spoilt girl.

But *ga je*, she's happy. You don't have to come and save her here.

Actually, you'd like it. It's in Mid-Levels, "miles away" from home in Hillwood Road. How faraway it seems to *ma mi* and *da di*, way across the harbor, even though it's only fifteen minutes from where they are in Tsimshatsui to Central by the MTR. You know, there's an escalator now that snakes from Central up to Mid-Levels, which stops at several roads. The Hakka women coolies of our girlhood would have appreciated this moving staircase cut into the hillside, even if it does go against the grain of the dragon. In fact, some evenings I almost see one of them around Staunton Street standing still on an escalator step, rising to the heavens, and dropping, for just a moment, the load of bricks balanced on two bamboo baskets hanging from a pole across her shoulder.

But the parents! We were always too "faraway" for them, weren't we? Sometimes, I think of them as frozen into a past tense of safety. The first time, at college, was at least invisibly faraway. I almost made it you know. The blood from my wrists was difficult to stanch, the nurse told you. But what I want to say is that I remember how you came to me when I called in the middle of the night, the night he asked you to marry him. Eight or nine hours on a Greyhound it must have taken from New York to my petty, little, Boston college world. How I must have terrified you. And perhaps, if I'd made it, you could have had a life.

This flat though. It's in an old, pre-war building, just like home. I bought some high wooden screens to separate the living and dining room, like the kind in Uncle Bian Lee's place in Mongkok, the ones in pawn shops *ma mi* used to take us to when she didn't want to show her face anymore at Uncle's place, entreating him for yet another loan, pretending she was pawning her family's jewelry because she didn't care for them. The ceilings are, oh, twelve feet I'd say. Two lengths of my current lover would almost fit to the top — no, I know you don't want to hear about yet another one so I'll spare you the details, but at least he isn't a husband, no, don't roll your eyes at me — he's a Northern Chinese dissident poet from Beijing, they're the best kind, dissidents, that is. But you! Living your almost perfect life. Married to an almost acceptable husband. You're the only woman I know of in this day and age who married the man who took her virginity — even Hong Kong women don't do that anymore. Even though he was French-American, at least he spoke beautiful Mandarin. *Da di* never had the grace to compliment him, but at least you could see how pleased he was to be able to converse in Mandarin with his son-in-law, after years of suffering the indignity of Hong Kong's Cantonese speaking populace who made fun of his accent. Yes, he was hopeless, wasn't he! And still is, despite all his years of Chinese school in Indonesia and his fluent Mandarin. But he gets his own back. A Cantonese trying to speak Mandarin is worse than an Australian speaking English — that's what he still says.

There's a tree outside my flat. A sprawling banyan. A pair of white cockatoos and a squirrel live in it. It reminds me of the tree we used to climb in the park near our school, the one out of which I fell and suffered a huge bruise on my forehead. You took care of me, took me to the hospital, and then rung the parents to summon them to fetch us because you didn't have enough money for a taxi. How old were you then? Only twelve at most I think.

But those cockatoos. They're not supposed to be there. Escaped from the Botanical Gardens, I think, or some such story. Who knows? All I know is that they shouldn't be in my banyan tree, no more than I should be in this city, this supposed home city of ours. I'm not like the squirrel; he belongs. He's got the right reflexes.

But here I am. It's a third floor flat, an easy walk up. The parents haven't seen it yet, haven't displayed even the slightest curiosity, but then again you know how they are. Did you know that they never visited my other place either, the one which my news-anchor lover rented when I lived here previously, and that was in Kowloon, albeit "miles" away on Broadcast Drive . . . Why am I complaining? Because they made it to your wedding halfway round the world, and gave you a dowry of jewelry and money fit for the queen that you are?

Why am I so sure you'd like my sanctuary?

When we were young, do you remember how I hated the sea, because, I said, it was always like taking a lukewarm bath. You were the queen who called me princess, and told me stories about my special *petit prince* on a flying black horse who would steal me away to another planet. Our new world had fields of poppies and daffodils, lots of them all over the hillsides, surrounded by an ocean of icy cold water into which I could dive and swim for miles. And it was quiet; there were no cars.

Remember the second time you rescued me? I had plunged into the Charles River in winter, and the nurses were trying to thaw me out. When you arrived by plane from New York, I was still hallucinating from the mushrooms and babbling about planetary horses. The nurse's aide said to you that I thought I was *le petit prince,* to which you replied, I was. How we laughed over that afterwards when you held me and welcomed me back! And I begged you not to tell our parents and you promised me you wouldn't. You kept that promise, too, didn't you?

*Ga je*! How did you love me so long?

Did I remember to say I moved into this flat in summer, at the beginning of summer? I missed the rains the day the movers arrived with all my things from New York. The very next day, it poured. Nothing could be worse than wet boxes brought into an old flat where damp rises, the way it does here. The ceiling in my study is streaking through the new coat of paint. The landlord did paint, and cleaned after a fashion. But he's off in Canada somewhere, and leaves these details to his sister who manages his property. No children. He refused to rent to anyone with children. The flat stood empty for a while. A three-bedroom 1,500 square foot flat simply doesn't get snapped up by couples with no children. It is a flat for a Hong Kong family.

You would know how to make a home of it, with your children and your Shanghainese man.

Don't you understand how much *da di* and *ma mi* would have liked him? Oh I know he spoke accented Mandarin, which *da di* would have commented on, but at least his English was good enough for *ma mi.* And you and he could have jabbered with the children in French. Funny but for all your intelligence, without a doubt superior to mine, you just never understood about bloodlines. All you had to do was leave that husband, show up with your man and children in tow on the parental doorstep, and they would never have turned you away. You don't believe me? No, I guess you would have a hard time believing me, divorced twice over the way I was, having affairs with local Hong Kong painters who exhibited my naked body across canvases in Hong Kong's art galleries with a distinctly clear representation of my face — poor *ma mi*, she couldn't face any of her friends for weeks when that happened. But I did it all here, not "faraway" in New York. It was we who were far, not they. Homage is paid to the Middle Kingdom — that is, to every Chinese parent that ever existed — not the other way around. I know each of my many returns was fraught with scandal, or the possibility of yet another familial loss of face. But I came home, like a dutiful daughter, for *ma mi* to weep over in shame. I didn't deny her that pleasure.

When Amelia was born, the parents diligently studied the photos you sent. How fortunate she came after Jean-Pierre. Don't you remember how all your baby things were embroidered with W for William, since they were convinced of your masculinity? Ah *non!* you say, our parents were not that Chinese, being as they were *wah kiu*, and never threading into Hong Kong society completely. Why do you think they waited so long before having me? Not to risk another disappointment? Or was I an accident? They'll never say, and we'll never know. So it's the guessing game, the favorite pastime of Chinese life.

But when Amelia was born . . . they studied those photos for a long time. Finally, *da di* looked up at both *ma mi* and me and declared, "She looks Chinese, thank goodness."

It was just before I took the trip to New York and OD'd on speed and Jim Beam. Remember that trip? That was my watershed attempt; you began your talking cure with me after that, once a week at great telephone expense to yourself and your family. And you stayed with me, sometimes for weeks at a time, or had me stay with you.

Do you wonder that my brother-in-law found himself a few girlfriends?

Stoic sister, you should be in this flat of mine with your wonderful Shanghainese man. He truly loved you, perhaps even more than your husband did. The only reason I can afford it is because I'm the "right profile". The landlord said he would rent it to me because his sister was my schoolmate and vouched for me, actually told him he had enough money and should see his way clear to supporting a penniless writer who was after all, "one of us"? So yes, I live in luxury for a song because the schoolmate was once my lover and this way she knows there's less chance (though not no chance) that I'll keep our affair out of my novels and away from her very wealthy and socially prominent husband's eyes. I'm not immune to bribery.

You haven't always liked my "right" profile, have you? I can't say I blame you. Being right the way it worked for me was about being wrong, but taking that wrongness to such extreme heights (call it selfishness, license, self-indulgence — whatever it was, it worked, and, unlike Miller, I didn't even have to prostitute my lover for my daily bread) that it became the only way to be, the way everyone expected me to be. It was my *libération*, my *jie fang*. I didn't always like your responsible nature, your willingness to accept the roles dished out by Confucius and other tyrants. The charm of my irrepressible irresponsibility, backed by just enough talent, squeaked me by, especially in our shallow home city where a little melodrama goes a long way for lack of anything deeper to observe. Besides, I was good gossip for the party circuit. You chastised me, scolded me mercilessly as all good *ga je's* are supposed to do. But you never blamed my writing, the way the family did, because they couldn't understand, could they, why I had to do what I did instead of getting a job or married properly, the way I was supposed to.

I know now I was born to write. In your own way, you tried to tell me, without placing the pressure of being accepted on me, without expectation of a livelihood or success (how I've appreciated your many bailout loans for my extravagances over the years), without condemning the myriad wrong turns I took in pursuit of what I thought the artistic life should be. You painted my real dream, made me think, despite all proof to the contrary, that it was possible. Things only came true if you said they would. I am about so much fiction and always have been. You are about fact, about facing life the way it is, the way it has to be.

So why has this farewell taken so long to say, since that departure on your fortieth birthday?

You told me once you would not live past forty. It was in Paris, at the worst point of your marriage. I was young and "recuperating" from my most recent attempt. Have you forgiven me for not really knowing what you meant? Oh what am I saying? Of course you've forgiven me. You've always forgiven me.

But I should have known what you meant!

I think I understand. We were close in time and space. You changed my diapers; we fought on our parents' bed. I went after you with a knife and fork once when we were little, angry over some imagined hurt. So how could I not understand?

If nothing else, we could have lived in this flat together with your children. It's big and beautiful and spacious. I don't have the married lover anymore. He comes to Hong Kong often, which is ironic because, now that I've moved here where it would be much easier to see him because he travels out this way all the time, I've dumped him back in New York along with the husband. You know, the one you never thought much of, but didn't have the heart to say so? I know. You were right. You looked upon my husbands and lovers with disdain, and rightly so. Men let you down, you always said.

So why did you believe in love and romance and promises of forever? (You were dreadful that way — despite my multiple lovers I didn't really fall in love the way you did). I think it helped you survive adolescence, and, for a time in Paris, your marriage. And then your Shanghainese came along. A Chinese doctor! And the son of a respectable businessman. What a perfect *wah kiu* son-in-law he would have made for the parents. He even wanted to come to live in Hong Kong. You should at least have had an affair with him. But no, it was only love you wanted, and love you got. He called me once, to see if I could convince you to leave your husband. You wouldn't listen. And in the end he married, and that was the end of your second chance at love and happiness. Of course your husband shouldn't have left you, despite the fact that we all knew it wasn't a marriage worth saving by then. Of course you shouldn't have disappeared to England that day the way you did, so that he could complain about how you just "upped and left your children" (what a hypocrite, he left you after all, and it's not like Amelia and Jean Pierre were left alone for any length of time since your mother-in-law was coming to visit that evening).

But it's too many years now to blame my brother-in-law any longer. He could almost be forgiven his flings with mistresses. After all, you were busy with the children, and me. Even I couldn't expect him to understand your devotion to such a prodigal, profligate and ungrateful sister. You never even told him about your own love affair, such as it was. What absolute fidelity your marriage inspired in you! As long as you could be in love, and if not that, as long as the marriage held, you could remain with me, with all of us.

Your children do remarkably well you know — I've been going to see them at least twice a year, and they still ask me to tell them stories every time. So I tell them about all the worlds beyond their own. It's the least I can do for my family.

You gave up on romance, didn't you? Perhaps if you had held onto the magic of falling in love . . . but for what happened in London afterwards I blame myself — for not going there when you called, for not being there on the one occasion you asked for help. Which is why I am no longer married to the man who stopped me, who whined his jealousy, even though you had never, in all those years, ever asked for a favor. Why didn't you shout? Why didn't you scream? Why didn't you din into my stupid head the real reason for your call, instead of coating your pain, the way you always do, because who I was, what I was, had to dominate the space between us? In the end, even that husband of mine wasn't to blame — he always whined.

Who wasn't he, the man who killed you? Why wasn't he there for you to fall in love with, to become starry-eyed over, like the heroines of all those romance novels you loved to read as a girl? Why didn't he materialize just one more time, to offer a bit of hope for surviving your divorce, your life?

Just like all your romance novelists, I let you down, didn't I? Me and the man who wasn't.

What triggered it that day? Why that day? I've turned it over and over again in my mind, to no answer, no lightening of the mystery. But it's not a mystery, is it? I can almost hear what you'd say — Death needs no pride, no *raison d'être*. It's life that demands our devotion and love.

I only know how to write my kind of novels now. Writing's the one promise I made to anyone that I've kept and will keep — when you told me that last time on the phone to write, always write no matter what, how could I know that my promise was what you needed to hear, to know you'd completed the last of your family obligations? I imagine you calling, first our parents, then your ex, then your children. And finally your *muihmuih*. "Little sister," how softly you said it.

Even when you asked me to come, it was less a plea than a request, understated, the way you always are in life, and in death.

You didn't even leave a mess. How like you to be so neat, to leave no blood, to have slept into your overdose in the bathtub so that cleaning up would be no problem. Just a body in a hotel room, with the exact cash payment on the dresser next to the hotel bill you had the foresight to ask for the night before. And my phone number on the envelope of that three-line note.

I keep it, along with your sketches of my sanctuary.

Dear *ga je*.
Until we meet.
All my love.
*Muihmuih*.

# A Final Appeal — Three Weddings at Tuen Mun

## 1996

*Yang Yi Lung (John D. Young)*

*An educator and historian, Yang Yi Lung was a respected academic and held positions in universities and institutions in America, Australia and Hong Kong. Born in China, he came to Hong Kong as a young child. He was active in local politics, publishing widely in the Chinese press on Hong Kong affairs. In the early 1990s, he began writing short fiction in English; a story and essay are included in this anthology. He died in Hong Kong in 1996.*

———

When once questioned about her family history by a visiting government dignatory, Mei-lin, the eighty-year old matriarch of Tun Village replied rather casually, "My family moved here from North China during the Sung Dynasty, about nine hundred years before you British arrived in Hong Kong." There was no genealogical evidence to support this claim, but because this visitor happened to be a Hong Kong governor, Mei-lin's brief encounter with the big-nose foreigner enshrined her as a living legend in the region; whenever she appeared in the local market, her fellow villagers would honour her with a thumbs up sign, shake their heads, and sigh, "What a wonderful response, *ho-yeh*, great."

But today Mei-lin did not feel so *ho-yeh*; for the first time since her husband passed away a decade ago, she had difficulty breathing. She told the Filipino maid to add a few more incense-sticks at the family altar. She prayed, long and hard, to the Buddha, to the Gwun-yum, to her ancestors. Three weddings in twenty-four months was a bit too much for her frail bones, and there was no certainty that things would go smoothly on this auspicious day (at least according to the villager astrologer), for with Ngau-ngau, anything was a challenge. Not that she minded the two million dollars spent for the last two weddings; a male to keep the family lamp lit was priceless. Not that she minded losing face in front of all the village people. The excuse actually had the opposite effect: These two girls could not satisfy Ngau-ngau's needs. It was as if she was saying to everyone, see, I don't care about money. I want the best girl for my only son, my little ox, and in turn she would give me a healthy grandson.

The family face only suffered minor bruising. But honour did not stop all the wild rumours. One villager swore he saw the bride running away from the Ngok mansion in the middle of night, leaving behind her a trail of blood. Ngau-ngau must have acted like an animal, and she could not handle him. He must have acted like a dog, another relative murmured. After all, Ngau-ngau had the habit of staring in amazement at dogs in copulation.

Another version of the story was that Ngau-ngau almost scared the bride to death on the wedding night, as they had never met before that evening. She thought five-hundred thousand dollars would persuade her to give herself to any ugly person — sadly for her, she had no idea that Ngau-ngau's face truly resembled that of a pig's; he even had similar flappy pig-like ears. After the bride went back to her own village, word came back that it was more the drooling and his dreadful smell that repulsed her; when questioned, Ngau-ngau insisted that he did take a bath the night before, the first time in six months.

If the first bride had an excuse, the second did not, for she had the opportunity to see Ngau-ngau in person, and she was told by the go-between that Ngau-ngau had a high fever when he was seven, and afterwards had become slightly "slow" in his interpersonal skills. "A virtue," Mei-lin declared. Because he was not so quick on his feet, he never developed any ties with the other rich kids in the village, who were spoiled by their parents and only indulged in gambling and womanizing. "My boy is kind and gentle, and he is not devious," Mei-lin repeated for the tenth time. True perhaps, but anyone who met Chung-jung — Ngau-ngau's formal name which meant following loyalty — for the first time could not help but be startled. His whole head leaned to the right, and he walked with a slight limp. He had bulging eyes, and most of his front teeth protruded outwards, somewhat like a smiling garoupa. And when he really smiled, his village "cousins" swore that he looked like a true replica of the lazy and woman-chasing Pigsy in popular folklore. Of course, known to every Chinese young woman was the fact that Pigsy was extremely *haam-sup*; he was interested in human flesh for other purposes as well, although in the novel *The Journey to the West*, every time he came close to cannibalism, he was stopped by the Monkey or his master, the T'ang monk, Tong-Tseng. The bride-to-be took a look at Chung-jung, and said, "a million." With a deep breath, she continued, "Another million if I have a son."

Mei-lin was furious. She took a glance at the family ancestral altar, and replied in a low voice, "Half a million, and another half if you have a son. Ten-thousand for a daughter. For the second try, a son, also half a million."

For the second wedding, the aging matriarch hired a professional beautician, to work on the groom. Over the phone the woman said she could do wonders, that she would turn Ngau-ngau into a handsome groom in a few hours. When she arrived, the minute she came close to Ngau-ngau, she screamed, "Give me a water hose." Ngau-ngau endured the cold shower in silence. He acted clumsily, as if he were a garoupa being prepared for steaming. His face turned completely red as the beautician helped him get into his Chinese wedding robe. Afterwards, Mei-lin gave her a five-hundred dollar tip, for Ngau-ngau did look rather becoming, almost like a painting and his hair was brushed to one side. Tidy, but nothing much could be done about his ears. "Big ears mean long life" was the parting quip of the beautician.

Half a million dollars of cash was deposited into the bride's bank, account or to be more precise, her family's account. Apparently the dowry did not do much good, for she arrived in her wedding gown with matching red eyes; she must have wept non-stop the night before. She must also have heard some of the wild rumours in circulation, Mei-lin thought to herself, or else why would she have refused to look at her son even once throughout the ceremony. The girl must be persuaded to perform her wifely duties, Mei-lin contemplated as the couple went around the tables, toasting all the guests and relatives.

But before she had had a chance to initiate conversation with her new daughter-in-law, she approached the matriarch with a question, "Can you give me another ten thousand dollars? My father insisted on keeping all the money you sent, and he beat me up last night when we quarrelled about it. This is why I have red eyes today."

What a relief, Mei-lin sighed quietly. She was in a good mood now, and stated graciously, "A bonus of twenty-thousand dollars if you become pregnant in the next 30 days."

\*    \*    \*    \*

It was such a loud deep shriek that every single soul in the village must have heard it. Before that, Mei-lin heard plenty of noise from the newly-weds' chamber. She curled her lips slightly, as she remembered her own experience from a long time ago; hopefully Ngau-ngau did not act like a bull, like his father. The loud noise woke her up from her nostalgic thoughts. The door to the chamber was flung open, and out came Ngau-ngau, with his make-up all smeared, and his trousers torn. "Oh my ancestors, she must have rejected him and couldn't go through with it at the last minute. Poor girl."

Ngau-ngau did not appear the next day, nor the next, nor the following one. After a week, the bride packed up her belongings, kowtowed to the mother-in-law, and returned to her village. A few months later, Mei-lin was formally informed by the village elders that Ngau-ngau was absolved from the marriage, as it was never consummated. However, the bride's family did have the right to keep the half a million dollars offered in the arrangement.

At first Mei-lin was on the verge of mental collapse. What did Ngau-ngau do to these poor women, these young virgins? Mei-lin endured the agony. The boy did not deserve a wife, obviously. But she remembered very clearly: even Mencius said, not to have descendants was the worst transgression of filial piety, and if she did not perform her family duties properly, she would probably end up at the bottom of the 18-level hell. "My ancestors will never forgive me," Mei-lin lamented.

So it was with a certain degree of joy that the go-betweens managed to find a widow with two daughters. Probability-wise, this meant she would have a son if she should ever have another child. A widow was worth a lot less money, but still, the agreed upon condition was not inexpensive for Mei-lin. Half a million dollars for the widow, provided that the two daughters were not brought into the new household. Clearly, Ngau-ngau could not become an instant father, as he must concentrate on having his own children.

Mei-lin had to appeal to her son again. He did agree to two weddings, although both were failures. "It wasn't your fault — maybe these girls just didn't understand the goodness in you. They pay too much attention to outside looks. What's the use of youth and beauty? In another ten years, with children, they will end up looking like me. Maybe they were only interested in my money. Anyway, Mrs. Li is a more mature person. She will be good for you. She will know what to do, too. Please, my son, I would like to live to see my grandson."

Ngau-ngau mumbled, something about not wanting to become an old bean, *lo-dou*, a father. And then he started to drool, and with his flappy ears, even his own mother thought he looked pathetic. No wonder these women did not want to sleep with him, she thought silently. But the doctor said he was physiologically normal; the Western medicine man was called a few weeks after the second bride ran away. He assured her Ngau-ngau was in good physical condition, at least in that department, he said in a whimsical manner.

"I hope the doctor did not hide anything from me," the matriarch murmured to herself.

The third wedding, and she felt exhausted before the day had begun. All the invited guests showed up, as if the last two events had never occurred. They ate and drank, and toasted the newly-weds, and whispered into one another's ears about Ngau-ngau and how forlorn he looked. This time, the beautician was not called.

The extra prayers and incense worked. The night passed away quietly, no screams, no noise from the bed-chamber. Mei-lin woke up startled, by a quiet knock on her bedroom door. The maid, who slept in the same room, came over and said, "Mrs. Li had already come three times this morning. She said she wanted to speak to you." "Tell her to come back in ten minutes," Mei-lin replied. She might be an older bride, but she was still a daughter-in-law, and she was given half a million dollars.

"I am afraid I am here to ask your permission to leave. I can no longer be your daughter-in-law as your son has asked me to leave."

Mei-lin almost fell out of her chair. "What has Ngau-ngau done this time? Was he rough? I know he is ugly by conventional standards . . . he didn't try to force you, did he? but he is really a nice boy . . ."

Mrs. Li frowned, and interrupted this woman so obsessed with filial piety, "No, dear old ma. I was the one who tried to throw myself on your son, just as the other two brides did. Ngau-ngau told me. He said they tried to tear off his clothes, but he did not want to sleep with someone whom he doesn't know, or doesn't care for. The other two wanted their half a million dollars, and so they were quite rough. I guess I took pity upon him when he started to cry. Poor, poor child."

# Lau the Tailor

## 1998

*Charles Philip Martin*

*Charles Martin is an American writer who lived for many years in Hong Kong where he was also a humour columnist, musician and copywriter. His story 'Lau the Tailor' won an honourable mention in the 1998 O. Henry prize stories award; it appears here along with one of his columns. He now lives and writes in Seattle, from where he continues to host a weekly jazz programme on Radio Television Hong Kong (RTHK).*

When I first saw him, he was peering through the glass of my shop, as if he were just another man on Portland Street with a minute to spare. But he didn't seem to have a minute to spare. He wasn't looking at the blazer Ah Ho had made. He paid no attention to the solitary mannequin, which I'd dressed so well it looked like a businessman who happened to misplace his head. No, he was looking at me, taking my measure in my own tailor shop.

He walked in and asked if I needed a tailor. I did, of course, and that's what I told him. Because I feared the future.

And there was something to fear: another tailor might not come along. People were one of the few things in short supply in Hong Kong, at least skilled people; they were moving to Canada and the States, taking their professions with them. A hundred and fifty years of capitalism had taught us to grab what we could, when we could. So I had to grab him.

How he knew I needed a tailor I never figured out. Maybe he knew the man who had stolen mine. A week ago Ah Ho had come to me with a sheepish smile, announcing that he had been lured down the block and out of my life. Probably because he feared the future too. No hard feelings. When you're that young, you go for the money. I certainly did, year after year, and when I had saved up enough to buy my own tailor shop, I approached my boss with that same self-conscious grin. It all comes around.

Lau was shortish, as lean as a coat rack. He wore a sport coat and tie neatly, and carried a valise made of dull, cracked leather. His face wasn't exactly likable, but he looked intelligent enough.

"Where did you work before?" I asked.

"Sun Kwok Custom Tailors, in the old Sun Kwok building."

"Why did you leave?"

"No more building." A common enough complaint. All they do these days is tear down everyone's place and build new, expensive malls with high rents.

I looked him over. No sign of drinking, thank God. Lazy, maybe? You'd get them sometimes, people who just didn't want to work, who'd do just enough to earn their pay in order to blow it on a Macau weekend. I had to be concerned about that — my place might be small, but it has a reputation. Portland Street is in Mongkok, far from the tourist business. Regular customers pay my bills. And there are two other tailor shops on this block alone. I'd get no second chance if my place went downhill.

"You don't find many shops like this anymore," I said. "With a sewing room in the back, I mean." These days you only need a phone and a list of numbers to run a tailor shop. That's what the Pakistanis do: take the measurements, call up someone to make the suit. If that man's too busy, call someone else. One tailor makes the trousers, another one the jacket. Not like it used to be.

"The back room is the reason I want to work here," said Lau.

Then silence. Maybe I should have thought it over. I certainly pretended to, pausing and looking out the window for answers that didn't show up. But in fact, I was merely stalling to avoid the appearance of haste. Or maybe because I feared the future, I was trying to put it off one more day. But Lau made that impossible just by being there. What could I have done? Already a shirt order had been sitting around two days.

"All right, I'll take a chance. It pays nine thousand a month." Less than Ah Ho's salary, but after all, Ho had been with me three years. Lau nodded and walked into the back room and carefully placed his valise on the table. I grabbed a piece of paper and followed him.

"Start with this one. Can you read my writing?" I handed him an order slip for three business shirts, rounded collars, French cuffs. "What's in there, anyway?" I asked, pointing to his case.

"Things I need."

"You'll find everything here already." As I spoke, Lau was unwinding and examining a bolt of pencil-striped broadcloth.

"You know," I said, "I'm a tailor myself. Haven't sewn a stitch in years, though. I used to have a shop in Wanchai. Once I made a suit for a member of the royal family — a duke, I think." Lau nodded, but he kept his eyes on the cloth that he had laid out on the table. His fingers pulled, stroked, tested, as if assessing the material for some great task it was to perform.

"Before that, I had a shop near the Peninsula Hotel. And before that, I worked for my father. He was from Shanghai."

Lau said nothing. Suddenly feeling useless, I went out front, lit up a cigarette, and took a few slow drags. Give him a chance. How much damage could he do in a day? I sat down in the soft leather chair by the counter and started to read the paper, but when I feel useless, the news seems useless too. So I turned the chair toward the window and looked out, into a street with crowds that never stopped moving.

A little while later I poked my head in the room to ask if he would deal with customers too.

"No problem. No English, though."

"Don't need it, out here. This isn't Wanchai. No drunk sailors."

His knobby hand sewed a seam in rhythmic motions. So smooth, as if he were underwater. "You shouldn't watch," he said.

Rather than think about the way he was behaving, I went out front and sat by the window again. Silence from the room; then, the sound of the shears' metallic clicks.

Ah Tak put down my iced lemon tea and sat on the edge of the bench, the better to jump up and serve customers, though there wouldn't be many till lunch.

Ah Tak is a stocky man who does everything easily: talking, smiling, and perspiring. His face is as fat as a pork bun, and his salt-and-pepper hair is cropped short, to save him the trouble of combing it. He has never taken the time to tuck in a single one of his cheap shirts since I have known him, nor have his trouser cuffs ever reached below his ankles. But then, he has never been my customer, only my friend.

"What does he mean, 'You shouldn't watch'?" I said. "Strange thing to say a few minutes after you're hired. How do you figure that out?"

"Maybe you make him nervous," offered Ah Tak.

"Ha. He makes *me* nervous. He's serious, though. I like that."

"Serious. Serious people are a pain in the arse, Kin. When's your son getting back?"

"Tomorrow night. We have to go out and meet the plane at nine. Another reason it's good I got this tailor: to take care of the shop. I want to spend some time with Wai. He was just a kid when he left, but he's almost a man now. You grow up a lot in university, especially over there." We then talked about the races. Ah Tak played the horses a little, just for fun.

Soon it was time to return, and I stepped out of Ah Tak's place into the throngs of Portland Street. From outside, the back room of my shop was visible; anyone looking in could see Lau was working away. For a while, conscious that I was disobeying his request — or was it advice? — I watched those hands describing precise loops. That was when I changed my mind about going to the shop, and walked the few blocks to my home instead.

Yu was in the sitting room, watching Ching-dynasty warriors battle it out on TV. At home she spent most of her time in that chair, which had faced the TV since we'd bought the place. Funny, all our chairs faced the TV; none of them faced each other.

"What are you doing here?" she asked, her eyes drinking in the blue light of the screen.

"I have someone taking care of the shop."

"Who?"

"A new tailor. Name's Lau. He started this morning."

She turned to me. "And you trust him to take the shop?"

"He knows what he's doing."

"What are you paying him?"

"Nine." I wanted to say less, but she'd find out anyway. She went over the books more carefully than I did.

"Hmm." With no more to say, she turned back to the screen, where one of the men shouted threats and drew a sword. Costume dramas never impressed me; I preferred police shows. When the news came on, I watched it, hoping for a mention of California. Ever since my boy started going to UCLA, I tried to keep up on events there. Just to have something to talk about. My thoughts, however, kept returning to Lau. Leaving a new employee alone in the shop was a peculiar thing to do. Why did I do it? Lau seemed harmless, but something about his appearance made me jittery. We were tied together somehow, I felt, but I was dancing at the end of his string. He showed no interest in me, as if there wasn't a thing I could have told him about tailoring, or anything else for that matter. I put it out of my mind and dozed awhile — the shopkeeper's prerogative. When I returned to Portland Street, the sky was beginning to darken.

Lau worked impossibly fast. One shirt was done when I returned. I stepped into his room and picked it up.

"Hmm. You didn't cut the fabric for all three shirts, I see. Why not? It saves time."

"They're different shirts."

"Same measurements."

I don't remember what he said, if anything. I just stared. God, what a shirt! It was lovely. I picked it up, and the sleeves tumbled out majestically, as if from a king's robe.

Five years ago I took a tour to Europe with my wife, and one of our stops was that big museum in Paris. Neither of us knows a thing about art, but I won't easily forget stepping up to the ropes that kept the crowd of tourists fifteen feet from the Mona Lisa. Someone else can lecture you about the beauty of the painting, the talent of the painter. What I remember is the feeling that an idea had suddenly become real. I was facing a greatness that before I had only known from a distance.

A shirt isn't a painting. But for twenty-five years I made shirts as well as I thought they could be made, tried my best to know what made a shirt a shirt and a tailor a tailor. It took everything my father had taught me about tailoring and a quarter century at the job just to look upon Lau's work. I had found a beauty that my craft could only parody, like the calendars and dish towels from which the Mona Lisa's serene eyes stare out, tolerating the absurdity of it all.

How it sang! Who could describe the song this shirt sang, a song of perfect geometry, of perfect love. This was a thing beyond my understanding. This was that greatest of man's works, unmechanical perfection, defying nature with frightening symmetry. For a moment, the shirt seemed to taunt me with answers to all the questions ever asked. Here's why I, and all men, were born, it said.

"How did you do this?" I asked Lau, but he said nothing. It was a foolish question. One might as well have asked how a tiger is put together.

Slowly I fingered the strip of cloth down the front of the shirt holding the buttonholes. "The placket. You made it a separate piece. Why didn't you just fold the cloth over the front edge, the usual way? You made a separate placket and sewed it on."

Ignoring me, Lau began to cut the cloth for his next shirt while I pored over the buttonholes, which were as perfect as any I have seen. And the way the sleeves tapered from shoulder to cuff, with pleats — God, how many pleats did he sew? — making the transition smoothly. The placket was one point among scores; new details flew up to meet my eye, clamoring for attention. The collar stitching had to be twenty to the inch — could it be twenty-five? more? — tighter than I had ever seen. And every stitch impeccable, as no man or machine ever had sewn before.

I buttoned the collar. Perhaps most people would not have noticed the perfect intersection of the fabric pieces at the seams. Nothing need be hidden by the tie. This shirt was more than perfect; it was inevitable, like the rise and fall of a song written long ago, that could be no other way than it was.

"Finish the others," I said breathlessly. "I want to see them." Leaving Lau to his room, I retired to the chair by the rear counter. I had to study the shirt.

When I looked up and out the window, the dinner crowd at the restaurant was giving Ah Tak a run for his money, so it must have been past my closing time, perhaps seven thirty or so. Tak was smiling, chatting as he ceaselessly walked the same path from the kitchen to the tables and back. The evening was warm, and against the leather of the guest chair my back was soaking. Clutching the shirt a little too firmly to be explained rationally, I walked back to Lau's room — it was Lau's room now, and that was that. He was bringing the second shirt to life.

"It's time to close. I usually close around seven."

"Can I stay here?"

"What?"

"I have no place to stay. I used to live in the Sun Kwok shop."

There was nothing plaintive or pitiful in his voice. It was up to me, and what was I to say? Ask him uselessly why he didn't tell me earlier? Say no, and put him on the street? I consented, and went to a drawer behind the front cabinet, the one that exhibited charcoal-grey Shetland wools.

"Here's a key. There's no alarm. You'll have to close the shutters, but there's a window in the bathroom, so you won't feel too closed in. I'll be here around eight thirty to open."

"Would it be all right if I open it earlier, when I get up?"

"I suppose so. You really don't mind living in the shop?"

He shook his head. Sensing the discussion was over, I placed the key in his hand; my fingers grazed flesh that was surprisingly soft. Perhaps I trembled slightly as the key went from my hand to his: that tiny piece of metal was letting him into more than just the shop, I knew.

My wife was eating when I got in. Not quite between mouthfuls she asked why I was late, and I told her I was taking care of details with the new man. It was going to work out well, I said.

"Good. You needed someone."

"In fact, this man is amazing. The best tailor I've had, ever."

"Well, I hope he's not too good. He'll be wanting more money."

"He's living in the back room."

She looked at me. "What? For how long?" A grain of rice dangled on her lip.

"Don't know. Permanently, I suppose. He didn't mention looking for a place."

"Are you crazy? You'll never get rid of him! If you want to fire him, he can claim you're putting him out on the street. It's out of the question! Tell him he has two weeks to find a place!"

"No, he's all right. I'd never fire him. For one thing, he's too good."

She slammed down the bowl and screeched, "Then make him pay rent! Why should he be given a tailor's pay *and* a house? No one gave us *our* house!"

"Oh, what does it matter? We're doing all right."

"Now, yes. But what about later? Think of *after!*" She meant after China came over the border and took our lives back.

We fear the future and long for the past. Funny, that means we're living backwards. Life is a train going in the wrong direction.

Lau was already at work when I came in the next morning, though the front room was dark. I switched everything on and went back to greet him. He looked at me for a second, then went back to his sewing. On a chair the other shirts testified that he had been at it all night.

They were superb, as the first had been. The buttons caught the morning sunlight. Where did he get mother-of-pearl of such quality? From that valise of his?

I had to tell someone. Like a child, I ran across the street, carrying the shirts over my arm, and found Ah Tak weaving through tables filled with rowdy people who were stuffing down their breakfasts in a hurry. My news intrigued him, but he had no time to look at the shirts right then. He chuckled and said he'd be over as soon as he could get free.

At nine o'clock I dialed the office number of the customer who had ordered the shirts, and told him he could pick them up anytime. Then I turned to Lau, who was arranging spools neatly in the cigar box he kept in his leather valise.

"Make me a shirt," I ordered. Begged. Lau looked up at me. I'd have been grateful to see some expression in his eyes, but there was none.

The minutes dragged until the crowd thinned at the restaurant, leaving a few stragglers that the hired waiter could take care of. From my shop I watched Ah Tak remove his apron, place it on the stool behind the cashier's desk, and walk over.

You can never quite tell with Ah Tak. He's tactful, always ready to share enthusiasm. But he must have been impressed with the shirts because he asked me to have one made for himself.

I laughed. "You, Ah Tak? You haven't worn a tailored shirt in your life, I'll bet."

"Maybe not, at least not since my wedding. But you're right, these are beautiful. How much would it cost?"

"No charge for you."

"Don't say that. You pay for your tea."

"Still, no charge."

"I insist."

We worked out that he'd pay for the cloth, but not Lau's labor, which was amusing in light of the commonness of the cloth and the magnitude of Lau's talent. I took out a tape measure.

Lau stepped up to me with surprising speed and said, "I'll do it." Smiling politely, but obviously determined to relieve me of the task, he took the tape and swiftly measured Ah Tak. Very swiftly, in fact, making notes in a scraggly Chinese hand. He was the first tailor I had seen since my grandfather's days who wrote the measurements in Chinese characters. When he was done, the paper held only a few numbers, far from a full set of measurements. Only I could have guessed the reason: he wasn't really measuring Tak, just confirming what his magnificent eye saw instinctively.

From the rear counter Lau brought back a bolt of fancy-check broadcloth, the thin blue and gold stripes crisscrossing cheerfully. Now Tak laughed, because the cloth might as well have borne Tak's family chop. It *was* Tak. The cloth was nothing less than Ah Tak's simple jolly face in a different form.

When Lau and I were alone together again, he told me that he would take measurements from now on, if it was all right. I shrugged my shoulders and extended my arms out to my sides. It was my turn to be measured for a shirt.

He did me more slowly than Tak. For some reason, as he drew the tape across my back and looped it around my arms, I found myself closing my eyes and swooning. Then I felt pain, as if he were drawing a sharpened piece of ice down my spine. The tape seemed to invade me like a surgeon's knife. Lau was laying open my body, exposing, like a lining in a jacket, the fear that hid under the skin. The fear behind the decisions I make. Behind the small talk I give customers. Old terrors, now out in the open, breathing the same air I was.

You shouldn't watch, he had said. Of course not. I'd never watch him again.

Around lunchtime the customer who had ordered the three shirts walked in the door. His name was Chang. He was perhaps my age, but no tradesman; from the looks of his suit he sat at a desk all day. For a long time the man looked at his new shirts without speaking. I urged him to try one on; finally, I would see one of Lau's creations animated by flesh.

He emerged two minutes later from the back room, the shirt buttoned and tucked in meticulously. And oh, how that shirt sang, how it made his body sing in harmony with it! Chang, however, said nothing. His head was bent down, his eyes on his shirt front.

"Well?" I asked expectantly.

"It makes me sad."

A pause.

"It's so sad. I was in prison once. This shirt reminded me of that. It was during the Cultural Revolution. Someone turned me in, I never found out who. One day the Red Guards hauled me out of my home, said I was polluted by Western ideas because I knew English and had a couple of English-language books once.

"They threatened to denounce me, throw me in prison forever. But I could go free, they said, if I would tell them who corrupted me, list three other friends who shared my depraved Western ideas. They beat me badly, and threw me in jail. It was a cold, cold November, and the prison was wet and freezing. My shirt was all I had to keep me warm.

"Finally, the pain and the cold were beyond anything I could resist. I called in a guard, told him I would give them what they wanted. I named a couple of friends as sympathizers, named someone I hardly knew as the devil who had twisted my mind. They let me go a while later.

"But you know the feeling, when you put warm cloth on your skin and you get a little chill before you warm up? You shiver — one last reminder of the cold that's still out there, even if you're protected from it. I just felt that chill. I shivered as I put on the shirt, before it warmed my skin. And I thought of the prison, where my friends must also have suffered from the cold. It made me sad."

He picked up the shirts and left.

Wai had grown a little, perhaps not taller but broader and more solid. He sunk into his seat and took over the cab, in the way that young Western people do. I wondered if he would lose that Americanness over his stay and revert to his old habits. It didn't really matter. If you send your son to university in America, you have to let him soak in everything. As long as he doesn't get into drugs.

"So how are things over there?" I said.

A tiny smile curled his lips, but he looked ahead, into the welter of Kowloon neon. SONY. FOSTER'S. TOPLESS. KARAOKE NIGHTLY. "All right."

"Are you studying hard?" Not a question a returning student loves to hear. He seemed absorbed in the streets of Mongkok and didn't answer, so I didn't press him. We passed nightclubs, appliance stores, restaurants, all lit up and out to make a dollar. A minute later he spoke.

"How's the shop?"

"Fine. I have a new tailor. He's . . . extremely good." The neon cast a red glow on our faces as we drove under a mammoth sign. "Actually, I've never seen anyone like him."

"Hmm. They could use him in the States. No one has suits made there. Almost no one wears suits, even the teachers."

"I used to get Americans in the shop."

"Yeah, well they must wear the suits to funerals. What's new? What are you making these days?"

"Not too much. People are saving their money to get out. First to go are the shirts — you can always buy a pretty good one at Crocodile. Still, it's not desperate. We get some orders."

"Looks like the full cut is out."

"Yes, especially trousers. No shoulder padding to speak of. Ties are getting less fancy again, thank God. Funny how you show an interest in this. You never wear anything but jeans." This time a real smile from Wai, and he looked into my eyes, which made me feel good. I never shared smiles with my wife anymore.

"Do you feel a lot of pressure at college? It's not easy, is it? I never liked school too much."

"Pressure?" He looked out at the city again.

"Lee's son got sick at college. Toronto, it was. One day the teacher was giving out assignments, and he started to cry in class. Whatever the teacher wanted, it was just too much. He started sobbing and couldn't stop. The doctor there said he had to rest, of course. It was the boy's sister who told me all this — Lee would never admit that he pushes his son too hard. Anyway, it got worse, and the poor kid had to miss a term and rest up, finally. That was almost worse than the overwork itself. He felt he had failed, that his parents had worked for nothing."

Wai shook his head. "Idiot. Let himself get whipped like that. Who has the right to hang the future of the family on a kid? It's not fair, is it, Father? You end up worrying about it all the time — I see it plenty at UCLA, not just the Asians either. They're wrapped up in the consequences of their every action every day."

The taxi driver stayed in a gear that was one too low, making the engine whine irritatingly.

"Did you ever hear of Merlin?" Wai asked.

"Merlin?"

"He was a sorcerer, a magician, in King Arthur's court. He was a legend — I don't think he ever really lived."

"What did he do?"

"He lived backwards."

"Eh?"

"He lived life backwards. While everyone else was going one way, to the future, he was going into the past."

"I get it. So he knew what was going to happen. He could tell the future?"

"I don't know. But I love the idea of it."

"Living backwards? Then you'd know the future. You could win on the stock market, the Mark Six, everything." But that was a silly thing to say, I knew right away.

"No, that's not it. If you lived backwards, consequences wouldn't matter. You'd never have to pay for your actions. That's what I'd like."

Lau presented the shirt to me. Fingering the ivory-colored Oxford, I remembered that I had forgotten to choose the cloth and Lau had not asked me. But the cloth was right for me. Lau indeed had the key to more than just the shop.

It felt neither cold nor warm on my skin: just a shirt. By now I was almost used to the seen and unseen perfections that permeated Lau's handiwork. It was no surprise to learn that the collar length, a little shorter than I had ever worn before, was better for my head size. There was just enough taper to the shirt to keep the line neat as it reached my belt. No exaggerations, no inappropriateness. And then I remembered something. "I had a shirt like this once," I said out loud, to no one in particular. "I was twenty . . ."

My voice faded; there was no use going on. It wasn't for Lau to hear anyway. Or maybe he already knew, somehow. It had been that terrible year. I was a journeyman tailor in my father's shop, earning next to nothing, and I had only one good shirt, which I wore to make a good impression when I took over the outside counter at lunchtime; most of the day it hung on a hanger in the back. I was wearing that shirt when my father returned from lunch early one day and took me upstairs. He told me I'd have to marry Yu. Why, I asked, since I hardly knew her. My father was worried about me, wanted me to be happy, and had found Yu. Her family had some money, and the match would be a big help to us. It sounds insane now, but things were different then. Like a good son, I gave up the woman I was hoping to marry and did as I was told. We were wed, and our son came early, seven months later. Stupid as I was, it took a year and a half for me to work out that my father had been paid to make the match — by some father desperate to marry off his pregnant daughter. Yu and I never discussed it. I never knew who Wai's father was.

I didn't love Yu, of course. Not then, not now. I had loved the sister of one of the tailors. But that ended the day my father told me what my future was to be. I hated him for it.

Lau went back to his room, and I sat out front, thinking about that afternoon twenty years ago. A while later my wife and son walked into the shop on their way back from a visit somewhere; I didn't ask where. Yu walked around the shop, looked in on Lau, mumbled a hello. Then she told me where we would be going for dinner, though I had to be told again later. Wai said nothing to anyone; he just stared at my shirt the whole time he was in the shop.

The day was very warm, the air a bit too still. We walked past the bonsai trees towards one of the garish pagodas, the one holding the Starving Buddha. It had been my idea to take the day off, and Wai had chosen the Tiger Balm Gardens, of all places. Yu had stayed home because she preferred air conditioning and didn't like being on her feet.

"You used to bring me here when I was little, remember? Mom liked you to do it, because it got me out of the tailor shop." And then, after a pause, "A man who can make a shirt like that is great." Wai said this deliberately, not with enthusiasm but as if expressing a fact.

"'Great.' I hadn't thought of him as great, exactly, but you're right. The fellow's so quiet." I lit a cigarette and offered one to Wai. He waved it away.

"But he *is* great. That makes you great too, in a way," said my son. "It makes your shop the best one there is. Even if no one else knows, as long as you have him you're part of something . . . I can't think of the word in Chinese. I'd give anything to be able to make something like that."

"You? Since when are you interested in tailoring?" But he was, of course, and always had been. As a young boy, he'd come into the shop after school and watch me sew — see the suits and coats being put together. I taught him the rudiments of it, but Yu had bigger ideas for him: he was going to be a doctor or professor, after he studied in the States. By the time he was a teenager I was discouraging him from coming, telling him he didn't want to be a tailor, convincing him that his future was much grander than mine would ever be.

We looked at the lunatic displays of plaster figures in the Tiger Balm Gardens. As a child, Wai had contemplated the morbid friezes that illustrated the fate of different sinners: one of them showed people being eviscerated; in another, sinners were consumed by flames. The sculpture was clumsily done, and there was no great horror to it — just a cartoonlike violence that absorbed kids' undiscriminating attention.

"Mother said that's what would happen to me if I was bad. Remember?"

"Yes. She was only joking."

"It scared me. But it didn't make me change much."

"You were a good boy."

"Yeah, but the point is, all this stuff is supposed to get people to change. The millionaire who built this wanted to show his fellow man the way to live. It didn't work for me. Did anyone pay attention to the message?"

"It's just a reminder. Of the consequences of evil, I mean. Not a whole sermon. It's always good to remind people that there is good and evil, consequences."

"But these aren't really the consequences, are they? They're just crazy scenes of torture and suffering. How do you really show the consequences of evil?"

The sun was relentless, and we were both a shade darker when we came back to our flat. Yu didn't remark on our lateness. I told her that Wai wanted to come to the shop tomorrow to see Lau work.

"Ah, that's crazy. Let him go with his friends. What does he want to stay around the shop for?"

"You should see Lau sew. The workmanship!" I went on despite Yu's sneer. "His clothes have an effect on people. Yesterday a man picked up three shirts — and forgot to pay." She looked at me as if I had just said something amazingly stupid.

Tired from the walk, I went to bed early. The sounds of Mongkok flooded through the window, and as I dropped off to sleep, I barely made out Yu's voice amid the familiar din. Some hateful words were all I heard.

*Get rid of him! We worked so hard to build all this. He'll destroy it.*

It was hard to get up the next day. I was later than usual getting to the shop. Wai was already there, sitting on a stool, as transfixed by Lau's hands as I had imagined he was by his lectures in California. Lau was stitching the shoulder seam of Ah Tak's shirt as they talked.

"Is a suit different from a shirt, then? I mean, when you make the patterns, is that when it happens?"

"The muslin is just a guide. The ultimate pattern for the suit is the man."

"And the measurements?"

"Like dates in history, they're guides, numbers. Things happen between them."

"Why did you make a split yoke?"

"You have two shoulders, which move independently. With two pieces of material it gives a little more, hangs — "

Lau stopped as I came in. They looked up at me. Wai smiled, but they didn't resume their conversation. My son had heard more words from Lau than I had since he was hired.

"Ah Tak's shirt is almost finished," Wai announced.

Sipping milk tea, Wai and I chatted about America while Ah Tak brought out order after order of BREAKFAST A: bowls of macaroni in broth with a few shreds of ham, fried eggs, and a grilled hot dog. The restaurant was full of hungry people, so Tak wasn't going to slow down for a while.

"I miss this tea. You can't get it like this in the States. They sell condensed milk in the stores, but they don't have it in the coffee shops. Always fresh milk. I tried to explain once that I preferred canned milk, but they thought I was crazy . . . Why did you send me away?"

"Away?"

"To college. I didn't want to go."

"You were a good student. It was the best thing for you."

Listlessly, Wai spooned a stray leaf out of his tea, and lay the spoon on the table.

"But I didn't want to go. It was Mother's idea, wasn't it?"

"We both want you to be a success."

"Aren't you a success?"

That was a good question. I'd clothed a few hundred men. Is that success enough? There was enough money. I owned a shop and paid a tailor to work in it. I owned my flat and rented another one out. There was little to say. "You could be more," I told him. "A lawyer, something important. You need college for that."

"That isn't why you sent me away."

"I didn't. She did." I immediately regretted saying it. Wai stood up and looked in my face. Then he walked out.

Inevitably he would blame someone, probably me, probably rightly. It was a natural consequence of our actions, of every step my wife and I took toward what we pretended was happiness. Everyone had to face the consequences. There are the consequences of marriage, the consequences of making love, the consequences of pursuing a dream and of giving it up. No one — except Merlin, I suppose — escaped them.

Tell me I shouldn't fear the future.

The truth was coming, I knew it. It was sure to be here soon; the signs were there. The way you can tell a typhoon is on its way — when the air keeps stirring all around, brushing your skin, taunting you with the inevitable. Wai wasn't going to leave this alone. Soon the truth would be on us like a storm. I returned to the shop. It was time to prepare.

"Make me a suit," I told Lau. I closed my eyes as he went for his measuring tape.

I was late again the next day. There had seemed little reason to get out of bed, and the forces that had given my shop over to Lau were the only ones I seemed to notice in my life.

When I finally arrived, around ten, Lau said, "It's ready."

"What are you talking about? The suit?"

"No. His shirt." Of course, Ah Tak's shirt, the one he ordered in a fit of contrariness. I waved and shouted to Ah Tak across the way and enjoyed watching his face as he walked over, his arms and legs slightly splayed from his early years of hauling vegetables for his father.

Tailoring is as against Tak's nature as sulking. Yet when he saw Lau's creation on the counter, his eyes widened and he let out a small sigh. He picked it up as if it were a new baby. Suddenly he laughed gleefully and tore off his imitation designer polo shirt, revealing his yellow, pockmarked undershirt. He put on the new one.

"You are a lucky man, my friend," Tak said, hastily buttoning the shirt. "We're both lucky men. We're friends, and friends are real. Security is an illusion. There's such a race for security in Hong Kong. Buy a flat, buy another, get a passport, send your kids away, get richer. If we pursued friendship the way we pursued security, we'd have both.

"I've lived life well. I'm not a smart man. Seeing this shirt makes me realize both of these things. Lau, you're amazing, you're everything my friend says you are. You're the smart man, the artist. I just put plates of noodles and glasses of tea in front of people all day long. But I know enough not to get trapped pursuing an illusion. When I die, my shop will go back to the landlord, my savings will go to my children, and they'll remember me as their father. No one will remember me as a tycoon, or a man who accomplished anything greater than breakfast, lunch, and dinner. And who cares? I have my friend Kin in the tailor shop across from me, I have a beautiful shirt, a job, and the memory of a fine wife. What more should I work for? How big can the smile on my face be when I die? And all of the people who were frantic for security in past years, what good did they do me?" He glanced across the street, still beaming. "Excuse me, a few more customers walked in. I'd better help out."

He walked out singing "A Bamboo Pole" to himself, an old tune that could be no other way than it is.

Business started picking up that day. I called Chang to remind him he hadn't paid for his three shirts. He didn't seem embarrassed. But he must have told some people about Lau. One man came to have a winter coat made. Two ordered suits, and one man wanted some shirts. That's a lot of orders in one day for a Mongkok tailor. People knew.

The funny thing is, they were different people. One of them gave me his card; he was from North Point. There were plenty of tailors in his district; why come to Mongkok? Why were they drawn to Lau?

All day long, Ah Tak's words haunted me. I thought of friends I had and friends I had forgotten. Around four, I made a decision. Bidding Lau good evening, I made my way through Portland Street, which was already filling up with evening hawkers trying to catch hungry commuters who couldn't wait for dinner. Food wasn't on my mind as I descended the MTR stairs and pushed the turnstile.

Causeway Bay. There were still oldish buildings here. The one I approached had a renovated lobby to lure a better class of tenant, but the lift was cramped, dirty, and overworked.

Apartment 4A. She peered at me through the metal grille, clutching a magazine, an empty look on her pleasant, plump face. I must have sighed, and she changed her expression to one of curiosity.

"Do you know who I am?" I said. She shook her head, so I continued. "I came back to understand something."

Her lips parted, and her eyes opened wider. I remembered that expression; it belonged to me still.

"You!"

"Don't worry. I just wanted to see you. I was thinking about people today, important people. You were the most important person there was, once."

"My God, what am I supposed to say? That was twenty years ago."

"You remember me, then?"

"Of course. I loved you. Tell me, are you all right? Are you still a tailor?" She flung the magazine to a chair behind her and held on to the steel bars. There could be no question of opening the grille, we both knew.

"Yes, of course. I have a son. He's in college in California. Things are all right. And you?"

"I got married about a year after you did. My husband is a policeman, an inspector. He works in the antismuggling operations."

"Children?"

"Three — two girls and a boy. Do you love your wife?"

"No. I loved you. It was all wrong, what I did to you."

"Forget it."

"But it was wrong. I hurt you, I didn't stand up to my father, I ruined everything for . . ." I was going to say "for both of us," but that might not be so. Maybe this policeman was a good fellow.

"I guess so. Kin, I really mean *forget it*. Bad memories aren't much help. Listen. When I had my first child, I was terrified of the pain. I knew it was going to hurt me as nothing had before. The doctor gave me a choice of two medicines: one got rid of the pain, and the other didn't, but it made you forget that you had the pain. Of course, I chose the painkiller. It was years before I understood what the other one was, why it was just as good. But you and I don't have a choice. We can forget, and that's all."

"Do you forgive me then?"

"Yes, Kin. If it will help you forget. Is your marriage all right?"

"I guess. Like my tailoring. I do the best I can."

"You're not cruel to her?"

"No."

"And do you understand what you came here to understand?"

There was no answer for that. Rather than wait for the elevator, I descended the dim stairway and left her a second and final time.

Back at the shop, the lights were off and the shades drawn. But Lau opened the door when I tapped on it.

"No, that's okay. I don't want to come in, I'm on my way home. Just one question: have you ever made women's clothes?"

He nodded.

"I'll bring an outfit of my wife's for measurements. I want you to make her a *cheongsam*. Drop everything else. I think we both should have a new set of clothes." Lau didn't bat an eye.

*We were all tailors, you know. My father, and his father. My son would have been one too, except I broke with tradition. You wanted it that way, didn't you, my dear wife. I loved Wai from the moment he was born. I wanted him close to me, because he was innocent of all the foolishness and treachery of the world that had made him.*

*Maybe you loved him too, in your own way. But you hated me — because you had to marry me.*

*So you took from me the only thing that might have made me happy: your son. You made sure I'd never get close to Wai. He wouldn't go into my trade, wouldn't share secrets with me, wouldn't depend on me for a livelihood a day longer than he had to. You were the one who decided that he would go to America, become something different from us. You did it to put distance between Wai and me.*

*Wai loved the tailor shop. He loved the smell of the cloth, the slow process of creating a garment. He wasn't bad with a needle himself (until you found out that I had taught him a little, and made me agree to keep him out of the shop).*

*He was never to become like me — that would have been another insult. Like having a man get you pregnant and then refuse to marry you, or having your father pay someone to make his son marry you. Or having to wed a simple tailor, because respectable society would start to blab after counting the months between the marriage and the birth of the baby.*

*No, those were enough insults. There was not going to be a closeness between surrogate father and son that you could be jealous of. And there never was, though Wai and I wanted to be friends. You kept us apart. But I've forgiven you. All I want now is to make things new again. Let's start with the clothes, shall we, my wife?*

In a week the suit and *cheongsam* were completed. Lau was working hard, seven days a week. Wai was in the shop too, watching, asking questions, absorbing as much as he could.

Lau had fitted me for the muslin pattern, but that's all. I never saw the suit, even in the making, and had no final fitting. Not that there was a question of a crooked fit, or a baggy seam. No, Lau had his own reasons for keeping the suit to himself. That was why he had already put the suit and the dress in boxes, contrary to the tailor's custom of proudly showing off his work. I took the boxes and carried them home without looking at the contents. Yu wasn't home, so I put her box on the bed, mine on a chair in the bedroom. Then I went out for a while.

Tak was wiping down tables as his assistant mopped the floor. I stayed out of their way, as I always did when visiting this late.

"You know, Kin," he said, "I've been thinking about my wife. I was making her an offering last night, as usual, and it suddenly struck me that someday my children will make an offering to me. We worship our ancestors, Kin. We worship the dead. Why is that?"

"We're supposed to. Out of respect."

"Right. Respect for our elders, respect for the dead. We can only respect what's closer to death than we are. Funny thing to think, isn't it? Death frees the spirit, and spirits have power. For us, the power really rests with the dead. I wonder about people sometimes."

The *cheongsam* lay on the bed, where it had been dropped, though not carelessly.

"Why don't you put it on?" I asked.

She stared at the yellow silk with the red trim, the loveliest thing in the room. Like a flower in its most radiant bloom.

"He did it! Lau did it! That bastard, he knew! I wore a dress like this one night."

"The night you got pregnant?"

Her stare shifted to me. "You knew about it?"

"Yes. Twenty years you thought you'd kept it a secret. But what does it matter now? Wai's ours."

"Ha! That's what you think."

"God, you hate me, don't you?" I said. "Because you had to marry me, and you didn't love me. You hated me because I reminded you that you could never have your real lover. You gave in to him, and that was why you couldn't have him. Was he rich, from a good family? Men like that don't marry pregnant women, do they?"

Yu laughed, almost cheerfully, then paused to regard me with her dull, wasted eyes. "You idiot!" she spat. "You think you've figured it out!"

"That somebody paid my father to make me marry you? I figured that out a long, long time ago."

She jerked back for a second. Her eyes swept the room, looking, it seemed, for a piece of sanity. They kept moving till they rested on my suit, which lay on the chair. Yu had opened the box and drawn out a dark sleeve, which hung down and touched the floor. "Put your suit on. Go ahead!" she shrieked. "It's too late anyway! You wouldn't get rid of him while you had the chance! *Put it on! Let's see you in that fine, fine suit!*"

I stood up, suddenly frightened. Something was about to be cut loose, thrown away, and I had no idea what. Worse, I feared, nothing would take its place — I wanted things to be as they had been.

Drawing the suit up by the wooden hanger, I smoothed the cloth with my free hand. It was an old-fashioned suit, brown with broad chalk stripes. You saw these suits sometimes — on old men who had been measured in more robust times, whose skinny necks now failed to meet the frayed collars of their shirts and whose ties were knotted self-consciously, probably by a wife or daughter. An old man's suit. And a heavy one too.

Then it came to me, a little revelation. Lau and the wool were key and lock; the cuts must have been in the wool, and Lau merely found them. The way he found the truth. The truth always fits, like the best kind of tailoring.

Wonder filled me again as I took off my clothes and donned the suit. "Where did he get these buttons?" I said out loud, to no one but myself. "I've never seen bone buttons like this; they look handmade. Where did they come from? I must ask him tomorrow."

"You can't. I fired him."

"My God . . . why?"

"Why do you think, for God's sake? He's destroyed everything. Wai's not going back to college, did you know that? He's going to be a tailor now. *A goddamn tailor!* After all we've done for him, trying to make something out of him." Secretly I smiled.

While she spoke, I got a pair of suspenders from the closet and hitched up the trousers, which were high on the waist. No, that *is* the true waist, I remembered, forty years of fashion notwithstanding. Then I put on the waistcoat and began fastening the small, perfect buttons. My fingers got faster as they learned their way over the garment.

"It's your wedding suit," Yu said.

No, it wasn't. My wedding suit burned in a fire ten years ago, and this was no resurrection. But something dawned on me now. Those broad, pale-orange chalk stripes. How could Lau have gotten the cut right? The shoulders were padded in a way that was unusual but oddly familiar; they drooped a little by modern standards. The suit felt something like a sack. The weight of the trousers was impressive, made so by the length of the legs. The cuff broke low on the shoe, obscuring most of my black loafers. The suit wasn't mine, though I was wearing it. It was my father's best suit. I remember it from the pictures.

*Why did you do it, Lau? What were you trying to tell me?*

"You had to fire him, didn't you?" I said. "I understand now. Your undoing was inside his little bag when he walked in. Because truth is your undoing. Like the mongoose and the snake, like the horse and the tiger. You and truth are natural enemies."

"You stupid bastard!" she screamed. "You idiot! Look in the mirror! What do you see?"

I saw I was wearing my father's clothes. I knew I hated my father for selling me to Yu's family. I hated him for tearing me from my love, my one inconsequential, selfish love. I hated him for pushing me away from the only thing I cherished. What was left to see?

"You don't see it, do you, you lover of truth?"

I saw I was wearing my father's clothes. I was my father. I had done to my son what had been done to me. I had pushed Wai away from me (and to him, I was his father) and destroyed his simple dream of being a tailor. Yu wanted success, the success of a wealthy son with a degree and a job of importance. She wanted things only a rich son could give her. I had helped exchange Wai for things, sell him outright, as my father had sold me.

That was it, wasn't it?

"You're no better than I am," said Yu, a bit calmer now. "You can't understand Lau, you can't know what he is. He's telling you everything, but you can't see it, because you're as far from Lau as anyone can be. You're no artist. You don't see things. You're blind. No one paid your father to marry me off. You want to know why I married you? I couldn't marry my lover because he was already married — to your mother! I was your father's mistress. Wai is your half-brother. You're the stepfather of your own half-brother."

*I was my father.*

"That's what happens with Lau and his clothes." A tear fell, ignored, from her eye. "We can't match him, any of us. All he cares about is the truth! That's why he's the artist and you're not. You wanted the truth — well then, take it. You weren't the only victim; I was one too. Neither of us had a choice. Men aren't fair, are they? You get wives to serve you, sons to follow you and carry on your work. We get men to make us suffer, and daughters who get taken away and who are made to suffer by other men."

I sat on the bed and thought about what was happening to me. Had this been inevitable, or was it Lau's fault? Would things have been better if Lau had never come along?

*I feared the future.* That's why I hired the first tailor I saw. That's why I put up with Yu and let her manipulate my son. What stupidity! I feared the future, and so I sacrificed it. And what I ended up with was a past I had made: a marriage that wasn't but should have been, and one that shouldn't have been but was. *How do we show the consequences of evil?* Wai had asked in the Gardens. Sometimes we are the consequences of evil.

Lau's gone now. And so is my son. Wai took off the next day, said he was going to find Lau. He didn't take any clothes with him, but why should he have? No doubt he has his first suit already. What did he see in Lau's clothes? Possibilities, I suppose. The truth. Everything he's been denied, everything I held back from him.

Yu and I are still managing. No endless possibilities there, but we're managing. And as for the woman upon whom I intruded that day — and who shall remain nameless — I've kept my word to myself and not visited her. There's no need to really. It was an impulse. Tak's words had set me in motion: he had made me remember my friends, and my responsibilities to them. I had to see that she was all right too, so my past would be in order. No regrets about that impulse.

Chang appeared one day to pay for his shirts and told me to thank Lau. He'd been thinking, since the day he had been in the shop, about the innocent people he had betrayed. He realized now that he too had been innocent, that there were only innocent people back then, innocent people and Red Guards. Someone had betrayed Chang to save his skin, and he had done the same thing to someone else. The inquisitors had preyed on people's fears to get what they wanted. To give in to them was human. That was Chang's sin: to be human. He could face the future with only that sin.

I never think much about the future. I doubt I fear it now. What we should fear is the past; that's where all our misery is. When our past comes to get us, we should take off as if we'd seen a ghost.

I don't know what Merlin would say, but maybe life's going in the right direction after all.

# Transcript t/23–098076/89

## 1999

*Simon Elegant*

June 7, 0235: ". . . no, no, of course, not. I keep telling you the same thing over and over; why won't you believe me? Yes, I was there, but so was everyone else in the city. If I'm guilty then you'll have to arrest the whole of Beijing. As soon as the troops were ready to move in, we ran away. I tell you, I was just a spectator.

What has happened since then, how many people were killed in the fighting? Who else has been arrested? Please tell me, it can't do you any harm . . ."

June 7, 0445

". . . well, of course I was interested. Everything was chaotic and it seemed like our society was turning itself upside down; you would have to be blind and deaf not to be interested. A million people were out on the streets that night. What person who truly cares about China in their hearts, who really loves China, wouldn't have gone out into the streets? You were all out, weren't you, even if you were off duty? No one was off duty on that night, though, I suppose . . .

Of course I wasn't involved with the student leadership. My students were all good students, all studying to be chemistry teachers, not counter-revolutionaries. I learned my lessons about becoming involved in the ten lost years. I suffered too much in the cultural revolution to want to risk anything like it again . . .

Can I go to sleep now, please?"

June 7, 0645

"Yes, my mother was a bourgeois intellectual and came from a capitalist class, but her family had lost all their money. You must know this already. You have my work unit file there on the desk . . .

My grandfather made a lot of money manufacturing umbrellas in Guangdong. While he was still alive my parents lived in a big house in our town, Wuwei, all of the sons and daughters living in one big compound. He died soon after liberation, though, and we were moved out of the house in 1955 when I was six years old. Most of the money was gone by then, some of it taken by the Guomindang, the rest taken by my mother's brothers who moved to Shanghai in 1946, then to Hong Kong in 1949 when the liberation came.

But my father's background is very 'red'. He was from a poor peasant family and joined the seventh route army during the anti-Japanese war and became a medic. My mother was a doctor in those days, that's how they met. They were divorced in 1966. Why? Well, you know already, I'm sure. A lot of people in those days divorced if one of the couple was suspected of being a rightist or had a bad class background. It was to protect the children. So I became a Red Guard. My mother used her maiden name anyway and I never mentioned her to anyone . . .

No, just because I was a Red Guard doesn't mean I want to overthrow the state: there were tens of millions of us and we all just wanted peace and quiet after we came back from the countryside. We wanted no more politics, just to be able to get on with our jobs . . .

I'm very tired. Please, can I sleep now?"

June 8, 0930

"Thank you for letting me rest, comrades. I still feel a little dizzy now, though . . . .

Why do you want me to tell you about the past? I told you my parents were divorced in 1966. Before that? All right, I'll tell you, if you really want to know: My youngest brother died in 1959 when I was ten years old. I remember it very well. It was during the great leap forward when we had almost nothing to eat. My father had been mobilized to help build a reservoir outside the city and was away for nearly six months, so only my mother was looking after us. We hardly had any food in the town, but father told us it was much worse in the countryside, with whole villages dying of starvation.

I remember that my brother cried all the time, at first because he was hungry, then because he was sick. I suppose I cried most of the time, too, but I tried to keep it quiet: he didn't know any better. He got the flu that winter and his body wasn't strong enough to fight it. One day he just wasn't there any more. Some returned students said books about China published overseas say 20 30 million people died of starvation or illness in those years. I . . ."

June 8, 1425

"All right, I'm ready to continue now. I became a Red Guard in 1966 when Chairman Mao called on the youth to 'Bombard the headquarters', and destroy the four olds, old ideas, culture, custom and habits. I'm sure you can all remember those days. For us youngsters, they were like a dream, completely intoxicating. 'To rebel is justified', and 'learn revolution by making revolution', do you remember those slogans? Now we have 'to get rich is glorious'.

I knew I had become a real Red Guard when I went to a struggle meeting and saw my mother up on the platform, her head bowed while the crowd shouted abuse at her, her arms stretched out behind her in the airplane position. She was teaching medicine at Longhua Normal College and some Red Guards broke into the hospital. She tried to stop them stealing the drugs and they smashed up her offices. They found western medical books in her office and accused her of being an imperialist, a spy.

The whole crowd was screaming and jeering. The people in front were even spitting on her. She fell down because of having to stay in the airplane position and everyone laughed at her, even her colleagues from the university. We Chinese laugh too easily at each other's misfortunes. I kept silent, but some of the other Red Guards noticed, so I started jeering at her too. I think she heard my voice, because once she raised her head and looked straight at me and smiled. She committed suicide that night. She hanged herself with her bed sheets. I think she was still hoping to protect my father and me . . ."

June 8, 1515

"After my mother died, that was in early November — I don't know the exact date, they never told me and no one remembered by the time I could ask — my Red Guard unit went up to Beijing for one of the rallies in Tian An Men Square. It was like a combination of a school holiday expedition and a revolution, thousands of us packing the trains, sleeping on the floor of the railway stations. We finally got to Beijing just before the last rally on November

26, I remember the date because I wrote it down with a few notes in my book of Mao's quotations. I've still got the book, but the notes are mostly illegible. I was trying to take them in the crowd just before Mao appeared at the top of the gate. Suddenly he was standing there, very far away, but you could tell it was him from the crowd, everyone just went crazy, all the girls weeping and waving their arms in the air holding the book and screaming, the boys hugging each other and jumping up and down and thumping each other on the back. I was crying, too. I was completely overwhelmed to finally see him and hear his voice, even from so far off.

I don't remember much he said. It was very difficult to hear and after a while I began to feel too cold to really try and listen anymore. It took nearly the whole day to get out of the square after the rally and we had to sleep on the floor of the train station for five days before we could get a train back home.

After that, we all went crazy. There was no one to stop us. The younger ones were the worst, especially the girls. Little girls in pigtails with shiny red cheeks urging on the bigger boys to beat some capitalist-roader cadre. Also the uneducated boys, the sons of workers. They really hated the intellectuals we caught and would beat them over and over again.

We tarred and feathered one woman we caught wearing nail polish. I don't think we actually killed anyone, not directly at least, but it was like what happened to Lao She. Our most famous living writer, nearly seventy years old, beaten for two days by Red Guards until he committed suicide. That's what they say, but everyone believes they killed him and then tried to cover it up as suicide.

The one I remember best was a physics professor. One of his colleagues had informed us he was a rightist who had questioned the leading role of Mao Ze Dong Thought. We were searching his laboratory and one of the boys started a fire. They burnt everything, twenty years of research destroyed in ten minutes.

The youngest of course enjoyed destroying things the most. We found a cache of old paintings and pottery in one old man's house and he watched weeping as we ripped the paintings to pieces and smashed the vases. Some of it was Sung dynasty, a thousand years old, but we didn't care. The older the better, I remember one girl saying . . .

Of course, I'm sure you've all heard these stories many times before . . ."

June 8, 1824

"After that we were all sent down to the countryside to learn from the peasants, as you know. I was sent to live in a small village near Amoy. I didn't even speak the dialect, and none of the villagers could understand much national language. When I first was dumped in the middle of the village by one of the produce trucks, everyone gathered around and stared at me. It was raining and cold, but they didn't seem to care, they just stood there staring at me, rain dripping off their straw hats. In fact, they didn't know what to do with me, didn't have any food for me, or a place to live, or even any work because I didn't know what to do.

They tried to put me in with a young bachelor, hoping at least that they would get one villager a wife, but I lied and told them I was already married. They didn't believe me and one of the men hit me over the head with a stick in exasperation, just like that. You can still see the scar. That probably saved me. The village women intervened and I ended up sleeping on the floor of a young couple who had two babies. After three months some other students came down and we built ourselves a hut, but it was very draughty and bitterly cold in the winter. For two years I looked after a flock of sheep and carted night-soil from the privies to the fields.

The clearest thing I remember from that time is a shirt my family sent to me. It had come from overseas, from my uncles living in Hong Kong, and was made of very thick flannel. Someone had left a piece of tissue paper in the pocket, pink coloured. It seemed to be the softest thing I had ever touched. I used to keep it under mattress and take it out every night and touch it to my face until it fell apart in my hands."

June 8, 1945

"Yes, after I came back from the country I studied by myself for three years, working in a doll factory, putting the eyes in plastic dolls, and managed to get back into school. I was lucky. I had just finished middle school when they closed down the schools in 1966. Then I became a teacher at Hong Qi Teacher Training College in Beijing in 1975. I've taught chemistry there for the last 14 years."

June 10, 1222

"Again? No, I've told you three times already, I won't go through it again. What's the point? It's all on tape, anyway, you can listen to it again if you want to so badly."

June 10, 1253

"All right, I can speak now. My mother was a bourgeois intellectual and came from a capitalist class, but her family had lost all their money. My grandfather made his fortune manufacturing umbrellas, the old fashioned oiled wax paper type. While he was still alive, my parents lived in the big house in Wuwei . . ."

June 12, 0255

"So, as I said, I joined the Hong Qi Teacher Training College in 1974 . . .

Yes, I'm sorry, maybe I did say 1975 before time. I'm very tired . . .

Then what happened? Nothing. My generation just want to be left alone, you know, to get on with life. I taught chemistry happily enough until you arrested me the other day . . . .

Of course, I followed political developments in our country. Yes, I was sad when Wei Jing Shen was put in jail in 1978 after the clampdown on the democracy wall movement. People say he has gone mad in jail, is it true? He's here in this jail, isn't he?

Maybe, yes, I did feel a little spark of hope then, before he was arrested, that China was finally coming of age, that the Chinese people would finally be allowed to stand up by themselves, as Mao said in 1949 at Tian An Men. And, yes, I thought that this time maybe it was really happening, too. We are always ready to hope, we Chinese, but we are always disappointed. Haven't we suffered enough? Why can't you just leave us alone? Why do you send tanks against children?"

June 12, 0340

"I'm sorry for my outburst comrades. I'm very tired. Yes, yes, I can go on now . . .

No, no, I've told you before, I hardly knew Wang Dan, Wu'Er Kai Xi and the others . . .

Yes, I knew them. I told you that before . . .

No I've never met Fang Li Zhi. I just knew a few students. If you have confessions from them implicating me then why do you need me to say anything? Just take me out and shoot me . . ."

June 12, 0525

"Yes, yes, I was in the square that night. As I said, when the army came, we all ran away. I already knew that something terrible might happen. The day before we were trying to persuade some soldiers to join us, chanting: 'The People's Army loves the people. The People's Army loves the people,' over and over again. After a while we stopped and there was a silence. Just then a young soldier with a very thick country accent — they must have brought in the real bumpkins who wouldn't mind shooting students — shouted, 'Who the fuck loves you? Not us, you spoiled bastards.'

That night, there was a vote. A few people spoke to the hunger strikers and the students left in the square, there were only about 300 of us. I helped to look after the hunger strikers in the tents . . .

No, I don't remember who spoke. It was very short. Some of the 'dare to die' types wanted to wait and face the soldiers. To die for China sounds very exciting when you are eighteen years old. Others said we should run away so that we could, so that we could . . . I mean others just wanted to live, the older ones mainly . . .

Well, I don't remember. Who said so? Perhaps I did speak, it was all very confused. I'm confused now. It's because I haven't had any sleep. How do you expect me to remember clearly if you won't let me sleep?

I don't understand. How could you have a transcript of what I said? Did you have spies even there? Let me see.

I certainly didn't say these things. No, certainly not. We were only asking for a few simple things, more democracy, less corruption. Nobody ever said anything about overthrowing the party or establishing a capitalist economy."

June 12, 0624

"We weren't 'a counter-revolutionary clique', we didn't try and 'foment anti-party, bourgeois capitalist ideas among the masses'. We were just trying to save China, I mean to help save China . . . I don't know."

June 12, 0755

"Yes, yes, I'll sign it. I admit the things I've told you are true. If what we did are crimes, I am guilty. Give me a pen."

(Transcript Ends)


Public Security Bureau, Chinese People's Republic
File FT2/23-098076/89

Name:                      Wang Bao Ming, female
Born:                      Oct. 1, 1949, Wuwei Township, Guangdong Province
Distinguishing Marks:      Scar Above Left Eye

| | |
|---|---|
| Work Unit: | Hong Qi Teacher Training College, Beijing; Chemistry Lecturer |
| Date Arrested: | June 7, 1989 |
| Subsequent Action: | |
| June 7 — June 11: | Interrogation, Wan Lu Prison. Partial Transcript Attached |
| Oct. 1: | Executed at City Stadium with 15 other counter-revolutionary elements and 355 criminals. |
| Status: | File Closed |

# The One-Legged Rickshaw Boy

## 1999

*Lawrence Gray*

*A screenwriter whose credits include the BBC, Lawrence Gray is from England and has lived in Hong Kong for over a decade. He also writes fiction and essays and runs the Writing Circle which regularly holds programmes and workshops for creative writers. He lives in Hong Kong.*

I was on a mission to find a one-legged Rickshaw Boy. I told Mr P. about my story idea and he said it was a very good one. Mr P was my producer, which means, as you can guess, that I am in the TV business.

My agent had arranged our initial meeting in a wine bar in London's Soho.

To my astonishment he told me the cheque was in the post and that I was his man and that he loved my shoes. "Policeman's boots," he called them and then showed me his moccasins. I didn't understand the significance but I think it was his way of telling me to relax and buy some more comfortable shoes. We drunk a bottle of Merlot each and then I told him my story idea. He said the one-legged Rickshaw Boy element was a hoot and I said I thought it a very important statement. This made him laugh.

That was how I came to be in a cockroach-infested apartment eight thousand miles away without toilet paper. More important, members of the film-crew were put up in a four-star hotel but there had been some deal over real estate and this apartment was available. Apparently I was very lucky to be put up there. Long-term stays in hotels, so Mr P. told me, were unnatural as well as expensive. Apparently someone once stole his shoes from his hotel room. He had a thing about shoes, did Mr P.

So I was met off the plane, dumped in the apartment by a driver called Larry Lau, and left without maps, food or phone numbers. Extremely annoying, I thought, but there was little I could do about it then. I had succumbed to jet-lag and was dreaming, for reasons that escape me, of three-legged turtles when the telephone rang.

"Where are you?" said the phone.

"What?" I said.

"Where are you?"

"I wish I knew," I said.

The voice at the other end said she was Mr P.'s secretary. Apparently it was ten o'clock in the morning and I was late for work.

"Then send a car for me," I said. "And have you found the one-legged Rickshaw Boy?"

I heard a giggle then the phone went dead. I could tell that my quest was a true crusade. We would have a disabled actor hired if it was the last thing I did. I would also have it credited that no tigers' penises were used in this production. Like I said, it was a very important statement. There were disability and environmental issues at stake here, all of which are very important in my world of wine bars and UK creatives.

When I looked out of my uncurtained windows I thought Hong Kong looked promising.

The sky was smog-laden. Dogs howled. Pile drivers drove. Horns hooted. And schoolgirls in white socks paraded below in the sloping mess of streets. I had imagined an anthill of snake-eaters in pursuit of money. And here it was. Just the place where an artificially legged Rickshaw Boy with a penchant for blowtorching his victims crispy-skinned might operate. It was an entertaining prospect.

I dripped like a rusty tap as I waited on the sweltering unknown street for the Toyota. The driver, Larry Lau, wore a yellow T-shirt rolled up over his stomach. He also had a mobile phone and pager strapped to his belt. I think he suffered Bandwidth Anxiety problems. For a man obsessed with communication I was surprised that he rarely spoke.

Larry pushed an LPG canister off the back seat onto the floor. I assumed this was to make me more comfortable. However, sitting with legs straddling the cylinder had an unnerving effect. It occurred to me that I was being taken off to have my blood drained and my body dumped piecemeal into the water tanks of tall buildings. This is cop-show writer anxiety syndrome. There is no known cure. I dreamt of falling off the roofs of financial institutions and plummeting with the Hang Seng Index. Then the car rumbled down ramps into a basement car park and woke me. Luckily it was beneath the studio and not the lounge of a chainsaw-wielding rolling-eyed madman. I do not know why, but somehow I associate such characters with this mission. Mr P. leaped about his office explaining that "Heroes never sat down."

"Heroes never sat down," I repeated as I jotted the words into my notebook. "Because?" I asked.

"Because they don't," he replied. "Heroes do what heroes do. And one of the things they do, is don't sit down."

"Except when they drive cars?"

"They'd do that standing up if they could," he explained. "But mentally, they are on their feet."

Then he regaled me with many stories about his buckskin moccasins. He took his shoes very seriously and since it pays to ingratiate yourself with the man who is paying you, I smiled and nodded appreciatively at his insight into life and footwear. As he spoke, he fed ant-eggs to Martian goldfish swimming in a small tank on his desk. Every so often, he had a bug-eyed expression on his face not too far removed from that of his fish.

"I tell you, thingy," he said. "Jet lag is shit lag. I haven't been for two weeks. Heh heh heh!"

"Yes Boss," I said, "It sure seems that way."

There were limits to my sycophancy and I suspected that he could see them approaching. So tiring of my company he pushed me through a door into a darkened room and introduced me to one of the film editors.

"Hi Ed," he said. "Here's thingy, you know, the writer, come to do some work. Heh heh heh."

"Hi thingy," said Ed. "Sit down."

"I'm being heroic."

"Ah, you know, he's right. Look at this lot. They don't sit down."

Ed had a grizzly look about him and sweated before images of scrawny sinuous men in greasy vests bouncing, kicking, dodging bullets and never sitting down. I recognised Larry on the screen in mid-death throe, screaming like a young Jamie Lee Curtis. Driving was obviously his forte.

Ed frantically cut and slashed at the rushes. He grabbed the strips of film from big wheeled tubs, slapped them onto the Steenbeck editing suite, and seemed able to run the film upside down and backwards and still know where to make the cut. Even so, he groaned, "Oh God! Call that acting! Don't they understand anything?"

"Well at least they don't sit down," I said.

On the screen a hairy-chested muscle-bound monster wielded a flamethrower and growled, "Eat death scumbag!"

"Oh Jesus!" groaned Ed. "Can't we kill that bastard?"

I was not sure whether Ed referred to the character, in which case it would have been my fault, or the actor. I plumped for the actor.

"He was cheap," I said.

"Well he's costing them plenty now."

Ed replayed the line over and over again and I realised that the hero was actually saying, "Eat beth thcumbag!"

"To think," muttered Ed. "I could have been in Hawaii working on an Eastwood movie."

Ed had not seen daylight for fifteen years. In the darkness I think he was secretly crying. He was definitely sitting though.

I escaped from the editing suite to look for the one-legged Rickshaw Boy. There had to be such a character or the whole episode would make no sense.

The Korean casting lady, an ex-porn star whose last acting role was a naked hog wrestler, said that I was insane. She snarled when she spoke and exhaled cigarette smoke from her nostrils.

"But in movies the serial killer always has a physical disability," I said.

"Never wear panties, darling," she snarled. "That's the only rule that means anything in this business."

She called herself a dragon lady. It was a well-rehearsed little speech for the likes of me. She was show business. I was an upstart. She was the old China hand. I was an ignorant fool. We got on like a house burning down.

"One-legged Rickshaw Boy!" she snarled, exhaling more smoke. "You *gweilo* have not got a clue have you?"

I felt ignorant but there was a moral imperative to hire a disabled actor. It was my contribution to human rights. Something that I felt more people should know something about.

The golden reflections of Hong Kong's unblinking lights swam across the wet windscreen of my black Toyota. I scoured the streets seeking limblessness. Larry, my driver, if I read his sign language correctly, knew a one-legged beggar who would fit the role. However, when we found the man he was sprawled on the concrete floor of an overhead walkway with two legs, granted crippled, but bipedal none-the-less.

"He has to be able to pull a rickshaw," I mimed to Larry, hopping and tugging at the air. Larry nodded as if he understood. "And of course, avoid sitting."

We bent over the beggar again. He was not sitting, but he was lying face down on the floor banging his begging tin like a Saturday afternoon TV wrestler begging to submit.

I dropped him a hundred Hong Kong in memory of my grandmother howling down an ancient English wrestling personality called Billy Two Rivers doing his stint of tag and grudge matches at Bridlington Spa. It was one of those moments when one wonders how one got here from there. Indeed the beggar was probably thinking much the same thing. One moment his mum was wiping his nose and drying his eyes, and then suddenly he wakes up a stain on the pavement.

"Even if we chop a leg off it won't work," I said. "And I don't think we can budget the recovery time for trauma."

Larry looked at me and grinned. I grinned back. We liked each other because although we could not speak the other's language, we could see in our eyes that we knew the truth.

I returned to my apartment saddened that I could not reach the day's goal.

Inside the room, it was dark. I switched on the lights and noticed that though I switched, nothing went on. On closer, groping, examination, I saw in the shadows that all the light bulbs had been removed and wondered if somewhere there was a god who knew the reason. Maybe they had never been there in the first place? Maybe I had a rare form of stroke that disabled light bulb perceiving brain cells? Maybe there was a market for stolen light bulbs in Hong Kong run by one-legged Rickshaw Boys? It was a mystery, like the source of our dreams and the course of our lives.

Since there was no light I went to bed and dreamt that I was in a sampan. An old woman in a black frilled straw hat sat at the tiller. She gnawed on a live snake that featured in episode three, and saw that I had fifty thousand Hong Kong in my wallet. She called to her husband who had a chopper.

It was the sort of dream that conjured up one-legged Rickshaw Boys who would spit on my dismembered parts, call me a devil, and tell me, curiously, that I had no right to appear in their dreams. Then I remembered how part of my research for this project had been viewing a documentary on Cambodia and it became clear whose dream was being dreamt and that the fragments of my reality were but bits of shrapnel randomly blown off in my direction.

I woke up, more or less, and telephoned Mr P.

"Landmines," I muttered to his recording machine. "Cambodia! Princess Di just before the mystery assassins caught up with her, or not. Good publicity for everyone, that is the cause, not the assassination, or not, but the 'Good Cause'. Anti-anti-personnel mines. Authenticity found in using a real victim. And a mere . . ."

I almost said: "hop away".

I did say "hop away".

I made a note to castigate myself for bad taste but also breathed a sigh of relief. I had discovered that I had not been completely crazy, merely geographically off-centre. The mission could thus be accomplished and I hoped, before I drifted off into exhausted slumber, that my crazed memo would not be taken as a sign of mental breakdown, more of inspiration. Either way, it was, as we say in showbiz, a done deal.

I spent the next day writing the script for episode six. It featured a story about doping horses for the Happy Valley Races. I thought it would be amusing to have a bunch of hapless criminals try to get a doped horse into a high-rise lift. When I told Mr P. this, I thought he would tell me what a hoot that was and that I was his man. Unfortunately, he told me what a pain getting a horse into a lift would be. He said I should do the same story with cockroaches instead. He had heard of triad-run beetle races and how in Mexico City people painted beetles, sprinkled diamonds on them and tethered them to their shoes as decoration.

It did not seem quite as challenging for a gangster to get a doped cockroach into a lift, diamond-studded or otherwise, but Mr P. told me to use my imagination. He said maybe there was one special cockroach and it got loose in the building and it had a small nuclear detonator attached to it. I said I was not quite sure that the animal rights angle would be fully exploited in this situation. I think he noticed that I was almost angry. He looked me firmly in the eye and told me that God had an inordinate fondness for beetles. "But," I said, accusingly staring him in his wild bug eyes. "What has he done with my light bulbs?"

Mr P. decided that he had to go to the toilet at that point — either that or that I was passing into a typical scriptwriter faze of unreasonable insistence on common sense, so I took my notes and decided not to write any more that day until I had digested all these ideas or got drunk enough. I settled on getting drunk. Then I'd get back in the correct state of mind for working like this.

Larry took me to a bar in Lan Kwai Fong, a ghetto for Westerners and thus a place held in much contempt by Westerners who liked to think themselves above the sort of Westerner who hung about with no one other than Westerners. However, nearly all the customers in the bar were Chinese and so Larry left me alone as he went off with friends. I did find one Westerner though, drinking pints in a corner. He was an English soundman from the film crew and a miserable pot-bellied man with podgy fingers. I told him all about the impossibility of trying to think up a story about cockroaches and he told me he hoped that I would fail. Like Ed, he too could have been on a shoot with Clint Eastwood in Hawaii. Instead, he told me, he was sitting in cesspools trying to catch the essence of the East, or, rather, avoid catching it. His main sources of complaint so far were lizards that could not act; trained monkeys that ran up sides of buildings to plummet to their doom before startled tourists; and the hog-wrestling scene . . . The Hog Wrestling Scene?

I thanked goodness he did not mention one-legged Rickshaw Boys, but my left eye began to twitch and I could feel sensations creeping through my mind like rats through the sinking corridors of the Titanic. "The hog wrestling scene?" I said.

"Whoever thought that one up must need his head examined," he said.

"Don't look at me," I said, becoming increasingly concerned because it was always possible that I had thought that one up, in much the same way as I had thought up the cockroach racing.

"Have you ever seen a frightened pig?" gurgled the soundman into his lager. This sound was supposed to represent the intestinal activity of a frightened pig.

I immediately went and dragged Larry away from a Filipina dressed in what looked suspiciously like a Minnie Mouse costume. Every time my eye twitched she said: "Fuck the British." I did not know whether she was making an offer or an insult.

"*Diu*," said Larry, which I guessed by the look of his face, was Cantonese and not an offer.

"Take me back to the studios," I demanded, discovering my voice had risen an octave.

He glared at me as I mimed him driving and then said "studios" three times in varying degrees of hysteria. He put a cocktail stick into his mouth, chewed on it a moment, then said, "*Che*," and walked out. I followed behind and he drove me to the studios in silence apart from the noise of a jiggling plastic cat on the dashboard.

"Hello Kitty," I said, pointing to the curious writing on its side. "The Trend Of Life Style," said a sticker on the dashboard and I couldn't help reading it out loud to try see if its meaning could be shaken loose.

"*Chi seen*," said Larry, spitting bits of the cocktail stick down the front of his T-shirt.

"I am doing this for us all," I explained to him. "Everything must have a meaning."

"Waah!" he said.

"It is what makes us human," I added, stating the essentially humanistic and benevolent goal that motivated my urge to make money through my writing and bring a little joy into the otherwise humdrum lives of the masses.

At the studios I went to see Ed, who was sat in one of the film tubs smoking a large cigarette and giggling. I told him that I wanted to see the Rickshaw Boy episode.

"Yeah," he said. "But I strongly recommend you smoke one of these before sitting through the whole thing."

"The whole thing?" I said, threading the film into the editing machine.

"They finished it without my politically correct anti-anti-personnel devices Cambodian?"

As Ed burnt what I hoped were useless out-takes of film and watched them melt and drip to the floor as they emitted startling whizzing noises, I sat back and watched a mad moustache of a Vietnam War Veteran in hot pursuit of a one-legged Rickshaw Boy.

As the stuntman hopped down Queen Street it was obvious that his spare leg was strapped behind.

Mr P. stepped through the door, perhaps alerted by Ed — I think there was an emergency red button that could be pressed when the writer demanded to see the rough-cut.

"Hey thingy, don't worry," whispered Mr P. "If we get hold of a stump for some close-ups, then people will be too frightened to look closely! Heh heh heh?"

"But he's got two legs!" I choked. "Didn't you get my memo about Cambodia? That country is full of limbless people."

"But can they act?" said Mr P.

"They can act limbless."

"No," he said. "The Americans wouldn't like it. And we're pinning our hopes on cable syndication."

I felt a sting of defeat. There was no arguing with American taste.

"Ah," said Mr P., spying a consolatory opportunity. "The Hog Wrestling Scene."

I sank down into my seat and saw my hairy-chested hero grab a squealing pig, slip on something disgusting and fall flat on his back like a clown.

"I thought you said heroes never sat down," I whined.

"The pig's good though," said Mr P. "He'll be a star. Or is it she'll be a star?"

"But it makes no sense," I cried. "It's a piece of shit!"

Mr P. placed his hand on my shoulder and pointed at the screen.

"With a bit of work, you can make it make sense. You can polish it till it shines. I believe in you, thingy! You're my man."

I looked up and studied the film from a professional perspective. The soundtrack was not yet finished, so I could add a few pieces of dialogue over the back of people's heads.

"Hey there, you guy," I tentatively ventured as Ed sat down beside me. "You not point that thing at me!"

"I don't think he'd say that," said Ed with a smoke-fuelled giggle.

"Well what would he say?" I snapped, trying to make sense of my pig-wrestling movie.

"Well," suggested Ed. "He's supposed to eat the guy so he'd say something like, 'You might be stirred but you ain't fried yet!'"

I looked at Ed, who burped and giggled, then I looked at Mr P., who nodded sagely, then heard a rumbling from deep inside myself. It was hysterical laughter. I suppressed it and calmly said, "The guy does not have any teeth. He cannot eat anyone!"

Ed examined the situation, running the film backwards and then forwards and then backwards again. "Why the fuck did you want a one-legged Rickshaw Boy?" he asked.

"God knows," I said burying my head in my hands.

Then something came over me. I turned to Mr P. and said, "You know, some people say that travel broadens the mind and that art is a means of increasing one's understanding, empathy, and spiritual health. But I'm not quite seeing it somehow."

"Whatever," said Mr P. with a shrug.

"Excuse me," I said. "I'm going to scream."

I slipped out of the door into the warmth of the night and took the lift to the roof. I found a washing line hanging with dried fish. I studied it for a moment and decided that once they must have been wet, therefore, to dry them one hangs them on the line. It made perfect sense. Then I looked down upon the hazy streets and imagined sending parcel bombs to prominent cultural figures. That too made perfect sense.

"It's a jungle out there, Mr Wong," I muttered as I looked down upon the people scurrying from shopping malls to housing blocks. They were crying as well. Which also made perfect sense.

I quickly returned to the editing suite, slapped Ed on the back, and gave him the "jungle" line that would lead into the end credits where it said, "No tigers' penises in this production."

"And you know what?" said Mr P. "There ain't!"

After that, work proceeded relatively smoothly, though there was a revolt by the camera crew over the cockroach story. It then became a grasshopper story, which they thought more acceptable.

"Right," said Mr P. "There's this singing grasshopper with the same frequency that sets off bomb alerts in the cross-harbour tunnel."

"And the guy who steals the light bulbs in my apartment lets off a swarm of these things to disguise the fact that he really does have a bomb!"

"But why?" asked Mr P.

"One of the mysteries of the East?"

"Exactly," he said.

"And my toilet paper keeps going missing as well," I told him, which seemed to make him smile.

I decided Mr P. was the result of a UFO abduction and artificial insemination. I suppressed the thought though because I suspected that it was crazy and also that I might have to work for him again.

At the wrap party a pig's skin was roasted and served. I was certain that we were eating the famous pig. The evening ended with Mr P. going to every table, yelling "*gon bui*" and shooting down several shots of X.O. brandy. He made a speech about synchronicity and then with a wink at me, told us how a Red Indian pro-wrestler called Billy Two Rivers warned him that his pig-skin moccasins were slippery when wet. Mr P., his eyes focused upon each other, said: "But I never really heard him until one stormy night — Heh heh heh!"

Even those who understood him failed to laugh, which must have meant that the job was over so we no longer had to. Mr P. thereafter sank into the shadows in an alcoholic stupor that apparently he never left until the next series was under way. Mr P. considered himself a people person and if he was not entertaining any, or the centre of attraction for any, or bullying any, he didn't exist at all. It was a sign of his calling.

Larry drove me to the airport. We shook hands and I presented him with a new T-shirt that he immediately put on over his old one. He handed me a box with a dried tiger's penis in it.

"We'll work together again," I said.

"*Che!*" he said. "Could a been in Hawaii!"

My mind immediately started to work on the next project. I was already late in delivering a script on *Country Nurse*. I needed an outline and the flight back to London would give me plenty of time to think and write one. I was on a mission to find a set of Siamese twins for Nurse Kilkenny to deliver. I was on a mission to encourage compassion. I was on a mission to stop the world crying, especially in Nicam digital stereo between the hours of eight and nine p.m.

# The Catholic All-Star Chess Team

## 2000

*Alex Kuo*

*Alex Kuo is an acclaimed author who has won numerous literary awards, including a National Endowment of the Arts fiction fellowship and an American Book Award for his story collection* Lipstick *(2000). Born in Boston, he grew up in China and Hong Kong and has taught writing and literature for almost forty years at American universities. He is the author of several books of poetry and fiction and has an MFA from the University of Iowa. In 1998, he organized and chaired the first conference devoted solely to Hong Kong literature in English at Hong Kong Baptist University, where he was a visiting Lingnan University scholar. One of his stories of Hong Kong and several poems are included in this anthology. He lives in the Pacific Northwest region.*

*It is the queen which gives the king most trouble in this game and all the other pieces support her.* — Teresa of Avila

My most immediate reason for recording this story is my suspicion that the monogamous obsession of the Chinese for the game of bridge will prompt them, when the island reverts to Chinese sovereignty in 1997, to dismiss from history a most incredible chess match that occurred in the middle of the century in the present British crown colony of Hong Kong. I myself do not play bridge, ever since I once read Arthur Schnabel refer to the game as a disease contracted by the demented. In fact, his warning was so severe that I have never even had a friend who played bridge. I do not pretend to understand the game, but I know enough about bridge and the Chinese to know that, like everyone else, they will most likely rewrite Hong Kong's cultural history and relegate chess to a game played by students at the King George V School during the colonial period.

As a matter of fact I did not attend KGV, but in the early 1950s played on the chess team for my required intramural activity at the Diocesan Boys School when Governor Grantham, a wood-pusher known for his quirky gambling habits, formed a formidable team with seven of the finest local players, including one International Master, an official with the Hang Seng Bank who also sat on the Legislative Council, with His Excellency playing in the last position to round out the eight, and invited local teams to a two-week June Tournament for the Governor's Challenge Cup and a HK$4,000 cash award.

The captains of the DBS and DGS teams got their players together one Saturday afternoon at my parents' apartment near the Royal Observatory to discuss fielding a joint team. The mood was at first pessimistic, since it seemed to most of us that such a junior tag team would be eliminated in the first round. But when Natalie Rodney, the captain of the DGS team who looked quite striking aggressively dressed in something other than her school blues and red tie, mentioned that we should do it if only to gain the competitive experience of playing under FIDE international competition rules, we became excited and were willing to enter the contest and be publicly humiliated by being seeded lowest in the field.

As we sipped our second shandy gaffs, we started putting together the starting eight in that living room, surrounded by light tapestries and several orchids whose bent colored the striped greens of an early Hong Kong May. They came singing, deft trapezists certified in ubiquity and unanimity, whose names came to rest on the official entry form:

1. Teresa Avila
2. Ruy Lopez
3. Pia Lindstrom
4. Donald Chow
5. Vincent Lombardi
6. Peter Pluhta (capt.)
7. William Perry
8. Natalie Rodney

It would be most appropriate to chronicle the stories of such a historical assemblage in that international city:

**1. TERESA AVILA:**   Her high school studies at DGS were cut short when her father was called back to Madrid. After a brief but trying early marriage to an itinerant poet, she turned to writing instructional books and moved to Carmel, California. Although Teresa gave up competitive chess quite early, she nevertheless used chess metaphors in her lessons, particularly her bestseller, *Way of Perfection*, which has since been translated into eighty-six languages at last count. She is perhaps even better known as the ecstatic model for the heir to the sewing machine dynasty, photographer Gianlorenzo Bernina.

**2. RUY LOPEZ:**   After his graduation from DBS, he went professional and both became Grandmaster and approached a 2,600 points Elo-and Clarke Rating before his twenty-first birthday. The lure of big money attracted him, and for several years he made a handsome living decimating rich fish in blindfold simultaneous and odds games. According to his brother Barry who also graduated from DBS and now teaches writing at Notre Dame University in Indiana, Ruy soon tired of this decadent champagne-and-oysters-for-breakfast lifestyle and joined the priesthood the morning after his thirtieth birthday. The latest word from the alumni office tells that he is angling to make bishop.

**3. PIA LINDSTROM:**   She took the Radcliffe team to a national collegiate team championship, and later an individual first in San Francisco in 1962 in the world's first televised chess match with a score of +4, =3, −1. Pia then joined NBC and is now one of its chief news executives.

**4. DONALD CHOW:**   Undoubtedly the megabrain of the team, Don went to M.I.T. and changed the spelling of his last name to Zhou. He later programmed the MANIAC computer at Los Alamos and the IBM 704 at Livermore to play chess, and the MAC SHACK VI which provided Bobby Fischer an opponent for his last published games. It is rumored that on April 25, 1980, the day after the aborted Teheran extraction mission, he was appointed by the Pentagon to develop an interagency and interservice informational system with a Cray computer that allowed the SEALS and Delta counterterrorist units to instantly retrieve up-to-date human and signal intelligence.

**5. VINCENT LOMBARDI:**   Always the optimist and the team's cheerleader, he urged us on with daily pre-match huddles and the rallying cry of *Go for daylight*, Vince toured Italy for a year after graduating from DBS before joining the meatpacking industry in Brown County, Wisconsin, giving up chess for bowling to keep himself trim.

**6. PETER PLUHTA:**   Having survived the Warsaw Uprising as a six year old, Pete was a natural for the captain's position, since such survival instinct and temperament were essential to maintaining order and decorum among such a miscegenated team. At only slightly over six feet, he made it as a point guard on the Duquesne University basketball team by virtue of his dunking skill. Sadly, he defected to the game of competitive bridge when he turned twenty-one, but has distinguished himself by playing on the team that has defeated the Dallas Aces on three consecutive 128-board matches for money.

**7. WILLIAM PERRY:**   He had a solid but unimaginative game, never known for chancy or aggressive moves. Away from the board, however, he was accident prone, and often needed others to move his pieces for him when he surprised everyone by showing up at matches with both hands bandaged. It was conceded that he could not hurt us in playing the seventh position. After DBS he charged through Australia's restrictive immigration policies and went into the mobile refrigeration business.

**8. NATALIE RODNEY:**   She was an enigma. We thought she was Russian. We knew that she lived near Causeway Bay, but that was all. Someone thought he saw her in Chicago's O'Hare Airport several years later, but he wasn't sure. I remember Natalie most for the image she projected that afternoon, and her name pencilled on the stone ledge of our apartment's veranda later, obviously put there by my sister to establish credibility for her allegation that I had a crush on her.

As it was that will never be again, we prepared for the challenge, tested each other on the variants of all the major modern openings, simulated each other's games, played blindfolded to increase concentration, anticipated the best and the worst, kept Perry out of accidents, and waited for June.

The challenge match began on the first Saturday afternoon of the summer vacation. Originally scheduled at the Governor's House, the site was moved to the Peninsula Hotel on Salisbury Road when His Excellency's staff discovered that there were more persons of color playing than expected. This change of venue did however allow Billy Graham, a chess patzer when he was not converting souls, who was in town for his schedule-crowded first Hong Kong crusade and staying at the same hotel, to watch at least most of the first round before he was ejected from the audience in the final and deciding game played at Board One between Teresa Avila and Paul Klee.

The team and reserves met and decompressed at the rectory of St. Joseph's before taking the short, Number 5 bus-ride to the hotel. In normal clothes instead of our stringent school uniforms, we all looked different to each other, particularly Teresa, stunning in an organdy skirt above brown leather flats and nylons, light brown sleeveless shawl falling from her shoulders and buoyant, white felt hat with a broad brim from which flowed a black flirtation veil. And with the single, seasonal hibiscus pinned to her scapula, she was silent but ready.

At the hotel Pete checked the seeding board and confirmed that our team was indeed last, and the governor's first, in an even field of sixteen. Having consulted the players at the rectory only half an hour ago, and seeing no strategic or seditious necessity to change the board positions at the last minute, he submitted our lineup: Avila, Lopez, Chow, Lombardi, Pluhta, Perry and Rodney.

An overflow crowed had gathered in the main ballroom in which Boards One and Two were to be played on the stage, with manually operated display screens instantly simulating play above the two tables. As the referee announced the conditions of contest, Billy Graham was escorted to his front row seat facing Board One. It seemed obvious that the crowd was excited in anticipation of the blood and carnage to be spilled in the top seed's slaughter of our team. Pete had picked up the Governor's Team's lineup, and knowing the strength of its eight players, we were perplexed by its order. While its strongest player, the Swiss banker and International Master, Paul Klee, was positioned to play at Board One, the strategy of the rest was not obvious: Moritz Rosenthal, John Elway, Lt. William W. Cooke, L. Frank Baum, Ron Guidry, George Gossip, and Alexander Grantham.

Vinnie Lombardi called a fast huddle of the team in an ante-room between ballrooms, *Go for daylight, Go for daylight*, but he was the only one above nervousness to say anything beyond two words.

So on that early June Saturday and Monday while the Day Star, North Star, Shining Star, Morning Star, Meridian Star, Celestial Star, Southern Star, Evening Star, Twinkling Star, and Leading Star sailed across the harbor two hundred and eighty-six times, chess history was made.

On Board Eight, Rodney's early refusal of Grantham's opening Queen's Gambit proved to be costly, allowing the governor to push unrelentingly up the middle. Always on the defensive, she was forced to resign on her twenty-third move, two hours before dinner break. Minus one for us. His Excellency was beaming with gin-and-tonics as he waved his two-fingered victory sign before cameras and reporters in the main lobby. Next day he was quoted in the *South China Morning Post* as saying, *In a crown colony the Governor is next to the Almighty.*

Further disaster hit our team before dinner, at Board Seven in the same ballroom, where Perry had drawn Gossip for his opponent. Drawing black, Gossip had put up a formidable Sicilian Defense. Steady but non-aggressive with his four-hundred-years old opening of pawn to king-four followed by knight to king-bishop-three and bishop to knight-five, Perry slipped on his timing in his fourth move and allowed Gossip, destined to become the worst chess player in the history of the game, to accidentally turn his defense into a king-side offense, forcing a nightmarish mate on the thirty-second move. Minus two for us.

Both Pluhta and Lombardi had better luck with their opponents, Guidry and Baum, on Boards Six and Five in Ballroom C. As white, Pluhta got off to a solid beginning with his King's Gambit, controlling the center with provocative but threatening implications. An early defensive king's-side castling by Guidry on the sixth move put him even further behind. Lombardi threw up a standard French Defense against Baum's Center Pawns' Opening, but on the sixth move, Baum abandoned its conventional continuation and inexplicably pushed his king's-rook-pawn up two squares, a move totally out in the ozone. At the break, both Pluhta and Lombardi were ahead, but the team was still behind, minus two.

In Ballroom B Lindstrom was playing Elway at Board Three, but they appeared to be playing more with each other than the game. A steady flirtation hampered their concentration as Elway followed his well-known motif and practically driveled down the front of Lindstrom's neckline. When he punched the time-clock after his second move, he grinned and said to Lindstrom, *You look very familiar, haven't I met you before*, and after his third move, *You know, you remind me of Ingrid Bergman*. Visibly distracted by this not-so-unwelcomed attention, Lindstrom botched the simple third move of her standard Queen's Gambit opening. From that point on, their games deteriorated. At the break they were tied, in bad moves, and it was anyone's guess how the game could be technically salvaged out of the terminal mess.

At the other table on Board Four in the same ballroom, Lt. Cooke was taking a bath. His premature attack evaporated and Chow encircled the unsupported charge and demolished Cooke's pawn structure and knights as well, in the process gaining both tempo and position. In this all-out slugfest that went only sixteen total moves before the break, eight pieces had been captured. It was clear however, that Chow was way ahead.

On Board Two in the crowded main ballroom, Lopez and Rosenthal were giving a masterpiece exhibition. Rosenthal opened with a Queen's Gambit, and Lopez responded with a deferred Dutch Defense, but on moves four and five pressed his king's-bishop forward for an advantageous bishop exchange. The main lines by both were simple and imaginative, and the balance supportive and flexible. It was clear that the spectators gathered here had come to watch the match on Board One, but by the fifth move, everyone but Billy Graham, started paying more attention to the Lopez-Rosenthal board. Before the twenty-third move when Lopez retracted his Queen in his sealed move for the break, the game was very even.

At Board One, the first two moves by Avila and Klee were identical to those by Rosenthal and Lopez at the table forty feet away, but they continued conservatively to the break with no surprises, Avila ever watchful of her verticals, and Klee protective of his horizontals. There was no deviation from the conventional, nothing remarkable, risky or exploitive, only the cautious exploratory, indulgently waiting for the middle game.

—

As we walked to the Jade Garden around the corner from the hotel for a bite to eat, Pete passed out the game records that he had picked up at the scorers' table and gave us his estimated score at the break: ahead in three, even in two, and behind in one, but in the official column, *Minus Two*. Natalie and Bill were mildly apologetic, but they had played their best, and the rest of us appreciated that. Vinnie was ecstatic and, along with the blitzing Don, wanted to have another huddle right there in front of the restaurant on crowded Nathan Road. Pete killed that suggestion when he stopped and looked up from the game record of the Lindstrom-Elway match: *What the hell happened here?*

At dinner, Vinnie's optimism continued, a coachless team seeded last apparently tied with the top seed. Pia and Teresa were silent, though I suspect for very different reasons. It was hard to determine what Teresa was thinking about during dinner, if she was thinking at all. In the only time that she lifted her veil, and that was to drink some water, she looked as if she was in silent meditation. Don was however famished, and after finishing Teresa's plate, started licking his chopsticks.

—

During the evening session at Board Six where Pluhta was ahead of Guidry at the break, Guidry's sealed move continued to give Pluhta the advantage. But on a surprisingly late king's-side castling followed by a Louisiana-Lightning fast concealed attack on the left verticals, Guidry managed to fight his way back into the game. Not having the time to reorganize his defense, Pluhta could not handle this slider and sought a draw on the thirty-sixth move.

At Board Five across the room, the meaning of Baum's ozoned sixth move became clear. Out of the west, out of the inexplicable pawn to king's-rook sixth move, came everything flying at Lombardi, straw, brick, metal, and a hint of a lion's roar. Ever stigmatic in his horizontals, particularly his pawn structure, Lombardi managed to fend off the attack, but at a devastating cost. Another draw. The score? Still *Minus Two* against us.

Chow was having none of that with Lt. Cooke at Board Four. Cooke's moves after the break suggested that he was obeying someone else's coaching, perhaps Governor Grantham's. They were belligerently aggressive, but they were also self-indulgent, inattentive and disconnected, approaching suicide. After Cooke refused to resign, Chow moved in with his three queens and totally decimated Cooke, leaving no prisoner to be taken. *Plus one, Minus Two*, for a net of *Minus One*.

At the other table on Board Three in the match between Lindstrom and Elway, nothing could be retrieved by either side, and the two of them went down to a dead heat, escaping mate their only consolation, for a net of *Minus One* for the Catholics.

The masterpiece exhibition between Lopez and Rosenthal continued at Board Two in the main ballroom. Everyone's attention was focused on this game, Billy Graham having left at the break to begin his crusade at the racetracks across the harbor in Victoria. As the evening went on, there appeared a certain natural inevitability in the development of Lopez's middle game, against which Rosenthal could only mount an accurate but temporary response. Anticipating the brilliant endgame unfolding as his shared control of center board faltered under Lopez's bifurcated pawn attack, Rosenthal resigned, stood up and graciously congratulated Lopez.

At this point the match was tied between the two teams at ten on a Saturday evening.

Between Avila and Klee at Board One, no strategic advantage had developed. Through their moves and body motions, it was quite obvious that they were cautious and respectful of each other. Both chess analysts in Sunday's *Tiger Standard* and *South China Morning Post* were to use the same word, *patience*, in their descriptions of this game. As it was in the afternoon, their game continued to be simple, unimaginative, but solid, waiting.

Joining the spectators in the main ballroom after his game was over, Pete noticed that Teresa's vertical strength was beginning to be apparent in her king and king's-bishop columns, but he also noticed that she appeared to be either getting nervous or losing stamina, from the way her hands held onto the front ledge of the table. It was approaching midnight however, and Teresa submitted her sealed move to the referee.

*Were you getting tired?* Pia asked, when Teresa joined us. She had also noticed, but Teresa remained silent behind her black veil. Not wishing to have an accidental leak of her sealed move, we waited until the continuation of the match on Monday morning just before the start of the game to ask Teresa what it was.

*I forgot.*

Undaunted, Vinnie called a huddle, several sisters and brothers from our schools joining his *Go for daylight*. When we looked up, Billy Graham, the governor and Paul Klee were standing in front of the stage, from which the second table and its simulation screen had been removed. The reverend and governor were smiling and exchanging a hegemonic joke, but Klee only looked distractedly in Teresa's direction for telltale signs.

Wanting an upset now, the spectators were exceptionally noisy as Klee and Avila took their places at Board One while the sealed move was opened and posted on the screen by the steward. Avila stood up to look at her move, studied it in surprise, and then turned to the audience, at once quieting.

Klee took twenty-two minutes to formulate his response, a knight move opening up his horizontal encampment and intended to increase his tempo and initiate some aggression. Avila responded by moving in her chair while her hands rose to grip the table. To everyone's surprise, on her next move she withdrew her pawn protection of her queen's bishop threatened by Klee's last knight move. He looked up at Avila, but decided quickly to capture her bishop, thereby increasing the potential of his attack.

At this point Billy Graham's whistling of Onward Christian Soldiers that coincided with Klee's first aggressive knight move, bothered Klee so much that he asked the referee to eject the reverend from the game. After the ensuing unsuccessful protest by both Grantham and Graham had subsided, Avila made another surprise move by exposing her other bishop. Klee looked up at her again, searching for a design, and just as quickly while she gripped the edge of the table, captured it, leaving her bishopless.

Now lifting one foot off the floor, Avila moved her knight to threaten Klee's king's-rook, at the same time disclosing a queen king-check. Three consecutive brilliant moves in a row, sacrificing her two bishops for a disclosed check that will at least achieve a draw. But both of her feet were off the floor now. The audience was speechless. Avila was clearly beginning to levitate while she was hanging on to the table. Klee's mouth was open, and as Avila rose higher and higher and the edge of the table started to tremble, his hands too reached out for the table and gripped it to hold it down. But it was futile. The table was tipped, the chess pieces, clocks, pencils and paper pads and water glasses all tumbled onto the stage as Avila went upwards, upwards until she was stopped by the proscenium arch.

Governor Grantham and the referee were the first to get up on stage, with the governor insisting that Teresa come down instantly, this very minute. But His Almighty was Protestant, Church of England, and by now the sisters and brothers had their crucifixes out and were kneeling on the ballroom floor in deep prayer. The cameramen who were not allowed into the ballroom now went up to the skirt of the stage and started flashing their bulbs; some of the reporters took notes while others dashed to the phones out in the main lobby.

Slowly, so slowly that her organdy skirt did not even balloon, Teresa descended. Klee walked over to help her down, bowed and closed his eyes.

This is outrageous, this is a sacrilege to the game, shouted His Excellency as he demanded our team's forfeiture. We had little choice. Things were too out of control.

—

On the hotel's promenade, in the bright sunlight of an early June in Hong Kong on that Monday morning, Teresa said to us, *We didn't win, it's not my fault,* as if after what happened winning was still an issue with us; but she smiled and added for all of us, *We'll never play like this again.*

It was a story that drew all of us into a magical event whose remembrance would stay with each one of us for the rest of our lives. And as we said our *Good-byes* to each other, we also knew then that we would probably never see each other again.

\*     \*     \*     \*

## The Reader's Purge Kit

Through the indiscretion of bright words that inform our dreamscapes, we are pushed to the limits of our patience or imagination, depending on our mood. But we do know that as long as we continue to confront such explorations, we cannot die, lest the story continue without us. It was at first awakening that this promise burst in, disquieting, an unmistakable reality, but it was ours. Then as we are swamped by our tedious complications — cooking, sleeping, counting — our histories become diminished, and we are left at the end gazing blankly at the sidewalks and front yards of other people's faces wondering if we are all looking at the same things without mercy. The denial of historical accuracy and assault on simple good taste have brought us this story with its bizarre metaphoric implications, as well as necessitating this questionable consolation. The author will however send you a xeroxed hand-record of the games when he receives your request and SASE, if that is the only way you have of approaching truth.

# Mysterious Properties

## 2000

*Nury Vittachi*

*In the 3rd century AD was written the Lieh-tzu. In this book, Yang Chu says: There are four things which do not allow people to have peace.*

> *'The first is long life, the second is reputation, the third is rank, and the fourth is riches. Those who have these things fear ghosts, fear men, fear power, and fear punishment.'*

*Blade of Grass, the things you want, are the things you do not want.*
*Hear the ancient story of the man who knew what he wanted.*
*He was walking by the riverside when he saw an Immortal.*
*The man was very curious. He looked at the person from Heaven.*
*'I suppose you want something special from me?' said the Immortal.*
*'Yes,' said the man.*
*The Immortal touched a stone with his finger. It changed to gold. He said: 'You can take.'*
*The man did not go. He stayed.*
*'Do you want something more?' said the Immortal.*
*'Yes,' said the man.*
*The Immortal touched three rocks nearby. They turned to gold. He said: 'You can take.'*
*But the man still did not go.*
*The Immortal said: 'What do you want? What is more valuable than gold?'*
*The man said: 'I want something very ordinary.'*
*The Immortal said: 'What do you want?'*
*The man said: 'Your finger.'*

*(Some Gleanings of Oriental Wisdom, by C.F. Wong, part 112)*

'You have to answer a question for me, Wong-saang,' said Biltong Au-yeung, leaning over the railing of the ferryboat, and shouting over the rushing of the wind and the churning of the engines. 'Why does everyone love the Star Ferry? Why do I love the Star Ferry? It's old, grimy, slow, crowded, out-of-date, and the terminus buildings are cramped and unappealing. Yet there's something almost — almost miraculously refreshing about it. Even in this city where everyone is rushing-rushing-rushing — even worse than Singapore, no? — people will make a special effort to put the Star Ferry into their schedule. Why do we do this?'

'Yeah. It's really kinda magical,' said Joyce.

It was dusk in Hong Kong. The green and white boat, shaped like a woodlouse, bobbed gently up and down as it lazily transversed one of the world's busiest waterways. They were only halfway across Victoria Harbour, yet already a dozen boats had crossed their path, some appearing to veer dangerously close.

So transfixing was the 360-degree panorama that Joyce eventually lowered her camera and just leaned on the wrought iron railing, soaking up the scene, and occasionally being showered by the spray. The variety of vessels visible was stunning. There were huge ocean liners, like white skyscrapers lying on their sides; there were freight ships, their decks piled high with multi-coloured cargo-containers, kindergarten bricks for giants; there were lighters topped with cranes, unloading cargo from ocean-going vessels on the edges of the central harbour; there were tiny tugboats, dragging large boats on what seemed to be ridiculously fine bits of string; there were old wooden Chinese junks, their hulls oddly upturned at each end (Joyce noted that they were powered by engines — not a single one had the romantic bat-wing sail that you saw on Hong Kong pictorials); there were sleek, aerodynamic jetfoils skimming futuristically across the top of the water with the sound of jet aircraft; there were tiny rowing boats, one of which had a figure with a traditional cone-shaped hat leaning over the edge, fishing with a string and a hook, but no rod; and there were the grey marine police boats, looking like water insects with spiky antennae protruding from their bridges, uniformed men standing stiffly at their bows.

'Not magic,' said C.F. Wong. 'Good feng shui.'

'Go on, fill us in then, please, C.F.,' asked Joyce.

'The harbour and the Star Ferry are the feng shui centre of Hong Kong. It is not the map centre. It is not the geography centre. But it is the true centre. Hong Kong island, on this side, 10 times smaller than Kowloon peninsula on that side. But Hong Kong island has very great ch'i energy. This balances the ch'i energy of Kowloon, also very strong. Look at the mountain. The mountain, the stars, the water — all combine to make ch'i energy flow into a pool on north side of the island.'

Joyce leaned over the lower deck railings and saw, behind them, the Peak, which stood like a huge green wall behind the buildings of the central part of Hong Kong island.

'The five ch'i elements are all here. Where we stand on this boat,' the geomancer continued. 'Water. It is under our feet and all around us. Wood. The boat itself is mostly made of wood. Wooden benches and wooden floors. Metal. The frame of the boat, the engine, the funnel. These are all metal. Fire. There is a fire in the centre of the vessel. Makes it move. Most of the day the boat is in the direct line of the sun. Soil. All around us on both sides of the harbour, are huge pieces of earth. Not just land. Big mountains of earth. Such big amounts of elemental energy can be bad. But here there is balance. It is not perfect. But it is quite good. The balance is quite okay. This is why many people feel strong when they are on the Star Ferry.'

It was dusk and the neon lights of the Hong Kong cityscape were flickering into life around them. The purples, reds and yellows of the neon logos were reflected as long, shimmering streaks in the water. To the west, the last light from the setting sun was captured as a thousand pieces of orange fire on the crests of the waves.

Joyce felt the wind-borne spray cooling her face and she was happy. She no longer felt that the feng shui man's world was one she could never enter. She was beginning to realize just how big her own world really could be.

Wong — whether because of the high ch'i energy of the location or just because he was in a holiday mood, Joyce did not know — was in an unusually talkative mood. He had bought a book of aerial photographs of the city, and was happily pointing out large-scale feng shui factors visible from on high.

'Hong Kong island is very good example of *yin* and *yang*, the two basic forms of elemental energy. Hong Kong north part is very *yang*. Noisy, busy, active, crazy, everyone running all the time. Then there is a mountain in the middle. Then Hong Kong south part is very *yin*. Quiet, lots of trees, restful, more homes, less offices. The houses are short, not tall, there are beaches instead of docks, you see, quite different. This is very obvious if you know something about *yin* and *yang*. But more interesting to the feng shui master is the influences of east and west on the island . . .'

'Beaches? Great. When are we going? I could just do with a couple of days on the beach. Make this the perfect holiday.' She wondered what Hong Kong guys were like. What was the name of that movie star? Fat somebody?

'This is not holiday. This is work. Please to remember,' said Wong.

'There's not much work,' said Joyce. 'We're only gonna buy a house. And Bill already knows which one. Won't take long, will it? Is it big? Does it have a garden?'

Biltong Au-yeung, a bespectacled executive in his late 30s, lowered his well-groomed but somewhat overweight body on to a wooden bench opposite Wong. 'Let me tell you about buying property. It's a bit different here than in other countries.'

He explained that nearly all homes were small flats in high-rise buildings. If you wanted a newly built one, you would look at the advertisements in local newspapers to see what developments were being started.

From his bag, he pulled out a folded newspaper and showed them a full-page advertisement from the previous day's newspaper telling readers that a residential complex in the rural area was to be sold shortly. It showed Dragon's Gate Court as a complex of tower blocks, with thick foliage draped over every balcony, surrounded by shops and gardens. There were no other developments nearby. Lush rolling hills stretched out on one side, and a tranquil blue sea dotted with white sailing boats ran to the horizon on the other. It was sort of paradise-for-skyscrapers.

'What's the address?' Joyce asked. 'It doesn't give any address. Is it anywhere near the Chim place C.F. was talking about?'

'It's on the edge of Ma On Shan,' Au-yeung replied. 'It's normal in Hong Kong not to bother with addresses, especially in new towns. You just name the area and the building.'

'Dragon's Gate Court. Sounds nice,' the young woman said. 'Now what? Let's go and see it. Have you got the keys? Where do you find the estate agent?'

'It's very different here. You basically get in a queue and put your name down for a unit. If it's a very popular development, they do a sort of computerized ballot, and then publish a couple of hundred winners' names in the newspapers.'

'You can win the flat? You don't have to pay?'

'No, no. You win the right to buy the flat. You still have to pay full price. At the moment, the market is in a bit of a slump, and these units are pretty pricey, even by Hong Kong standards, so the developers reckon a ballot won't be needed. We just need to go down there tomorrow morning. If you all come to my office by six-thirty, that should be enough time. Do you remember how to get there?'

'Six-thirty? Like in the morning?' She was shocked, and sat down, suddenly tired.

'Yes. There will almost definitely be a queue, and the first site bus leaves at 6.45. Bring your passports.'

'It's that far away? Like in another country?'

'No, but it's high security. Flat sales always are, here. Everyone needs formal identification.'

'Yikes. Six-thirty. That's only 12-and-a-bit hours away,' said Joyce, looking at her Swatch. 'And I have at least 10 hours' worth of shopping to do. And can we go and have tea at the Peninsula?' This question was aimed at Wong.

'I think we cannot afford it,' he said.

'Oh, go on, C.F. Daddy will pay you back. Put it on expenses. What about the shopping? Where is this Chim place you were telling me about, where you can get knock-off Prada bags and the shops are open till 4 a.m.?'

'Tsim Sha Tsui. Just docking there now.'

Wong whispered to Au-yeung: 'Please excuse my assistant. In *Putonghua*, there is a phrase. She is a bit *p'ei ch'ien huo*. Understand or not?'

The Hong Konger smiled. '*Mingbaak*. Waste-money-merchandise.'

With a gentle bump, the Star Ferry nosed up to the side of the jetty on Kowloon-side.

*     *     *     *

By 8.05 the next morning, Wong, McQuinnie and Au-yeung were in a long and sleepy queue of would-be property buyers which snaked along the outside of a construction site in Ma On Shan, a semi-urban district 30 minutes' drive from central Hong Kong. The developers had provided free transport from the major urban centres to the on-site showroom where the blocks were to be sold. Au-yeung had explained that this was partly for the sake of convenience, since there was only one access road to the development. But he added that it was probably also because triad elements often tried to infiltrate apartment sales. Each would-be buyer had to provide identification before they were allowed on to the bus.

Subdued by the earliness of the hour and the boredom of the bus ride, most people were initially too somnambulant to talk. But as the sun became bright in the sky, a buzz of sleepy conversation started to run down the length of the queue. Wong appeared to be asleep on his feet, his eyes open but unseeing.

There was a little drama soon after Au-yeung and his two feng shui advisers had taken their place in the queue. Two large dark cars pulled up and stopped dramatically in the road in front of the sales office. Some tough-looking men in dark suits emerged and marched towards the front of the queue. They were soon seen arguing with the guards that were planted thickly around the office.

'Who are they? People pushing in?' Joyce asked.

'I don't know,' said Au-yeung. 'Possibly triads. They often muscle in to flat sales and try to get the best slots, which they then re-sell for huge profits. I don't know, though.'

The argument got more heated, and the security guards were seen calling for help on walkie-talkies. More men in uniform arrived and soon physically grabbed the six men and hustled them away. There was much struggling and shouting, and the incident caused the queue of people to become completely silent for several minutes.

The whiff of danger served to wake the young woman up. She noticed that Au-yeung's briefcase was handcuffed to his wrist. 'Jeepers. You must have some pretty important stuff in there.'

'Yes,' the Hong Kong businessman said. 'My lunch. Someone once stole my *cha siu bau* and I am taking precautions to make sure it doesn't happen again.'

'Really?'

'No, not really,' he said with a smile. 'You have to pay deposits on flats like this in Hong Kong in cash. The deposit for this is one-point-five million Hong Kong dollars, which is about two hundred thousand US dollars.'

'Like, you have two hundred thousand US dollars in there?' she squeaked.

'No, I have what is called a cashier's order for that sum. It works like cash, but is not quite so heavy. But some people bring actual cash along. Some people in Hong Kong pay the whole bill in cash — not just the deposit but the whole price.'

'Wow. Two hundred thou seems a lot of money for a deposit.'

Wong added: 'Yes, and that only one-tenth of the full price. Even worse than Singapore.' He shook his head.

'Yes,' said Au-yeung with a sigh. 'That's why it's really important to get the right place. So damn expensive. We are going to use this flat as a launching pad for our family. My wife is six months' pregnant, so it is really important we get the right place.'

'Birth coming,' said Wong, who took from his pocket a brochure containing a floor plan. 'Need to harness the influence of the east. Must smooth out the darkness of the north. Also fix water element. So baby can grow big and strong.'

The businessman smiled. 'That's it. Anyway, when we get to the front of the queue, we will be shown a plan which will reveal which flats are still available, and you must help me choose. You only get a couple of minutes to decide, which is why I need you with me.'

'This map very bad. Gives room size for each room, but no directions.'

'Yes. They never give enough information. They just rush you all through, take the money and run.'

'I think it's hilarious,' said Joyce. 'I mean, look at the picture in the ad. It's nothing like this.'

Instead of the elegant blocks surrounded by greenery, there was nothing but a large, dusty construction site filled with half-built blocks, some of which were covered in green netting. Nor were the surroundings in the illustration — green fields and blue seas — anything like reality. The development seemed to be circled with other large, dusty construction sites.

'I can't see a single tree in any direction,' said Joyce. 'In fact, I can't see any plants at all. And where's the sea? According to this picture, it's supposed to be right next to the sea.'

Au-yeung said: 'This is what they call an artist's impression. The artists usually use their imagination quite freely.'

'Rip-off,' said Joyce.

'Yes,' said Au-yueng. 'It probably is. Now, how are you getting on, Wong Seen-saang?'

'You are sure it is phase one, that is for sale today, on this page?'

'I am.'

'Then you must buy block two or three, not block one. You should go for flat which is on east side, so must choose Flat D or Flat E. You say you like high floor, so you can choose which floor, does not matter. Block two I think is better than block three, but I need to see proper big map to be sure.'

'They have big area maps in the main office, when we get to the front of the queue. The upper floors tend to sell out first, so that might not be possible.'

'If you cannot buy upper floor, I suggest buy floor five. Good feng shui. Fourth floor also good.'

'Fourth? I thought fourth was always bad luck?'

'No, only in Hong Kong superstition. In true feng shui, historical feng shui, four is very often a good number.'

'That may be so, but my family are Hong Kong traditionalists. I don't think they would let me buy anything on the fourth floor. What about the roads?'

'Yes. I am considering Big Picture. But difficult with such bad information. There is only one road approaching. This goes northwest. But travels past gate facing northeast. There is one more road behind. But hard to tell. Not finished building it yet.'

The queue was gradually moving forwards. Just where they were standing, there was a gap in the fence, and Wong poked his head in to see a carpenter, white with sawdust, trimming a plank to fill in the hole. The man shouted something to another worker, and Wong visibly started, recognizing a familiar accent.

'*Wai. Lei haih Guangzhou-dong-yan, hai-mm-hai-ah?*' Wong said.

'*Hai, lei-la?*' the man replied in a gruff voice.

'*Bai Wan ngoh heung-ha*,' said the geomancer.

The carpenter smiled. '*Bai Wan ngoh sek. Ngoh sing So. Ngoh dai-lo Bai Wan ju.*'

Au-yeung told Joyce: 'They are from the same *heung ha* — that means ancestral town. Wong is from Bai Wan, northeast of Guangzhou city. There are a lot of Guangzhou people in Hong Kong; not so many in Singapore, I think.'

Wong talked animatedly with the carpenter, and eventually stepped in through the hole in the fence and continued to fire questions at him.

The queue moved slowly forwards and Au-yeung and McQuinnie were carried along, losing sight of the feng shui master. 'Will he be all right?' asked Joyce.

'Sure. He'll fit right in. I mean . . .' Au-yeung paused and gave a guilty grin. 'I don't mean to be rude or anything, but an oldish, craggy fellow in rumpled clothes, and, speaking with a strong Guangdong accent — he's just like most of the illegal immigrant types they have working on construction sites in Hong Kong. He'll fit in just fine. Also, he'll be able to have a good look round. He might find out something useful to us. As long as he doesn't get arrested or anything.'

The Hong Kong businessman opened a thermos of hot water and a pot of instant noodles. He offered to share his breakfast with her. The early start had given Joyce a queasy stomach and she decided she couldn't eat anything. Au-yeung munched through the noodles, and then started making phone calls on his cell phone. He seemed to have an endless list of people to speak to.

Joyce stood bored. She wished she had brought something to read. Biltong's newspaper was all in Chinese, and seemed to be full of pictures of accidents and ambulances. She passed the time by examining the other people in the queue and trying to guess what they did. Directly behind them was a tall, shaven-headed man who kept trying to sneak in front of them, edging forwards around the sides of the queue. She caught him leering at her, his tiny eyes running over her body. He must have some villainous occupation, she decided — running a shop selling pirate VCDs, maybe.

She stood her ground to prevent him moving forwards, and was shocked when he continued to move forwards until he was actually touching her. She crossly changed places with Au-yeung.

In front of them were two women, bespectacled, smartly dressed, each with identical hairstyles. They were wearing expensive-looking, designer suits, which seemed a ludicrous idea on this dusty construction site. Accountants, she decided, buying property as an investment.

'How long will we have to wait?' she asked when they had been standing in the slow-moving queue for almost an hour.

'Probably another hour or so. Let me find out.' There were several slick-looking young men in dark glasses who regularly strolled up and down the length of the queue. Au-yeung stopped one of them and spoke briefly to him in Cantonese, and then turned back to Joyce.

'He reckons another 40 minutes.'

'Who are these young guys? The one on the left is kinda cute, I mean, if you like that sort of thing.' She smiled, slightly embarrassed by her own comment.

'They are people hired by the developers to help with organization and security. You always get a few of these "aides". I mean, if you want my honest opinion, I would say that they are almost definitely a rival group of triads themselves. But they have some link with the developer and are helping to make sure things go smoothly.'

'Why are they walking up and down?'

'They are just imparting information to the crowd. For instance, this guy just told me that the eight penthouse flats on both blocks have already gone. Most of the upper floors have gone, he says. There's a 12th floor flat facing northeast still available. That might do us, but if that goes as well, I don't mind lower floors. The fifth floor facing east, like Wong suggested, would be fine. Probably not too many people after them, either, so we've got a chance of getting one, I hope.'

After another 20 minutes passed uneventfully, Au-yeung and his companion found themselves 12 places from the door to the main office. 'Won't be long now,' the businessman said. 'I wonder where Wong is?' He was starting to become anxious, and kept turning around to see if the old geomancer was anywhere in sight.

The young men in dark glasses were standing to one side, counting the people from the door, and then moving along the queue, chatting to each buyer. This time, the conversations were more animated, and the buyers in front of them seemed to be pleased by what they heard.

Joyce watched while the young men spoke to the two be-suited women in front of them, and then swapped a few words with Bilton Au-yeung. The businessman smiled broadly.

The one that Joyce decided was attractive took off his wrap-around petrol-coloured sunglasses and caught her eye. He grinned, showing an old woman's gold tooth unexpectedly placed in a young mouth. 'Hello? Spik Chinese?' he said.

'No, sorry. Do you speak English?' She gave him her just-slightly-interested smile.

'No.' He turned to Biltong and asked him something in Cantonese.

The businessman replied in the same language, and the young man instantly lost his smile, replaced his glasses, and walked on.

Au-yeung turned to Joyce. 'He was asking whether you were my girlfriend, although he didn't use that word. I told him you were my second sister-in-law and you were due to marry an extremely wealthy businessman in the interior decoration industry next week.'

'Why d'you say that? Did he like me? You didn't have to put him off. He was kinda cute.'

'Yes, but, believe me, I did you a favour. You wouldn't want to get involved with someone like that.'

Joyce shrugged her shoulders. 'Dunno. Whatever. I've always wanted to be a gangster's moll. Guess it wouldn't have been very romantic if we like, couldn't speak to each other. Wish you hadn't said I was marrying an interior decorator though. What a poncy job.'

'Pon-si?'

'I mean, it's all gay men, mainly. Decorators. Gay people are cool but you can't marry them.'

'Ah. Well it's different here. Certain jobs here are closely associated with the triads here. Interior decoration is one of them. It's a real tough-guy job in Hong Kong. I was basically telling him that you belonged to someone more powerful in his own line of work.'

Joyce thought about this for a moment. 'Interior decorators are tough guys in Hong Kong? You're having me on.'

'No.'

She shook her head. 'Too weird. So I guess I am a gangster's moll in his eyes. Cool. Why did they stop and talk to you, anyway?'

'They said there are 20 more flats left in block two, eight of which are on the fourth floor — fourth is always the last to sell in Hong Kong. If you calculate the number of people ahead of us, we look like being the last people to be able to buy a block two flat which isn't on the fourth floor. Apparently both the flats Wong picked out are still available: E and D on the fifth. Fifth floor isn't very popular. It's too low, and too close to the unlucky fourth. We're in luck. Thank goodness we took the earliest bus.'

The shaven-headed man behind them groaned with disappointment after talking to the same young men.

'He's upset,' Au-yeung translated, needlessly. 'He'll probably have to have something on the fourth, or go for the next block.'

'I don't feel sorry for him,' said Joyce. 'He's been trying to push in and get in front of us ever since we got here. He's got wandering eyes too. Wonder where C.F. is?'

They had to wait another 10 minutes before Wong returned, arguing his way back to his companions with some difficulty. 'Hard to get back,' the geomancer said. 'Thought I was trying to get in front. Went back to building site. Borrowed hard hat. Then I can walk anywhere.'

'Pushing in is a capital offence in this sort of situation,' said the businessman. 'The British left an awful lot of good things, and a few bad ones, but the habit of orderly queuing is one of the best. Did you find out anything interesting?'

'Yes,' said Wong. 'Very many things. Important things.'

He took out the brochure and opened it to the floor plan. 'One. This plan is a bit wrong. A lot wrong. South should be here, not here.'

'Oh dear. Does this change your recommendation?'

'Yes. Very much change.'

Au-yeung, suddenly worried, leaned over to look at the map. 'You better tell me fast, Wong. We're nearly at the front of the queue. We've only got a few minutes before we have to decide.'

'But listen first. There are some other strange things I found out too,' said the old man. 'The main gate, the entrance, when it is finished, will be here. Will face northeast. Big ornamental gate very nice. Back gate will be southeast.'

'We knew that, though, didn't we?' said the businessman.

'We knew the gate was here. But we did not know the direction. This means the name is wrong. But So told me that the feng shui master for this development was Pang Si-jek.'

'Wait a minute. Who's So?' asked Joyce.

'The workman. His brother lives in my village. But listen. Pang Si-jek was the feng shui master for this development, he says. I know him very well, before. He usually does not make mistakes with names?'

'What's wrong with the name?'

'Northeast, the name should be Tiger. Tiger's Gate Court, if it is an animal. If it is not a star animal, then any name is okay. But cannot use astrology animal and use wrong one. Dragon's Gate Court is a southeast name. Where back gate is.'

'Probably just carelessness,' said Au-yeung. 'I'm sure there's nothing to be worried about.'

'But Pang never makes such mistakes. Listen please. New foreman and new bosses and new workers arrived yesterday, he told me. To make place ready for sale today. So said there is something wrong. Usual foreman did not come to work. The workers, they call it Ma On Shan Lot 2761. But they thought it was going to be named Blossom Garden. Until yesterday. The new foremen ordered the new name, Dragon's Gate Court, to be put up last night. These signs, all new.'

'That does sound a bit odd.' The cheek muscle under Au-yeung's left eye gave a worried twitch.

'There's something like weird going on here, right?' said Joyce.

'Have more news,' said the geomancer. 'The people you said were triads. Those men who came early, had argument. I found them. They were locked up in a how-you-say? Metal room? Portable room? Portaloo?'

'Portacabin,' said Joyce.

'Yes. Portacabin on west side. I pretend to be worker. Got close. Speak to them through the window. I think they are not triads. They are too old, some of them. I think they are real owners. Bad men took their mobile phones.'

'Real owners? What? What do you mean? What's going on here? This is all too strange for me.' Au-yeung got out his mobile phone, although there was no one obvious for him to call. It just seemed to be a nervous reaction. He started to put his phone away, and then got it out again. *'Mutyeh si?* What's happening? You've got me really confused, Wong.'

Joyce was trying to work it out. 'You mean, like, these bad guys turn up last night and take over the site and give it a new name and try and sell it and stuff? But you can't sell someone else's building. I mean, didn't the real owners object? They must have seen the ad.'

'Usually they do not put addresses on the ad. Also the what-you-call-it? Artist impression? All artist impression look the same, I think.'

Au-yeung gasped: 'What's the idea here?'

'They just want the deposit I think,' said Wong. 'How many people here? Much cash deposit.'

Au-yeung tried to speak but his voice was just a croak. His throat suddenly felt constricted. He coughed. 'Erm. *Ngoh mm ji.* I don't know. About five hundred, I reckon.'

'The deposit is how much?'

'One point five million Hong Kong dollars,' said the businessman. 'Five hundred times one-point-five million is, about, 750 million Hong Kong dollars.'

'Wow,' said Joyce. 'That's probably like a lot of money even in real money.'

'One hundred million US dollar almost,' said the geomancer.

'Pretty good for one night's work.'

'Very good for one night's work.' Au-yeung was breathing deeply and quickly, like an asthmatic. He checked the handcuff holding his suitcase to his hand, and then hugged the bag to his chest. He was sweating. 'We have to escape.'

By this time, the queue had moved on again and they were standing at the door of the main office. They saw a desk, surrounded by guards and men in dark suits.

'Heavies,' mumured Joyce. 'Like in the movies.'

A man at a desk was greeting a buyer, taking a cheque from him, and ushering him to the next desk, where he was shown a map, a list of apartments, and handed some papers to sign.

Au-yeung, looking over the heads of the women in front, kept his terrified eyes firmly on the progress of the man's cheque. It was slipped into an envelope and then taken to a third desk, where a man put it into a metal security box — a container that held a large stack of similar cheques, plus some thick wads of cash.

Wong was talking to the large shaven-headed man in the queue behind them.

'I can see what's happening,' Au-yeung said to Joyce. 'Look, they're collecting all the cash and cashiers' cheques in that box, and they'll make a break for it before someone realizes that they are selling someone else's unfinished property development. What a scam. We have to get away.'

'Will they let us leave? Do you think they'll have guns?' whispered Joyce, suddenly noticing the large number of unsmiling guards and staff representatives around the showroom.

'Wong,' said Au-yeung, grabbing the old man's arm. 'What do we do?'

'We just go,' said the geomancer, starting to move away. 'I told man behind us the apartment we want already sold. We don't want other ones because of feng shui not good for your birth chart.'

The man behind was gleeful to see Wong, McQuinnie and Au-yeung step out of the queue, and he hurriedly closed up the gap, standing unsociably close to the young women who had been ahead of them.

The slick young man who had spoken to Joyce earlier approached the three as soon as they stepped away from the queue. '*Wai. Mut-yeh si?*'

'*Ngoh-ge chaang maih-jo,*' said Wong, with a pained expression on his face. '*Di-yi-di chaang fung shui mm-ho, ngoh lum. Mo baan faat.*'

'Mo ban fat,' repeated Joyce, trying to look tough, as befits an experienced moll.

With a dismissive toss of his head, the young triad let them leave, and the three climbed into a waiting taxi to head back to the urban area.

'Phew. Thank God we are out of there. What do we do now?' asked Joyce, as the vehicle slipped on to the main road. 'This is a major scam. Shouldn't we like report it to the police or something?'

'Already did,' said Wong. 'Used a phone on site. Before I came back.'

As they proceeded towards Shatin, three squad cars raced past the taxi, and turned, tyres squealing in the best Hollywood tradition, into the approach road that led to the site.

'Do you think they will catch them?' asked Joyce. 'Won't they try and escape round the back or something?'

'Yes,' said Wong. 'I think they will try that. They will take the money box. They will use the road that goes to the southeast in the direction of the dragon. I told the police to put a road block there. So I think it is no problem.'

Au-yeung remained sitting frozen with his briefcase in his arms, stunned by the turn of events. 'I almost lost you, my poor baby,' he cooed to his savings.

'Does this mean you are not going to buy a flat after all and we can go on holiday now?' asked Joyce.

Au-yeung, in shock, did not answer.

'Yes, I think so,' said Wong. 'I think he will not let go of that bag. For a long time.'

'Can we like, go to the beach or something now?'

'Yes. But first, I think we go and have breakfast in the Peninsula hotel.'

'I thought we couldn't afford it.'

'I sold our place in the queue to man behind us,' said the geomancer. 'He gave me three thousand Hong Kong dollars. I think it is enough.'

The taxi picked up speed as they topped a hill and row after row of glittering towers beckoned them.

# Conversion of a Village Ghost

## 2001

*Jane Camens*

*A fiction writer and journalist with long experience in mainland China, Macau and Hong Kong, Jane Camens is originally from Australia. Her stories have been broadcast on the BBC World Service and she holds an MFA in fiction from Vermont College, Norwich University, USA. She is a founder of the Hong Kong's International Literary Festival and lives on Lantau Island, Hong Kong.*

Every autumn, after the moon festival, when the sea turns almost too cold to swim, the old Hakka Chinese women of the village sweep up the remains of summer. They light small bonfires of fallen leaves, crumpled cellophane lanterns, broken paper kites and polystyrene noodle buckets, which smoulder in a series of anonymous cremations that take the village into winter.

It was one of the golden afternoons when the evening sky had turned red and the sea had turned into a burnished pathway to the islands of China which lie in the distance out beyond the bay, their peaks like upstretched tongues swallowing the sun. It was the time of year when weekenders from Hong Kong finally leave us, residents of the island, in peace. The air had lost its moisture-heavy thickness so, at last, you could breathe again. I remember coming back from a run, climbing up the cement path from the beach, breathing heavily and feeling my pulse to check my heart rate.

I hardly noticed the old woman in black pyjama trousers and a faded floral blouse squatting next to a pyramid of leaves. I suppose I must have seen her, though only from the corner of my eye, like a shadow. If I'd thought about it, I'd have realized I'd seen her often enough scuffing along the beach in the mornings, stooped beneath the weight of cane baskets hanging on either end of a bamboo pole. But I could not have said then who the old woman was. Strange, really, because a part of me knew she lived with the parrot-bald deaf old man in the tiny, squat house next door. It was the old man, not the woman, I noticed, and him only because he drove me crazy, sitting out there in front of his house on the cement, his legs splayed out in front, black pants tied with string and rolled above skeletally-thin knees, banging soft drink cans flat. Bang, bang, banging. I'd deduced that he was profoundly deaf since he gave no response to my repeated requests to *please* shut up. I'd tried frowning and shaking my head as I mimed banging. But he also appeared to be cataract blind. When he stood, he flayed his arms like feelers until he found the wall, and patted it towards the door. His grunts sometimes brought the old woman out to guide him.

The old villagers and I barely registered each other. They were, for me, no more than part of the scenery. Equally, I was irrelevant to them. "*Jo sahn,*" I sometimes said, bidding good morning, any hour of the day, in my limited Cantonese to a line up of women in black sitting on a wall like old crows. They never responded; didn't even make eye contact. They held conversations among themselves, looked right through me as I passed as though I was as insubstantial as air. I was the village ghost, *gweipoh,* the foreign devil woman.

My anonymity suited me. I could concentrate on my work. I'd lived alone in the isolated village for two years, rarely talking to anyone, which was what I wanted. I didn't want people coming near me after my divorce. Didn't want to be touched.

The only person in the village I had much to do with was Emma, my landord's daughter-in-law. She was — still is — the only other person along the bay with any grasp of English. She helped me negotiate my lease and it's her I call if a typhoon blows in one of my windows or an air-conditioner packs up. I wouldn't then have called us friends — not in the sense that I'd ever shared anything personal with her. Though she referred to me as a friend. I used to think hers was an entrepreneurial Chinese idea of friendship, based on one person doing another a favour and expecting favours in return. I was wary of such friendship. But, occasionally, Emma said something that suggested a different quality of friendship, like the night before the moon festival that year, when I asked her by to put right some miscommunication with her father-in-law. She sat in my living room among all the English-language books and promised to explain the situation to Mr. Wong. I thought that was it, readied myself for her to go when, unexpectedly, she said she was going to sit up on her flat-topped roof at midnight waiting for the clouds to part so she could catch a glimpse of the full moon.

"If you wait long enough," she said, "the clouds blow away and then you see the hopes in your heart."

I smiled, uncomfortable. Did she wish to reveal something? I wanted to get back to work. I'd taken on a freelance job and was nearing deadline. She didn't seem to be about to go.

She looked straight at me and said, "Even if the clouds don't go away, you know the moon is there."

Efficient, reliable Emma, seemed almost vulnerable. Was she trying to tell me something? Frankly, I was too busy to worry.

I had a routine. Work all day until the flicker of the dying sun on the sea, then run along the beach for twenty minutes before returning to my desk. I wanted to get back to the desk that evening, which could have been why I paid no particular attention to the old woman crouched by the small smoking pyre. As I climbed the path, a breeze that had blown out the humidity lifted my hair.

My house stands at the top of the path overlooking the bay. The other houses crouch behind, the Hakkas believing it bad luck to face the sea. "The tide comes in, the tide goes out. Same with money," Emma told me. "Better to face the mountain," she advised when I negotiated the good rent on this place. My house is the only one that stands exposed to the elements, but it also has a view. A couple of bougainvillaea I'd planted in dragon pots by the front door clawed the wall almost naked, their few remaining leaves singed brown from winds.

Apart from Emma, all the neighbours are old, most of them in their eighties and nineties. All the young people have moved to the city to find work. Out here, there are not many ways to make a living. Emma cleans for a corporation that keeps a holiday beach bungalow for employees. She considers I'm clever and lucky because I don't do physical work and am not married. I force myself to smile, wrap my arms around myself against the winds.

A few tan chickens along the path pluck-plucked through the villagers' collection of junk. Sheets of tin, wooden planks, broken air-conditioners, tin cans, an old refrigerator . . . . Why did the old folk hoard this stuff, turning the village into a junk-yard? Thinking this, I followed the path up to the house, noticing that the breeze had enough muscle to turn into a wind. It was then I looked back briefly at the woman beside the smoking leaves. "She's going to smoke out the entire village," I thought, in the same way I irritably dismissed thinking more about the rubbish bordering the path.

It must have been about an hour later that I looked up from my work, a strong smell of smoke in my nostrils. I'd been working on a conversion problem as part of the job I'd taken on to localize a student text book. "If Macau jewellery shop owner, Ah-Wing, earns nine thousand Hong Kong dollars from the sale of an ivory bracelet and two gold rings, fifteen thousand patacas for an apple-jade disk on a gold chain, and eight thousand renmenbi for eight gold figurines of lucky cats, how much has he earned in U.S. dollars?"

If I'd done the maths, I'd have figured out the consequences of smoke and a rising wind to my house, the closest and most exposed structure on the cliff.

But I didn't see or hear the fire until sheets of tin on the junk heap began lifting and dropping. I'd taught myself to block out most sounds. Sounds like the deaf man next door banging those wretched cans pancake flat; firecrackers exploding in the middle of the night to ward off malicious spirits; fishermen out in dinghies in a quiet dawn slapping the sea to scare fish into nets; and high, flat, discordant exclamations — *"Wah!"* — that flew through summer evenings like sound-frisbees when teenagers from Hong Kong held barbecues on the beach.

But, the clanging tin — like the repetitive clashing of Chinese cymbals — drove me to the window. I looked into the dark and saw clouds of smoke billowing towards the house. The smoke had begun to engulf the house, and beneath the sound of clashing tin cymbals and the roar of the wind, I heard a crackle that was unmistakably wood splitting under fire.

My first thought was to call Emma. Emma could deal with this. I didn't want this nuisance to enter my psychological firebreak. I leafed through my address book and stood while I dialled, peering into the night. Through the smoke I could now see a line of flame stretching up the slope, eating its way through the pile of rubble. Why hadn't I been more aware of what was happening out there?

For three, four rings, no answer. She should have finished work by this hour. She should have been home. Then, the phone was suddenly answered. A man barked, *"Wei? Wei?"* Emma's husband.

I tried to tell him in my toneless Mandarin, panting exaggeratedly to relay panic. *"You wenti.* Have problem. Big problem." I know my Mandarin is so poor that I have as much chance being understood if I repeat myself in English. But Emma's husband spoke no Mandarin and no English. *"Wei? Wei?"* he repeated. "Emma?" I raised my voice, not knowing Emma's Chinese name. I stumbled to retrieve some Cantonese. "Em-ma *haih bindo-ah.* Where is she?" Still no response. Then I tried mixing dialects, Mandarin and Cantonese. *"Ninde furen,* your wife," I said crossly, *"haih bindo-ah?"* Surely he'd understand that! He hung up.

I switched off the computer and took the phone to the loft where it seemed to me, at the time, that I could monitor the progress of the fire better. Of course, I should have left the house, but it was my "safe" house, my bolt-hole from the world. I looked down at the beach towards the Spanish-style bungalow where Emma worked. The lights were out. The only lights on the shore came from two or three fisherman's huts in the distance.

It was then I remembered that among the rusty tools and broken chairs my landlord kept in the plywood shed by the entrance of my house, were two or three gas bottles. How empty were they? Would they explode? What the hell was the number for emergencies?

I rang directory assistance and was put through directly to the local fire brigade. Thank God that one of Britain's legacies was an English-fluent emergency services switchboard. Ten minutes, they said.

Twenty minutes later the downstairs living area was thick with smoke. But as it filled the room, my sense of urgency became clouded. I felt I'd done what I could. Now the outcome was out of my hands. Perhaps, I'd become more Chinese over the years; become a fatalist. I didn't for a moment seriously believe the house would go up in flames. I figured that if it did start to burn I'd throw open the door and make a run for it. In the meantime, however, I sat on the bed and pulled the quilt over my head to avoid inhaling more smoke. Anyway, who'd care if I incinerated? I was only a ghost woman. Not real.

Yet, I listened for hints of salvation. Instead of blocking out sounds, I now had to strain to make out anything above the white noise of flame blowing up against the outside wall. A series of explosions as the fire found something, perhaps the gas canisters. It seemed to me that I'd wake up soon and this would have been only a bad dream. Or, perhaps, like paper effigies at a Chinese funeral, I really would burn along with the house, the computer, my phone and all my books, and the explosions I'd heard were simply fireworks let off to frighten away my hungry ghost spirit.

"Holy Mary, mother of God, bless me now at this hour of my death . . ."

The sound of the approaching fire engine siren reached me distantly, as though sensed from underwater. I heard the villagers *wah*-ing, firemen shouting instructions, the sound of boots running on cement. The shush of a hose. And then Emma, calling my name, her high voice coming through the din.

"E-laaaine, are you in there? E-laaaine."

Something knocked directly on the other side of the wall. I lifted the quilt to see a ladder positioned by my window and shortly afterwards a young fireman dressed in black fireproof gear with yellow tape over his uniform climbed through.

"You're safe now," he said in confident English. Somehow, when I'd thought about rescue in the past, it was different. Rescue had meant "take me away from all this," not deliver me back to the same choking reality. But later, looking back, I figured it was right to be rescued by a Chinese guy who didn't fit the fairy tales. This was the real world, after all.

"Why didn't you leave the house?" Emma asked when the fireman brought me down.

"I don't know," I told her. How could I say I was afraid? Afraid I'd been so smart I didn't have any burdens of responsibility left to tie me to the world. I could hardly say I'd ceased to believe in my own existence.

"You can't stay here tonight," she said, looking at the smoke-blackened house, the paint on the outside blistered, the metal door — which I'd planned to open and race through — buckled from the heat. "Come with me," she said, and took my arm. She led me across the beach to the Spanish-style bungalow.

She fetched me blankets and made tea, pouring the hot water from a plastic urn into the pot. We sat together on a green leatherette sofa, in silence at first, until Emma said, "You know the old woman who lit the fire?"

"No," I said. "Who is she?" Thinking, "Stupid old thing."

"She's your next door neighbour. Mrs. Lai. You must have seen her carrying big baskets full of vegetables from the paddyfields behind the beach here. You must know her!"

I nodded. Yes, I knew her. I realised I'd known all along what was in those baskets she carried. I'd seen spring onions tied in bunches to her clothesline, peanuts spread on the concrete to dry, and sweet potatoes piled by their door. I hadn't registered the old woman worked paddyfields not a hundred metres from where we sat.

"Yes, of course I know her," I repeated, to make it real.

"These old people aren't very educated," said Emma. She liked to divorce herself from the villagers, pointing out that she was from Kowloon. She'd had her pick of husbands, she said, choosing Mr. Wong's son because he'd needed her more than anyone else. His family, and all the old people in our village, had come from the mainland by boat over a hundred years ago, and had lived on the edge of the bay, longer than the British had had the lease over this part of the New Territories. They still made their living the way they always had, fishing and growing vegetables.

"They sell to the pirates," she said.

"Pirates!"

"Haven't you seen the boat? Every Monday, three o'clock. Next week you watch. A junk from China comes every week. It brings rice and hami melons and Marlboro cigarettes. It's not very legal." She laughed. "The police know, but they're like you. They look with one eye closed." She poured more tea.

"And the old people make enough money from a few basketfuls of vegetables?"

"They also sell tin and old electrical goods," she added, which solved the mystery of the junk heap. "But they make only very little money. Their life is simple, but very hard." I knew she was leading to something.

Again, Emma filled the cups and I tapped the table.

After a suitable pause to sip the tea, now well seeped, Emma said, "Mrs. Lai is sorry for what she's done." She put down her cup and put the lid over it. "She says she wants to commit suicide."

"That's ridiculous!" The old woman was not like me, would never think of giving up the ghost, would never say die. I'd seen her make cement and turn it into sets of stairs leading down the slope, split thick planks of wood by banging in cleverly placed nails. On top of this, she cared for an invalid husband, tended paddyfields, carted vegetables and cleaned up the village after the summer season.

"Mr. Wong says she must pay damages," Emma said. "You could see how his house looks now. Very terrible. Mrs. Lai can't find so much money."

"Mr. Wong can't insist on the impossible," I said.

Emma really didn't belong to the village. She said, "He has the law on his side."

There's something therapeutic about painting. It's a form of meditation with visible end results. The scraping was hard, removing all the blackened, bubbled paint. But once I'd finished the undercoat, I enjoyed applying the top two coats, reaching up with the squeegee and bringing down each stroke so it blended with the last. Mr. Wong agreed that if I painted the place, not only would he forgive Mrs. Lai the damages, he'd extend my lease another year at the same low rent.

I was reaching up with squeegee to the last section of wall when I saw Mrs. Lai head down to the beach with her baskets. I looked out into the bay and there was a junk.

At the bottom of the ladder, I heard Emma. "Have you forgotten?" she called. "It's Monday. Three o'clock. Do you want to meet the pirates?"

I climbed down and ran inside for my wallet, then walked with Emma down to the shore. A dozen villagers had gathered by the water's edge. Some stood beside baskets of lettuces and sweet potatoes. One old man had brought a broken television which sat crookedly on the sand. Everyone watched as a young couple in a dinghy motored in from the smugglers' wooden boat. As the dinghy came close, even the old women rolled up their trousers and helped it land. Then they broke into waves of chatter, exchanging goods, negotiating prices.

The dinghy was laden with eggs, cigarettes, toilet paper, bags of mandarins and assorted Chinese vegetables for less than market price. I bought a bag of tomatoes and some garlic. I was about to add to this a bunch of spring onions when Mrs. Lai grabbed my wrist. She pushed a bunch of her own spring onions into my hand, more than I could use. I wanted to pay, but Emma said she wouldn't take it.

Mrs. Lai smiled. She pumped her arms backwards and forwards, miming a runner's action. "*Pao Bo*," she said. She'd apparently seen me run in the evenings.

I laughed. "Yes."

She reached out with a gnarled finger and touched me.

# Until the Next Century

## 2001

*Xu Xi*

"*Qingfu*." He handed her the chilled champagne.

She took it and kissed the tip of his nose. "Quick, close the door." Even now, she welcomed him this way, recalling the first time when, embarrassed by his presence, she wanted to pull him in, to conceal him from the neighbors.

He loosened his tie. His jacket hung untidily over his arm. "Are you well?"

"Same as usual." She hung his jacket in the closet. Long before she knew better, she would drape it on the back of a chair, thinking, there were plenty of chairs and this way, when their time was up, he could grab it and run. But he proved careless, sitting in the same chair his jacket was on, leaning against it, rumpling it further. In the end, she'd given up and put it away, out of his clumsy reach.

"It's been awhile."

How like him to be vague. "Six months."

"*Shi ma?*"

He had lapsed into Mandarin, but she held her tongue. Why argue anymore that reality was lived in Cantonese? Besides, Hong Kong's transformation was already well underway; their city would enter the new century as "China." "Things have changed a little." Seeing the flicker of disbelief in his eyes, she added, "It does, you know, with time."

"Time, what's time? We're forever 'young at heart,' aren't we?"

She winced. No imagination, ever. "You're almost seventy."

"Sixty-eight," he corrected.

"Only for one more day." That would get him. Still the pursuit of youth. A moment's jocularity passed; the familiar irritation rose, stuck in her gullet. "Why did you want to see me?"

"Don't I always want to? Besides, who else looks after you like I do?"

The presumption! "I'm fine."

"I thought we could celebrate." When she did not respond, her face hard, he added, "You like remembering. It is our anniversary after all."

"Would have been." The words leapt out, more sharply than she intended.

"Would have been," he repeated.

They had met on a New Year's Eve, about half an hour before midnight. The party was a large one, at the home of an artistic Shanghainese family who had Westerners as friends. She came along reluctantly with a girlfriend, her classmate from university. Her own upbringing was strict. Had her parents known she were consorting with such cosmopolitan types, from Shanghai to boot, she would have hell to pay. She was nineteen.

"Remember how I kissed you?" The quaver in his voice interrupted.

"Only because I let you."

"You were my first Southern girl." Because he was originally from Beijing, having escaped, nine years earlier in '49, alone.

"But you've kissed others since."

"No, only you, my *Gwongdung* love."

They had held this conversation many times, improvising variations to amuse themselves. She insisted he make love to her in Cantonese, *Gwongdung wah*. When he wanted to tease, he would speak Mandarin all evening, and she would laugh, holding her hands over her ears, saying *mouh yahn sik teng* — no one "knows how to hear," no one comprehends — and he would pull them away and whisper Northern endearments. After all these years, her Mandarin had become proficient; her ears were attuned to his accent. However, his *Gwongdung wah* never did sound quite right.

It wasn't a game anymore, hadn't been one for a long while.

"Will you drink with me?"

She considered a moment. "All right."

"Get us some glasses?" He began unwinding the wire on the cork.

She obliged, but noted the inexpensive brand, wondering, why couldn't he at least have brought Dom or something, if he must celebrate. She would have liked the treat, and it wasn't as if he couldn't afford it.

A quiet pop, unlike the shouting bullets of old. Before, she would let the froth and foam wash over her hands and lips, wetting her clothes, laughing as they fell upon each others' hearts. He still had beautiful hands, free of the welter of veins that plagued hers. Only the slightest tremor now as he poured.

"I'd have brought it over this morning. With a big bunch of pink roses and wild hybrids from Holland, and arranged them in your mother's vase before you got home, the way I used to surprise you."

She sipped rapidly at the overflow, in time to halt the spill. "At our age, we don't surprise."

He clinked her glass lightly before he drank.

In 1984, she had asked him to return the key to her flat.

"But why?" His shock was palpable.

"It would be more . . . convenient."

He had given her a sapphire and diamond bracelet that very evening, a gift for her forty-fifth birthday. What he didn't realize was that she knew it was originally a present for his wife who hadn't liked it because she wanted a certain Qing porcelain instead. He planned at first to return it to the jeweler, Linda Chow, but changed his mind at the shop. Her discovery of that fact had been entirely circumstantial. Linda Chow had wondered aloud about his decision to Jane Ho at their weekly *mahjeuk* table. Jane, being the incurable story-teller, repeated this when they'd run into each other one day, the way she'd probably told countless others, mindlessly, without real malice. Jane, of course, didn't know about them. Nobody did.

But that wasn't the reason she wanted her key.

"Convenient? For whom?" He almost shouted.

"Me of course. It is my home."

"I've never presumed otherwise."

"Then it isn't a problem?" She could not restrain the challenge in her voice.

He glared in cold anger, unyielding. "Tell me why."

"I think it's better if I don't, for both of us."

"I need to know," he insisted. And then, grazing her cheek with his fingers, "Please?"

She refused to look at him. Since their life together began, she felt he adopted too Western a face, practically staring at people, and asking the same of her, insisting always that she "look at me." She complied out of consideration but found it alien. Right now, however, she looked away because she wanted to be honest. "It would be preferable to avoid unnecessary surprises."

When he left that afternoon, he did so in a fury, and refused to return for over a year. His absence saddened her a little, but did not cause heartache. She only wanted parity, but by then, she had lowered all expectations of him to virtually nil. It sufficed to embrace the memory of love. A pity, though, that she could never wear the bracelet publicly since Linda would be bound to recognize it, something that simply didn't occur to him. Discretion was her burden, not his.

Yet he did return, tortured by their time apart, unable to sever the connection. There isn't any reason to be angry, she reassured, as he undressed her, tore at her garments, drew her in greedily, desperately, reviving his soul.

He refilled his empty glass. "Do you still see . . . ?"

She tried not to smile, but failed. He couldn't, had never been able to ask the question outright, despite all his demands of others to be straightforward, railing against business associates, staff, friends, even family. His lack of diplomacy bled ink on the social pages.

"Not since the year before last."

"He was only the . . . second, right?"

"I believe in longevity."

Amusement lit his eyes, despite the jealous flash. He was youthful yet, and handsome; black strands lingered among the gray. He stood straight, conscious of his stoop. At nineteen, she had pledged passion to his image — hair like coal and eyes as warm as the sky on a summer's night. This afternoon he appeared tired; he allowed his shoulders to slump.

"I believed too, once."

Such maudlin tendencies! How she hated them. "You've had a good life."

"It's far from over. I still can, you know." He stretched an arm around her waist.

She pushed it way, exasperated. "Enough."

"Please."

"Don't make me pity you."

"I don't need pity. Just you."

"You don't need me. No one needs anyone."

His arm retreated and he sat down. "More champagne?"

She shook her head. When he had showed her the Viagra last year, gleefully, like a child, she almost lost her temper. That was when she told him not to visit again. He did, of course, because life could not keep them apart. "I'm tired," she declared.

"You don't eat enough." His voice rich with concern. "Let me order you some Hainan chicken rice. You like that. The broth will do you good."

Chicken rice again. Did he think she ate nothing else? "No. It'll spoil my appetite."

"Oh, are you going out tonight?"

"Why ask? You know I do every year."

"I'm sorry."

"Stop apologizing."

He took hold of both her hands. "*Qingfu*," he said. Love-wife.

"Don't call me that. It's not what I am."
"I'm sorry."

And what she could recall of the night he first kissed her was that he said, afterwards, "I can't take you home."

She had been startled by the sensation of his proximity. Her whole body swayed dreamily, encouraged by the champagne. Everything about that almost midnight moment had been new, delicious, swaddling her legs, hips, waist, breasts, arms in a heavenly wrap. She hadn't quite heard what he said. "I'm sorry?"

"I can't take you home."

"Oh, that's all right." She supposed it was, because from the moment they met, a mere twenty minutes ago, reality disappeared, flushed away into nothingness.

"In fact, I have to find my partner. Before midnight."

She stared at him quizzically.

"I came with someone tonight. A woman."

She giggled. "Then you better not let her find us."

He scribbled her number in his notebook and promised to call. During the year that followed, she went often to meet him at cinemas, in parks, at bus stops. As long as her parents didn't know. They wouldn't have approved of this older man, this entrepreneur who rented out property for a living. Shameful, they would have called it. Exploiting your own kind. His later wealth and social standing would have justified nothing in their eyes.

All that year, he had begged her to surrender. Such nonsense, she'd say. You men make too much of all that. Then it shouldn't matter, he argued. Privately, she agreed, although she wouldn't say so to him. What she wanted was to know the certainty of her love. He persisted. She found she needed to see no one else. He would wait, he said, until forever.

There was a moment she finally knew.

It was summer. Her mother had been coughing, and she was making soup for her as prescribed by their herbalist. As she hovered over the bitter aroma, she heard the faint cough. It brought her back to the day when she was four, holding onto her mother's hand as they left their home in Guangzhou. "We'll stay with uncle until we find our own place," her mother said, between coughs. "Will I like it over there?" she wanted to know. "Oh yes, your father has set up a nice shop for his antiques. On Hollywood Road, imagine, what a name for a street! We'll have a good life, you'll see." "How long will we live in Hong Kong?" "As long as you want. Until . . ." her mother searched for words to make her laugh. "Until the next century. How would you like that?"

Later that day, after her mother had fallen asleep, she went out to meet him. He reached for the tip of her nose in greeting. "Where to, today?"

She grabbed hold of his hand, cool and comforting in its closeness, and kissed him below the ear. "Forever," she replied.

He gripped her so tightly she could scarcely breathe. "You've made me the happiest man in the world."

Two days later, he told her that Janet Ogilvy had accepted his marriage proposal, and that they could no longer meet. The following year, her mother died. Her mother was fifty-two.

"So why did you want to meet?" It was almost five-thirty. She had to get ready soon. Tonight was exceptional. She was going to dinner and the Philharmonic's concert with Linda

Chow, whose children were all in Canada, and who was alone since her husband's death three years ago. They were both expected at Jane Ho's party for the millennium moment. Linda was the punctual type; besides, there was no explaining him, especially not now.

"You haven't drunk yours."

"I don't drink much anymore." She did not hide her impatience.

He swiveled his champagne flute on its base. "I have to go soon too."

Then stop wasting time, she wanted to say. Out with it. Instead she waited, thinking, he had become, not exactly annoying or boring, but something she didn't recognize.

"Janna's getting divorced. She called from London." He meant his third child, the daughter after Janet's first miscarriage.

"That's a shame. I hope she knows she can come home if she wants." Because Janna didn't get along with her mother.

"My children, they're all so . . . English."

She almost shouted — well what did you expect? Hadn't she warned him, urged him to be a father, to show his children his love. They can't read your heart, she'd told him over and over again. You have to show them you care by the things you do, not by what you say. He had been at home so little, and Janet was an Anglophile. It was useless repeating herself. Things were hard on all five kids since Janet floated off into her own "spiritual" space after the cancer. Yet as she looked into his troubled eyes, she failed to connect, failed to feel anything more than a polite sympathy. Neither he, nor anyone, deserved the sorrows of life.

Yet surely their paths forked and always had? Unlike her, he had no family and tried to create his own. Janet Ogilvy was beautiful once, and Eurasian, with privileged access into colonial English society. It was what he chose in marrying . . . no, it was more than mere choice. He desired, lusted after, craved all that Janet represented so desperately that it became something else, something stronger. A feeling like love.

"I don't have anyone to talk to," he complained.

"You have family, friends, your club, the world. You've been knighted by the queen and shaken hands with Deng. All of Hong Kong knows who you are."

"I need you."

"No you don't."

"You're still angry."

"No."

"Forgive me?"

"I am not angry at you. I've never really been angry."

"Then why won't you love me anymore?"

He had drunk too quickly and too much. She had to get him out before he made a fool of himself. Taking hold of his glass, she tried to wrest it gently away, expecting his fingers to loosen. He surprised her by gripping the stem.

"Don't patronize me."

She pulled up her hands as if he'd pointed a pistol at her. "Done."

"Marriage is the beginning of death," he told her when they met again, seven years after his wedding. She had not attended. Her presence would have upset Janet, who suspected, but did not know of their little affair. At twenty, she had had no great expectations after her virginal sacrifice. He had been fun, a break from life's routine, a passion tornado.

By now, he was rising in society and reasonably wealthy.

They had run into each other on Hillwood Road near her home. He was driving past when he spotted her.

"And what about you? Why haven't you married?"

"No one wants me," she smiled.

"Still the joker."

"Life isn't so serious."

"That's easy for you to say, with no family responsibilities."

She wanted to say, parenthood can be planned, but refrained. Her father taught that incivility did not become a lady. "So how many now?"

"Three. Another girl. Janet wants at least two more."

"How nice. Well, pleased to see you again. Give Janet my regards." Her father wasn't well and she wanted to get back to him.

But he dallied. "You're still very beautiful."

"We spinsters keep well."

"Can I come see you?"

"And 'be the number three'?"

He laughed. "Why not? It's quite 'expected,' as you Cantonese say."

Afterwards, she regretted it. She hadn't meant at all to suggest . . . she had no desire for an affair. No reason either to tell him about Joseph Chan, the civil servant who wanted to marry her and would have made a fine husband. She couldn't explain her reluctance. Love was deaf to mere declarations, and marriage, at least to Joseph, seemed unnecessary.

Perhaps if her father had lived, she would never have quit teaching or gone abroad for her Ph.D., and their lives could have progressed as friendly, if distant, acquaintances. She did not regret starting what they called their "silly people's secret thing" when they became lovers and continued during her time in the U.S. Wonderful memories, sweetened by age. He looked so tired now, so burdened by life. What did his ambitions matter anymore?

He poured himself more champagne and sipped, wistfully perturbed.

"What do you want from me?" she asked.

"I don't know."

"Things aren't the same."

"But why not? Why won't you tell me? We've been together so long you've become a part of me. Don't take that away. It's pointless to separate now. Let me see you. We belong to each other." His voice trembled. "Besides, you owe me, just a little don't you think?"

"I don't owe you. You told me yourself the very day we met." The day, she knew, he gave the gift of love, without expectations or demands.

"It isn't about that. I love you."

"Don't confuse yourself."

"Then what? Because you think I can't?"

She grimaced. "Don't be ridiculous. It was never just about sex."

"Then why won't you love me?" When she gazed at the ceiling and did not reply, he repeated, "It's because you think I can't, isn't it? Isn't it?"

Always, always. It would always be about him. She refused to break her gaze.

Thirty, she mused, had been her year to take a stand. It was the year she quit teaching and attended, reluctantly, a New Year's Eve party. He was there alone. Janet was ill.

That night, he took her home and made her feel nineteen again.

His visits were sporadic at first. Her father was already dead and she owned the family flat where she lived alone. He came more often; it became like his second home, but without his contribution. Had he offered money, pride would have insisted she refuse it.

She wanted more of him, but did not demand, knowing it wouldn't be fair. Two years later, she left for graduate school in Massachusetts. Away from home, their relationship became real.

He declared love a lot, and most of the time, she ignored him. He needed to brag; the rest of his life did not allow such space. After each visit he paid her abroad, he would report back greater successes, in business and social affairs. That's excellent, she'd tell him, now don't talk too long or your telephone bill will clear out your bank account. Olden days. Easy hours peering at art slides and researching her thesis. Days to dream about going home, to take over the modest business her father left behind. Daughter, we're proud of you, she could hear her parents say. Their voices softened her loss, making it possible to go on.

Only once did she believe his declaration.

It happened when May flowers bloomed. After four years, he was impatient for her return. "I hate leaving you," he said. "Why don't you come home?" He said that often now, which she usually dismissed with a joke. But this time, something stirred. Perhaps it was the darling buds. "Why should I hurry back? It's more awkward for us there." He kissed the tip of her nose. "We can change that." For a moment, life burst open in magnificent radiance, although she remained cautious. "What is it you intend to do?" That was when he declared, "I love you. I'll leave Janet."

For once, she was silent. A promise of life demanded real attention. "You're not serious."

"I am."

"Why?"

"She doesn't make me happy the way you can. She doesn't understand me."

"What would we do?"

"I'd buy us a new home and I'll begin again. It would have to be a bigger place than yours, so that my children can visit. I won't be cruel to Janet. I know you wouldn't want me to do that. Everything will be fair."

Forget!

"What's the matter?" He had come out of himself and the champagne. "You look upset."

"It's nothing. I haven't been well."

"You see, I knew it. You haven't been eating enough, have you?" He stood and gripped her shoulders. "You need me."

Dirty dishes and stained sheets marched past the years. Her friends marveled that she never kept a domestic helper. How could she, if she didn't want word to get out, if she didn't want people to know? No, it was impossible. People in America do their own housework so why shouldn't I? She faced their world, defiant.

On the table, a puddle of spilt champagne.

"Stop it," she said. "Leave me alone."

He attempted an embrace, pinning her firmly against him. "One more time, please?" He licked her neck.

How could she tell him she felt nothing, that she had stopped feeling years ago?

"I'm not angry at you anymore," he reassured her. "Not even about your young men, when you made a fool of yourself. It was some mid-life thing. Tougher for a woman. I've forgiven you."

She shoved him away. "You're the fool."

"*Gwongdung* dragon." His voice was teasing. "My only love."

"Leave, please. Or I'll tell Janet." It burst out, escaping her lips. The words whirled chains before his eyes. She had never threatened. Not once.

He gazed at her in silent horror. "After all this time? Why?"

Because, exploded the silent scream, because you were unfair. To me, to all your children, to Janet. You perpetuated what you had no business doing. You made a mockery of truth and a fool of me. You promised without the intent to fulfill and worse, expected forgiveness. Life isn't about forgiveness and the wasting of our energies. Life is about love, not just the feeling of love.

The silence gripped her. She was sixty and still she hadn't spoken.

"You don't mean it," he said.

"I do."

He froze. His whole body seemed to shrink. And then his eyes searched round the flat. She removed his jacket from the closet.

"Oh," he began.

She knew what would follow — you hung it up, how kind of you — uttered in obtuse surprise. His words would have unleashed the scream completely, and then there would be no going back. She spoke before he could. "I'll be your *qingfu*."

The day she first said that was two years after her return from the U. S. They had not seen each other in months, not since he admitted he could not leave Janet and his family, and begged to end their relationship.

"I shouldn't be here," he said when he arrived, his arms filled with roses.

The petals were too open, she thought, as she placed them in water. "What do you want from me?"

"I can't let you go."

"Why not? I did." Only lightness and air, no betrayal of hurt. When her mother was dying and she knew it, she hadn't been able to stop her tears. *Don't,* her mother told her. *Live for love, not pain. Only fools carry pain as if their hearts depend on it. Look after your father. That's all I ask.*

"It destroys me to think of you with someone else."

Joseph Chan had taken her to the last New Year's ball, and she knew he'd seen her. "That's ridiculous. You ended it."

He became curt. "We've been through all that."

"Then there's nothing more to say."

He reached for her waist. "I love you."

She held herself away from him. "I know that."

"But it wouldn't be fair to make you my . . ."

"What?" Her eyes glimmered with laughter and tears. "Your *qingfu*?"

"No! I wouldn't waste your life like that."

"It isn't yours to waste."

"What do you mean? Don't you want someone to look after you?"

That was the first moment her burden of shame lightened. If she kept him, the power would be hers. She had looked after her father and because of it the pain of his death hadn't cut as deep. If she cared for him too — he brought laughter, after all, and at least the feeling of love — her life might be a little less empty.

"*Qingfu*. It's just a word," she told him.

His eyes lit up with the exhilaration of success. "Then you don't mind? You'll take me back?"

Very well, she decided. There wasn't really anyone else she wanted. Had she become his wife, marriage might have been the beginning of death. But to be his *qingfu*, the "wife" who gives the feeling of love . . . even if she would never forgive him, she could at least forgive herself for indulging in sorrow over his betrayal, and absolve herself of that intense, unbearable, private shame, more painful because she couldn't shout it to the world. Their "silly people's secret thing." Like the secret of the king's donkey ears, the words floated away with the winds, freeing her.

"You will?" Hope returned to his eyes.

"In memory."

His face fell. "But we've been together . . . over forty years."

"My parents didn't even have that many," she replied. "Besides, it was really thirty. I count us only from after your marriage. Thirty good years, though."

"But what will you do?"

"It's not like I depend on anyone. I'll do what I've always done. Look after the store, travel, see people, celebrate each New Year's Eve because my friends throw the best parties. These days, I may even meet another Beijing man." She giggled like a nineteen year old.

He frowned. "But what will I do?"

You, she wanted to ask. Do you really think this is still about you? His voice betrayed such worry that she had to choke back her laughter.

"Well, I'm glad you're amused." He put on his jacket, miffed but resigned.

Kissing his cheek, she was struck by its papery texture. "You, my love," she whispered to the air, "are a freed man." The door closed behind him.

Six o'clock. Heavens, how late. She really must make a move. She needed to get ready for the night ahead, for the pleasures that were yet to come.

# Walking on the Melting Ice

## 2002

*Hark Yeung*

*Hark Yeung is the pen name of a former Chinese-language journalist who writes fiction and essays in English. A native of Hong Kong, she studied translation at the University of Hong Kong. An essay from her book* Our Elders *(co-authored with photographer Fong So) and a story from her first collection appear in this anthology. She is now a full-time writer.*

When I woke up, Naja, seven dogs and I were on a piece of broken ice floating on the rough, thick sea. The midnight sun had disappeared. In the north, there was a pale blue light. The edge of the sea ice could not be seen.

Narwhals were talking.

Naja was facing the sea.

'The ice has broken,' she said in a normal voice without turning to me, as if our situation was part of an ordinary hunting trip in the Arctic Sea. 'It's not yet day,' she added before my question came out in words.

I gradually got used to Naja sensing my needs, problems and feelings. Most Greenlanders could do that. Naja was just a bit more sensitive. We met two weeks ago when I was walking in Qaanaaq, the northernmost city in Greenland, looking for a woman hunter who could take me to the place where the meteorites were found. Naja walked to me, stopped and asked, 'Are you looking for a hunter?'

She did not introduce herself, but I could tell the woman was Naja, whom other Greenlanders had told me so much about.

I could not take my eyes off Naja's back; I was waiting for her to speak again. Hunters did not speak to each other often in the wild, even if they hunted together.

Hunting, it seemed, was a hunter's personal dialogue with Nature.

'The storm came when we were dreaming,' Naja's words came again, after a long while, among the voices of the narwhals.

'It was a nightmare,' I said. I was not sure if it came during the night. The midnight sun had frozen my sense of time so that I could not distinguish between day and night. The sun was part of that nightmare. A seal was sunning itself on the shining silver ice. There was a gunshot. The seal struggled towards the crack on the ice. On its way, it stopped moving. With a knife, I walked towards it. The carcass turned into a human corpse. A scream pierced the vast icy silence.

'What was in your dream?' I asked Naja.

'I talked to Nature.'

'About . . .'

'We did not talk with words.'

Our piece of ice shook a bit, as if its bottom was melting.

'Will the sea freeze again?'

'Once that happened, when many narwhals were talking. The ice came during the night. In the morning the narwhals were trapped in a bit of water surrounded by the ice.'

'We can wait for the ice.'

'We have to wait for the men. The midnight sun has already come.'

'So the ice won't come?'

'Once that happened. The men will come. We have to wait for the helicopter.'

Naja turned and sat in front of me. The white fur of her polar bear skin breeches rested on the ice. On my lips, some words were hanging but they did not come out. In my mind, my nightmare replayed itself again like an out of order videotape. Here, in Greenland, my dreams refused to stay as dreams. They were vivid enough to convince me that I was living in two interlocking realities.

About a month before that, I had watched the slaughtering of a seal, but was not impressed. A ringed seal, twice as big as a human being. The intestines of the seal made me tipsy, but I continued to eat them. 'The intestines are like alcohol,' a Greenlander said. 'We'll soon forget everything and just feel happy.'

Another said, 'This is a male seal. We're thinking of sending its . . . to China. We always receive letters from China asking for them . . . Ha ha . . . They said they would make medicine with them . . .'

The dogs, their chins flat on the ground, made some sad, low sounds, as if they were recounting the events leading us to this broken piece of ice. On the ice, the frozen Arctic Sea, we were travelling with darkening clouds that gathered around us like a pack of wolves. The footsteps of a storm were audible. Naja told the dogs to go faster with her whip. It was icy cold and I could feel myself getting number. I wanted to call for help but was too weak to say anything.

Naja stopped. She set up the tent and lit a fire. She knew that I could not go on.

The storm had broken the ice and sent us floating away on this piece. The waves were still beating the edge, threatening to break it again.

The dogs were looking at Naja. Out on the ice, the dogs were calmer. They had stopped producing the low sounds I always heard during my sleepless nights. In the city, they were chained. As they walked, the iron chains rubbed against the hard ice like old, helpless saws working on a never-ending job.

I missed that noise. The narwhals had stopped talking and the silence sat on my mind like a piece of heavy stone. Towards the dogs, I walked, to see if there was fear in their eyes. Big White lifted her head and made some muted calls to the sky. The calls made me laugh. It sounded like a challenge to the overwhelming silence around us.

Naja also laughed. She said, 'I used to have fifteen dogs. During the winter eight died. A severe winter, many dogs in the city died. My grandmother said she had never seen so much snow before. The lover of this Big White also died after a hunting trip. He fought alone with a polar bear. He was one of my younger brother's dogs, a black one. Big White was deeply in love with that black dog. They could see each other far, far away. When they were separated, she always gazed into the distance as if her soul was out of her body. I asked my brother to sell me that black dog. He refused. After the black dog's death, Big White has become thinner and thinner.'

I thought of Dog, one of the largest meteorites ever discovered in Greenland. It was lying, as silently as the dogs in front of me, in the American Museum of Natural History in New York. So deep was its silence that it was not just haunting but also inviting.

Naja took out the big piece of ice she had cut from an iceberg on our way, cut out a small piece with a knife, boiled it in a pot on a soapstone lamp, as she did right after she had set the tent up on the sea ice. She always looked thoughtful and locked up in her own world. I wanted to ask her something but could not.

'What can we do now?' I heard myself saying.

Naja turned to the sky and then to the ice.

'Do what we did,' she answered, I looked at my watch. Once we were on the sea ice, it had stopped. Naja had no watch.

Over us, a black and white little auk flew. 'Abadiasuk,' Naja called the bird softly.

Before this hunting trip, thousands of such birds were swirling around a cliff in a village near Qaanaaq, looking for mates and homes, making sounds like echoes of a far away carnival. In a crack, a pair stayed together and did not move even when I tried to catch them. The Greenlanders caught them with long-handled nets. Holding a bird in his three fingers, an old hunter pressed the bird's heart gently with his thumb until the bird gradually closed its eyes in his big palm.

That old hunter's daughter told me how her father's dogs ran away on a hunting trip with the sledge, leaving him standing on an iceberg with his telescope. 'On foot, he followed the tracks made by his dogs and sledge. On the ice, they were the only marks. He walked and walked until he found his dogs. Many kilometers. That trip cost him two fingers.' The young Greenlanders spoke much more than their parents. With the coming of television to this part of the world, perhaps they had lost the ability to communicate silently.

Over my head, another little auk flew.

'Shoot it,' I heard myself saying.

Naja shook her head but handed me her gun.

A small, thin bird. Those birds stayed near water before they flew to the cliffs.

Those little auks were delicious. With their feathers, the birds were boiled. Tents were set up at the foot of the cliff. From the cliff, the tents looked like living creatures. Even the hot steam from boiling pots could be seen. I ate ten birds and the Greenlanders laughed. When they were not laughing, they always looked a bit sad.

'The Danes don't like our food,' one of the Greenlanders said. 'There's another way of eating these birds. We put about a hundred of them into the belly of a seal, leave them under some stones, let them ferment with the blubber of the seal until we can smell them. That takes several months but we made some last year. When you come back from your hunting trip, you should try it.' I told them that in China there was a special way of eating birds: wrapped them in soil and baked it until the soil was hard. Then broke the soil. 'But we don't have soil here,' the Greenlander said. 'That's why we can't bury our dead in the ground. We pile up stones around them.'

On our piece of ice, what we could eat, besides chocolates and instant noodles, was a piece of seal meat. We had taken it from a hut built for travelling hunters. A lonely little hut at the foot of a mountain. 'Hunters used to travel from one such little house to another, they didn't have a home,' Naja said when we went into the hut. 'There's always some meat in these houses, left behind by some lucky hunters.'

From the seawater a narwhal jumped up. Naja watched it. Another jumped up. Then came a small one. Naja shot it, harpooned it and drew it to the edge of our floating ice. The blood of the narwhal coloured the seawater. In the red water, the narwhal's ivory tusk, more than a metre long, stood like a messenger from Nature. That was the tool the gentle narwhal used to protect itself in a fight.

It was still smiling, the narwhal. The edge of our ice was as red as sunset. But the sun would never set at this time in this part of Greenland.

The dogs followed Naja with their eyes. They were too weak to pull the narwhal up onto the broken ice. 'It's about six hundred kilos,' Naja said. 'Too heavy for seven dogs.' Naja cut some meat from the back of the narwhal and threw it to the dogs. The narwhal, tied to a hook anchored on the ice, rose and fell with the rhythm of the waves. The dogs ate the meat hungrily. Hunters used to feed their dogs after a hunting trip, not before, perhaps to make sure that in case the dogs chose to run away, they would not have energy to go too far.

In front of our tent, Naja was making narwhal soup. Hot steam came up from the pot. Tent was the name of one of the biggest pieces of meteorites ever discovered in Greenland and was still one of the biggest ever discovered in the world.

Those meteorites were the Greenlanders' source of iron. The tent was our home on this piece of ice. I knew why that meteorite was called Tent.

Naja stirred the soup, as respectfully as the old hunter handled the little auks. Greenlanders believed that animals gave themselves up to the hunters they had chosen, they could never be 'caught'.

'Ka la lu ye da lu gull. Ka la lu ye da lu gull. Ka la lu ye da lu gull.' Naja shouted and then turned to me, 'Repeat that, it means I got a whale. I got a whale. I got a whale. When we get big animals like whales or polar bears, we always say that to Nature.'

That was the first narwhal hunted that year in that part of Greenland.

# ESSAYS

## Why Compromise? Get Divorced Instead

### 1993

*Nury Vittachi*

Chen looked like he was about to burst into tears. "Three of my clients are in the throes of messy divorces," he said, sniffing. "And two others have this week started trial separations."

He dabbed his eyes with his handkerchief. "I'm SOOO happy," he exclaimed, emotionally. "Why is life so good to me?"

You think Chen is a divorce lawyer, right? Or a solicitor's tout? Well, he is not. He is a property agent. He rents out flats at exorbitant prices and takes a fat percentage.

But this evil genius has a wonderful get-rich-quick formula that cannot fail. He calls it the Slammed Doors Principle.

Statistics show that for every 100 married households that go through divorce, 153 dwellings will be needed. "That's an instant 53 per cent growth in the market," boasts Chen, which is not his real name.

For him personally, the figures are even better: he specialises in providing services to couples likely to argue. He can spot them a mile off.

"My best bets are self-centred young yuppies in the rapture of first love. They earn a bit of money and quickly move in together without much thought," he said.

Chen has studied the subject. In the UK alone, divorces are directly responsible for a demand for 80,000 new homes a year. A similar phenomenon is just starting in Asia, with a new generation of impetuous yuppies lining up to do the wrong thing with their partners. "Yuppies make the same mistakes as real people, but they make them more expensively," said the property agent.

Personally, I blame Hollywood for raising false expectations. In movieland, escapees from bad marriages are always whisked away to a fresh adventure by someone such as Dudley Moore or Kathleen Turner.

In real life only one in three divorced people find anyone at all to move in with straight away. And who is that person?

Statistics reveal the shocking fact that that person is almost always your mother. Well, not YOUR mother, but the individual concerned's mother, if you see what I mean. Of course, in the case of you, the reader, it would be YOUR mother.

This trend is particularly profitable in places such as Japan and Hong Kong, where a demand for ever-smaller pieces of birdcage-like accommodation is what the market caters for best.

Chen proudly points out that divorces have benefits (for him) that last for years. Splintered couples tend to go off and start new families. They then need larger homes to accommodate extra children visiting at weekends.

When I showed the first half of this essay to someone, she commented: "You should write that this property agent is a complete slimeball."

"I would," I replied. "But the editor dislikes tautology."

What worries me is that there is only one short step from profiting from the arguments of couples to actually interfering with relationships yourself.

Chen's biggest temptation, he admits, is to try to sow the seeds of discontent himself. I've seen him do it. This is the sort of thing that happens: a Yuplet and Yuplette in their early 20s come into his shop.

Yuplet: Have you got a one-bedroom flat in this area?

Chen: Certainly . . . (Nods in direction of Yuplette.) You're not thinking of moving in with her, are you?

Yuplet: (surprised) Yes. Why?

Chen: Oh, nothing, nothing. (Directs next question at Yuplette.) Are you sure you wouldn't prefer two bedrooms, you know, to have one spare?

Yuplette: We only need one bedroom.

(Chen restructures his cheek muscles and eyebrows to convey the silent message: if I could tell you half the things I know about this young man, you'd think differently.)

I asked Chen what he would do if all the couples on his book were unexpectedly getting on well for a long period of time, and not generating any new contracts.

"I might be tempted to stick my oar in," he said.

What precisely he meant by this phrase I did not wish to ask.

But I am going to be suspicious the next time he tells me he is spending the afternoon doing an in-depth probe into highly desirable places.

# Thanks for the Memories

## 1996

*Yang Yi Lung (John D. Young)*

It was yellow, stinky, and squarish. I pinched off a small piece and placed it in my mouth when someone behind me shouted, in Cantonese, *chu-si*. So ended my first taste of cheese. Who would want to eat pig excrement?

After all, there were plenty of other marvellous goodies available — chocolates, chewing gum, and beans, as well as shoes, blankets and on this particular occasion a US Army canvas bed. But the redheads and big noses handing out these free items were not military people, as the trucks they came on usually had huge red crosses painted on them. 'They are Jesus people,' I was told by some of the old ladies in the crowd.

I returned the cheese, and carried the bed home with my elder sister, and we slept in it for years. In those days, one of my mother's favourite sayings was 'Foreign goods last forever'.

Today, reflecting on my childhood years in Hong Kong during the 1950s brings memories of how different life was then. There was no running water, no supermarkets, no electricity (for a number of people), and certainly no television sets in most living rooms, at least not in the public housing estates of Diamond Hill where 'foreign aid' came to take care of us refugees from the mainland.

But there were plenty of opportunities to become familiar with Western things — although at that time I was not consciously aware of 'them' versus 'us'. One hot summer day, television finally came to our district's only herbal tea store, and everyone in the neighbourhood showed up in wooden clogs and pyjamas. There were old men who came in just in their underwear.

I have no recollection of the date, but I distinctly remember what I saw — *Robin Hood,* with Errol Flynn and Olivia de Haviland. I was glued to the tiny black-and-white screen, watching arrows fly and the man in the green suit fencing a bad guy with a beard.

Afterwards, I made my own bow and arrows. They lasted a long time, until one day I shot a rooster and was forced to eat it for dinner.

I also started to learn the Latin alphabet, not because I wanted to understand the movies, but because I needed this knowledge to get into school. It was a simple approach. I sat on a small wooden stool, and repeated out loud whatever my mother pointed out on a makeshift blackboard.

I also got language lessons from my best friend who lived across the road. At times, he would say to me: 'I have to learn the foreign language so that I can get a job in a hotel. But I hate foreign food.'

The first time I saw a sandwich, I asked my father, 'What is this triangle bread?' That was also the time I first tasted ham. I soon gave up sandwiches for something even more magical: ice-cream, or as the locals named it, ice-cakes. On special dates, the family would go to a restaurant called King of Kings and there we had the world's most wonderful round ice-cakes, in pink, orange, white, and brown.

Ice-cream became an important reward for my mother who rewarded me with a scoop when I recited the alphabet in the correct order. By the time I was seven, I knew all 26 letters by heart. With this 'foreign knowledge', I enrolled in a school called Good Hope.

After a year, I was kicked out for changing my grades in the report card. I wrote over all the red marks with a blue pen, got my parents' signature, and returned it to my teacher.

I don't think I left with a very good impression of the nuns, but I was grateful to some of the doctors at the local clinic. They all practised Western medicine.

I remember being terrified of their needles — but what was even more frightening was the thermometer. My concern was: 'What if I swallowed it?' Then one day a nurse with orange-coloured hair and a big nose told me I would be in trouble if I took the thermometer out of my mouth too soon. I did not know if trouble meant I would die, but I made sure that I held on to this instrument with tight lips.

The clinic was always full of people, many spitting indiscriminately although there were 'do not spit' signs on the walls. Perhaps because most of the spittoons were full from kids using them as urinals.

Good or bad, rich or poor, post-war Hong Kong was a society where East and West lived side-by-side. The East, willingly or otherwise, explored and experimented with different dimensions of the West, and subsequently came to terms with those aspects that had universal appeal.

This unique historical experience is vital and necessary, albeit painful at times, for Hong Kong to become what it is today. No other Chinese community in the world has experienced anything quite like it. Hong Kong as a confluence of the Occidental and Oriental, if nothing else, is worth preserving post July 1, 1997.

# Colonial Life and Times*

## 1997

*Charles Philip Martin*


**1841**   Dear Subscriber, Welcome to the world of *Colonial Life*, your magazine for all things relating to life in the far-flung outpost. We know you'll enjoy our many information and entertainment-packed articles. Watch out each month for new and exciting features guaranteed to keep you on the cutting edge. Here's what the well-read colonist will enjoy in coming months: new beauty treatment from the north (foreign mud facials), product review, durable new umbrellas that stand up to repeated thrashing of locals.

Enjoy *Colonial Life!* Please look over the terms and conditions of the enclosed treaty, which will remain in force indefinitely, all things being equal.

**1898**   Thank you for renewing your subscription to *Colonial Life*. You'll be delighted to know that starting next issue, a supplement called *The New Territories* will be added to your already feature-rich offering. In fact, we've got enough great material to keep you satisfied for, oh, 99 years. Happy reading!

**1910**   We know it's only been 12 years since you last renewed your subscription to *Colonial Life*, but we thought that now would be a great time to consider sending in your cheque and extending your subscription. Something might happen soon that would keep you preoccupied — who knows, an extra-long cricket match, a world war — and you might forget to renew. That would be a shame, especially with such great features coming up as: Sun Yat-sen ("Flash In The Pan") and "Win A Cruise On The Titanic" — White Star Line's newest and largest luxury ocean liner.

This is too good to miss! Renew now!

**1946**   Well, with the war and detention camps, there are probably plenty of reasons why you haven't got around to renewing your subscription to *Colonial Life*. Not to worry. Your subscription still has some time to go. And there's never been a better time to make sure you keep on enjoying all the wonderful features that *Colonial Life* brings you each month. Coming up soon: "The End Of An Era" (locals allowed on our beaches) and Mao Zedong ("Flash In The Pan").

So don't delay. Renew now!

**1967**   Have you forgotten? We've been waiting for you to renew your subscription to *Colonial Life* but we haven't heard from you. Remember, you only have 20 years left, so don't be left

---

\*   Reprinted with permission from South China Morning Post Publisher's Limited.

out in the cold. You don't want to miss out on coming features such as: "Artificial Flowers
— Too Bloody Expensive By Half!" and "Corruption In Hong Kong: Storm In A Teacup."

**1982**    Our records show that your subscription to *Colonial Life* is about to expire. You don't
want to be caught napping. Now is the time to show your determination and let everyone know
that you intend to hold on to *Colonial Life*, no matter what. Features include: "Home Decor
— The Three Legged Stool . . . Passé?" and "Property Investment In Hong Kong? Too Late!"

**1996**    Beware. You have just one year left of *Colonial Life*. It would be a shame to miss out
on all the great features that are on the way, like "Last-minute Gift Ideas — 60-second
Democracy".

**July 13, 1997**    Our records show that your subscription to *Colonial Life* expired two weeks
ago. Was it an oversight? We hope not. It's too late to take advantage of any special offers now.
However, as a consolation for a long-time subscriber, we have a special offer for you. Please
see the enclosed brochure on our new offering, Pitcairn Getaway. And thank you for your past
patronage.

# Lives in Transition*

## 1997

*Jesse Wong*

*A native of Hong Kong, Jesse Wong wrote for* The Asian Wall Street Journal *for over twenty years where he held various positions, including Hong Kong bureau chief. He attended Washington State University and worked in Canada as a journalist. An essay from his first book,* Lives in Transition, *appears here. He is now a freelance writer and lives in Hong Kong.*

———

## Uneasy Riders

Shenzhen, China — It is 1:30 a.m. on a six-lane stretch of superhighway. With only 20 kilometers to go before reaching China's border with Hong Kong, J.Y. Yung can look forward to the end of a working day that began more than 18 hours ago. But he isn't there yet.

Driving his container truck up an access road after stopping at a gas station, he spots two leather sofas in the glare of his headlights. It is an odd scene: In the dead of night, with open fields all around him, someone's discarded furniture is blocking his way in the middle of the road. But Mr. Yung has seen worse on the highways of south China, including dead animals and human corpses.

The corpses "could be genuine hit-and-run victims, or they could be props for some highway robbery or extortion scheme," he says, steering carefully around the sofas. "The important thing is to keep going and not stop."

Dodging trouble is all in a day's work for Mr. Yung, a streetwise 43-year-old who hauls cargo between Hong Kong's Kwai Chung container port and the clusters of boomtowns along the south China coast. The job keeps him shuttling between two worlds. In British-run Hong Kong, everything hums like clockwork. Once he crosses the border, he is in a chaotic society plagued by banditry and corruption.

To some outsiders with an eye on Hong Kong's July 1, 1997 reversion to Chinese rule, it seems a worrying contrast. Mr. Yung, who drives with a polyester red rose wired to the top of his dashboard, is content to take things as they come. "It's going to happen whether I like it or not. So why bother?" he says of the sovereignty transfer.

In the dark, his two-way radio crackles with the chatter of two drivers who speak of themselves as being "freedom-bound" — drivers' shorthand for the return trip to Hong Kong. Switching off the radio, Mr. Yung continues, "As long as business is OK, as long as the containers keep moving and I can drive my truck, I can't complain."

Business is most certainly OK with the Chinese Communist Party of the 1990s. If anything, it has replaced the radical politics of the past to become a national obsession, with government departments and the sons and daughters of many high officials in business either

———

openly or on the side. Evidently reassured, the Hong Kong property and stock markets are coasting to record highs even as the July 1 handover draws near.

The optimism isn't without foundation. With poor infrastructure and a rudimentary legal and financial system, China relies heavily on Hong Kong in business dealings with the rest of the world. That makes many of the territory's 6.2 million residents beneficiaries of the same economic liberalization that has spawned the seamy, money-grabbing side of modern-day China.

As an occupation, cross-border truck driving didn't exist in the early 1980s. Now there are about 20,000 drivers plying the routes — cogs in the machine that churns out the Barbie dolls and Nike shoes and Lee jeans that help make China an exporting power. (Chinese citizens aren't allowed to work as cross-border truck drivers because of concerns in both China and Hong Kong about illegal emigration from China.)

But money doesn't buy everything. Mr. Yung, with 10 years' experience on the highways of Hong Kong and south China, knows that well. "In Hong Kong, I have my dignity," he says. "I do my job, and the people in uniform do theirs. Over here, I'm at their mercy completely. All day long I plead and beg and go, 'Yes sir this' and 'Yes sir that.' But people get used to this kind of thing, I suppose."

On this day, he has delivered one container from the Chinese city of Shenzhen to Hong Kong and is now on the return leg of his journey, hauling a second container from Hong Kong to the northern edge of Shenzhen. The distance adds up to only about 120 kilometers; most of his time is spent waiting — waiting to clear customs, waiting in traffic and waiting for cargo to be loaded and unloaded.

A little after 8 p.m. finds him by the roadside. He stretches, gazing lazily about him. His hair is a thinning mop of scraggly curls. In his soggy T-shirt and shorts, with socks that slide down to his ankles, he looks like he has been moving a ton of bricks.

He has just made it past Wenjindu, one of two main border checkpoints in Shenzhen, after four hours snaking along in a kilometer-long line of traffic. All that is left for the day is to deliver his shipment of plastic pellets to a factory 50 kilometers to the north and then head back to the border checkpoint. By the time he reaches it he will have been on the road 19 hours.

For such a workday, which gives him time to go home and see his wife and son just a couple of times a week, he will be paid the equivalent of US$176, or US$88 per container. In his old job in a metal working factory in Hong Kong, he would be making half as much. But the money is hard-earned; many cross-border truck drivers acquire it at the cost of broken families. Some have paid with their lives.

In March a Hong Kong driver died after being shot during a robbery near the Wenjindu checkpoint. Muggings and murders happen in Hong Kong, too. But word among drivers is that the victim in this case bled to death after being refused hospital treatment for lack of a cash deposit. Shenzhen authorities denied the rumor, although reports are common of Chinese hospitals demanding disproportionately large deposits from would-be Hong Kong patients.

Mr. Yung hasn't run into any serious mishaps except for a couple of break-ins into his truck. Break-ins, however, can cost a driver dearly. To get around in China, a driver must carry about a dozen documents. Replacing any of them could take months of shuffling from one surly bureaucrat to another. So criminal gangs have taken to ransoming stolen documents. The going ransom for a yellow customs-registration book, without which truck and driver would be immobile, is 5,000 yuan (US$603). Its official replacement cost: 70 yuan.

Back on the road at 8:15 p.m., Mr. Yung says, "When you see these guys with nice shirts and bulky money-and-document bags strapped to their backs, you know right away they're Hong Kong truck drivers. They might as well walk around with 'Rob me' signs on their chests. Me, I just try to look Chinese."

Is the money he earns worth it, after all the hassles and the potential hazards? The question fills him with ambivalence.

Like many Hong Kong residents, he is a onetime emigrant from China. The country was dirt-poor in 1978 when he left, and so was he. In Hong Kong he toiled in the factories, saving enough money to start his own plastics molding plant but losing it all when the business folded. He saved again to buy a container truck, only to stumble a second time over cargo owners who didn't pay their bills. Now he is a hired hand driving for a trucking company.

His life has certainly improved over the years. But in his hometown in Hainan, an island province off the south China coast, some of his relatives are living better thanks to the country's economic boom. Compared with them, he is freer to speak his mind and freer from fear of bullying by government functionaries. Some days, though, that doesn't seem like enough.

"There are times when I regret having gone to Hong Kong. But there's no use thinking about it," Mr. Yung says, staring straight at the road ahead.

An hour after leaving Wenjindu, he approaches the Baimang checkpoint. Such inland checkpoints, strung along an east-west line some 40 kilometers north of the Hong Kong-Shenzhen border, are intended in large part to be a second line of defense against smugglers and illegal emigrants seeking to cross the international border. In practice, they pose an additional hassle for truck drivers.

Coming to a halt in front of a customs officer who stands with legs apart and hands behind his back, Mr. Yung rolls down his window and puts on a bright smile. "Good evening, sir," he says.

Expressionless, and with a cigarette hanging from his lips, the official gestures with a tilt of his head for Mr. Yung to pull into the parking bay for an inspection. It is Mr. Yung's unlucky night: Several trucks following his are allowed to continue without being stopped. "Yes, sir," Mr. Yung says cheerfully. After pulling away, he erupts into a string of expletives.

Hong Kong, which levies high import duties on tobacco, is a hot destination for cigarette smuggling. Coming the other way, everything from videocassette recorders to luxury yachts is in demand, given China's stiff import tariffs on a range of items. Mr. Yung once got a nasty surprise after he had delivered his load to its destination. Concealed in the shipment of plastic pellets without his knowledge were sets of heavy molding machinery.

To provide incentives for enforcement, China's central government permits each customs unit to keep as much as half of all fines and fees it collects. That has turned into an incentive to find fault. A detailed customs inspection of just one container can take several days even if the cargo is legitimate. To save time, drivers and cargo owners often are prepared to pay bribes.

Several months ago, Mr. Yung was stopped for carrying only 7 1/2 tons of plastic instead of 15 tons as his shipping documents specified. A customs officer declared on the spot that a 20,000 yuan fine had to be paid. After conferring with the cargo owner, Mr. Yung negotiated the payment down to about half the original amount.

Recounting the episode, Mr. Yung says, "I said to the customs officer, 'The owner wants to know if this could be settled for 5,000 yuan.' The officer turned around and walked away at once, saying, 'I don't sense any sincerity here.' As soon as I heard his reply I figured that it was going to be OK."

So was it a fine that the cargo owner ended up paying, or was it a bribe? "I didn't get a receipt," Mr. Yung replies.

He has been through similar situations often. "You must understand that the government hardly pays these customs guys enough to live on. It isn't so terrible for the Chinese to learn to appreciate the value of money and to want to have money. For China, that's real progress," he says, resting his bare feet on the steering wheel and massaging his toes while waiting at the Baimang checkpoint for customs inspection to proceed.

The inspection tonight proves a tame affair that lasts only 40 minutes. Three barefoot laborers are instructed by the customs officer to unload the container. With about 100 sacks of plastic pellets on the ground, the laborers stop to argue among themselves over whether the shipment totals 640 sacks as declared by Mr. Yung. No one bothers to examine the bags' contents.

Mr. Yung pays a 215 yuan inspection fee, accepts an official receipt, and is off. Another driver in a similar situation might have offered a payoff to avoid going through with the formality, Mr. Yung figures. "The customs people expect the drivers to pay them off because they know that to the drivers, time is money. But I don't want to spoil them," he says.

His destination is on the northwestern edge of Shenzhen, near a community called Songgang that has little besides low-rise factory buildings and dormitories. It is close to 11 p.m. by the time the shipment is unloaded and he is on his way again, finally ready for dinner. A few minutes later, he pulls up at a cheap hotel along the highway.

In the dimly lit gravel lot, a figure approaches him as soon as he jumps off his truck. It is a young woman, about 20 years old, wearing tight blue jeans and a low-cut blouse. The contrast between her lipstick and face is accented by the pale street light.

He says no and, after she has merged back into the shadows, observes that it is a bad idea to pick up women in unfamiliar locations. Later, eating in a restaurant inside the hotel, he mulls the widely held perceptions in Hong Kong of cross-border truck drivers as philanderers.

"If you ask me if truck drivers care about their families, my answer would be yes, 90% or more of truck drivers care a lot about their families. If you ask me if truck drivers play around, my answer would be yes, too, for 90% of us. We aren't bad husbands and fathers. It's just that sometimes the pressure gets to a point where we don't know how to cope."

With dinner over by 12:30 a.m., he is back in the cab of his truck. He is going nowhere in a hurry, as the Wenjindu checkpoint is closed for the night. But he wants to get into line early so he doesn't have to spend all day waiting after the checkpoint reopens in the morning. Already, he figures, a line of trucks a kilometer long, their drivers sleeping inside the cabs, will have formed at the border.

At a set of traffic lights, he stops and lights a cigarette, waiting for the red to change to green. It does, and his truck begins to roll into the intersection.

From a distance, a van no bigger than the rear wheels of Mr. Yung's container truck comes at him against the red light. The van shows no sign of slowing as it approaches the intersection with its horn blaring and its high beams blinking. Having spotted it in good time, Mr. Yung stops and allows it to pass. Then he calmly shifts into gear again.

"Most drivers from Hong Kong wouldn't have stopped for this guy," he says, gazing at the van's vanishing tail-lights. "Coming from Hong Kong, you'd expect him to stop, if not for the red light, then certainly for a truck 20 times his size. But here, Hong Kong logic doesn't apply."

*November 13, 1996*

# Our Elders

## 2000

*Hark Yeung and Fong So*

## Chapter 7

I got interested in my mother's sense of insecurity when a friend told me that her own mother had become terribly nervous after her aunt suffered a fatal stroke during a burglary.

'Didn't you say that your house was looted when you were young?' I asked my mother. I was having tea with her and my father in a Chinese restaurant on a bright autumn Sunday nearly a year after the trip to *xiangxia*. I had finished two essays about them and had got more interested in their stories.

'Oh, yes! Bandits looted the whole village! Rumour had it that some of the family were working for the bandits. The village was walled and had a drawbridge. It was not easy to break into . . . At that time my mother had taken us to my maternal grandfather's house.'

'Why?'

'Because my paternal grandfather had been kidnapped and my mother was afraid that the bandits would come to take my elder brother as well . . .'

'Oh, kidnapping was very common at that time. One of your uncles narrowly escaped a kidnapping because the bandits knew that he was the only son in the family. That's why he came to live in my village . . .' my father interrupted.

'What happened to your grandfather?' I asked my mother.

'Ha, he was really funny! After living in South Africa for many years, he wasn't afraid of anything . . . He said to the bandits, "Don't ill-treat me! I'm sure my sons and daughters-in-law will pay the ransom. One of my daughters-in-law is very rich. I eat green bean soup everyday. Please prepare that for me. If you happen to go to a teahouse, bring along some dim sum for me. Take good care of me. If I die, you won't get any money." At that time, there were only women in the family. My mother was the one who negotiated with the bandits. My father was dead and my uncles were in South Africa. After talking with the bandits two or three times, my mother paid the ransom, with money from my maternal grandfather, something like a hundred thousand Hong Kong dollars. At that time the bandits wanted Hong Kong dollars and they called them Western dollars . . .'

'A hundred thousand Hong Kong dollars? That was a huge amount of money in the thirties. How come your mother had so much money?'

'Perhaps less, I'm not that sure. I was just a few years old. But my mother's family was very rich. They had a wholesale business in Guangzhou, selling peanut oil. The ransom was not just the money. The bandits also demanded more than a hundred pieces of men's underwear made in England, a famous brand called 555 . . .'

'Of course 555! They were really popular and everybody wanted to have some. They could only be bought in special shops in Guangzhou. That was always part of a ransom at that time . . .' my father interrupted again.

'The bandits also wanted large cartons of a very popular brand of cigarette called . . . Black Cat? A carton had ten small packs . . . There were twenty cigarettes in a pack . . .'

'Twenty! No! No, at that time the packs were smaller, only ten cigarettes . . . Black Cat was not the most popular brand . . .' my father said.

'Your grandmother said, "How can I let them kill an old man?" So she paid. Also she believed that the bandits had come for my elder brother. But we happened to be out, so they took my grandfather instead. My grandma was shot by the bandits. She tried to stop them from burning her silk. My grandparents used to have a small silk factory. She bled to death.'

'Do you think that's why you're always afraid when you are alone?' I asked my mother seriously.

'No. I've never thought about it. Perhaps . . . Yes, perhaps that's why . . . But also because of the bombing during the Japanese invasion,' my mother said after a while. 'My father used to do business in Shanghai until the Japanese dropped a bomb right next to his shoe shop. He had a terrible shock. He came back to our village and died a few months later.'

I turned to my father. 'What do you want me to write about if I want to write about you?'

'Of course you must write about my *xiangxia*,' my father said proudly. 'Listen. We had young soldiers even before the Japanese invasion, can you imagine? One of my uncles was a graduate of the Huangpu Military Academy, the top military academy in China at that time. But he didn't like the war so he went back to his home village and gave military training to the boys there . . . You'd better record the couplets in our home village as well,' he recited the couplet.

'How about you? What do you want me to write about you?' I asked.

'I haven't finished talking about *xiangxia* yet . . .' he recited the couplet again.

Knowing that he would go on to talk about his *xiangxia* for some time, I turned to my mother.

'What kind of child was I?'

'You?' She said with a scornful smile. 'If you saw a chair was in your way, you didn't even bother to push it away, you just went round it . . . You just read your books.'

'I remembered that you used to say to me, nearly everyday, "What use are you? You don't teach your younger brothers! What's the point of you getting good results? You are useless! You are selfish!" '

'Of course you were useless! You didn't teach your younger brothers!' my mother said angrily. Then she turned to Fong So and said, 'Can you imagine what she said to me? "I study on my own and they should study by themselves. They should pay attention during lessons . . ." '

'What else do you want me to write about?' I turned to my father again.

'Once, during the Japanese invasion, your uncles and I wanted to visit a place near the railway. At that time, the Japanese soldiers occupied the big houses near the railway. When we were there, the Japanese soldiers suddenly appeared. They probably thought that we were trying to destroy the railway and they chased us. We jumped into a fish pond. They used a speedboat to go after us. That was the most dangerous moment in my life . . . Normally the Japanese soldiers were nice to the children in the village. When they were on a train, they threw those one-cent coins into fish ponds. Sometimes they threw bread into the ponds as well. Many children in the village, including me, would jump into the fish ponds to get those coins and the bread . . .'

'Only people in your village would take things thrown away by the Japanese soldiers!' my mother interrupted. 'The people in our village never took anything! The Japanese always threw rice out but no one in our village took it. They cooked wheat with rice. Strange! We only ate our own food . . . We never took any food from the Japanese . . .' she said proudly. My mother has a special kind of sentiment towards China. Twenty years ago, when I was travelling in Nanjing in Central China, I spent all the money she had given me on an expensive antique inkstone. I thought she would scold me when she heard what I had done. But she did not. She just held the inkstone in her hand and said there were many good things in China and we should try to keep them.

'The vegetable trolley is coming, what kind of vegetable do you want?' Fong So asked me all of a sudden.

'No. No. Eat vegetables in an expensive restaurant like this? How ridiculous! For a few dollars, we can buy a big bag in the market! Tens of dollars for a dish here . . .' my father objected angrily.

'Get a dish of vegetables,' Fong So looked at me. 'You have nothing to eat. All the dishes we have ordered are meat dishes . . .'

'You're hopeless! You don't eat meat!' my father shouted at me. 'What's the point of being a vegetarian? You are useless! Useless! You don't eat meat, how stupid . . .'

'OK OK, don't order any vegetables,' I said to Fong So.

'But you haven't eaten anything . . .' Fong So was still trying to attract the attention of the woman serving vegetables.

'Ordering vegetable dishes in a restaurant like this! How stupid!'

'Forget the vegetables, Fong So . . . Get another meat dish . . .' I said.

My father started talking about the allocation of the shares of the newly privatised Mass Transit Railway. That had been the talk of the town and nearly eight percent of the local population had tried to buy the shares.

The chandelier in the restaurant made me think of the Sunday dinners my parents used to hold and those uncles whose families were on the mainland. In my father's *xiangxia*, I met one of them. He had gone back there to live, after he retired, like my old uncle. I had met another recently in Hong Kong and he told me that he would never consider living in his *xiangxia* because his friend had died during a minor operation in a hospital on the mainland and he did not trust the hospitals there.

The old man sitting at the table next to ours was leaving, he had been sitting there alone for a long time. He was wearing a pair of old glasses and looked bewildered. He reminded me of the old man in a photo I took in the eastern part of Germany in mid-1990, shortly after the West German mark become the official currency. That old man was trying to cross the road but could not, as if the road had become, all of a sudden, too busy and difficult for him. Then I remembered my mother telling me how unstable the currency was on the mainland before 1949. 'What was worth a bag of rice in the morning could be worth only half a bag in the afternoon.' My mother said that after the handover of Hong Kong in 1997, when the Hong Kong dollar was under pressure and there were daily rumours that it would be devalued.

When the waitress was making the table next to us ready for a new customer, she asked him, 'Should I buy some shares in the stock market tomorrow?'

'Yes, buy more in the morning, the market will go up at least five hundred points tomorrow,' the customer said to her.

'You should also write about your grandfather,' my father said after taking another meat dish. 'Your grandfather used to work in a gambling house. He was the banker of the game because he was well known for his honesty. Also he kept calm, no matter how big the bets were. Whenever he won some money, he always gave his children dumplings as a treat. I was very happy if I had dumplings to eat when I was young. But when you were young, even if I wanted to take you to a teahouse to have dim sum, you refused to go . . . In my *xiangxia*, there were professional gamblers . . .'

It was true that I was not enthusiastic about those treats my parents gave us after they had won money in mahjong or horseracing. It was because when my parents lost money, the children were often accused of having done or said unlucky things.

'There were professional gamblers everywhere at that time,' said my mother. 'If there were no professional gamblers in a village, the village would be very poor.'

'Yes, in my village, there were gambling houses and places selling opium. That was why my village was rich,' my father said.

'You know, your grandmother's shop, the one your great-grandfather gave your grandmother when she got married, was rented out. The ground floor was a gambling house and the first floor was a place selling opium. They used to pay rent every day, not every month. At that time, only that kind of business could survive,' my mother said.

'How about after you came to Hong Kong, what do you want me to write about?'

'There's nothing worth writing about,' my father said.

'And you?' I asked my mother.

'There's nothing worth writing about,' my mother said.

I looked around. The headline in the newspaper on that day, October 15, 2000, was about the past: the Premier of China was visiting Japan and the TV audience there had asked him why the Chinese endlessly asked the Japanese to make a proper apology and pay compensation.

After the tea, I looked at the photos of old people I had taken in the past ten years. One of them was taken on the day of the handover of Macau when I happened to walk past a crowd while the lowering of the Portuguese flag was being broadcast live. Many people were watching the television, among them an old man whose expression I could not forget. Perhaps he had come to Macau as a refugee and suddenly found that he was back in China again. When I saw that photo, I thought of my parents who had stayed in Macau for a while in the fifties.

'When we go to Macau again, perhaps I can invite my parents to go with us,' I said to Fong So.

'Are you sure?' Fong So asked.

'Didn't you encourage me to be kind to my parents?'

'Your parents are much more easy-going when they're with your younger brother, but with you . . . I won't encourage you to spend time with them any more. I thought my family was problematic enough, I could not imagine yours could be worse. One of the reasons that your parents dislike you so much, I think, is that you don't eat the food they eat.'

'You think that's the reason?' I laughed. 'But it's true that I was not enthusiastic about food, especially meat, even when I was small.'

'They don't let you have the food you need, even if you're the one who pays,' Fong So said. 'I won't encourage you to spend time with them any more. You won't make them happy.'

'Can I make anyone happy? The only thing I know is that I will be happy only if I am determined to look for happiness by myself.'

I looked at the photos of the old women in the former Soviet Union. There were so many widows, created by wars and dictators. There were always old women selling eggs and potatoes in the bitter cold at the railway stations along the Trans-Siberian railway. In big cities like

Moscow, they usually sat idly in the open, very much like many of the old people in Hong Kong, as if there was no other place for them. Fong So told me that once, on his way to a bus terminal near my parents' flat, he saw my father sitting in a small open space under a huge flyover, along with other old people, doing nothing. Coming from a farming village, my father has never got used to the small flat he has been living in all these years and likes to stay outdoors.

The place where I took a lot of photos of old people was Greenland, a Danish colony. In Upernavik, a city north of the Arctic Circle where most of the Inuit population were still hunters, I stayed with a woman, half Danish and half Greenlander, who managed the old people's home. It was a paradise compared with the old people's homes in Hong Kong: each resident had a spacious room with a spectacular view of the Arctic Sea.

'In the past old people used to tell stories in winter and children used to listen to them. Now children spend their time watching television. Our society is changing too fast, there's no ground for old people to stand on. It's difficult for their children to take care of them . . . It's impossible for me to live with my mother-in-law,' the manager told me. Her own mother-in-law, who had three sons, also lived in that old people's home. 'In the old people's home, the residents have all they need but they are not happy.'

# North Wind

## 2001

*Nury Vittachi*

The rain doesn't fall in Hong Kong. It attacks. It leaps from umbrella to umbrella until it finds an opening through which it can find something expensive to ruin, like suede or silk. Sometimes the rain falls *up*. It deliberately misses you on the way down and then ricochets from the pavement toward your lower limbs. The moisture establishes a beachhead at your ankles, from which it scrambles up your trousers until your thighs become clammy and cold. And then, when you finally reach somewhere warm, dry and sheltered, it stops.

So it was on the night of June 30, 1997. An ocean of tears fell on Britain's farewell "Sunset Ceremony" that evening, soaking fresh school children and over-ripe statesmen alike. But when dignitaries entered the halls for the midnight handover of sovereignty from Britain to China, the precipitation halted, halfway down the sky. It then scurried back up to clouds, to bide its time for a morning rush-hour attack.

So now, half an hour after the flags had been changed, everything is wet, but the air is crystal clear.

It is past midnight, but it seems as if every light in every building in Central is on. Some children are carrying glowing light-toys left over from the Mid-Autumn Festival. Sweating TV crews are heaving painfully bright floodlights, like portable suns, across Statue Square. People recoil as it sears their retinas. The dazzle from the heart of Central is changing the midnight sky into an opaque, shifting, grey mass, like a huge ghost.

\*    \*    \*    \*

It was Thursday, June 26, and I was in a *baaaad* mood. Every day, a representative of the many-headed monster called The Meeja (the media) had been tramping into the newspaper offices and plonking itself down in front of me. Now these weren't the intelligent correspondents who had been in Hong Kong for years. No, these were what were called *Firemen* in newspaper slang. Something dramatic happened, and these guys were sent off to deal with it. They knew nothing about this region and had no real interest in it. They just wanted a few headlines to fill their pages or broadcast time slots.

Earlier in the year, Fenby and I were running pretty much neck and neck in terms of the numbers of television crews that came and filmed us, although in the past week or so he had overtaken me. I was getting a full television crew twice every three days, whereas they seemed to be trekking into his office on almost a daily basis this week. In every interview I ever saw him give, he reiterated his commitment to total independence and said that there was no interference from the proprietor. I was troubled by the ease with which my friend managed to maintain this line.

I was in a bad mood because yet more interviewers had grilled me that morning, and I knew from their questions what their stories were going to be. They were all missing the point.

Everyone was focusing on Hong Kong: how it was going to change, whether its freedoms would remain, when its character would be subsumed by China and so on. They liked to focus on Hong Kong, because it was like their home cities. It was full of capitalists, and first world families worrying about human rights and the rule of law and so on.

— But this story isn't about Hong Kong. This story is about China, I said to several news crews. — What is Hong Kong? A pimple. A city of six million people. It doesn't matter what happens to us — not for our own sakes, anyway. What is China? A fifth of the human world. What really matters here is what effect the handover has on China. The mainland will change, once Hong Kong is a part of it. It has to. And that is the significance of the event that would happen in four days' time. That was the question that we should be asking.

The bimbette who was interviewing me looked baffled. She turned to simpler matters.

— And what do you think of Mr Hwa?

— That's Mr Tung.

I decided to use my Saturday column for an essay pointing out that the media were asking the wrong question. How China would be changed was more important than how Hong Kong would be changed.

*July 1 is the birth date of the new Hong Kong, yes.*

*But that's not why that date is important.*

*The reason July 1 is important is because it is the birth date of the new China.*

*A China with us in its belly is not the same as a China without us.*

*The best analogy I can think of is that Hong Kong is a bran tablet. These things are small and inoffensive when you take them, but they kind of invisibly expand in your stomach once they are in there, and have a beneficial effect.*

*They also produce huge amounts of gas and hot air while the adjustments are being made, which I think fits the analogy rather neatly.*

*And let's be honest about this. As Hong Kong changes, some 6.3 million of us will be affected, and the rest of the world isn't going to be much bothered, whichever way it goes.*

*But as China changes, it is going to make a HUGE difference to the future history of this planet.*

*And that's the real reason why July 1, the birth date of the new China, matters.*

# Myself a Mandarin

## 1968

*Austin Coates*

*The author of several books about Hong Kong, Macau and other parts of Asia, Austin Coates spent most of his adult life in Hong Kong. He was posted from England in 1949 as assistant colonial secretary and also district officer magistrate in the New Territories, an experience that was the basis of* Myself a Mandarin *(excerpted here). He later moved to Sarawak where he was secretary to the governor and adviser on Chinese affairs. In 1962, he returned to Hong Kong and became a full-time writer, living on Cheung Chau. He died in 1997 at the age of 75.*

In the district I had to conduct many negotiations with Chinese people — commercial negotiations, usually involving land, and political negotiations, some with communist organizations; others — more complicated — were with local power groups. Some of these negotiations were by no means easy, and had it not proved possible to bring them to agreeable conclusions, some of them would have led to public disorder, and to the imposition of government orders by force — the mark of failure.

These negotiations taught me a number of things, some of which — stepping once more from the smaller to the larger dimension — I believe to be relevant to the greater general question of negotiation with China.

A Chinese negotiation differs from negotiation elsewhere in two respects: in its indirectness, and in what may be termed a margin of indefiniteness.

The degree of indirectness required in a Chinese negotiation is something which is apt to reduce any but the most patient Westerner to exasperation. Everything, from start to finish and at all levels, must be done indirectly, to avoid all possibility of any kind of confrontation or show-down. No contrary word should be uttered except to a third party, who will transmit it in his own way — often, be it added, in a wrong sense, which has subsequently to be rectified by similar indirect methods.

It is all but useless for a negotiator, whether diplomatic or commercial, to go to China and expect to discuss matters with his opposite number. Negotiation is the work of underlings, who on the Chinese side will be provided. If the Western negotiator arrives without underlings of his own, he has instantly lost his status.

The very last thing that a negotiator is expected to do in China is to negotiate. The duty of the principal person in a negotiation is to meet his opposite number, engage him in delightful dinner parties and pleasant country excursions, give well-chosen presents to his hosts and hostesses, and be amiable. The perfectly conducted negotiation is one in which neither of the principal persons concerned ever has to refer to the matter in hand.

This may sound like something out of an antique fairy tale, but it is not. It is China as it was, as it is, and as it will be. The Chinese dislike of direct confrontations is exceedingly deep, pervading Chinese life from beginning to end. A Westerner who reckons without it will get nowhere.

To take an absurdly small example of how it works, there was a time when my cook was not making bacon and eggs in quite the way I like them. I did not dare tell him so, since this, in its very small way, would have been a confrontation. Instead, I telephoned his 'back mountain', the man who years earlier had recommended him to me, and said, "Please ask him not to overcook the bacon." The speed with which this message was transmitted was reflected in the bacon and eggs next day being entirely to satisfaction. As he brought them in, my cook gave me a knowing look and was happy, because the matter had been conducted in a proper way. Never a word was said.

Six months living with a Chinese family is, I reckon, just about the time required to ensure that the unprepared Westerner will end in a mental institution. Matters which, in the West, would be settled by a three-minute telephone call and prompt delivery of the goods, in a Chinese family often take hours, days, weeks to achieve, while the family try one go-between, who turns out to be the wrong one, then try someone else, then give up hope for a week, and then suddenly think of the right person, and the matter is settled in minutes.

Life in the family house is delightful; everything is beautifully run; the food is marvellous; and people are considerate of one another to a truly remarkable degree. The outcome, in other words, is the same as in a Western home — in some ways better — but the mechanics by which this is achieved are entirely different. Matters which in the West would take a long time to fix are resolved on the instant. You never know what to expect. All you have to remember, as a Westerner, is to be patient. Family dramas which in the West would set any family into commotion — such as the eldest son running away with a call-girl — will be received with such complete calm (because the family are doing something about it in their own way) that you would never know anything was wrong. Then one day you will hear the whole house in uproar, and wonder what on earth is the matter, only to discover that father has come home with mud on his trousers, having been sprayed by a passing car.

Staying in a Chinese home — this is a digression, but it may perhaps help to illustrate the main point — nothing will be explained to you, and you must learn never on any account to ask questions, even the simplest ones, since propriety in matters of conversation is yet another matter which differs entirely from the West.

Hilarious and ribald conversations, in which even grandmother will participate, will be held on subjects which in the West would be enough to reduce any dinner-table to stunned silence. Yet a simple inquiry — about a member of the family, perhaps, and which in the West would be considered thoughtful and polite — may easily prove to be indelicate, and cause embarrassment.

One of the difficulties here is that Chinese take it for granted that nothing is said without a motive; and thus, if a motive is not at once apparent (the Western motive simply being to say something polite), it will set people thinking, wondering what you are really up to.

In the West, though most of us are unconscious of this, we say many things without a motive, it often being polite to do so. In the West, for example, we say, 'I hope you are well', when it has never occurred to us to hope either one way or the other; we have simply said it 'in a manner of speaking' — a phrase which to Chinese is very revealing of the West, since it implies insincerity. In China you do not say things 'in a manner of speaking'. You either say, or you do not say. And where we say, 'I hope you are well', Chinese say 'Are you well?' — in which case, if they hope you are not, at least they have not had to say they hope you are.

It is from such small points that the angles between China and the West widen into great differences, and into much misunderstanding. To use the same illustration, to say 'I hope you are well' in Chinese has such a strange ring about it, that it would instantly be deduced you hoped the exact opposite. Thus, as a Westerner arriving in China, even when shaking hands with someone, you have to remember where you are. Nothing — *nothing* — is as it would seem.

The other unusual aspect of a Chinese negotiation is the margin of indefiniteness which must always be left at the end of it.

Earlier on, discussing religion, and again discussing geomancy, just when it seemed that the moment was drawing near when the absolute fundamentals of Chinese belief would be revealed, it was found that these were situated in the empty spaces between two Western words, and could not be brought within the tactile grasp.

This is so true of China, when it comes to submitting things to Western analysis, that it could perhaps be called the most important point of all. I have many times said privately that the only sure way of discussing the deepest aspects of Chinese philosophy and life is after a little liquor, and in pidgin English. The liquor allows for inexactitudes, while pidgin English, albeit rigidly exact, has between each word those merciful interstices of indefiniteness, without taking account of which, and without recognizing as being *permanent* interstices — sheer blank space — China cannot be understood, far less enjoyed.

Here the difficulty is that the Western mind simply will not leave such blank spaces alone. What is *in* them, people ask? How *can* there be such a thing as a blank space in the thinking of an entire civilization?

There is a blind spot in everyone's eye. When it is brought to anyone's attention, the fact is recognized. But what do you see when you try to look through it? And what advantage is there in trying?

The point is that, despite its blind spot, the eye is a perfect organ of the human body. So, too, is it with the Chinese interstices. They are not a deficiency. The thought and reasoning in Chinese civilization are complete. It is simply that there are certain points on which Chinese thought remains deliberately indefinite; and to seek to define what is there in those interstices is as foolish as to try to see through the blind spot in your own eye.

This factor of the indefinite has a most important relevance to negotiation as well as to manners, the making of arrangements, and many other things. The Western insistence on obtaining exact facts, making precise definitions and drawing absolute conclusions, breaks down in China somewhere between ninety-five and ninety-eight in the hundred degrees. A Westerner who persists in demanding exactitudes after ninety-five is a bore, after ninety-eight rude. Contracts, oaths, sworn statements, and suchlike are other features of the West which can never be more than 95 per cent respected in China — if that — since they deal with absolutes; and to the Chinese mind, the absolute is essentially absurd, because it does not exist.

The West, with its transcendentalism, dogma, anathema, and similar concepts, will not accept the truth of this. The West instinctively *seeks* absolutes, *desires* them. Its philosophical books reek of them, and to the Chinese mind are consequently indescribably dull, since the philosophers are dealing with what they should surely have realized before they started was *unreal,* as Chinese see it.

Similarly, in the West, people desire a perfect car, a perfect servant, a perfect house, all of which denotes the same striving for the impossible, and is — when one comes to think of it — ridiculous. If one can arrange matters 90 per cent to satisfaction, one can already consider oneself extremely fortunate. After that, relax. What happens if you fill a glass 100 per cent full? The wine spills on the tablecloth. Even in the West, it is recognized that a wineglass should not be more than about 90 per cent full. In China a wineglass should be filled 98 per cent, with the meniscus just reaching to the brim. 98 per cent, in other words, means full.

Ah! the Western mind exclaims. What you are actually recommending is a policy of *laisser-aller,* the thin end of the wedge, agreements that need not be scrupulously adhered to.

When an agreement is scrupulously adhered to, it is because of the *character* of those who have agreed to it, and the degree of understanding that exists between them. It is not because of the written contract, which, when it comes to it, is merely a reminder of the points that have been previously agreed to. It is this element of *character,* which throughout the Orient is the most important of all criteria of judgment, which might in a sense — and here I succumb to my own Western dislike of blank spaces — be said to lie in those subtle interstices of indefiniteness.

Because of this element in Chinese thinking — the element that has no time for absolutes — a Westerner has to be careful not to press too hard or too far in negotiation. The Western technique of making extreme demands, then moderating them, until an agreed balance is reached, is of course fatal in China. Moderate a demand, and you lose face. In a negotiation, the moment reached when you have created the position in which you can make demands, have in mind clearly what you want, and demand 70 per cent of it. In most instances, the next 25 per cent beyond this will be understood by the other side, and thus can by gentle steps be gained. The last 5 per cent is sacrosanct.

I remember once being sent into another country to conduct a Chinese negotiation, and having with me a European colleague unfamiliar with the Orient. I spent more time arguing with him than with the people we had been sent to negotiate with. He simply could not understand why, at a Chinese dinner, when we had our host perfectly poised in the position wherein we could make our final demand, I would deflect the conversation into some channel of frivolity and let the opportunity pass. Returned to our hotel, my colleague would be furious with me. Had I no sense of responsibility?

I tried to explain to him that, had we pressed our advantage, we would have ruined the dinner party, and by bringing matters to complete definiteness — the one thing at all costs to be avoided — would have soured up the entire course of the negotiation, besides giving our hosts a poor impression of our *character* as negotiators.

He never understood me; and when we finally left, with various points still undecided, he did not know what to make of it, complaining afterwards that we could have struck a far harder bargain, had I not so consistently bungled matters.

Indeed, we could have struck a far harder bargain. But Westerners who strike hard bargains do not last long in the Orient. In the nineteenth century, the nations of Europe struck hard bargains with China, made exact demands, and got everything they wanted. By the 'unequal treaties', China was humiliated. The humiliation, however, did not lie in the fact that the West was strong. That, with a hard swallow, could have been tolerated. The humiliation was that China was dictated to by people who behaved like boors.

Moreover, what was the outcome? Where are all those treaty ports and special concessions today? Losses such as Europe has suffered in China exemplify what will always happen if Chinese are pressed too hard.

An agreeably concluded negotiation can leave many things unsettled; and in all negotiation, something should always be left uncertain, to be decided by goodwill. This also leaves matters open to revision in the event of possible future ill-will, which is useful. Francis

Bacon put much the same thing in a different way when he wrote, 'Love as if you were sometime to hate, and hate as if you were sometime to love.'

Finally, in a diplomatic or governmental negotiation, in which the Western negotiator will naturally have his own principles of proceeding, it is important never to forget the principles which will be guiding matters on the Chinese side. There will probably be no visible signs of it, but the Chinese officials will almost surely be sticking closely to their own maxim of the three principles, or duties, of sound government. These are:

to simulate friendship;
to express honeyed sentiments; and
to treat your inferiors as your equals.

Thus when a diplomat in China — or indeed any Westerner engaged in formal business — finds himself being treated on terms of delightful equality, let him be on his guard; he is almost certainly being used for some ulterior purpose. The ambassador of the most powerful nation, with nuclear warheads and other mighty armament, is basically, from the instant of setting foot on the soil of China, and despite everything that may suggest the contrary, just another foreigner, i.e. inferior to the humblest farmer or shop assistant. A foreigner in China *is* inferior. He is inferior because more than 700,000,000 people all around him think so. There is no argument about it.

Then surely, it will be asked, it must be impossible to make true friends. Strangely enough, this is not so. As anyone who has lived among Chinese people will testify, Chinese friendship, once established, is of the truest.

But, in China, who *are* your friends? Your friends are those who have come to know and esteem you sufficiently to enable them to forgive, but not overlook, the fact that you are a foreigner. They are those who are aware that you are genuinely trying to behave properly, according to Chinese canons, and who, though they will be embarrassed, are prepared to forgive you when you unintentionally say or do something indelicate or indiscreet. On their side, they are in addition people with sufficient courage of their convictions not to mind being seen with you in public, since it should be remembered that in normal Chinese society, to be seen with foreigners is lowering.

The Chinese top-level, Westernized segment of society particularly demonstrates this quality of social courage, looking as they often do beyond the frontiers of China, and seeing things in a wider perspective. But when it comes to it, they too none the less regard themselves as innately superior, as you quickly discover if you accidentally rub them up the wrong way.

I was once in conversation with one of Europe's most eminent sinologues. He was married to a Chinese lady from a family of high standing, and I happened to know that the sinologue was *bien vu* by his Chinese in-laws. He thus seemed to be the right person of whom to ask a question, about which I had long wondered, namely, surely the circumstances — albeit rare ones — must exist in which a Chinese is capable of regarding a foreigner as a brother?

He thought for quite a long time, then nodded, and said:

"As a younger brother, yes."

To the reader familiar with China and the Chinese, all of this will seem very old stuff; but it will be agreed, I believe, that these are things that need to be stated and re-stated, since without taking them into account, no real understanding between China and the West will ever be possible.

The world is changing so quickly, its nations and races are drawing so markedly closer to one another in understanding, and in their material desires, that each year it becomes progressively more difficult to take in the fact that similar changes are not taking place among the Chinese, even in non-communist Chinese society. The Chinese do change — they have changed immeasurably since the turn of the century, and a great deal in even the past twenty years. But these changes are changes occurring within the orbit of Chinese civilization, which is distinct and separate, having, as was seen in the illustration of the Chinese family home, a different mechanism.

Within their own society, in other words, there is continual change; but in all that pertains to relations between a Chinese and a member of another race, there has been no change of any real significance; and this is something which has to be remembered by anyone who engages in the conduct of a Chinese negotiation.

A Cantonese friend of mine — and this is referring to Kwangtung, the dictionary — once explained the matter to me thus: the traditional Chinese psychological reaction to a foreigner is, firstly, not to hurt him, and secondly, to remember he is an enemy. The reason for not hurting him is the same as for not hurting animals; and, to give the completing touch to the complexity of it all, it has to be remembered that the very word for 'foreigner' in Chinese, when written down, has beside it the radical strokes denoting the genus 'animal'.

# Crusade for Justice

## 1981

*Elsie Elliott (Elsie Tu)*

*A political activist, champion of the underdog and educator, Elsie Tu originally came to China from England in 1947 as a missionary and later moved to Hong Kong which became her home. She is a former member of the Legislative Council. Among the many awards she received in recognition of her work was a CBE. Her autobiography* Crusade for Justice, *published under her former name Elsie Elliot, is excerpted here. She runs the Mu Kuang School which was founded by her late husband.*

---

Others besides myself had problems in setting up schools for the underprivileged. It now seems clear that the government was hedging, not because Nissen huts were unhealthy, but because they did not want to provide education for the underprivileged. Several missionaries who were running schools mentioned that the government put every obstacle in their way, and it seemed they simply did not want them to provide education for the poor.

Was it because the legislators were business people and wanted to keep a cheap labour market? Was it because the Financial Secretary did not want to spend public money on the education of the underprivileged? Whatever the reason, free primary education for all children only came into being in 1971, a century later than it had been introduced by a Japanese Imperial Government in Japan. By 1971 it was clear that crime began with some primary school drop-outs, as well as with children who did not attend school at all. Most homes could only manage if both parents worked, so the children were often left without supervision. One-parent families could not exist on the pittance of public assistance, and those children too were left to their own devices. Some found jobs for their children. It was probably a lesser evil than idleness, child labour was an open secret. I have myself seen children of four or five years old sitting in a dirty gutter packing biscuits into packets with dirty hands, while the van of a local biscuit factory stood by to collect the packets.

Encounters with government departments were educative, if frustrating. I cannot remember how many times I have stood on the stair landings of the Education Department (now the temporary premises of the Supreme Court) to choke back tears of frustration. It was hard to believe that every well-intentioned effort to provide education for the underprivileged children was crushed by petty-minded officials, tied to a book of rules, but completely oblivious of the results of the policies they carried out. One can only feel thankful that the younger generation of education officals can at least plan for universal free education up to the age of fifteen.

To register a private school one has to satisfy the requirements of the Public Works Department for loading, the Fire Services Department for fire risk, and the Education Department for academic standards. No one could complain about that, because ostensibly it was for the protection of children in schools. But in those early days it was almost inevitable that one must pay one or all of them a bribe, and my problem was that I offered no bribes. Very few Europeans, I suspect, paid bribes, because corrupt officials knew that they might report corrupt practices. It was easier to intimidate Chinese people for it was a case of pay up or no registration.

After the Nissen hut episode, we had to look for rented premises for our school. It was no easy task to find a building that would approximate to the requirements for loading, fire safety and health standards.

One of the buildings we rented was on the top floor of a building which had shops on the ground floor. When the Fire Services came to inspect it they said that the premises were too high: they had no ladders long enough in case of fire. I wondered what domestic tenants would do in case of fire. I discussed the matter with the Director of Fire Services personally, pointing out that rooftop schools in government housing estates were even higher than our building, but they were registered. He agreed. He sympathized, and it was unusual to get sympathy from a bureaucrat.

"Technically," he said at last, "your building is too high, but how can I apply rules to you which I am not required to apply to government schools?"

Finally, he agreed to count the distance to the floor of the top storey instead of the ceiling, which he was supposed to do.

"After all," he mused, "we rescue people from the floor of a building, not the ceiling."

I shall forever be grateful to this understanding official.

But another snag arose on that same building. The shop below our school had applied for a licence to sell kerosene. If they had obtained a licence, we could not have registered the school. A different official inspected this point.

"Never mind," he assured me, "we'll accept your application because it came first, and reject the application to sell kerosene." We thanked him.

A few months later an official came rushing into our school.

"You'll have to close your school," he said. "The shop below you is selling kerosene and the children are in danger."

I explained what arrangement had been made about it. I took him to the office to confirm with our manager, Mr. Tai, that this was true.

Mr. Tai looked hard at the man.

"Yes," he said, "that was the arrangement, and *you* were the one who made it."

He had obviously forgotten his promise.

"All right," he said, embarrassed, "forget about it." And he left. We heard no more of the matter, but I did worry in case the kerosene continued to be sold and the children endangered.

We had some problems in that building because drug addicts used to climb the stairs to the roof and sit there smoking. Eventually with official permission we built a hut on the roof and installed a caretaker. We also put an iron gate at the top of the stairs and gave a key to every tenant of the building as a fire precaution. There were two staircases to the building, and there was little, if any, risk. But in the end the Fire Services Department forced us to remove the gate. Apparently it was better to have drug addicts using the roof than to use a little common sense. People everywhere kept rooftop gates locked. But we had to obey the regulations to the letter.

Even so we fared better than some schools. I dealt with one case that made me furious. A school had been operating for several years as a kindergarten, when someone opened a fireworks shop right beneath it. The shop then obtained a permit to sell fireworks, and the school was ordered to close. It was useless to talk of fair play in such cases, because everyone was determined to stick to the book of rules, but no one wanted the trouble of considering what was fair play.

A more hilarious experience was the inspection of another building which we rented in 1965.

This building consisted of four storeys, with pairs of flats on either side of the stairs. As they had been domestic flats, all the doors opened inwards. In fact, they could not have opened out without blocking the stairway, as each door opened onto the stair landing.

The fire inspector came. I knew the book of rules by this time and was prepared for his observation that doors of a school should open out, to allow emergency exit in case of fire. Indeed, I too was concerned for the safety of the children, and had arranged for doors to be kept latched back all day during school hours.

When I explained it to the inspector, he replied, "All school doors must open outwards."

I explained that by opening outwards, the danger was worse, as the doors would cut off exit down the stairs. He was adamant. Whether or not the end result was worse, the book of rules must be obeyed. In frustration I rang up the most senior officer, and requested him to send along someone who was prepared to use his brain. He agreed to come himself.

As soon as he saw the premises, he said, "Of course you could not open these doors outwards. That would only increase the danger." He agreed that the premises could be registered if all doors were kept open during school hours.

Inspections by education officials were just about as difficult. Admittedly very few private premises were entirely suitable for school purposes. The shortage of school places required some relaxation, but by and large we did try to stick to rules. The safety of the children required that, even without the book of rules.

What surprised me was the number of premises being used as schools without carrying out any regulations whatever. All they had to do was to operate without registration and anything went. For example, seating arrangements were intended to protect the children's eyesight. No child must be too far from the blackboard. If the room was too long or too wide, the number of pupils permitted in a classroom would be considerably reduced. One room in our school was large enough to accommodate over forty children, but when other regulations came into play, the number was reduced to twenty-six. That made it impossible to pay the rent and the teacher. But the illegal school next door to us divided a room of the same size into two parts and taught sixty children in each part. When I asked why they were allowed so many children in the classrooms, I was told that as the school had not applied for registration the rules did not apply. Theoretically, an illegal school was subject to prosecution, but this law was seldom used. To operate illegally was infinitely easier than to obey the law. So it was in many aspects of life in Hong Kong.

The book of rules said that fluorescent lighting could be used in classrooms if the windows did not meet the requirement of being placed on the students' left side. Permission had to be obtained.

In one building we rented, we installed the required fluorescent lighting and duly obtained permission. Later we decided to open a night school in the same building. But when the inspector came he refused to register the school because the windows did not admit light from the pupils' left side. I pointed out that this was an evening school, and there was no light coming in from any side, so we had fluorescent lighting instead of daylight at night. He refused permission unless we made special application to waive the regulation about day light.

Perhaps he expected us to produce sunlight after darkness fell! I explained that we had permission for the day school to use artificial lighting.

"There is no record of that," he said.

I showed him my letter of permission.

"We don't have a copy of that in our files," he replied. "Please send me a copy." This was not the only time I had to send copies of official letters. One official confided that it was the practice for some officials not to keep proper records, but leave their successor to argue the matter each time with the school supervisors. It was believed that each time a bribe had to be paid.

Running a school was no joke in those bad days of corruption.

But occasionally we scored a point. I remember one obliging inspector who stood facing the class of students and said benignly, "Good, I see that light comes in the windows from the left." I did not enlighten him that it was his left, but the students' right side. I could not have turned the windows round anyhow.

Sometimes we just have to laugh and try to keep a sense of humour.

Most schools in Hong Kong now operate from purpose-built premises. I seldom need to look at the book of rules today.

In one school our students wanted a tuck shop, so they built it on the rooftop, brick by brick, all by themselves. It was very small and hurt no one, as we had rented the rooftop. It took weeks to complete, and on the day it was due to open, an inspector of the Public Works Department ordered it demolished as an illegal structure. It was commonly believed that an illegal structure was usually left until ready for occupation, because then the owner is more likely to pay a bribe to save demolition. In this case I argued that it was not a squatter hut, that no one would live in it. He insisted it must come down at once. If we wanted to build a rooftop structure we should hire an architect, submit plans, and apply for permission. I stood with him on the rooftop and surveyed all the illegal structures on the nearby roofs.

"Did they all have an architect?" I asked. The question was ludicrous because no architect could have drawn those contraptions.

"You are accusing me of corruption!" he said.

"Am I?" I asked. Perhaps the cap fitted, but in fact I was only curious.

Even today, almost twenty years later, people still build rooftop structures and action is seldom taken against them. When I recently inquired about this I was told that action is only taken when there is a complaint. This provides a good way for getting revenge on a neighbour, but seems to have no relation to law and order. Some structures built against the wishes of landlords and tenants seem mighty hard to have removed.

The students were heartbroken to lose their tuck shop on its opening day, and they had to demolish it brick by brick just as they had built it. We tried to compensate them by buying a cupboard from which to operate.

I was certainly learning about people. I learned how hard it is for the small man to get permission to do anything.

"Money speaks," was the first thing my students taught me. I found that it did. Without it, each step of the way was frustrated and agonizing. That we managed to survive and continued to make progress however slowly, made me feel that some power was driving me on and giving me strength by the way. I often felt the inspiration of my father, who had always wanted me to serve the poor of the community.

*    *    *    *

## Transport, Triads and Intrigue

The 1967 RIOTS had shown how easily life could be disrupted if legal transport workers went on strike and illegal transport operators took over. Illegal transport consisted of all kinds of cars used as taxis (*pak pai*) and all kinds of vans as minibuses.

Public transport had never been adequate, probably because more profit can be made from overpacked buses than from adequate services. Hong Kong has always provided its monopolies with maximum profits and its people with minimum services. There had for many years been illegal taxis, some run by triads, some by ex-police, and some were jointly owned by triads and police. I once went to the Kwun Tong Ferry Pier to watch the operation of triads. While licensed taxis had to line up at the taxi stands and were prevented by police from picking up passengers at the pier exit, the unlicensed taxi drivers were permitted to stop right at the exit and steal passengers looking for taxis. Sometimes when I took a taxi in Kwun Tong, the driver would refuse to take me to my destination because he was afraid of the triads which operated under police protection in that area. One of them drove me to see for myself, and there I saw illegal taxidrivers hobnobbing with police. I am glad to say that this operation has been greatly reduced since the Independent Commision Against Corruption came into being in 1974.

Wherever there is a shortage of supply in Hong Kong, the triads are smart enough to take control. In this way they control illegal water and electricity supplies in hut areas for example. The authorities are well aware of the opportunities they give to triad operations, and one is driven to the conclusion that they prefer to keep the triads happy rather than to eliminate them. That they extort money from people and terrorize those they squeeze is of little or no interest to the government.

It was to be expected, therefore, that minibus drivers had to join the triads, or be beaten out of operation.

In early 1968, I mentioned the transport shortage to the Transport Advisory Committee. As minibuses were already operating, I proposed that they should be licensed for a period of three years, during which time the bus companies should be given an ultimatum to get enough new buses on the roads or have their franchises cancelled. I figured that, with enough new buses in operation, the minibus drivers would be sure of employment when their licences expired after the three years' grace.

My proposal was supported by one senior government official, but it was met with derision by the Commissioner of Transport.

"Legalize those things?" he laughed. "Never."

Three months later, after a trip to Japan, the same Commissioner announced that he had decided to legalize the minibuses, not for a limited period, but as a permanent form of transport. It soon became clear that the minibuses would have to be of a standard size, supplied by one Japanese firm. Thus, minibuses became a permanent form of transport in Hong Kong, and every effort by their owners to use a more suitable and cheaper vehicle has failed.

If the type of vehicle was standardized, everything else connected with the trade was left to its own devices. Each route was controlled by triads. Every driver who wanted to stay in business had to pay the triads. Those who failed to pay were not allowed to enter the loading areas. If they continued to operate they were subject to summonses for careless driving or other traffic offences, thus establishing a connection between triads and police. Some were threatened, while others were beaten up; one driver was beaten to death. Some had their vehicles damaged during the night.

Just about this time a new head of the Anti-Corruption Branch of the police took over. His name was Peter Law, a British policeman who had served in the Special Branch. He called me to his office to tell me that he was determined to get rid of corruption and he wanted me to tell him all I knew about it. I may be too suspicious in feeling that sometimes I am asked that question not to help the authorities in their work, but to find out how much I know. However, I put aside my suspicions and told Mr. Law all I knew. I particularly asked for action against a policeman named Lam (or Nam) Kong, who had been involved in my frame-up in 1966. I had been reporting his activities and he had reason to want to be rid of me. I knew that he had some connection with the drug trade. He was also quite a senior policeman.

"Oh, Lam Kong?" replied Mr. Law. "Yes, I know about him. Don't worry, I have about thirteen charges against him. We will certainly get him." I wished him well in his new job, and promised to pass on to him any information I obtained about corruption and the drug trade.

Several months later, Lam Kong was still at large, so I rang up Mr. Law. "What about Lam Kong?" I asked. "Any further news?"

"I don't know what you are talking about," replied Mr. Law. "Who is Lam Kong?"

"You said you had thirteen charges against him," I reminded him. "Don't you remember?"

"I said nothing of the kind," he replied.

I know I was not dreaming up our previous conversation. I would be prepared to take an oath about that first interview.

The mills of God grind slowly, but they grind exceedingly sure. More than ten years later I picked up my newspaper and read, "A High Court judge and jury in a dangerous drugs conspiracy trial yesterday heard of a meeting presided over by former Chief Police Detective Staff Sergeant Lam Kong with the head of a Hong Kong and a Thai drug syndicate. The meeting was for the purpose of recovering a consignment of morphine which was said to have been seized by the police . . ." In fact, Lam Kong was then one of those corrupt police on the run in Taiwan. The same newspaper (*South China Morning Post,* 1 November 1978) also reported: "Police are still unable to confirm a newspaper story that said a runaway Hong Kong detective was shot dead in Thailand. They said they have no news from Interpol on the reported death of former detective station sergeant Lau Cheong Wah. According to the report in the Chinese newspaper, Lau was shot three times by a Thai during an argument over 'Business'." Lau Cheong Wah was involved in the Cactus Apartment murder in 1974, and had a prison sentence of seven years passed *in absentia.* This is the kind of policeman to whom we had been looking to enforce law and order. Had I tried to expose his activities, I should most certainly have been sternly criticized by the authorities.

By mere coincidence Mr. Peter Law was, in later years, sent to investigate drug trafficking in Thailand.

Shortly after the minibuses had been legalized, a driver came to report that a gang was extorting money from drivers at the Jordan Road Ferry Terminal, as well as in many places in the New Territories. He suggested that we should invite Mr. Peter Law to go and see the racket for himself. With some hesitation I accepted the invitation. I was afraid that the driver who made the report might find himself being penalized. I had had ample experience to show that informers on corruption could hurt themselves without stopping the rackets. I therefore warned the driver, Mr. Mak Pui Yuen, of the possible outcome. Mr. Mak was determined on his course and went to see Mr. Law. Soon after Mak complained that he was being persecuted, with shoals of traffic summonses, he suspected that his visit to Mr. Law had become known to the traffic police. Mr. Law assured me that was impossible as the file was locked in his own desk.

Mr. Mak then suggested taking Mr. Law on a trip to the New Territories, a trip for only three of us, unknown to anyone else. Mr. Law would then see what was happening.

One morning I took a special trip across the harbour to see Mr. Law and asked him face to face. I avoided using a telephone because I know how easy it is to listen in to extension calls. I put the plan before him, emphasizing that no one was to know about it, and we would not talk on the telephone. "Right," he said, "anywhere, any time." The time was arranged, but I did not specify the places we would visit. He checked his diary. He was free and would be glad to go with us.

When I returned home that morning I received a phone call from Mr. Law. He said he had just discovered that he had a meeting with the government on the afternoon of the day arranged. Would I tell him where we were going so he could make his plans. I was reluctant to talk on the telephone, but he gave me no alternative. I explained that we were going to the New Territories, but would get him back in time for his meeting. He agreed.

A little later, however, Mr. Law rang again. His meeting, he said, scheduled for the afternoon, had been changed to the morning. Would I mind if he sent his second-in-command, Mr. Morgan? By this time I could not have cared if he had sent the devil himself, because by now everyone in his office would know about our visit. I also found it hard to believe him, because my contact with government offices had taught me that except in extreme emergencies, the government does not suddenly change the times of meetings. I was no longer interested in the visit, but agreed to whatever he suggested.

On the day of the outing, to my great surprise and disgust, Mr. Morgan arrived with two carloads of detectives. Mr. Mak at once recognized one of them as a corrupt policeman who had squeezed him when he was a hawker. He thought I had double-crossed him. I felt that Mr. Law had double-crossed me. Neither of us had the slightest interest in going on with the visit.

When I questioned Mr. Morgan about all the police coming with him, he explained "I must have witnesses in case we find any corruption."

"Would not your word with mine and Mr. Mak's be accepted?" I asked.

"No," he replied, "we must have other police witnesses."

But why two carloads? Mr. Morgan then proceeded to laud the honesty of the police. I felt utterly sickened. After a short time, when we found that no minibuses were in sight, we called off the operation. Everything had been arranged to prove Mr. Mak to be a liar. He was soon listed as an "Unreliable Informer".

I was so angry with the whole operation that I wrote a record of what had happened, and asked Mr. Law to sign that it was correct. I pointed out that failure to sign would be accepted as non-opposition. If my record was incorrect, he should write and tell me. When he replied, Mr. Law just repeated why he had not taken part, and why the police were present. I referred no more cases to Mr. Law.

So the racket on minibuses continued. And Mak continued to oppose the racket. Other minibus drivers held a meeting and complained of threats, summonses and beatings. Two drivers gave details of beatings and agreed to have their names used in a report.

It seemed useless to try Peter Law again, so this time I sent my report to Peter Godber, giving my reasons for not approaching Peter Law. At that time Peter Godber was head of the Traffic Police. I asked him to interview the two witnesses who had been beaten, and do something about the racket. I did not tell Godber at this time that I had photographs showing the racket going on: I wanted to see what he would do first. The photographs showed money being handed over by drivers in the presence of police.

A week later, Godber replied that the matter had been investigated, and no evidence had been found. The Anti-Corruption Branch had been informed, and they too could find no evidence.

I was absolutely livid. I made up my mind to do my own investigations. The task was easier than I expected. I chose a public holiday when I had time and could take one of my English teachers with me as a witness. I was armed with a camera. The ease with which I was able to locate the racket exposes the police lie that there was no evidence.

At the Jordan Ferry minibus terminal, several gangsters were operating, collecting money from every minibus that stopped to pick up passengers there. Police stood by watching but taking no action. I took a number of pictures. Amazed at their non-action, I approached the police and asked them why they did not stop this extortion.

"No need," they replied. "These drivers *want* to give money to the men who regulate the terminus."

I took photographs of them and the racketeers right before their eyes.

"Come with us," the police said, "and we'll ask the drivers if they want to give this money." The police then went to speak to the driver of one minibus, accompanied by the gangsters. It was clear by their threatening attitude that no driver would dare to deny that he wanted to pay them.

Finally, my friend and I decided to board a minibus and pretend we were going to the New Territories. We sat in the front seat to talk to the driver. When the minibus was out of sight of the police, I asked the driver, "Is it true that you drivers like to pay money to those men."

The driver laughed bitterly, and drew his finger across his throat. "We die if we don't pay," he said.

We then got off and I went home to make my report. A few days later the story, with the photographs, appeared on the front pages of the newspapers.

One TV station arranged an interview with the police and myself at different times, but synchronized the questions and answers to make it appear like a conversation between the two sides.

"Did anyone report to you a corruption racket on minibuses?" the police spokesman was asked.

"No," replied the policeman. "We knew nothing about it until it appeared in the press."

Then I appeared on the programme and was asked, "Did you report this racket to the police?"

"Yes," I replied, showing my letter to Godber, and his reply.

By the time this programme ended, the police were clearly lying, and in shame they made an announcement that there had been a breakdown in liaison. The police spokesman had not received information from Godber in time to put it on the air. But by this time no one believed what they were saying. They had to take some action to convince the public.

So they arrested several men and charged them with collecting money. I wrote again to Godber, asking if he would not like to call me as a witness, since I had actually seen the men collecting. I had photographs of the gangsters, and wanted to make sure that the right people had been arrested. Godber did not reply, and to this day I do not know if they arrested the real gang, or if some innocent person was arrested instead, as this was the common practice.

The racket did not cease. It simply took a new form. But that, too, was reported to me.

This time, the racketeers, led by a traffic policeman whom I can name, and who later figured in a corruption case, set up a phoney cleaning company. For a certain sum of money each month, the company would clean the minibuses. Anyone who did not pay the company was subjected to threats and summonses. Of course, no cleaning was done, but each minibus was given a sticker when the money had been paid. Detectives boarded those mininbuses without stickers and issued threats. In fact, it was illegal to put stickers of any kind on minibuses, and later when some drivers voluntarily put my election posters on their minibuses, they were threatened with summonses.

Again, by means of press publicity, I was able to expose this new racket and put the "cleaning company" out of business. But that did not stop the racket, because a new and better way was found. The money was then collected right inside the police premises at San Po Kong, where I could not enter with my camera.

Did the Independent Commission Against Corruption put an end to this racket? Certainly not. The racket simply went underground. I am told that even now, minibus drivers in some areas have to pay a large down payment to become members of a phoney association which still controls the minibus routes. The drivers have probably learned that it is useless to complain, because officialdom just continues to tolerate gang law. And all the top cops involved have escaped to Taiwan, are still in their jobs in Hong Kong, or they had light prison sentences if convicted. There is seldom sufficient evidence to convict. Yet in convicting an ordinary member of the public, no real evidence is required. The word of a perjured policeman is frequently sufficient evidence to procure a conviction.

So has it always been in Hong Kong.

# I Am Jackie Chan*

## 1998

*Jackie Chan with Jeff Yang (co-author)*

*Jackie Chan is one of Hong Kong's leading international film stars. He is best known for his kung fu movies and comic roles. His life story* I am Jackie Chan *is co-written with Jeff Yang.*

## Breaking in

And so for the first time in my life, I found myself alone — and free. I was seventeen years old, in the prime of my youth. I was determined to make a life for myself, and a name, and maybe even fame, in the wild, beautiful city of Hong Kong.

But first I had to deal with some loose ends.

You see, when I was thinking of leaving the school, I'd called my parents, to tell them that my ten-year contract with Master was ending soon. My father immediately told me I should join him and my mother down under.

Well, I'd lived under the eyes of adults all my life, and I wasn't going to pass up the chance to finally kick up some dust.

"Kong-sang, you will like it here," said my father, his gruff voice broken by the static of a bad international connection. "I'm sure we will be able to find you a job, and of course you can stay with us until a flat is available."

"I can't hear you, Dad," I said, even though I could hear him quite well.

"Kong-sang?" he shouted. I held the phone away from my ear and winced.

"Dad, I'm not going."

"The line is bad; I thought I heard you say you are not coming."

"I'm not."

"You certainly are," he said, his voice taking on a familiar edge. "Your contract is up, there is no more opera company for you to join, and you are old enough to begin earning a living for yourself. There are many jobs here in Australia, much opportunity."

"I'm working already, Dad," I retorted. 'I'm doing movies. I'm a stuntman."

"How much do you think you can make doing movies?" he said.

I realized that I had absolutely no idea. All of my movie fees went directly to Master, and the amount he gave us as our spending money was barely enough for snacks. Could I live on a stuntman's pay? Maybe I *was* crazy.

"There is no way you can survive," said my father, breaking into my thoughts.

Nothing makes me more determined to succeed than someone telling me something's impossible.

---

"Of course I can, Dad!" I said. "In fact — "

I gulped, because I suddenly knew exactly what would force my father to let me stay, if that was what I really wanted. And it was. *Right*?

"In fact, the reason I have to stay in Hong Kong is that I've signed a contract with a movie studio. I'll be working for them all the time now. A *contract,*" I said.

There was silence on the other end of the line. I mentioned before that my father is from Shandong. Well, the people of Shandong are known for two things: they always face death without fear, and they always live up to their word. A contract, even a verbal agreement, is unbreakable, no matter how unfair it is, or how terrible the price of keeping it. That's why my father had kept me in the school, even though he could have afforded to bring me to Australia years earlier. No matter what happened to me, even if I'd been crippled or worse, I was committed to stay there by the contract he'd signed with Master — and if I'd run away and somehow managed to join them in Australia, well, he might have killed me himself. No son of Shandong could live with such humiliation, and no Shandong father could bear to have such a cowardly son.

So if I'd signed a contract, I was untouchable. I was bound to fulfil its terms.

"How long is the contract for, Kong-sang?" said my father, after a long pause.

I told him the first number that came to mind. "Two years, Dad."

"And where will you live for these two years?"

"I — uh . . ."

He had me there. I couldn't stay at the school, and with most of its students leaving or already gone, the school wouldn't be around much longer anyway. We'd often overheard Master discussing the possibility of leaving Hong Kong, to start over in a place so culturally backward it had barely even been exposed to Chinese opera: Los Angeles, in the United States.

"Kong-sang, it would be shameful for you to dishonor an agreement that you have already made," he said. "But it would be even more shameful for a son of mine to be living on the streets."

I knew it. He was going to demand that I give up Hong Kong and my last chance at freedom.

"I suppose," he continued, "that I have no choice but to buy you an apartment."

"But Dad, if I go to Australia — what?" I reevaluated what he'd just said through the static. "I'm sorry, the line is bad . . . I thought I just heard you say you were going to buy me an apartment."

"I did," he said.

"You aren't!"

"I certainly am," he said, and I swear I could hear him smiling. "You may consider it a graduation gift."

So on the day when I finally walked out the door of the academy, I had somewhere to go: my own apartment. It was very small, and not in very good shape, but it was mine, and it was home. My *first* home. I'd spent my entire life in other people's houses, and while I lived under their roof I had to obey their rules. But in my tiny seventeenth-floor flat on Xing Pu Jiang, I was the king, and I could stay up as long as I wanted, and sleep as late as I chose.

That apartment cost my father HK$40,000 — a huge amount for him to spend at the time. It's the nicest thing he's ever done for me, and something I can never forget.

In fact, I still own the place. I've thought about selling it, but my father told me that the *feng shui* of the place must be very good, since I've had so much luck since then. Maybe he's right, maybe he isn't. I'm not a very sentimental or superstitious person, so even though I never went through with a deal, I had a real estate agent come and look at the flat. She said that if I sold it, I could get more than *HK$3 million*. Which should tell you something about how much Hong Kong has changed over the past three decades.

(It's gotten a lot more expensive, for one thing.)

\*    \*    \*    \*

## A City View

That first night in my new place was very strange.

I had no furniture, so I lay down on the floor — but I was used to that. The thing I wasn't ready for was the feeling of being alone in the dark. Without the muffled noises of other bodies, the snoring of Biggest Brother, and the creak of the old wooden floor as it moved under our shifting weight, the night seemed terribly empty.

I couldn't sleep. I got up and walked across the room to the window that faced out into the street. The glass was faded with old dust, but I could still see the lights of the city beneath me: blinking neon and the occasional flare of automobile headlights.

I pushed at the window, grunting as I struggled against the layers of rust and old paint that stuck it to its frame. When I finally got it loose, the night came alive with noise. Even as high in the air as I was, I could hear the sounds of Kowloon after dark.

Hong Kong had always been crowded; now it was a permanent mob. It had always been fast, but now it swarmed with constant motion. There was action in the streets, the kind of action young men were told to stay away from if they wanted to grow up into old men — women, drink, drugs, fighting, and gambling, always gambling.

This was the early '70s, when Hong Kong was just beginning to turn into a real economic power, one of Asia's "Little Dragons." The postwar wave of refugees had fueled the growth of the island's industry with their labor, first pouring out their sweat in tiny basement workshops, and then in big factories, making garments and toys and plastics.

Some people had become very rich. But even those who hadn't — from shop owners to businessmen to the hawkers in the streets — believed that, with enough determination and hard work, they could, too.

The city I was named after was growing up, and so was I. We would grow big enough to take on the world together. There wasn't a doubt in my heart.

That night, there in the air above the streets of Kowloon, I made a vow. I was Chan Kong-sang, man of Shandong, son of Hong Kong. I would survive. I would succeed. And all of them — my ancestors, my city, my father — I would someday make them proud.

And with that thought in my mind, I shut the window, curled back up on the floor of my new home, and slept.

# POETRY

# A Hong Kong House*

## 1962

### Edmund Blunden

*Best known as a war poet in his native England, Edmund Blunden was the most significant international poet of his time to write extensively of Hong Kong. He was head of the English Department at the University of Hong Kong from 1953 to 1965, and later held the Oxford Chair of Poetry. Several of his poems from his collection* A Hong Kong House *appear here. He died in 1974.*

———

'And now a dove and now a dragon-fly
Came to the garden; sometimes as we sat
Outdoors in twilight noiseless owl and bat
Flew shadowily by.
It was no garden, – so adust, red-dry
The rock-drift soil was, no kind root or sweet
Scent-subtle flower would house there, but I own
At certain seasons, burning bright,
Full-blown,
Some trumpet-purple blooms blazed at the sun's huge light'.

And then? tell more.
'The handy lizard and quite nimble toad
Had courage often to explore
Our large abode.
The infant lizard whipped across the wall
To his own objects; how to slide like him
Along the upright plane and never fall,
Ascribe to Eastern whim.
The winged ants flocked to our lamp, and shed
Their petally wings, and walked and crept instead.

'The palm-tree-top soared into the golden blue
And soaring skyward drew
Its straight stem etched with many rings,
And one broad holm-like tree whose name I never knew
Was decked through all its branches with broidering leaves
Of pattern-loving creepers; fine warblings
And gong-notes thence were sounded at our eaves
By clever birds one very seldom spied,
Except when they, of one tree tired,
Into another new-desired,
Over the lawn and playthings chose to glide'.

---

\*   'A Hong Kong House', 'An Island Tragedy', and 'On Lamma Island' by Edmund Blunden are reproduced
   by permission of PFD on behalf of the Estate of Mrs Claire Blunden.

# An Island Tragedy*

## 1962

Among the twinkling tree-tops on our hill –
It was perhaps an afternoon illusion –
Above, I saw poised absolutely still
A wood-god, a giant earth-god, – no confusion
At least to my awakened sight: he stood
Head and shoulders aloft the far-off green,
The steady straw-haired monarch of the wood,
As one defending his disturbed demesne.

What was he if not he? I used my eyes.
There that Form stood, as ancient as that hill;
He had no right to strike with such surprise
Me! There he stood, for me he always will,
Poor giant, poor doomed straw-hair, staring down
From his starved rock towards the advancing town.

\*    \*    \*    \*

# On Lamma Island*

## 1962

This quiet place is changing as all do.
Builders have new ideas, shoppers too.
Even pigsties somehow pass from old to new.

And still these fields with brightening seedlings lined
By kindly handiwork, of old designed,
Remain the same, wherethrough the footpaths wind

As yet, so I recall them for a brief
Passage of years, the same on my relief
Memory-map; and still we have our chief,

Not on a charger, but afoot ahead,
Greeting the well-pleased toilers round us spread,
And then at the foot of the hill, by the shrubs and the shed,

Delving once more, disclosing what has been, –
From us to them three thousand years between!
Simple survivors, what a world they mean.

A factory, he decides, here nigh the sea
Three thousand years ago sold pottery;
He hands drab shards in proof to you and me

Beneath the old calm sky. We cannot hold
In hands untrembling these skilled works of old
He takes them gently, richly, like red gold.

And change is working meanwhile round us, friends,
And him our merry wizard; here ascends
Ere long some such great factory . . . or, here ends?

# At the Cemetery Above Happy Valley Racetrack

## 1977

*Dean Barrett*

*Dean Barrett is an American writer who has authored several books of Asian fiction and non-fiction, and previously lived in Hong Kong for a number of years. He is trained as a Chinese linguist and served with the Army Security Agency in East and Southeast Asia, and is also a scholar in Chinese and Asian Studies. He currently lives and writes in Thailand.*

We're neighbors now, who would have guessed?
I wonder how we would have got on had we met, had we known.

No matter. We'll get on fine now, won't we?
Although – my earth is a darker brown; might
I even say more fine?
Ah, well, it isn't mine
to say.
It's theirs.
And, before long, no one will notice the difference.

I say, they race horses down below. Although, I think
it's fixed. Would you care to wager? It passes the time.

Oh. You're not a betting man. A pity. But still,
I think it's true. It must be fixed. Else why would
mine be a darker brown? And might I even say more fine?

But, no matter, we're neighbors now.

# Lok Ma Chau*

## 1977

*Joyce Booth*

*Joyce Booth lived in Hong Kong for many years and was the mother of author Martin Booth. She returned to England and is now deceased.*

I remember him
From long ago,
Toothless then as now
One long, cultivated hair
Growing from a mole upon his chin
He shambled from his
Gloom shaded hut
Into strong sunlight;
His old eyes screwed against
The stab of brightness
Nobody was there –
Just he and I –
So he smiled
As his wrinkled, indrawn lips
Mouthed a greeting,
Wide brimmed bamboo hat
Bowing in courtesy.

Pitifully poor he was,
Filled with the majesty
of mandarins

I sat on the stubbled grass,
Watched the stiff movement of his legs
As they carried him downhill
To his watercress bed

So still the air
At Lok Ma Chau;
So soundless below my hillocked seat
The pattern of paddy
Rambled into China,

---

\*   Reprinted with the permission of Martin Booth.

A patchwork *min toi*
Created for the growing of grain,
Varying shades of green and silver
Where rice began
To thrust delicate spears
Sunwards.

He looks the same today,
No older than the old man
He then was
No more fine wrinkles
Could trace themselves upon a face
Already lined to capacity
His shreds of clothing
Hang from angular shoulders
As they did years ago,
Faded as ever into nondescript rags

But now it's all a sham,
A monumental deception;
Tourism had discovered him,
Made him star attraction
Titled "Rural Peasant".

Big squat coaches,
Air conditioned,
Straddling narrow roads,
Biting deep tracks on muddy lanes,
Whining, coughing noisily,
Polluting still, country air
With diesel fumes
At Lok Ma Chau they come to rest,
Tourists pouring from their bellies –
Ants from a mobile ant hill;
Past the stalls of carved curios,
Coca Cola, ice cream, chewing gum,
Straw hats, satin skull caps
With flat, scarlet buttons

He steps from the same old hut,
Bares his gums,
But the smile is a set grimace
Donned for the occasion;
No formal bow – extended open claws

# Those Not Swimming*

## 1977

*Martin Booth*

quite how often we
'd queued just
there, at Big
Wave Bay, I've no
idea, but we
did – for
beach-tents

and took a
sanded plot for
hours on the
heavy afternoons that
swagged upon
the heavy months: the
man came
round with tin
pails holding
sanded water

we splashed and
those not eating pickled
squid, or singing, or (maybe) dancing, or having
a laugh, went
swimming

those not swimming
slept

and it wasn't for
some years that
they found the

---

\*    'Those Not Swimming', 'Dead Bones', and 'Martin Booth on a Poet' are reprinted with the permission of Martin Booth.

skeletons, in their
sanded plot, still un-
armed, still braided
but by sand, just where
we'd queued: it was
they still wore ID-
tags, had chipped
teeth, some still
wore tattered
uniforms, wore rings (I
was too young to
grasp a war upon
our bathing beach)

and we still ate pickled squid:
we still sang, danced,
laughed and all
the rest
while those not swimming
slept

\* \* \* \*

# Dead Bones\*

## 1977

littered the hills
in serried rows of pots
we peeked upon
and wondered: paper
money blew
across us
like a blessing

lay snuck in the old,
dank corridors of
derelict gun emplacements:
found a fibula there
once, by casting
matches out

washed in the sea

hid in the hoofmark
graves upon the mountainsides, secret
as those in the
gun emplacements

bleached on the island
with the arch out
Ninepins way, sailing

there were dead

those I saw boiling
in the mortuary gods
tucked away under the
hill near Yaumati, with

steam rising in a sweat
that stank well into
every nightmare, were
living

the dead were there
upon slabs: the piping
band had been dismissed
and this was where we went

I was eight
and unknowing: light
came late

and bones were dead
up to that date

# Martin Booth on a Poet*
*(for e. b.)***

## 1977

I came to you
along the path
beside the palm
and up the steps
– and you were kind.
We talked,
drank sherry
and it was peaceful.
The palm stood
erect and final
and everlasting
while the city hummed
through the creepers
and night slipped.
The next day
we took a photo
of you
with a mantis
praying on your hand
before it flew off.

I last saw you distantly
across a student audience,
gowned and still,
and I saw kindness
not knowledge:
it is better to be kind
than clever
– you taught me that.

---

** e.b. in the title refers to Edmund Blunden.

# A Matter of Time

## 1977

### *Joyce Hsia*

*Joyce Hsia compiled an anthology of poetry in English and in translation titled* Hong Kong: Images on Shifting Waters *(1977) with T. C. Lai. Several of her poems appear in that volume.*

———

Hong Kong House: a soon-to-be relic
of a passing era of leisure and space
where sun pierces verandah windows
splaying a red carpet and acquiescent piano;
hibiscus bloom in an untended garden and
a vine's tendrils straddle a king palm.

Ceilings soar with lazy fans pertinent
in long summer days heavy with heat.
A high-voltage air conditioner alternates
but kills the solace of French doors
swinging open to the wild camelia's bloom
and the call of cockatoos in their white
armour and sulfur crowns, replete with
raucous call from mates or contenders
in their luxuriant green enclosure.

Insects run rampant, but so do lizards
whose work is clean and knife thrusts quick
The mother cat hides her brood deviously but
with ease and need not readily capitulate.
Children are free to spread inexhaustible wings
as elders expand on alien themes without
partitions reverberating on either side.

Dust settles expansively; high polish is
forfeit to well-worn leather but antiquity
rubs off and one is mellowed by place.
Rembrandt's focus on light and shadow is
manifestly comprehended as the house
beckons and welcomes the elements.

Winter brings its particular charms
despite drafts echoing through corridors
as the family must draw closer to test
fire's veracity as logs crackle and
fantasies form in pedestrian grate.

Memory's eye remains at play until
a particular eve when dying embers
recall the expectant tree awash with
tinsel and gifts splashed with red
awaiting the auspicious day and Birth.

Chinese New Year asks for dusk to dawn curfew;
tempers remain in the temperate zone as
narcissus within and peach blossom without
display, hopefully, their eloquence
at the ascendant hour. Celebrations flow
like the ribbon dance long beyond
official holidays, when this dynamic city
waits on festivities and one longs
for the balm of a Hong Kong house.

Pillars support white-washed walls and
upper verandahs open to harbour view now
overgrown with concrete but the sky still
tantalizes with city glow while the king palm
stretches to an icy web of stars and the
moon's clarity over peaks in abeyance
before the striking sun rises to
spill over verdant slopes.

The house stands as a memorial
to an easier breathing space –
a luxury Hong Kong can no longer afford.
As the bulldozer moves it must go to
allow for the utilitarian skyscraper
but where will the wilderness of birds
find retreat and who can resurrect this
oasis of green where the azalea hailed
its profound profusion –

In an eclipsing cage of glass and steel.

# Western Approaches

## 1977

*Peter Moss*

*Peter Moss is the author of 'Western Approaches' and several other poems about Hong Kong that appeared in* Hong Kong: Images on Shifting Waters.

———

Journeying abroad
through junk cluttered corridors
between mist-edged mountains,
we near the perimeter
of our spring day
and the end of our return
into antiquity.

Stone piers,
fishing nets,
lichen printed walls
release us from this last
fingerhold on history,
as we round the final headland
and leave the outer isles.

The tide, the dusk,
the patient inevitability
of time present,
catch us in their current
and carry us back,
silent and submissive,
to the western approaches.

We escaped,
but only for a day,
and now our rock piled fortress
beckons us
in mocking blaze of borrowed light,
searing the sea
with reflected brilliance.

Terrible to watch,
that anguish of a dying sun,
bleeding from a million windows,
extinguished,
pane by pane,
in the artificial stare
of chandelier and neon.

No chimera this,
no sailor's tale,
no Babylon of fancy
rearing turrets in the breath
of vagrant clouds,
no vision in the night.

The city is reality,
and all our fickle day
a passing mirage,
lulling us,
momentarily,
with its sweet conceit
of centuries retrieved.

# Hong Kong — An Unfinished Symphony
# for Five Million Instruments

## 1977

*Walter Sulke*

*Walter Sulke came to Hong Kong from Shanghai after the war. He was an Urban Council member and also the former chairman of the Museum of Science and Technology and the Museum of Art. Known as the man who brought Mercedes-Benz to Hong Kong, he had many interests, of which writing poetry was one. He died in London in 1994 at the age of 71.*

———

### Allegro

High rise Buildings squeezing the breath out of
    the city
humid heat cloud pressing down
NOISE reverberating reverberating reverberating
piledrivercementmixerdieselbuspneumaticdrill
    shipshornstraffictraffic
and time shoving escalating deadlines through
telephonelinessateliteeearthstationstvsetsradios
    telexmachines
clattering cacaphony culminating in sixtysecond
    pulses
of screaming jet take offs and landings.

### Andante

The seafog gently silklining the velvet water
caressing the boat as it quietly makes way
to the open sea . . .
there straight ahead is Mexico
nothing between here and there
but immense ocean . . .
the thought overwhelms and turns to look
at the old Tang built fort
astride Fat Tong Mun
the local Scilla and Charibdis
an entrance to the fragrant harbour
fishing junks still use
currents and tide as treacherous as its
Sicilian counterpart . . .
Today smoothed by the fog
all silent the sea and the fort:
The Tang was a long time ago.

## Molto Vivace

Fluorescence of poverty
like a thousand diamonds
Wah Fu estate sparkles in the night:
EIGHTY THOUSAND souls in one block of flats
the future here and now.
"you should have seen them ten years ago . . ."
Here around the corner it's still ten years ago
hut upon hut upon squatters hut
and multiply this by ten and ten and ten
"and look here is an estate mark one"
give me the huts anytime
"Ah, yes, but now of course we are building
　　Mark fours"
"and they now three share one hundred feet"
An improvement:
From the greatest population density in the world
To a lesser greatest population density in the world!
"So can you do better?" and
"Why don't you go and live there then?"
The luck of the draw
and "They'd be worse off over the border"
I wonder . . .

## Adagio

In the bay of the leper island
the summer sunlight explodes
on a gently heaving sea
cicadas shrilling drowns out
the distant drum of hydrofoil diesels
but not the insistent Chinese tune
piping reedily across lapping water.
The leper island now houses
a different kind of sickness;
convict drugaddicts roadbuilding up the hill
the whiteclad nurse now a stickwielding warder
posing the nice question of who really is sick:
the Lepers moved to crowded city hospital wards,
the guard swinging his stick of superiority,
the prisoners yielding to society's force?
In the sun's noise there is the music of indifference . . .

# A Commodity in a Pure Competitive Market

## 1983

*Ho Hon Leung*

*A native of Hong Kong, Ho Hon Leung emigrated to Canada where he studied poetry with Vancouver poet Stephen Bett. He published several poems in Canada about Chinese culture and Hong Kong during the 1980s. He has a PhD in sociology and teaches at universities in North America. He now lives in Canada.*

My heart is negotiating with my mind.

Organic substances
seek pleasure
& avoid pain
— so do I.

Like being chased

        I am proud of it.
        (which may be the effect of society
but . . . to be an individual . . .

        In curing loneliness
        it's best
        to accept competitors.
    (& tho I am not a monopoly,
     demand for me is high
regardless of (the) agreement with
my first trader
who is in a far land.

My frustration
invested
by my       conscious mind
is         to max. the profit
in a        pure competitive market
I benefit from my   competitors,
to bare
this thanklessness
is something I'm    willing to do.

I would rather believe
that I'm unconsciously
breaking my agreement.

# After the Three Characters

*for Stephen Bett*

## 1983

1.  After I read yr poem
    I felt despressed.

    Once a bird evoked his intention
    to creat      our language
                  wch has flowered the
                  "Son & Grandson of the King"

    After I went thru      the tunnel
          & saw the unity no more
    I cried loudly.
                    I had confronted
                      the chaotic world.

        W/out light I cldnt
          see images      thru wch
    I sought forms

    One told me      the "  ⊡  "
                      symbolized the flame ball.
                      The brightness.

    As I learned more,
    I REALized the images/
      (REALity)
    wch went thru the symbols
    as light thru      a prism
    were being      crystallized &
                      formalized:
                              the sun rises
                            behind a tree
                  wch is the "EAST.")

2.  Later, characters travelled
          beyond themselves
    & became the subject matter
          of a work of art.

                  A deep emotion about
          a flying bird.

The imagination of
an ideal bird        wch
    stands as still as itself — the ideal language —
          (that you comment on: "[it]
          echo[s] the world both as seen &
          thought"

Tho the Yin conflicts the Yang
in the art work
      the balance
has been restored.
      [We're fighting w/ technology on the Libra.]


3.   We've been living as
        a river

            but we're meeting     a reservoir
            wch is also our        creation
               & civilivation.)

I see a horse
   run across
     a bar of
    my prison.

     The horse evolves
     as I evolve

But I can see it
    no more.

A car runs
   across my eyes
      (It reminds of the old
         RED WHEELBARROW.)

I turn my head aside &
see     two squares.
I think
it is a     tunnel.
Oh!   Yes.   It is the
   character:   RETURN

         (Maybe it is the prophesy
         from our ancestor.)

   . . . RETURN.

4.  But the horse wants
    to race &
    wants to be a superhorse
    competing in the computer world.

>                   Darwin, you may be right.
>                   Fitness is a matter of
>                   surviving.

The horse rides
on a flying carpet.

>               It cant bear two knowledges:
>               intuitive & descriptive.
>               The former is mercury.

Today          speed is
as important as simplicity.

>                   (The evolved flying-horse
>                   had undergone a bloody
>                   Revolution.    Improvement.
>                               (Improvement?)

[One told me, "the world is of computers, of numbers
101010 . . . to simplify our language is good for development
. . . easier to be learned by the machine-brain . . ."]

Art works are not rice.

5.  We've stepped on
        the misleading, non-stop
        conveyer-belt

>                   The flying-horse never
>                   glances back,
>                       only runs forward on the track

We cant return, but
        where can/will we go?

                    a loose horse

# An Old Man in Hong Kong

(written in 1982)

*for my uncle*

### 1983

His hair is whiter & whiter.

Now he doesn't care
which day is his day off,
either "The First Day of Oct"
or "The Queen's Birthday."

He lives in a room as big
as a rat hole.
He eats as cheap as cat.

No matter what the two
top guys' decision that
doesn't change him
since he's too old to
bother.

The only thing he does
every year is to put
a bunch of flowers
on his peer's grave.

Then he sits on his chair.
Waiting.

# fourth uncle

## 1984

*Jim Wong-Chu*

*Born in Guangzhou, Jim Wong-Chu lived in Hong Kong as a child and emigrated to Vancouver at an early age. He is a poet, editor and literary activist who formed the Asian Canadian Writer's Workshop. Swallowing Clouds (2000), an anthology of Canadian Chinese poetry which he co-edited, won the British Columbia Book Award. His poetry collections and individual poems are published in Canada, and four of his poems are included here. He lives and writes in Vancouver.*

we met in victoria

we talked and discovered
our similar origins

you a village relative
while I a young boy
sitting quietly on the other side
of the coffee table
cups between us

we are together
for the moment
but I feel far from you

you said
you travelled and worked
up and down this land
and now you have returned
to die

to be buried
beside the others
in the old chinese cemetery
by the harbour
facing the open sea
facing home

at the end of my life
will I too have walked a full circle

and arrive like you
an old elephant
to his grave?

# the old country

*(for tony hoy)*

## 1984

she gave me three letters

her daughter's son
wants to marry
send a thousand

a sister's nephew
has a first born
send three hundred

her stepson
in hong kong
gambled his wages
anything will do

aunt ling has a pension
and no savings

she asked me
to help her
divide ten dollars
and send each an equal share

# old chinese cemetery    kamloops    july 1977

### 1984

like a child lost
wandering about
touching    feeling
tattered grounds
touching    seeing
wooden boards

etched in ink
etched in weather
etched in fading memories
etched
faded
forgotten

I walk
on earth
above the bones
of a multitude
of golden mountain men
searching for scraps
of memory

like a child unloved
his face pressed hard
against the wet window

peering in
for a desperate moment
I touch my past

# The Immigrant

## 1986

*Alex Kuo*

This is a door
that remains intact
opening to this house

and what it changes.
Inside, it is
full of paintings

of other houses and doors
and it is
murky up to this table, up

to these documents
where I sit
disturbing names and dates

and the TV's uninterrupted news.
So let the laws
harbor this displacement.

Through the door-cracks
of this single world
I begrudge that it knows

my life, but I remain
silent. I get up
and move the paintings

around, changing my references
paying what I owe.
Can it be that

this door is still open
surviving on its own?
And where are the parents.

# The Picture

## 1986

## Preface

*O Peggy, Peggy! wherefore art thou Peggy?*

Whatever happens, I am ready with my eye. It is my first eye that sees, but when I want to remember, I use the camera to hold it forever.

\*

Have you ever sat down and thought about the camera? How it turns an innocent moment into an exhibition, something we don't want to have happened, or be seen in that way. However it is recorded in that one moment, someone will always be keeping an eye on it, even when they are not looking at it, like the picture hanging in your bedroom.

\*

But let me tell you also about betrayal. It is always there, that lie between the moment and the picture, since we rarely find in it what we foolishly want to record. The instant we look at the picture, we know something's been betrayed, and what we're looking at is something entirely different from what we want to remember.

Sometimes this betrayal is physical, like a blemish or a slight hitch of a leg in anticipation, which we only notice or regret in retrospect. When we know that someone else is also looking at us in this same way, we involuntarily begin to make allowances for it, and since then nothing is ever seen as truthfully.

Other times it is purely spiritual, like leaving the church the way we have learned to leave home or children or companion to live in a separate pain far away, the way Monet walked into the 20th century on lily pads, barely paying any attention to the details.

\*

Some will even say that this is where one's real life begins, after we have stepped away and betrayed our confidences.

\*

But mostly what's seen in the picture comes a little bit too late, and then we have the echo of catching up to the tedium and swamp of everyday living, the difference between plateau and surf.

The camera they bought with change saved over several months was first kept for weeks at his apartment, then at hers, even though they don't sleep without the other, haven't since they started saving money together. It went where he or she went, whomever it was with that day, and wherever they were to spend the night. But being forgetful, sometimes they would be without it, left at his or her other place. At such times they would be helpless at sex, feeling something missing in their lives. The last time this happened sleepless at three in the morning, they thumped out of bed into his car and drove through flashing yellow traffic lights to the other side of town to her apartment in record time. In the clarity of those two hours waiting for the sunrise, they discussed if the first roll of film into the camera should be black-and-white or color, Japanese or German, since it was made in one country with the other's optics. That was the morning they also decided that the camera should be kept at her apartment, since they are more often together there — that way they'll always know where it is, even if they're not there by mistake. This is the way reason prevails, and why we suck on each other's tit. You better believe it.

# There Are Many Ways to Listen

### 1986

I am the heat of drifting dust
Expanding in light, I would call you

Listen, this is what it means:
I am heat, I am dust

I live in foliage
My hair, the flicker of nests

There are words in my mouth
Eat them when you can

There are promises in my lust
Swallow them in your alphabet

When I rise against tolerance
Look for its gift in the window

When I touch my dread
Be shapeless as the wind that has stopped

This is what it will never be again
Listen, listen, what can be calling

# At the North Point Car Ferry

## 1992

*LEUNG Ping-kwan (Ye Si)*

*Leung Ping-kwan (also known by the Chinese pen name Ye Si) is one of Hong Kong's top Chinese writers. The author of over thirty books, his work includes poetry and critical essays on local literature, film and culture in both English and Chinese. He is also a translator and teacher of creative writing at Lingnan University's Department of Chinese. Several of his books are translated into English. In the last decade or so, he has chosen to translate and co-translate some of his own poetry as well as write poems in English. Several of these are in this anthology, including 'Leaf of Passage', written in English, which first appeared in his essay 'Writing between English and Chinese' (*World Englishes, *19:3, Oxford and Boston: Blackwell, 2000).*

The chill was through to the bone.
Bussing all day along dusty streets,
in a window slid wide open,
one knew the muteness of the lines of trees.
On an afternoon of numerous dull errands
one hardly saw the earth at all, just concrete.

His eyes were as black as coal;
the fine smoke made his silence visible.
A tire factory across the bay was aflame,
plumes of black smoke billowing.
Rolling black clouds worried the day.

Stifle yourself, save electricity!
The suns of our good old songs go out, one by one.
Up close to the body of the sea
her rainbows were oilslicks.
The images of the skyscrapers
were staggering giants on the waves.

We came through cold daylight to get here,
following a trail of broken glass.
The last road signs pointed to rusty drums,
everything smelling of smoke and burned rubber,
though we couldn't see fire anywhere.
In the narrow shelter of the flyover,
cars and their people waited a turn to go over.

# The Leaf on the Edge

## 1992

Sorry the food doesn't get to the leaf at the pond's
edge, still, you accept the homage due the beauties
at the center, being the center, leaf battlements and all,
reprising the regimens like an old regime. On the edge,
I'm nowhere in particular, a smoke-signal in a sandstorm,
a border legend, a plotless detail in the weeds of history.

Please don't make an imperial scene, or shout
anthems to the down-pours; don't pretend, with the breezes,
to grant us our ditties. Have you ever noted a marginal leaf,
observed the veins converging like noisy streets,

that challenge your blueprints' rectangles? What about this?
Beneath the solemn appearances of the sacred blooms,
under water, roots grow together, new leaves furl in the heart.
Beneath the winds' quarrels, a hidden song needs other listening.

# An Old Colonial Building

1.
Through sunlight and shadow dust swirls,
through the scaffolding raised-up around
the colonial edifice, over the wooden planks
men live on to raise it brick by brick, the imperial
image of it persisting right down, sometimes,
to the bitter soil in the foundation, sometimes finding, too,
the noble height of a rotunda, the wide, hollow corridors
leading sometimes to blocked places, which, sometimes,
knocked open, are stairs down to ordinary streets.

2.
Down familiar alcoves sometimes brimming
with blooms sometimes barren I go to xerox
glancing at the images caught in the circular pond,
now showing the round window in the cupola as duckweed drifting,
day and night caught in the surface, no longer textbook
clean, but murky, the naive goldfish searching
mindlessly around in it, shaking the pliant lotus stems
and the roots feeling for earth, swirling orange and white,
gills opening and leeching, in and out of the high window bars.

3.
Might all the pieces of ruins put together present
yet another architecture? Ridiculous the great heads on money,
laughable the straight faces running things. We pass in this corridor
in the changing surface of the pond by chance
our reflections rippling a little. We'd rather not bend;
neither of us is in love with flags or fireworks.
So what's left are these fragmentary, unrepresentative words,
not uttered amidst the buildings of chrome and glass, but beside
a circular pond riddled with patterns of moving signs.

# Images of Hong Kong

## 1992

I need a new angle
for strictly visual matters.
Here's an old portrait shot originally
in Guangguang's studio in Nathan Road;
They don't paint on them like this any more.
For no reason of mine, Mid-Levels scenes are on the television.
She'd come from unforgettable Shanghai, from glamorous
Jaffe Road, with its White Russian coffee shops, violins
playing into the night. How does it add up?
A bottle of lotion, Two Sisters, smashed forever on the floor.
Imagine the old vendors throwing olives up into a postmodern tower.
Even the lady who knows only we're all different has a point.
Here's a man who studied anarchism in France and came home
to work for "Playboy," then "Capital."
The tiniest angles divide our views of the moon
when we look up. The Star Ferry clock-tower,
sunsets in Aberdeen: too familiar. Only now
somebody plans to redo everything.
One has only to push buttons to change pictures
to get in on so many trends one can't even think,
too much trivia and so many places and stories
one can't switch identities fast enough. When can we — ?
And here's the Beijing journalist who became
an expert on pets and pornography under capitalism.
When can we just sit down and talk?
Our attentions get lost in factories of images and songs;
appetites are whetted in the hungers of the tiny screen.
Reach out and touch — what?

History, too, is a montage of images,
of paper, collectibles, plastic, fibres,
laser discs, buttons. We find ourselves looking up
at the distant moon; tonight's moon —
does it come at the beginning or the end of time?
Here's another from Taiwan, who thinks
she's Eileen Chang writing Hong Kong romances, with neon
dancing in the back-churning waters of the Star Ferry, on the old *depot*,
with Repulse Bay Hotel rendezvous produced on cue.
All this exotic stuff, of course, is for export.
We need a fresh angle,
nothing added, nothing taken away,
always at the edge of things and between places.
Write with a different color for each voice;
OK, but how trivial can you get?
Could a whole history have been concocted like this?
Why are there so many good at Oriental spy novels?
Why are there many things that can't be said?
So now, once again, they say it's time to remodel
and each of us finds himself looking around for — what?

# Trying to Find the Name of Love, Again

## 1993

*Brent Ambacher*

*An American born in Hong Kong, Brent Ambacher attended both local and American schools, and studied English literature at Trinity College in Hartford, Connecticut. He returned to live and work in the city where he founded* Partners in Rhyme, *a monthly poetry reading series, and published the English-language poetry anthology* Vs: 12 Hong Kong Poets *(1992). His most recent work appears in the anthology* Outloud *(2002). After some thirty years in Hong Kong, he moved to London in 2001.*

———

She is light inside the prism,
The beauty of the primary,
The coldness of old crystal.
She is trapped within me,
There to haunt me
As the melodies tormented Beethoven.

I am floating in the amnion
Of love's salt liberation.
I am listening for the lorelei,
Though there are no reefs to claim me.

We are not beyond pain's grasping,
Flight may not be eternal,
But we are inching towards the shoreline
Out of this once cold sea.

# Learning New Steps

### 1993

Think of these
As words for later;
Evening's end.

Think of these
As words to measure,
Gauged for pressure.
Think of these
As words of danger
Threatening love.

Think of these
As ballroom words
Brocaded and beaded:
Sure of themselves,
Grave and graceful.

Forgive slips
Of a tongue untutored
In such intricate dancing.

# A Four-Inch Beam Seems Narrower
# One Hundred Feet from the Ground

### 1993

What is it which makes us
So hard to hold,
So difficult to turn to?
Where is a middle road,
The mattress to pad
Inevitable
Falls from grace?

What is this lens
Which microscopes our anguish,
Compresses all our unbelief
Into an image
Small and square?

Where is the light
So incandescent
That our shadows
Turn the sand to glass?

In the razor touch of love,
In the blatent glare of needing,
The grip of leprous want,
One kindness may unhinge us
And plant the doubting seed.

# The Hot Bus

*For Ki Chun-kit, 1981–1992*

## 1993

*Liam Fitzpatrick*

*Born in Hong Kong to Irish and Chinese parents, Liam Fitzpatrick grew up in Hong Kong and attended Oxford where he graduated from Christ Church with a first-class honours degree in Modern History. His journalism is published internationally and his poems have appeared in* AMF *and* Vs. *He now lives in London.*

———

He knew the head swim of TV and gasoline,
denim ridge of dollars, the nowhere of evening,
Low sky crowded with radio waving.
A dusk, a life, a vanishing.
Cool geometry of apartment living.
Podium, block and walkway, sodium lighting,
amber floods illuminate the nothing
of metal and tarmac breathing.

Here, heat shadow of a motor.
Demented whoop of a car alarm, somewhere.
He a mile overhead; flat rooftops bear
the proximity of oblivion, a step into air,
lung full of tears, soapy despair,
with babyhood gravity, cartoon care,
he mounts the final stair
leaves air ripples behind him, there,

falls like a young swan
sinking, sad, in petrol ponds.

# The Garden

## 1993

After you had gone I planned
to restrain the garden, prune the tree.
But the garden is not governed by my hand.

Even now you undermine my modest husbandry –
new flowers emerge and fight for space
with the long grass that surrounds me.

Until finally there is no trace
of plants that grew as I meant them to.
Riotous blossoms have taken their place.

And despite what I have tried to do –
train the vine, trim the bush –
the garden sprawls and thrives for you.

\*    \*    \*    \*

# The Passing Train

## 1993

The sound of the train built up an attack
and passed triumphant on the swerve of the track.
You could not hear what I was saying.
*My words are gone like the train.*

Its noise after reaching fierce crescendo
fell away in the air as an echo.
Rather like the point I was making.
*My point is gone like the train.*

You were untroubled by the sound's belligerence
and through it maintained indifference.
As you did to what I was asking.
*My question is gone like the train.*

# Home

*For Veronica*

## 1993

You have another home,
one that lives in you.
Two homes, of now, of Kodachrome,
one you know and one half-knew,
of stone and images of stone
and if you move between the two

You find the road to be a ring,
and being in this round
is to be both leaving and arriving,
then and now in this way bound
by memory circulating
over once forgotten ground.

The way to affirmation
is this course from there to here,
a wheel that in completion
will renew the wasting year,
receiving life from that horizon
where home, both homes, appear.

# In the Forum at the Chinese University

## 1993

*Andrew Parkin*

*Andrew Parkin is the former chair of English at the Chinese University of Hong Kong. Born in England, he emigrated, by way of Hong Kong, to Canada where he wrote and published poetry. The author of two books of poetry, numerous essays and academic works on Yeats and Canadian drama, he also edited an anthology of Chinese poetry in English,* From the Bluest Part of the Harbour *and compiled* Tolo Lights, *two publications of poetry readings at the Chinese University of Hong Kong. Several of his poems appear in this anthology. He now lives and writes in Paris.*

In the shadow of white stone
and climbing silent columns
the colours signal a brief life
vivid as girls
surrounding the resplendent bride.

Fish, fluid as mercury,
slink through thought's shallow pool.

On the stone seat
the old ones sleep in the sun.

The scent of roses
haunts their dreams
like favoured daughters
who were lost
and then returned.

*February 1991*

# Unfinished Poems

## 1993

*Yuen Che-hung*

*A native of Hong Kong, Yuen Che-hung is an award-winning Chinese fiction writer. His books include story and poetry collections as well as essays on education. He occasionally translates his own work and writes English-language poetry, and two of his poems are included here. He has worked in theatre and is now a freelance storyteller in Hong Kong.*

———

In my drawer
there are poems
unfinished, lines
struggling to become shape.

I know them well.
Desperate. Every time I fumble
inside and touch, a guitar
still captive in its case

the music not made.
A song cut short
by the closing doors
of a subway train.

A singer or a violinist
buried by the hurried paces
these out-focused faces
in this

drawer of the city
I am now talking about
this old man outside Harrods
dancing his Tap Tap

to the music of sand.
I know him well
what he carries inside his clown's dress
all these same dreams

incomplete

*October 1986*

# Grandma Is Dead

## 1993

Dreamwalks
in the middle of the night
we were not worried
the corridor was safe
the neighbours did not complain
and you returned.

You returned and
returned
like the incessant tides
of an ancient ocean.

Splash.
Worlds in your eyes
night wind, moonshine.
What did you tell
our forgetful city
in your mumbling walks,
your age
maybe.

Then how old is
ninety-seven:
a decaying dynasty,
two world wars and
two revolutions.
Now a dying colony.

Must we not talk about
time and its promises
not kept:
the war to end wars
and our saviour saved
in the crystal coffin.

When you looked at me
and smiled without a word
I hear voices:
another generation
some other time
one more world.

When you looked at me
and smiled without a word
it reminded me of the time
when I slept, pressing
against your breast
the summer window
of everlasting rain
the smell of your old flat
in the old quarter of town
where I was born
grew up and learnt
to understand the world.

You kept on with
your dreamwalks walking
until at last
you disappeared
through another corridor.

I was not there
to say goodbye
but I was not sad
not exactly
even if I knew
you'd only return
as shadow on the window.
Something has been said:
>       people die
>       dreams come back
>       children learn to forsake
>       their lullaby.

# City

## 1994

*Louise Ho*

*Louise Ho is Hong Kong's most recognized contemporary poet in English. Born and brought up mostly in Hong Kong, she has lived in Mauritius, England, America and Australia. She is an associate professor of English at the Chinese University of Hong Kong, where she teaches creative writing, Shakespeare and English poetry. The author of two collections of poetry, her poems have been published internationally in literary journals. Several of her poems appear in this anthology. She now lives and writes in Australia and Hong Kong.*

No fingers claw at the bronze gauze
Of a Hong Kong December dusk,
Only a maze of criss-crossing feet
That enmeshes the city
In a merciless grid.

Between many lanes
Of traffic, the street-sleeper
Carves out his island home.
Or under the thundering fly-over,
Another makes his own peace of mind.

Under the staircase,
By the public lavatory,
A man entirely unto himself
Lifts his hand
And opens his palm.
His digits
Do not rend the air,
They merely touch
As pain does, effortlessly.

# Prose Poems

## 1994

### I

It's been snowing heavily and streets with cars
and other things are completely covered with
snow. Funny, snow always (especially at two in
the morning) gives a sense of permanence,
unchangingness. It arrests time and things
stay. Like a flood it covers all and swamps
all but unlike a flood it moves nothing and is
in itself unmoving. It reminds me of a
Japanese sand garden with patterns raked into
the sand. It stays for as long as you leave
it, then you flatten it and rake up a new
pattern. Cars come and make furrows in the
snow, these stay until other cars make other
furrows.

### II

For every mask that we take off there is always
one more left on — an endless recession of
masks, of depths of withdrawal. As long as
there is life, there is the ability to recede
further. The self is infinitely reductive and
is never reduced to nothing. Alternatively,
one can reach out and touch infinitely into the
other person, the other thing, the outside, and
having always to reach yet further.

# Pop Song 1 'At Home in Hong Kong' 1964

## 1994

feet that paddle
in the shallows
hands that sieve
through slimy weeds
eyes that reflect
the thousand lights
give only
secondary sensations
the toes are booted
the fingers are gloved
the eyes are shaded
we talk of cultural vacuity
we talk of flux
and instability
the sophisticated
talk of inevitabilities
to explain away inconsistencies
nevertheless
we walk firmly
though we walk
on stilts
we walk only
where stilts
are safe
schooled
in our system
of indirect transmissions
we run
like clock-work
and go on ticking
till we stop
on the dot

# Pop Song 2 'Hong Kong Soul'

## 1994

One has to be vulgar
To live in vulgar times
In vulgar places
They land on your lap
On moving buses
There are too many bodies here
The trouble is
They are alive
If dead they can be buried
Bodily stench
Twirls into a dance
Becomes an abstraction
Reality is
Which elbow
To use
Whose elbow
To avoid
Have piecemeal what piecemeal can
Heaven and earth conspire the moment
Have get make what you will you must
Minute
Elegance of much
Washed in gutters
Near the resettlement areas
By the Carlton Hotel
Seeps into our guts
And makes Hong Kong what it is

# Home to Hong Kong

## 1994

A Chinese
Invited an Irishman
To a Japanese meal
By the Spanish Steps
In the middle of Rome
Having come from Boston
On the way home


\*   \*   \*   \*


# Well-spoken Cantonese

## 1994

How praise the beauties of a gracious man
Except that they are the graces of a beautiful man?
Tone, stress, diction, timing, all combine
To make the texture of his voice:
So rare anywhere
But rarest of all, here.
His modulated resonance
Creates a civilized space
Or a proper silence,
Which was not there
Before he spoke.

# Shadows of Morning

### 1995

*Andrew Parkin*

The voice of the shadows of morning
whispers across the inner court
along the swaying branches.

The voice opens like an eye
that is focussed on one sound,
The voice closes.

The silence is unexplained.
And without rhyme or reason
sharp birdsong unstitches

a seam of silence
frayed by the low murmurs
of nodding pigeons.

I need no pursuit of the ideal,
nor insistence that all is vain,
no bias against beauty.

I desire no absence of this tree,
no refusal to favour the bird, the song,
in the pursuit of a clever phrase.

I find all my privilege
in this simple, cracked sill,
with geraniums, a few snapped stems,
their scent on your fingers still.

*23 July 1992*

# One Perfect Kiss
*(for Clare)*

1995

*Brent Ambacher*

Here we are.
Again, the dark
Clean and quiet,
Catweighted knees companionably close;
Let us talk.
We'll speak of days
Of wildflowers, wild flight,
Hard-won freedom and
Willing bonds of love,
Of Jesus in a temple lurking
Just behind the door,
Of things beautiful and monstrous;
Yes, we'll touch, hands just
This side of moist,
Shiver to the thrill
Of staring deep at death
Questioning his motives —
Or hers —
Mothers kill
their young
Never quite understand.
But I digress.

Ah,
Here we are again
In the clean darkness
with our knees
Close companions,
Touching lightly at
Fingertip and thigh.
Let's plant gardens
In this fertile blackness,
Trees and fountains,
Let's plan cities of
Air and ice,
Pluck beauty raw
And struggling
From seas not ever
Even seen.
You and I may map
Most perfect planets:
We'll sing of heroines
bold and warlike
And heroes who
Are frightened but
do not falter.
The worlds will
Spill like wine
From lips so ready
For one perfect kiss.

# Face

## 1995

### Juliette Chen (Tran Ngoc Linh)

*Born in Vietnam to a Taiwanese father and Vietnamese mother, Juliette Chen (who also writes under the name Tran Ngoc Linh) came to Hong Kong at the age of two. She went to university in Tokyo where she lived for seven years. Her poetry appeared in* From the Bluest Part of the Harbour, *and three poems are included here. She now lives in the United States.*

Old man, here she is —
led through clichéd labyrinths
where incense smokes the air,
where humped women pass
with an animal stare.

Your Cheshire Cat chauffeur
whispers on the phone.
He has seen this all before.
A glance in the mirror,
a button locks the doors.

Old man, she is here
to observe you in your lair.
Mirrored walls and ceiling
pristinely replicate
your fly-blown looks.

Your beckoning hand is fat,
singularly devoid of hair.
Let her tread your hirsute carpet
and admire the furs that toupee
the bald expanse of your bed.

Take care, old man, take care
that you do not ensnare
more than you can bear.
She has come to see one
of an endangered breed.

As you dine on ginseng
and tasteless sea cucumber,
you point out paternally
aphrodisiac properties
and comment on her charms.

You start on her before
dessert is half way through.
Your hand, a travelling salesman,
attests to the firmness
and rigidity of her back.

She looks at your soggy hand.
She looks at your speckled face.
No amount of cajolery
will budge her from her place
to take a spin with you.

In measured tones she informs you
that it is one of her rules
never to dance when she is full.
She thanks you gravely for lunch
and expresses a wish to leave.

As you wait for the car,
you make polite chitchat.
You speak of your daughters
as you recline in bed.
She sits on a distant chair.

In the car the chauffeur
glances in the mirror.
A button locks the doors.
He has seen it all before.
Old man, your face is saved.

# Dinner with an Eligible Bachelor

### 1995

There he is
but you can't see him —
the ghost at this Chinese banquet,
casually eavesdropping
as my father flatters you
with a remark
about the longevity
of your university.

Your smile indicates
such strain at the corners,
such blank politeness.
Surely there is more feeling
in the eyes of the garoupa
we have just devoured,
whose head is being debated
for its culinary merits

By ladies in diamonds and wigs
who profess themselves connoisseuses.
The selfsame women
and their masticating husbands
offer toasts to a future
they have no part in
and one which I decline
to share with you.

Too much stands between us:
this rotating animal boneyard
of fowl, fish, and mammals,
shrimps thrashing on the platter,
our elders' relish
in their own mortality,
lipstick stains
on fake ivory chopsticks,

Not to mention
the uninvited guest
whose letter smoulders and threatens
to burn a hole in my pocket.
You have no need of tea leaves
to predict the gall of coming years,
nor is there need to make it clear
that after tonight — we part company.

# Night Folk

## 1995

Only the night folk see us
as we haunt our usual grounds.
The bus driver catches us briefly
in the glare of his headlights
and wonders at our closeness,
at the distance between us
as we walk with bowed heads,
staring at the paw prints
in the cold cement
of animals long gone.
The night watchman passing by
may be excused for thinking
that the ghosts of cranes weave
in the fitful moonlight
to the music of the spheres.
The old woman who clears the tables
and the soft-drinks vendor
smile knowingly to see us
sitting silent in the dark.
They suspect the worst
with the best intentions
and refuse to believe
we are not lovers
whose fates are destined to twine.
Perhaps only the bats
hanging from the eaves
can see us for what we are:
strangers in transit
from different points in time,
intimate for a hurtful space
before we embark
on our separate flights
and never return.

# New Year's Eve, 1989

### 1995

*Louise Ho*

Yes, I remember Marvell, Dryden,
Yeats, men who had taken up the pen
While others the sword,
To record the events of the sword

That would have vanished
Were it not for the words
That shaped them and kept them.

The shadows of June the fourth
Are the shadows of a gesture,
They say, but how shall you and I
Name them, one by one?
There were so many,
Crushed, shot, taken, all overwhelmed,
Cut down without a finished thought or cry.

Presumably, that night, or was it dawn,
The moon shone pure,
As on the ground below
Flowed the blood of men, women and children.
The stunned world responded, and
Pointing an accusing finger, felt cheated.

But think, my friend, think: China never
Promised a tea party, or cakes
For the masses. It is we,
Who, riding on the crest of a long hope,
Became euphoric, and forgot
The rock bottom of a totalitarian state.

Then, this compact commercial enclave,
First time ever, rose up as one.
Before we went our separate ways again,
We thought as one,
We spoke as one,
We too have changed, if not 'utterly',
And something beautiful was born.

As we near the end of an era
We have at last
Become ourselves.
The catalyst
Was our neighbour's blood.

Whoever would not
For a carefree moment
Rejoice at a return
To the Motherland?
But, rather pick ears of corn
In a foreign field
Than plough the home ground
Under an oppressive yoke.

Ours is a unique genius,
Learning how to sidestep all odds
Or to survive them.
We have lived
By understanding
Each in his own way
The tautness of the rope
Underfoot.

1997 has become a focus,
A cause, a point in space,
A date to live by,
A topic for conversation.
There's always something deadly
About deadlines,
They haunt before they occur.

Let the bells of all the years
Jingle and jangle
To bring in the new.
Let them distil
Out of their clamorous babel,
One single clear note,
That it may make sense,
And we shall listen.

# Meeting

## 1997

I met a man yesterday
On the walkway
By the park
We tried to talk
But he spoke a different dialect
He was from the Mainland
He said
That was why
He didn't qualify for welfare

With a withered face and yellowed teeth
Thinking or not thinking
Of the next meal or the next shelter

How dare I
Find value to reside
Only in the works of the human intellect

# Island

### 1997

We are a floating island
Kept afloat by our own energy
We cross date lines
National lines
Class lines
Horizons far and near

We are a floating island
We have no site
Nowhere to land
No domicile

Come July this year
We may begin to hover *in situ*
May begin to settle
May begin to touch down
We shall be
A city with a country
An international city becoming national

# Flags and Flowers

*for N. E. R.*

## 1997

O to be here
Now that the Bauhinia is in bloom
In its mound of purple flowers

They sound the last post
For the last time
At the Cenotaph
Remembering
The eleventh day
Of the eleventh month
And the fields of poppies
For the last time

We too had our fields of red
Flowing beneath
An azure sky
A white sun
It'll be five stars upon red next

Change our flag as you must
But let us keep our speech
Our local voices
Our nine tones
Our complex homophones
Our own configurations of meaning
Our own polite formalities
Our resonances from the Hans of old

# Hong Kong Riots, 1967 I

## 1997

At five this morning
The curfew lifted.
Receding, it revealed
Shapes that became people
Moving among yesterday's debris.
Stones, more so than words,
Are meaningless,
Out of context.

# Hong Kong Riots, 1967 II

## 1997

Stand your ground
even if for only
two foot square.
The sentry's box
the railings
the imposing gate posts
were plastered
with posters.
People stood
upon others' shoulders
plastering posters
outside
the Governor's house.
Many months
and nothing broke through
the marching
the chanting
the burning
the bombs.
The stiff upper lip
held tight.
The anti-riot police
grouped
like so many Roman turtles
stood their ground.
Rain or shine
surrounded by crowds
outside
the Governor's house
the sentry stood
khaki shorts
rifle in hand
still as a statue
and held his ground
of two foot square.
This too is pomp and circumstance
without fanfare.

# Migratory

## 1997

You want space
You've got space
Now what do you do with it

I floated alone in my kingsize bed
I steered between abysses
To my left 1997
To my right 1788
I hugged the shorelines
Crossed the high seas
And drifted here
Landing on terra firma
Terra Australis

A part of ancient Gondwanaland
Its unique flora and fauna are young
Fossils mirror their living counterparts
The hundred million year Wollemi Pine
Will one day propagate in our gardens
The echidna, spikes on a meat slab
Has tunnelled through the ages to us
Having walked with dinosaurs

Another Anglophone settlement
Irish, Cockney, North country
Transported cultures
Transformed in two hundred years
Into new shapes new sounds
And endless possibilities

At first the heart longs
For the absent familiar
Cosmopolitan Hong Kong
Its chaos, its anomalies, its power
Or England, my other world

Or some landmark somewhere
A villa by Serlio on the way
To Erbusco, outside Milan
Or family, relatives
In New York, San Francisco
Vancouver, Toronto . . .

Then, like lightning
The shock of the void struck

The neighbours are kind, the dogs are friendly
The land is veritable Eden, the roads are straight
Tender is the meat, tasty is the fruit
It is the loss, the loss
That grips like a vice
That tightens the spine
And the legs go soft
Space-tost, land-lost
I float, I drift, I hover
Cannot settle
Cannot come to stay

Concentrate
Minutely on
This time, this space
Measure the land
Foot by foot
Step by step
These eight acres
Study each weed
Each blade of grass
Follow each flow of air
Sink the ankles
Touch the ground
Walk normally

These are my songlines
Claiming by declaiming
Over my land
O land, walk with me
May the dust settle
Wherever I may stand

# from kid inglish

## 1997

*Jam Ismail*

*A 'Hong Kong returnee', Jam Ismail has lived and worked in Calcutta, London, Canada and Hong Kong. Her poetry has been published in several Canadian anthologies and literary journals, as well as Hong Kong anthologies, most recently in* Outloud *(2002). Several of her poems are included here. She currently lives and writes in Hong Kong.*

———

: "didi" meant big sister (bengali), little brother (cantonese), DDT (english). to begin with, inglish had been at home, with cantonese & hindustani. one of the indian languages, the kid felt in bombay. which british hongkong tried to colonize. descended on all sides from the Idiosyncracy, the kid disdained grammar class, refused to parse, opted to be inherent parsee.

: at school wrote her first poem *Damon Nomad*      & what mean while was writing her, what *nom de womb?*      reverbed '47 (india, pakistan), '48 (koreas), '49 (chinas, germanies), '54 (vietnams).

: "hey," he bellowed, pants down in quebec, "bring in some english mags, i can't shit in french!" claude nearly kicked him in the anglo. macaulay's minute & roosevelt's second unearthed in canadian library digs. chattel feared english had him in its grip. spooken for, punish.

\*      \*      \*      \*

## 1997

# translit

eration tends to be rather sub rosetta (make that sub rashid)
    e.g.  look say      one sec      goosey      piping      jigsy
king      caught      woo way      e-nigh      or      as in
*oolemma.* suddenly (so it seemed) the british word for *kie dan fa* irretrieved, tip of tongue

: well, so when her sister was doing her hair — "do you want it more *been* (flat)," she asked, tugging at the plaits, "or less *been?*" they giggled. she was feeling pretty down at the mouth. weeks rushing to finish the prototype for the software conference & what!? she dreamt last night she served some thin vegetarian stew with celery. probably anxiety about salary cutback. "celery . . ." her mother mused. "that's *kun lik.* you're giving them your strength, your industriousness." it had never occurred to her she dreamt in cantonese. "ma!" she blushed.

: in lit hillside colossus of aquaria      gigantic fish moves
plain silver black slow,      its body filling tank
   in tank below, shelled headless prawn, leviathan of sashimi
hangs diagonal
   some will sometime soon read,      swimming treadmill
journalists & writers out of a limbo      like single carp

\*    \*    \*    \*

## goon yum

### 1997

forgot you're not yet in vancouver
didn't bring you flowers, goon yum
what to present Your Mover?
will you accept this dim sum

\*    \*    \*    \*

## wooway

### 1997

"it was my 7th birthday, there was a family party. i was standing in the dining room looking out into the parlour at, on one side a square table of women playing mahjong & on the other a round table of men at poker. the children were playing in the verandah."

"thing is, i was 7 & i thought of them as children. there's something else. it was a moment alone, but with something behind me, some spectral presence, in the form of a taller, man. the seeing was clear, without hype."

the recital often drew respectful & puzzled hms in coming-out story-circles. but pal prairie nipper tom mix synopped: "typically asian . . . mhmmm . . . ghosts." he nodded between puffs, silent upon a peek in *de rien,* wake of kinship soothing gene autre's cyrano

# First Draft

## 1997

*Agnes Lam*

*Born and brought up in Hong Kong, Agnes Lam left home at nineteen to study in Singapore and America, and completed her PhD in linguistics at the University of Pittsburgh. The author of two poetry collections and numerous critical essays, she is one of Hong Kong's leading poets in English. Her poetry has been published internationally. She is also recognized as a Singaporean poet and an academic in English studies and linguistics. Several of her poems appear in this anthology. She formerly taught at the National University of Singapore and is now an associate professor at the University of Hong Kong. She lives in Hong Kong and actively encourages local writing.*

My life is a first
draft printed on paper once
used for other drafts.

*1 June 1994, Eliot Hall*

\*    \*    \*    \*

# Petals

## 1997

in three countries
I can grow
if but a little
each time
I transplant

the air
pollen dusted
allergic to spring
dripping with sodas
in the heat of summer
a chlorine bath later
smelling burnt

and crackling
on autumn trees
in the clear winter
icicles break and bite

extremes in America
modulated in Hong Kong
negligible on the Equator
but always
petals unfurling
I thrive
on the spectrum
of colours smells noises
temperatures humidities

degrees of pollution
in the pervading air

ready to be
watered by droplets
pressed between a child's
small fingers
a gift for Father

without roots
I grow

with but the scent
for a season
even a moment
translucent petals
dancing in a raindrop spectrum

mere petals
of scent and light
dissipated and mangled
in an afternoon storm

as the traffic
halts on the red light
and pedestrians
cross in their umbrellas

*28 June 1986, LRDC*

# My Mother-in-Law

## 1997

### I

My mother-in-law –
I am supposed to be
always quarrelling with her,
according to Chinese folklore.

But I do not speak Teochew,
nor is her English even basilectal.
Mutual learning is a possibility
but she's too old and I'm too busy.

Many times though, my sisters-in-law
have called me to post-umpire
a verbal score between one of them
and my mother-in-law.

You tell me, Agnes –
who is right?
Have I not tried hard enough?
Such a small thing and she curse and curse –

And I, your favourite daughter-in-law
have only ears and no words
for my mother –
or sisters-in-law.

### II

My mother-in-law
had a sudden fall –
caused by a tumour
benign in the brain.

The operation was successful
– too much so,
a wicked daughter-in-law
would have thought.

But why should anyone worry?
Even before the operation,
you had decided to come and live
with me – your favourite in-law.

Gone – my roaming in shopping centres,
pizza dinners by special delivery
or last night's leftovers
microwaved for another meal.

No longer can I work
late beyond air-con time
or early in the morning,
switch on the music.

My last vestiges of pampering,
my meagre distractions
when husband is out-of-town
or if in-town, out-of-home.

Oh, my mother-in-law,
why must I, the youngest,
least able to communicate,
be your favourite?


III

Six PM –
the fan is whirring,
you are dozing,
an S-tube protruding from your nose,
coiling like a worm
feeding on your skull.

The sodium chloride drips
drop by drop –
another one,
another one –
the phlegm
chokes –

Always when I come,
you draw my hand to ease
the phlegm in your flatted chest.
For one-and-a-half hours, I row
the tiny oar of my white hand
on your trachea thinking –

thinking –
of how
my father died,
my mother died,
leaving you,
my mother-in-law.

thinking –
this woman has brought up nine children
and five or six grand ones,
this woman who could quarrel with such spirit –
is now seventy-odd pounds, unable to talk,
hands tied to bed rails –

this matriarch from of old,
who is supposed to scold,
lying flat, skin peeling
as if sunburnt but without the glow
and happiness
is when the phlegm will flow.

As I row my small hand,
you turn,
look at me
with your one remaining eye –
I smile
and you smile

and I
remember
my mother's words,
'Be good
to your mother
-in-law.'

*1 October 1989, Tan Tok Seng*

# Hong Kong Tanka

## 1997

*Andrew Parkin*

Behind the hills
across from Taipo's towers
lightning flicks night sky
with a dragon's white-hot tongue.
Thunder rolls in from China.

# Astronaut

## 1997

School kids and working parents
desert these tidy West Coast suburbs.
My link with life
the mailbox at the corner,
dripping with rain day after day
in my soul's grey blank.

I slit the airmail and unfold the blue
backing the Queen's young head,
bauhinia waiting there to blossom
everywhere: Government House,
Kowloon clock tower, harbour,
narrowed tub of bobbing toys,
Legco Building, echoing with new voices,
and Victoria, surrounded by penile monuments
well-oiled with wealth.

Black characters dance across the sheet
and I'm back on the tram to Central,
haring up Pedder into Queen's
for coffee and Danish at DeliFrance
with you and your friends from Pokfulam
now the old Hilton and its coffee shop
have collapsed, rubble of demolished memories.

Over the page I'm with you again
in Theatre Lane planning a jaunt
to Wan Chai's neon galaxies
where life spills its seeds in alleys and streets.

Alone in soft West Coast rain
holding an airmail in my hand
I hear the roar of racing crowds.
I make my solemn vows:

fly wife and parachute kids to passport-land,
fly back, astronaut, coming in above love hotels
of Kowloon Tong for a Kai Tak splash down.
Rent a flat again in Happy Valley
with a view of the races,
whatever the cost per square inch
to my karaoke soul!

# On a Mountain above Tolo Harbour

### 1997

Chuntering trains meet and pass
meet and pass far down by the shore:
in this moist afternoon
the sea's a stretched grey cloth.

I climb further up beyond a rocky outcrop
high above the permitted future
approved by planners, legislators,
elected or not, and the lawyers
and the whole pack of architects,
engineers, quantity surveyors, accountants,
and I can hear already the clatter and thump
of yet more construction
really the destruction of a previous sense of place.

And this brief time is sold,
sold over and over again
like the land, our only earth.

On sheer rock, nature grins
despite the shock time future brings,
for through time and weather
a shy green wisp clings in a cleft
and waves minuscule trumpet petals
of deep red heraldry.

Suddenly there's a sense of occasion.
For a few seconds, human and rootless,
I feel welcome.

# Song of an Illegal Immigrant

## 1997

I'll hit the road and quit this place!
I'll hit the road and grab a better life!
I'll skip the propaganda sores
that bring the spirit to disgrace.

I'll shun the stopwatch and the gong
as time runs out on hope and faith
and dodge the one-child-bearing brides!
I'll pay a snakehead for the night trip to Hong Kong.

And there I'll live at a dizzy height
or under some dusty staircase doze
or prowl abandoned village streets
or work from a shed on a building site.

I'll scale the scaffolds of bamboo
on a concrete spine in a porcupine town
and at New Year I'll climb the hills
to search for a girl that's just like you!

And under the shade I'll mend my shirt
and drink a toast to the pin cushion town.
I'll meet a sweet-smelling modern girl
who's pretty and rich and born to flirt.

Even in dwindling countryside
she'll be svelte in her green track suit
and her sports shoes will be costlier
than any trousseau for a village bride.

I'll stroll my city streets as sun begins to fade
I'll smoke long cigarettes between my teeth
and from a pure gold chain around my neck
will hang her heart of precious jade.

I'll master the use of portable phones
and I'll carry brown notes but no I/D.
Our kids will go to a school abroad,
but when we die, they'll polish our bones.

*October 1994*

# I Fear I May Grow Old Before Frost Fall

## 1997

### *Laurence Wong Kwok-pun*

*A noted Chinese poet and translator, Laurence Wong Kwok-pun has published numerous collections of poetry, 'lyrical essays', critical essays, essays on translation as well as several translations of Chinese, English, French, Italian, German and Spanish poetry. A native of Hong Kong, he obtained his PhD from the University of Toronto and has taught in universities in Hong Kong and Canada. He writes most of his poetry in Chinese, but translates a significant amount of his own work. Several of his translated poems are included in this anthology. He is currently the head of the Department of Translation at Lingnan University and lives in Hong Kong.*

Why do my thoughts, like water,
before White Dew has ever come,
flow into the vast emptiness?
Beyond emptiness my long-awakened eyes,
weary, perplexed, like two ancient wells
beneath the evil wings of bats, fearful of nightfall,
in the hour before sunset,
amid broken walls and the lalang grass,
await a distant dawn.

Across the wide river, the southern bank looks north in silence.
In silence the northern bank awaits a small boat
bringing home the scattered clansmen,
scrutinizing through the sheen of tears faces long missed;
awaits a bridge, even if roughly built,
to span the heart-breaking divide,
so that after the storm the unworthy son, long exiled,
can hasten home by the light of the moon:
trembling, push open the creaking door,
gaze into the house and, with a long sigh,
try to know again through tears the ruined courtyard;
then, kneeling down, lips quivering,
stretch out his trembling hands, close his eyes,
and touch the shrine of his ancestors under the moon . . .

But gazing north, I fear I may grow old before Frost Fall,
standing atop the mountain like a stone figure,
alone with the vastness and solitude of heaven and earth,
fearful of the storms
that sweep darkly across immensities of mountains,
bringing with them from afar the bleak despair of dusk.

*[Note: White Dew is the fifteenth solar term in the traditional Chinese calendar, while Frost Fall is the eighteenth.]*

# The Great Bell of Yongle

## 1997

Small gongs and cymbals may vie with each other,
but you are the River of Heaven, a stilled flow,
quiet in time's night sky.
Like the Tanggula Mountains,
you gather the roar of Qutang Gorge
into the glaciers of Geladandong;
like a mighty river, frozen in thundering surge,
billows abruptly checked; like a cavalry charge
from six hundred years ago suddenly reined to a halt;
like a coral-pink shell in starlight,
drawing in soft waves and ripples that lap upon sand.
For six hundred years, your voice
has been a dark wave
a thousand fathoms deep,
quieter than the warm current that slips between seaweed.
When small gongs and cymbals have worn themselves out
and every ear is weary of noise,
then you will awaken, a giant
wiping moss from your curling whiskers,
stretching yourself, lifting your head.
At each breath
every ear will hear a cataract from the River of Heaven,
dark thunderbolts stampeding in a myriad valleys.
In the highest firmament
the billowing firs will roar, echoing the surging tide of the
                                            moonlit night.

\*    \*    \*    \*

# Rhapsody on a Rainy Night

## 1997

Rain drips from the eaves,
drips, till the world sleeps,
drips, till all sound dies,
quenching every star in the sky.
Now the universe is a shell,
ethereal chamber wherein echo only
water beads dripping from the dark eaves.

# Courtship in Hong Kong

## 1998

*Barbara Baker*

*Barbara Baker is an English poet, writer and editor who spent six years in Hong Kong. She has edited books about writing and China, and her poems have appeared in British literary journals and in a co-authored book of poetry and photography* Round *(1998, with Madeleine Slavick) and most recently in* Outloud *(2002). She currently writes and lives in London.*

'Do you feel adored?' he asked 'because you are.'
Shops of wrought iron, rattan and rosewood furniture.
In the botanical gardens cockatoos
Kowtow to the rubber necks
And chilblained knees of flamingoes.

'I want you to be happy always.'
Velvet headed children; pink swellings
Of mosquitoes and their terrifying siren.
Lush verdancy and glass and concrete.
Hurrying at a shuffled pace.

Swathed in love, cocooned
Like a child before a birthday.
The bougainvillaea glows, while
The exhausted hibiscus produces
Endless flowers which only last a day.

'I love you millions.'
In the market crates of live chickens
Stacked on top of dead ones.
The smell of durian and decay,
Heat suffusing.

'Will you marry me?'
The champagne bottle wrapped in
Orange cellophane makes noises
In the corner of the room
Like a budgie pecking seed.

# Passage

## 1998

*Madeleine M. Slavick*

*A poet, photographer and writer born to American and European parents, Madeleine Marie Slavick has lived in Hong Kong since 1988. Her work includes several poetry chapbooks, two books on China and multimedia projects incorporating words and photographs. Her co-authored book of poetry and photography* Round *(1998, with Barbara Baker) won a Bumbershoot Book Award. Several of her poems appear here. She currently organizes several poetry reading series in Hong Kong.*

Red lights of the family shrine
Red door gods
You see third sister behind the pink cloth
Hung from the top bunk like a wrap-around skirt
You hear *lo sam* in her bed of a world
Her lips moving with prayer to a new god

Red lights of the family shrine
Red door gods
You know *a-ma* and *a-ba's* sleep
Inside their plastic-walled mattress
You know he'll rise at five to breathe good air
And she'll take exercises at six
In the empty school playground

Red lights of the family shrine
Red door gods
Summer hallway air drags itself
Through the bars of the gate
And wades in the living room
*Gwai-po* daughter-in-law is awake on the sofa bed
Do you see her?
Is she protected?

# Mongkok Market

## 1998

Blood at the neat hand
Shout
Buffet for the quiet eye
Wide
Sweet leaves of heaven
Sing

Brown feathers are pulled silent from a young hen
the small body a single organ
a fallen cloud
Cold tofu blocks stand in formation like frozen corporals
then are sliced
and wilt
into a white blubber stomach
Crisp blood shimmery on opened fish brings ice
a quick knife
a long red-spotted apron
*Choi-sum* winds like a whirlpool, kaleidoscope leaves
green, light stem green
yellow speck flower green
And chickens make their cages whiter and whiter

# Dawn in the Mid-Levels

## 1998

*Laurence Wong Kwok-pun*

Resting my head on the dawn chorus,
I am a green waterweed
Quietly listening to the soft silver ripples
Streaming into the golden glass of dawn.
Deep in the glass, a transparent vein of light
Is slowly flowing over lock upon lock of lilac wind.
The lilac wind is your soft hair
Floating noiselessly over the golden comb of dawn.

# Coming into Beijing, 1997
## — *for Moling*

### 1999

*Alex Kuo*

Don't tell anyone about this
But I feel as if I'm coming home
Grass browning, coal smoke drifting
In this even November sunlight

Concrete block buildings in all colors
Dark figures in narrow hutongs*
With less than a little money to spend
They have been here for generations, sweeping

Everywhere the carefully planted trees
Tendered rows of elms, willows and locusts
Above them the flitting magpies and higher
Always the crows that have witnessed all

And all have come to this, like me
Stones and people from every province
Still able to be astonished
Still doing wrong or right in different directions

Did I arrive with the right currency?
And enough cigarettes for everyone?
Unlike the Hong Kong I've just left
My Chinese is better understood here

The familiar, differing warm expressions
Their all-day tea jars warming in the sun
In the shadow of another Mao talisman
Or any other remediable mistake

I enter the city writing this poem
That has become important to remember
Holding back tears the entire ride
A 30-km trip I used to bicycle everyday

At every intersection hundreds of bicyclists
Negotiate past truckloads of cabbage
Testament to another government surplus
Distributed free to every work unit

---

* Lanes or alleys in Beijing.

The same traffic signs are still cautious
Saying the exact same thing to cyclists
And the working horses that have refused
To pay attention for centuries in their toil

Next morning I will watch early dancers
Face the rising sun at the pavilion
As if they've just jumped out of prison
Onto the back of a dragon vexing everywhere

Early next morning I will also pick up
A fallen gingko leaf, wipe off the dew with my fingers
And press it deep into my passport
So dear, where it will stay, where I am not

\*     \*     \*     \*

# The Day the War Ended

## 1999

I was six the day the war ended in 1945
But I don't remember which flag I waved

There were carnivals everywhere
The regulators were beginning to disappear

The radio station sent out free news
Prison doors opened for fifty today, one hundred tomorrow

One by one they came out, the Red Cross relocating
The head in one place, the feet in another

Most said nothing, others still stood in line
Promising to vote "A" or "A" in the next election

There I am, in that photograph trying to look away
The day the war ended on this street corner

Those others gathered around me were waiting
Blowing out kisses to Movietone News

They lingered, trying to believe whatever happened
Will not be repeated in any history that day

Now at more than a half century since that war ended
Our stories are still hedged between hurt and hope

Most of the time I'm watching eyewitness news
As if I'm seeing something taking place in the past

Or between there and here, whatever the time
These intolerances have not stopped, whatever the place

This is what it was like exactly that day after
With nothing left to be taken away

Someone is tracing a distant coincidence
Another is doing the same in his head

No one is waiting for messages or decisions
Our fists gripped in ambiguity, between wars

\*    \*    \*    \*

# The River

## 1999

We live by it, bank deep
By choice near where some ducks
Have also come to believe
This fierce geography that the wind
Will not forget in the next change

We live in it, in its echo
That is a question, and that it asks
Is a breath forming its words
There on the opposite century, here
On this seamless shore, this abundance

One year I followed it back
To its beginning in a glacial gap
The next night all the seasons moved
A half moon over my head rising
At last released from all counting
We live for it, in its story

Dispersed as we are flesh in its eddies
Of meaning, this wider water
And its settlement among leaves
Glittering with teeming assertion

We live like this, our voice
Over this river's edge, reason
Collecting at the changing waterline
Where only a vague mark forms
Between promise and possibility

# The Last Beach

## 1999

*Mani Rao*

*Mani Rao is the author of five books of poetry and has lived in India, New Zealand and Hong Kong. She is one of the organizers of the Outloud poetry readings. Some of the poems from her Hong Kong publications are included here. She currently lives and writes in Hong Kong.*

―――――

### 2

Can't read
Can't talk
Teeth soundless
Tongue short
Push breath Push babies
Wait under palate gate
of lost meaning
Wash words of meaning
say iggy ugga buga luga wari oh numm numm

\*    \*    \*    \*

### 14

Somewhere
In vacuum

No sky above
Nothing
North South East West gone
Pinheads scattered
Blew this way and that

Light opens
Inside bright lies red
Inside red, black
Inside black, countless tiny arrows

Like all the phone numbers of the world
in the air, ringing

# how feel I do?

### 1999

*Jim Wong-Chu*

your eyes plead approval
on each utter word

and even my warmest smile
cannot dispel the shamed muscles
from your face

let me be honest
with you

to tell the truth
I feel very much at home
in your embarrassment

don't be afraid

like you
I too was mired in another language
and I gladly surrender it
for english

you too
in time
will lose your mother's tongue

and speak
at least as fluent
as me
now tell me

how do you feel?

# My Father-in-Law at Twenty

## 2000

*Timothy Kaiser*

*Originally from Canada, Timothy Kaiser makes his home in Hong Kong. His poetry has been published internationally. Several of his poems appear in this anthology. He teaches English and creative writing at the Canadian International School of Hong Kong.*

————

when mother-in-law is in China
father-in-law will take off his shirt
unwire the ancestral wok from the ancestral nail
mix salt and steam and cigarette ash into the fried rice
he learned to make in London.

in London when he was twenty
standing by a snowy statue in Trafalgar Square
someone taking black and white snapshots of him
wearing an impressive white woman
in an expensive white hat.

he handsome in a dark suit
speaking dishwasher English yet
the way he holds his cigarette
the way he leans towards her
dismisses the camera the cold
the woman must have understood.

I have seen those pictures
my wife knows where they are hid
and he once told me when others were in bed
how on the ship from Hong Kong to London
there was more than one fistfight with *gwei loh*
except when the ship stopped in Egypt
a ceasefire to see the Sphinx
he has lost the photos, he says,
smiling
coughing
checking his heart
blowing smoke away from me,
too long ago.

for my father-in-law at twenty
the sands of Egypt spicy under his feet
fists bloodied against condescension
stacks of unwashed dishes awaiting his arrival in London
and a mysterious white woman
smiling at him from under an expensive white hat
the riddles of the Sphinx must once have seemed
no more difficult than striking a match
on ice.

# Apology

## 2000

*Agnes Lam*

When I arrived two days ago,
you apologized so
for not prearranging a schedule
of lunches and dinners
for my visit to your university.
'It's all right.
I already know when
I should teach.
That is enough.'

We came to your guesthouse
and you expressed regret
about my room condition,
though it had a television,
a refrigerator, a telephone,
an attached bathroom,
from the tap, hot water,
embroidered flowers
on a bed in apple-green,
white sheets clean,
a window facing east,
leaves fluttering in the breeze . . .

In the last few days,
I did see a tear in
the seat cover, the vacuum
flask with only a cork, stains
on the dark green carpet, a dusty spider
hanging from the ceiling, paint peeling
at a corner, next to the bin, a dried
centipede, rust on the bath door latch,
a strip of mercury lost
on the edge of the mirror . . .

But there is no need
to apologize, my friend.

I too am Chinese.
This too is my country.
I have already been given
more than you have received.

If you must apologize,
then should I?

For my navy Ferragamo shoes,
my Max Mara suit a darker blue,
my white blouse from Episode,
Guess sunglasses a turquoise frame,
Nina Ricci skin, hair by Rever
clipped by Alexandre?
My IBM Thinkpad, HP deskjet?
My minimal outfit without
jewellery or make-up
seems too foreign still
for a Beijing campus.

Appearances aside,
how should I feel
about my unlimited access
to the tools of our trade?
International journals, latest
books from major publishers,
grants to attend conferences?
Freedom of choice
to cross academic borders,
travel intellectual distances?

Moving back
thirty years, when
leeches were sucking your
blood as you were
bending to plant grain,
I was feeding in Hong Kong
on the harvest from China.

My friend,
when I think of you,
I ask
who am I,
what have I done,
to deserve what I have,
what you have not?

Ten years apart in time,
a few thousand miles in space,
exchanging parents,
I could have been you
and you,
me.

*5 May 1998, Sanhuan Lu*

# Leaf of Passage

## 2000

*Leung Ping-kwan (Ye Si)*

Is this a jade or a wooden canoe? Sailing through wails from both banks,
Only to be stranded near customs officers, amidst immigrants waiting in line.

Myths of Haida Gwaii at your elbow: Bear Father with young son sits at the bow
Looking back at the past; Bear Mother rowing hard, gazes into the future of her children.

The sharp-teeth beaver paddles away, the dogfish woman converses secretly with the mysteries
of the ocean.
The Wolf, vying for position, tramples on whose back? The reluctant recruit aids in silence,
clinging on.

Has our Chief with great vision disappeared from sight with his talking staff?
Under our eyes only the amphibious frog crosses over the boundary between two worlds.

Not an astronaut bringing home legends of space odysseys. Not at all.
Just a lonely father shuttling back with heavy twigs to build new nests.

Worries add to one's age, diseases accumulate. Transit is never as smooth
As sages on blades of weed. See those mottled stamps on a suspicious passport?

Not so easy to roll a house into a backpack; lost forever are the familiar
Land and language. Departing, you imagined yourself a snow goose flying south,

Crossing the frozen earth in search of a warmer port? What one foresees
Are sneers from both soils: how can a leaf move that many woes?

*December 1998*

# Passports

## 2000

### *Shirley Geok-lin Lim*

*Born in Malaysia, Shirley Geok-lin Lim is an acclaimed poet, writer and educator who has won numerous international literary awards, including the Commonwealth Poetry Prize for* Crossing the Peninsula *and an American Book Award for her memoir* Among the White Moon Faces. *She is also the author of many collections of poetry and short stories and most recently a novel, and has edited several anthologies. The former Chair Professor of English at the University of Hong Kong from 1999–2002, she launched the 'Moving Poetry' project in Hong Kong schools and* Yuan Yang, *a journal that publishes the work of university creative writing students in English. One of her poems from her time in Hong Kong is featured here. She currently lives in California where she is a professor at the University of California, Santa Barbara.*

Having arrived at
the celestial kingdom, I
Refuse to enter.

Even now they live on wet boards
 in Aberdeen, once nameless,
unCeltic, an inlet of water
 safer than shore. Lured to land
sons and daughters forget the east wind
 and the north. Somewhere, grandfather
had passed through, looking for Nanyang.
 A woman of my family waited
for the patched junk sails to fill.

I am walking backwards into China
 where everyone looks like me
and no one is astonished my passport
 declares I am foreign, only envious
at my good luck. Speechless, without
 a mind of China, I remember
grandfather's hands, grandma's tears.
 On Causeway Bay, a hundred thousand
cousins walk beside me, ten hundred
thousand brothers and sisters.

# Keep Talking

### 2000

*Mani Rao*

Keep talking
Make words live longer.
Add vitamins to words.
Write poems full of You-s and I-s.

# ratio quality

## 2001

*Jam Ismail*

young ban yen had been thought italian in kathmandu, filipina in hongkong, eurasian in kyoto, japanese in anchorage, dismal in london england, hindu in edmonton, generic oriental in calgary, western canadian in ottawa, anglophone in montreal, metis in jasper, eskimo at hudson's bay department store, vietnamese in chinatown, tibetan in vancouver, commie at the u.s. border.

on the whole very asian.

# Lunch Hour Detention with Little Ming

## 2001

*Timothy Kaiser*

Little Ming,
Chinese *mestizo*,
mother a distant Malay,
stares down at his unfinished grammar,
his classmates chirping outside with a basketball.
there is no god he says,
tapping harder with his pencil,
no Buddha.
no Jesus.
no Mohammed.

Little Ming's Malay mother
was once his god.
she soaked his 22-hour delivery,
clubfoot,
nightly in gin,
shared in the laughter,
as he stumbled after kites,
far far behind other boys.

Little Ming's Hong Kong father
was next his god.
after many phone calls his father agreed,
he would,
yes he would,
mind you he wasn't pleased about it,
take Little Ming
for awhile,
No, just for awhile.

They met at Kai Tak.
no hug.
no handshake.
no smile.
his father god brought along one of his angels,
who filed her nails through Ming's hair,
leaned over,

peered into his eyes,
checking for lipstick smears,
cute
clubfoot

>     Again I go to China, Ming.
> business
>         you go to school.
>         lots of food in freezer
>     *siu mai*
>     *ha gow*
>     microwave.
>     don't let in stranger
>     see you in few days

>     oh and if Uncle Six calls
>     tell him
>             tell him
>     make something up
> when you're thirteen
> and the voices of the gods sound much the same before the beep,
> and the waiters at Pizza Hut change their names every week,
> and the wind rattles keys at your door in the night,
> what good is grammar?

# eradication

### 2001

under a battered tin roof
of Ha Wo Che Village
a seventy-eight-year-old
hangs herself

makes the noose from Park'N Shop bags
eyes good
    steady steady stool
    dog fed
    floor mopped
    curtain drawn
    rice covered
    radio . . .
    forgot to turn off radio

    or leave on?
    news then Chinese opera then news . . .

    steady
    steady
    stool

    at the market tomorrow
    will fruit vendor and vegetable vendor argue about
    last words?

the seventy-eight-year-old
cradles the framed picture of her deceased husband
her soldier her soldier
he never let the Japanese enter

shouts of glass awaken the dog

two days later shards return to sand
under the boots of police inspectors

nervous neighbours cluster
in whispers behind red and white tape
fretting that wind and water
have been irrevocably disturbed
rumours have been circulating
about the government
now is the time
it is being said
for all squatters
all rats

# White Dust

## 2001

*Agnes Lam*

I had lunch with a colleague
from another department
and said how much I liked
the high ceiling in their seminar room.

And she told me about the ants,
the white ants
eating away
at the foundation of their building,
the oldest on campus,
part of Hong Kong's heritage.

A few years ago,
the ants got so bad
four banyan trees with roots
deep into the ground
had to be cut down.

One day she moved
a chair. The back came off
swarming with ants all over her floor.
The Estates Office called in the pest exterminators
who poisoned the whole department
but still advised vigilance.
'They will come back.
The building is full of wood.'

Another time,
her colleague took out a book.
It fell out in white dust
between intact covers.
The whole bookshelf had been infested.
He sued the university.

He got back a few thousand
but not his books.
'If he had not touched them
for as long as it took the ants to eat them,
they could not have been of much utility.'
The lawyer had argued.

I remember vaguely
this British colleague of hers who left
some time ago. There was a write-up about him
in the papers. He looked intelligent,
charming. He had died in England.
Was he sick? Was he drinking?
Did he kill himself?
I do not remember.

He was a man with talent.
Was he eaten up
before he left Hong Kong?
Or before he came?

Who else
around me is but white dust?

*12 November 1999, Senior Common Room*

\*    \*    \*    \*

# You Say

## 2001

we do nothing right,
we abuse human rights,
refuse Tibet independence,
order tanks on unarmed students,

steal scientific information,
export too much, import too little,
pollute the air and rivers,
destroy tropical forests.

You say we are communists,
a political nuclear threat,
an environmental time bomb,
a looming economic disaster.

But how often do we invade
other countries in alliance,
drop bombs on civilians,
demolish national treasures?

Our head of state or his children
have no mistress on television.
We find adultery illegal,
prostitution distasteful.

We love our parents and
children, respect education,
are open to co-operation,
international visitation.

I could go on —
but if I do,
I shall sound
just like you.

*17 April 1999, Rodrigues Court*

\*    \*    \*    \*

# Writing in the Middle of the Road

## 2001

On my way home one Sunday afternoon,
turning into the new Bisney Road opposite Queen Mary Hospital,
I saw a woman writing in the middle of Pokfulam Road
at her blackwood study table astride the white divider.

The traffic passed by her on either side, avoiding her table.
Some people stared at her as they drove past but no one stopped.
Sheets of her writing flew into the air, brushing against passers-by who read
a few words and let them glide down the slope into the cemetery below.

Night came. The woman was still writing in the street light. Fewer cars were passing.
With the morning, the traffic returned but no one called for the police to come.
The woman did not leave. All hours of the day, she was there writing.
She did not eat, sleep, use the bathroom, change her clothes or talk to anyone.

At last I stopped to ask, 'Why do you write in the middle of the road?'
She replied, 'Where else can I write but in the middle of the road?'
'You could write at home.'
'What is home?
My home is only an enclosed space
in a building next to the road below.
At some point in the past, that space was right above the sea water.

Would you rather that I should write in what was the air above the sea?
Where I write is only the middle of the road now.
In the past, it was a mountain slope.
This spot could have been someone's hut.
In the future, it may also be.
I am not at the wrong place.
Perhaps you are asking me from the wrong time?
Why should the present matter
more than the past or the future?
A second in the future
in the next second is the present
and then the past.
If you split a second into milliseconds, then the present millisecond is neither
significantly different from the future millisecond nor the past.'

*9 April 2000, Pokfulam Road*

\*    \*    \*    \*

# Water Wood Pure Splendour

## 2001

*Shui mu qing hua,*
water wood pure splendour,
four words across the lintel.

This courtyard of low tiled houses
connected by covered walkways
like in the Summer Palace,
two stone lions guarding its entrance,
bamboos and pines shading a garden.

Behind the courtyard is a lily pond.
Beyond the pond, white stone bridges
cross a vast expanse of water, lily
leaves floating, not moving. Touching
the water are drooping willows.

Little patches of land connect the bridges.
Islands of trees grow to a hundred feet.
Buds in deep red blossom into pink roses.
One pavilion named 'Lily pond moon scene'
by a writer leads to a statue of Confucius.

This wood and water was once
the residence of the fifth prince.
The fourth became the emperor.
On a stone memorial, I read
its history, how it once was

part of Yuan Ming Yuan,
now in ruins after the fire
in 1860 set by the English
with the French when
China refused to yield.

After more invasions
by various nations, in 1911,
with indemnity money returned
by America, on these grounds,
Tsinghua was established.

On the twenty-third day
of the second month
in the year 1990, the Beijing
People's Government declared
parts of Tsinghua historical.

If the Anglo-French fire had
spread just a little further,
all these would not have been.
And no one could now study,
walk, sleep, fish, write poetry

in the wood by the water.
As colours change through spring,
summer, autumn, winter, shadows move
east, west, south, north. Over this land
of thousands of years,

as earth becomes heaven
in water wood pure splendour,
can the Chinese not forgive?

*19 May 1998, Tsinghua*
*with reference to a couplet on the door of the President's Office in*
*Tsinghua University*

# A Song from the Moon

## 2001

'You ask me how much I love you,
how deeply I love you.
Think a little, take a look —
the moon is my heart.'

She sings still,
a lightness in the air,
as I bathe and soothe
with forest fern.

The heart had stopped
somewhere in Malaysia
after a life
away from fans.

Every newspaper
wrote about her.
Every music shop
brought out her CDs.

The story goes.
The body rots.
Her photos fade.
The voice remains

as light travels years
from the moon,
from the sun,
clear and fast,
the present from the past.

*17 April 1999, Rodrigues Court*
*for Teresa Teng*

# I Have Walked on Air

## 2001

Last night
I had the dream again . . .

. . . a quadrangle,
on all four sides,
walkways with high ceilings,
smooth stone columns.
A garden in the centre
filled with light.

I was sitting
on the cool tiled floor
in the shaded verandah
leaning against a column,
looking at the garden in the sun,
in a white nightgown,
a tinge of blue light,
thin cotton, loose and
long beyond my toes.

I heard footsteps coming
and started to walk away.
Lighter and lighter,
my feet a few inches
above the ground,
I did not climb the stairs.
I floated into the air . . .

So many times
in my dreams,
I have walked on air.

I move over houses,
mountains, water, fields,
between the clouds
into the stars

as my body sleeps.

*2 November 1997, Rodrigues Court*

# Still-Life

## 2001

*Leung Ping-kwan (Ye Si)*

At the beginning, there was someone sitting on the chair
At the beginning, there was someone sitting at the table
At the beginning, there was someone watering a plant
At the beginning, there was someone looking up from the books

Where have they all gone now?

The one who danced to the music
The one who liked eating noodles
The one who liked drinking plain water
The one who wore a hat to keep off the sun

Where have they all gone now?

Was someone who wanted to have a good talk with you
Was someone who wanted to hold your hand tight
Was someone who wanted to sing loud with you
to look at the sky together with you

Where have they all gone now?

Turned into one who shared a drink of water with total strangers
Turned into one who went on hunger strike for what he believes in
Turned into one who dissuaded armed police with tears in eyes
Turned into one who fended off bullets meant for friends

Where have they all gone now?

Squashed to pieces
Riddled with bullets
Blown into sand
Scattered as dust

Where have they all gone now?

Turned into the constant shadows by our sides
Turned into the sun and air of our days
Turned into the plants and furniture in our lives
Turned into the book we read over and over again

# Let Us Move from Lonely to Alone

## 2001

*Mani Rao*

Let us move from lonely to alone
Walk into crowded spaces and be one of them — any them —

Go back to the same place until they expect our face
Salesgirls, bartenders, banktellers
All the public people
Counters that tick for anyone — everyone —

You know the man who runs the corner shop.
And the guard with no name who knows you by your floor
Give friendly strangers the liberties you give strange friends
From love to rugby to poetry, don't join the club

Don't decide don't divide
Home is where the heart is and the heart is full of habit

Hum the schoolsongs that failed to teach you to love your country
Pack up your loneliness and shift it from place to place
Into the unknown
Voices at the other end of random phone numbers
Leave your eyes on in the dark

Stare back

Sleepwalk

# Looking

## 2001

*Madeleine M. Slavick*

When he puts
his loved brown hand
on her
loved white arm
men on noodle shop stools
stare
why-don't-you-
have-a-Chinese-girlfriend
monologues

Women who know
their beauty
give body-looks at him
her
then her again
and make a sum of it

Entire eyes
come from tiger balm pajama
men and women
in metal history elevators
which have never carried
a Chinese man with a white woman

\*    \*    \*    \*

# Mid-Levels Front Door

## 2001

The soil is seventeen stories away,
swept diagonally under a lunar lawn

Trees pretend to stand at the entrance
The moat pretends to be a harbor

# Tiger Balm Gardens

### 2002

*Leung Ping-kwan (Ye Si)*

Tourists come and stop at this point
in front of a world already falling apart.
The wire fence cannot hold together
loose rock layers disintegrating from within.
No external repairs could redeem
such heavy falls, such entangled tortures.

When young, we felt disgusted and thought
such a tourist spot could only attract the philistines.
Today we visit this place again – why not?
Among gaudy scenes of melodrama
we deliberately look for the stone that is most ordinary,
that carries no parable.

They claim to be shepherds and fairies? Whatever.
They do not lie simply because they fear the tongue-pulling torture.
Kneeling or standing in their own pose, they are content with
simple moral lessons. Facing the same smooth cement surface,
we too have our fears. Beside that huge frying pan, a device for torture,
tourists take pictures while we imagine other hells.

*1994*

\*    \*    \*    \*

# Leafing Through Wingo and Holly's Photo Albums

### 2002

Someone on the radio is saying this is a historical moment,
yet you continue to use your second-hand Polaroid
to record our arguments over the video just seen:
That old Beijing Opera actor now lost in our modern city,

how could his personal feelings be better linked to the flow of
history? I look out of the window, and see the lights stretch afar.
We have seen many things tonight: Donna's prints
blooming with black and white flowers, Antonio's sculpture
resting in the toilet, and snapshots as I leafed through
your photo albums: shy Chinese children standing before
a pavilion, holding up their hands, "Friends!"
a statue of the almighty leader holding up his hand, kung-fu style.
Images of ancient cave paintings projected on the wall
(Who is it that stands up so suddenly and blocks the flying flags
from our view? What subtle shadows have made history questionable?)
Would you consider those patterns personal expressions
or the solemn recitation of an orator not necessarily
recording the people's hopes and fears?
The faint form born between two lines – a baby?
Yours, approaching three, healthy and strong, is waddling
through the complex hybrid art works by young parents,
laughing she toddles around bronze torsos with raised hands.
Friends, I've been leafing through your albums the whole evening.
I never thought you have captured so many moments: the first
poetry and painting exhibition we did together,
the first trip back to China, groping with curious lens
to understand the shabby kids on the streets.
Tumultuous events have changed the age, yet friends went on
to get married, raise children, lose their jobs, divorce,
and meet yet other fates on unexpected occasions.
Old photos remind us not to ignore personal details:
that first assignment in commercial photography, first design job,
first woodblock print, first daughter born.
The political situation is unstable but daily photos stay forever.
The curious camera has developed into an inclusive camera with
commercial colours juxtaposed on the solemn negatives,
images we strove to collect eventually changed the shape of the product.
Your hair was cut shorter and shorter, your drinks got stronger.
From a suspicious camera to a relaxed one
you in your own way have recorded history in your family albums.
My pictures have been lost, our past is out of shape, until
one day an old photo reminded us of things we'd gone through.
And now I look out of the window at the immense darkness
with its silence and glittering lights, cold, scattered, some fading out,
Some lighting up again, all in the same frame
until the camera zooms out, revealing to us
there are people in the scene, there are spaces
to live in; more than images in a still photo, all could be
recycled, merging and changing with different times.

*1984*

# NEW VOICES

# The Monkey Trap

## 2002

*Andrew Barker*

Well, that was my last shift at the *Post*. I don't know if you can get sacked anywhere else in the world because your superiors don't like your friends, but . . .

"This is the third time," Diane told me. She was referring to Nenuthar. "First there was that lunatic with the cuddly-toy who just wouldn't leave even though he didn't work here."

"Peter."

"Yes Peter. Then that . . . that . . . that oaf with the sandwiches."

"Ernie."

Yes Ernie. Then . . . I don't even want to know what that fucking bitch's name is."

I didn't get sacked anyway. I resigned. And I had the last laugh. They told me I had to give them a month's notice. So I gave them a month's notice.

And left.

\*　　\*　　\*　　\*

Michael's infectious enthusiasm for tuition has had little effect on Peter. After Michael told him it was *that* simple, Peter promised to check it out, left the flat, checked into the *Jump*, checked out with Clive and, as it was Halloween, checked into the old colonial building that everyone wants to buy. I now know one of the reasons it hasn't been bought yet. It was a lunatic asylum prior to the Second World War, so one can imagine the atrocities that went on in there then. During the Second World War, it was used as a prison by the Japanese, so one can't even imagine the atrocities that went on in there then. Basically it is thought to be the most haunted building in Hong Kong.

Being in the building on Halloween is supposed to bring bad luck. Being in any building at any time, blind drunk in the dark is likely to bring bad luck as far as I'm concerned. The fact that Clive has now got no skin over his right kneecap has nothing to do with Cantonese curses or fung-shui and everything to do with the rotting floor boards that ran under the length and breath of the colonial carpeting being removed by the building's renovators. Peter is having none of this, however, and sees sinister forces at work.

Sinister forces were at work, but there was nothing supernatural about it. Having four *Flaming Lamborghinis* Peter dragged Clive off for a cultural experience. This to assist assimilation in Cantonese culture by way of helping them to comprehend Chinese superstitions. Andy and I found them outside the building. A cold Clive asked to borrow Andy's tweed coat.

A crazed Peter asked me to time how long they were in the building. Had Clive not fallen through the floorboards Peter seemed prepared to last the night out comporting with spirits, other than those he had emptied from the vodka bottle. I stayed outside the building with Andy who explained the building's history to me.

"It was a prisoner of war camp during the war," he told me. "Can you imagine the atrocities that have gone on in there in the past?"

I shuddered to think of the atrocities that were going on in there now.

"The Chinese are very superstitious about things," I said.

"Caucasians are superstitious too," he said. "Most superstitions are there for good reasons. Not walking under ladders for instance."

"What's the good reason for that?"

"You might get a tin of paint dropped on your head."

"What about black cats."

"What about them?"

"What's the good reason for black cats being unlucky?"

"How's your friend Christine, by the way?"

"Point taken. What about dogs?"

"I think dogs are lucky. They can see the dead."

"Why are moustaches unlucky."

"Is that Caucasian or Chinese?"

"Chinese?"

"Have you ever seen anyone look good in a moustache?"

"No. Burning paper money?"

"Better than burning real money."

"Arrrrrrrgh!"

"Not wandering drunk around derelict buildings in the middle of the night."

"He's been in there thirteen minutes incidentally."

"For Christ's sake don't tell him that." Peter came out carrying Clive over his shoulder.

"Anyone still want to say that place isn't cursed?" he shouted. "My god, man you're lucky to be alive. Don't speak. I'll get you to a hospital."

Peter put Clive in a taxi.

"Can I get my fucking coat back?" shouted Andy, as they sped off.

*    *    *    *

### Superstitions, Festivals, and Halloween with the White Ghosts

After Chinese New Year, Halloween is the most conspicuously celebrated festival in Hong Kong. There are, of course, numerous Chinese festivals: Lantern Festival, Ching Ming Festival, Tuen Ng Festival, to name but a few. But Halloween is special. It's an American festival that attracts a Chinese turn-out in Lan Kwai Fong. To a lesser extent, non-Chinese New Year does this as well. Chinese people go *gweilo*-watching.

And what do they see?

Well, they don't see us at our best; that's for sure. Marching down streets in ghost costumes with painted faces, wailing and moaning Caucasions often take on Chinese traditions and superstitions. It's carnival time! Michael didn't come. The Rubicund Old Rottweiler who pays Michelle's bills was out of town so he was partying elsewhere. His appearance would have made four; the unluckiest number, sounding as it does in Chinese like death. My wife and Peter took the ceremony seriously; seriously enough to wear their own Chinese talismans. "Traditionally these are written in the blood of a dog, chicken, or human," my wife told me. A chicken, I prayed.

My wife is becoming adept at understanding Chinese superstitions. "Talismans are lucky," she told me. "Children and adolescents often wear them when it is believed they have not grown sufficiently to fight off malign influences by themselves."

"Why are you wearing it then?"

"Keeps me young," she smiled.

Halloween is having a strange influence on my wife. I caught her saving her fingernail clipping last week. Nail clippings, apparently, should be carefully collected and disposed of in a place unknown to others as it is believed they can be used to curse the person from whom the clippings have come. I was cutting my nails last night. This was dangerous too: "You can't cut your fingernails at night" she told me. "This may cause a visit from a ghost."

Peter is worse. He's become afraid of barking dogs because dogs have the ability to see supernatural beings such as ghosts and phantoms, and howl when they see one. Howling continuously, presages an imminent death. Incidentally, fluid from a dog's eye can enable humans to see the spirit world. A medium will smear the fluid on his/her eyes in order to see the supernatural world for the purpose of exorcism. However it is believed that ordinary people who smear the fluid from a dog's eye on their own eyes may die from the shock of seeing the afterlife. Hence my wife was reluctant to attempt a visit to the vet's to search out the winners of next month's race-meeting.

Traditionally, Chinese superstitions do not claim to predict the future exactly however. The point is not so much to have a clear picture of the future, but an indication of the possibilities that lie ahead. The Chinese are not exactly fatalistic, though they hold many superstitious beliefs. Therefore, having one's fortune told is more an indication of the conditions ahead rather than actual events. The opportunity therefore exists for people to make the most of their lives by being more aware of the 'environmental conditions' surrounding them. Hence our room has now been harmoniously arranged: fung-shui a concept taken very seriously here. In Repulse Bay the apartment block built on the prestigious site of the old Repulse Bay Hotel has a hole in it: a loss of several flats. The reason? Fung-shui. The dragon that lives on the hill behind the hotel needs to get down to the water to drink in the morning. And big business the hotel does too. Hence — spurred on by Halloween — my wife's current interest.

And there's the drinking of course. Streets are crowded with Chinese out to watch drunken Caucasians. Even Dr. and Mrs. Cheng were there. So many were out to watch in fact that they were nearly denied the pleasure of three performers — my wife, Peter and I — because we couldn't get into the packed streets.

## Bid for Carpet Woven with Memories

### 1999

*Divya Vaze*

I see myself now, lying on the carpet in my father's study. We weren't talking to each other, but that was not important. I loved watching him, at his desk, his throne. Controlling his world and ours with a quiet conviction, a quiet devotion. A gilded fan was squeaking slowly from the ceiling, turning, and stirring the smoky air. His hands turning the pages of his book — the only other sound in the room. Rahul lay next to me on the floor, driving the tiny matchbox cars along the imaginary roads we had traced into the carpet with our fingers.

I like to think that my father wanted us there, that our presence comforted him. I asked him questions occasionally; not just to receive answers, but also to hear him speak. He had a tuneless voice, precise as a soft stick of charcoal on paper. Mr Ashraf often sat with my father in the study and together they would talk of music, literature and the politics of the world. So I was not surprised to see Mr Ashraf that night, but there was something tense in his manner, an anxiety I had never seen in his easy smile. He brought nothing with him, as he usually did, no fruits from his garden, no clumsy hats made from old paper bags.

When he spoke to us his voice was barely audible; I later realised that it was fear that made it so. Fear. Despair. Tenderness. My father presided over the heavy teakwood desk, surrounded by the grandparents and the uncles. The eldest four sat in armchairs; the others stood close to the table. We heard them talking all at once in low animated tones, but we only paid attention to a few words. "Jinnah will have his Muslim state." "It is not safe for Hindus anymore." "Maybe you can return later . . . when it's settled. But now is a bad time." They all listened when my father talked. "We will make arrangements." And he looked up, as if suddenly remembering we were there. He hurried us out of the room, and the loudness I felt in my ears, as if I had been slapped, was the door clicking locked behind us.

* * * *

The taxi jerks to a halt; we have reached. He rounds the finger on the meter to the nearest five dollars, and slaps the change into my hand. The people in Room 802 walk like those in a dream, muted by the beauty around them. There are exhibits everywhere; many are hung on the walls, a few of the older ones are framed. Each is accompanied by a history pasted neatly on a card. I saw them all for the first time three days ago when I came for the viewing. Now I see only one. It seems to follow me around the room. We seat ourselves around a low stage, ready for the bidding.

Again I see it, exhibit 10. The lighting is thin to protect the display. I can almost hear the pulse thump through my hands.

* * * *

We children were playing on the terrace; from where we were, the city sprawled out beneath us, red as an anthill. My mother ran up to us, her feet bare on the scorching tiled roof, knocking down our matchbox cars. She picked up my youngest cousin, and she said to the rest of us, "Come on. The train's leaving. We have to go."

And we left, just like that. My mother crammed some of her expensive clothes and jewellery into an innocuous-looking paper bag. My father said: "It's too dangerous carrying those around. Leave them behind." He sat in the driver's seat of the domed black Hillman; my mother and I beside him; the four wheezing grandparents pressed into the back with four grandchildren on their laps. The others drove in the Ashrafs' truck. The late-morning light was mean and streaky. I had questions that I didn't ask: Where are we going? When are we coming back? We rolled up the windows to keep out the grit and the air inside grew sullen with fear. Sounds seeped through the glass: the weary shuffle of thousands of feet; the creak of wooden wheels. Everyone was going to the railway station. One people, pulled into two. The roads seemed to wince beneath us. Wincing and trembling, like a body being flogged.

I saw an old man supporting himself on the shoulders of two boys slightly older than Rahul, his hair and beard maggot-white. He stumbled over a body slumped in the road, and he crumpled, a heap of hair, clothes and loose grey skin. They picked him up, and for the first time I saw his face. The eyes, grimy with asphalt, dry and drawn with the dust of the road, protruded far out of the ghost-pale face. There was no certainty in his face, only fearfulness and doubt. The eyes were wide, making the white parts larger than the irises. I looked at my father, and his eyes, too, were white and waxy.

\*     \*     \*     \*

Now they are talking about number 10, my number 10. Owned by a wealthy family, in Lahore before the Partition, who fled to India leaving everything behind. A fine piece. See the workmanship. Unparalleled.

I think of how out of place it looks here. Yes, they nod their heads gravely, a fine piece.

\*     \*     \*     \*

The train station was a tangle of platforms, writhing and churning with thousands of zombie people. We climbed out of the Hillman; the Ashrafs had not yet arrived. My uncle had to shout over all the voices around him: "We should have come hours ago. Look at all these people." He pushed me forwards, into the crush. "Go on, get on the train. We're just waiting for the Ashrafs; we'll join you soon. Go on, boy. Go. Go. Go." He shoved me into the pressing, elbowing crowd. When I turned back, I could not see the family; only the bald black head of the Hillman.

\*     \*     \*     \*

The bidding is over, and I am exhausted. Someone has come over to congratulate me on my purchase and I find myself writing out a cheque for an enormous sum of money. He wants to know my address: "For delivery, you understand, sir." No, I hear myself saying, give it to me now. I will take it now. Now.

\*     \*     \*     \*

I remember very little about the train. It was black and terrifying. My mother had once told me about the monstrous black beasts which took millions of Jewish people to Auschwitz and Dachau before the war ended two years ago. I wondered: Was it like this? Were they numbed with fear, as I am now? Did they, too, feel, as I do, like a blind person groping in the dark for some cool, quiet place where everything made sense? I remember shouting out of the window: "Here I am, Rahul. I've saved a place for you." But a large marble-eyed woman sat in the seat next to me. She seemed to understand what I had been thinking. She told me to sit still; she said I would find my family when we reached Amritsar, and that I would enjoy living there. "Not to worry," she said, as she put her thick arms around me, "you will be safe in India. They will come for you. Or you will find them." I never did.

*     *     *     *

A different taxi is driving me back; it smells flatly of synthetic lemon. Hong Kong, this city of my escape, this place I have loved as my home ever since I left India, sweeps past, frame by blurred frame. But I am not escaping now, I am returning. Beside me, hidden from my eyes by layers of brown paper, is a painting woven in silk. My mother once told me it had been part of her dowry when she married. The tassels have frayed now, but this is where we raced our little matchbox cars, through this garden of night. I imagine where I will keep it in my home, and I imagine my father behind his heavy teakwood throne, pausing from his books to rest the half-moon eyes, glancing across the leather room at his carpet. We are one now, he and I.

With this carpet — this beautiful survivor — I am taking home a childhood, a house in old Lahore, a family. I am taking them home.

# Press Enter

## 2000

*Lex Lao*

Return-Path: solwan@hkglobe.com
Date: Wed, 8 Dec 1999 19:20:28
From: Sol CW Wan <solwan@hkglobe.com>
Subject: The Dowager Empress
To: helenyu@canadanet.com

hi helen!

u know what? saw The Dowager Empress sneaking out of my room again yesterday. she was smiling like a lap-sap yan asking for a lai see. ignored her. as usual. bundle of stuff in her arms. looked like laundry, trash, paper & plastic bags.

migod! what's with the olds these days? they keep piling up garbage like third world war's coming. of course, it's good coz she keeps my room clean. but i'd be more comfy with a maid. at least nobody nags u if u ignore maids coz they're not like family anyway.

been telling dad to put The Empress in a nursing home. or maybe send her back to guangdong. but u know dad. can't make up his mind. kinda like The Emperor of Ice Cream really. ha-ha! (yups, we're still literate over here, despite the return to the motherland blah-de-blah-de-blah.) anyway. hope he melts soon. maybe The Empress can make tea out of him. but it would probably taste bad & bland. ha-ha!

so, how's ur life? u also live with weirdoes? u also have short circuits over there in vanc? guess everybody needs new motherboards in their heads these days. anyway. really excited about my english theme. just finished the draft. it's gonna be ubersuper! wait till ms bumsy ramsey reads it. (remember her? big as ever la!) she'll be floored. she might even refer me to a literary agent in london. yeah, right. ha-ha! oops . . . The Emperor of Ice Cream's here. he'll probably need the mac. gotta go!

cya! pls email soon . . .

sunny sol:-)

*    *    *    *

9 December 1999 Sheung Wan Hong Kong

My Dear Daughter,

I am now here. Death separates us and I can no longer see your smiling eyes — your father's eyes. But I can feel you. And that is even better than seeing.

I arrived here four days ago, in this always hungry city that has swallowed you in your youth yet spat us out like fishbone. On my first day here, I asked Siu-man to take me to your resting place. But your husband has retreated to the deepest wells of his lonely soul, like a turtle that has finally decided to die in its shell.

Siu-man said he was busy. Instead, he asked Chit-wing to take me to the cemetery. But your daughter also said no. She left the dining table without finishing her dinner and huddled in front of that strange TV-looking typewriter. At first, Siu-man didn't say anything. Then he started banging the pots and plates and chopsticks in the kitchen. Chit-wing started crying. I tried to comfort her. But she turned away and ran to her room screaming that she hated all of us.

I told Siu-man to just give me the directions and I could go myself. But he said I'd probably end up in Tai Po or somewhere. So he took me there himself the next day, but only up to the cemetery gate. He pointed me to a clump of trees, turned his back and lit a cigarette. I knew it would be useless to persuade him to walk me to your resting place, so I went alone from there.

I left some flower seeds around your grave. Remember the fast-blooming yellow ones you loved to put on your study table back home in Guangzhou, before this gluttonous city took you away from us?

You looked very beautiful, smiling in your picture on the headstone. You reminded me so much of your Papa: the eyes of a wild fawn, nose as stubby as dried abalone, and forehead as wide and smooth as the Gobi, cradle of our clan.

Oh, my dear daughter! You cannot imagine how it broke my heart that I wasn't there when you needed me most. I tried to plead with the authorities in Guangzhou to push my papers. I paid them the money that Siu-man sent me. The little savings I had and the money left by your Papa also went to the travel people.

But they made me wait. They said it was not easy to get the right papers. That it was very tight at the border. That there was no place for us old people in Hong Kong. Forget it grandma, they told me, Hong Kong doesn't like mainlanders, especially greying mainlanders. I could not understand why some people continue building borders and divisions. But this city had always been aloof, a fortress built on the fears and loneliness of merchants and thieves.

I almost died myself when I received Siu-man's letter in October last year. I cried until my heart cracked. If only I could have made Death wait for a few more months. I would have given him the old house your Papa built for us, given him the little vegetable garden that had sustained us during those terrible years, given him the last few years of my own life in exchange for more of yours. But Death is a greedy dog. It devours everything — flesh, bones, even its own vomit.

My travel papers finally arrived last month. But it was only for a temporary stay of about 30 days. I didn't complain. It was better than nothing. I sold our old house and I took the first morning train to Shenzhen. Siu-man was waiting for me. But he was not really there. He is so alone, like a bamboo weeping by a riverbank. I know he is crying inside, but he does not want to show his tears. So he grieves alone. But he will find his way. Your husband has kept himself busy with his work at the university. He's also helping at the public library on weekends, much like what you did then, showing children the books and those TV-looking typewriters you had told me about in your letters.

Siu-man will be all right in time. It's Chit-wing that I'm worried about. Siu-man said she'd been having fights at school. She hardly eats at home. Her room is a mess. And she spends most of her time in front of that TV-looking typewriter. Sometimes I find her staring into the eerie emptiness of that machine, her eyes dead and unblinking as she twirls her ponytail in her fingers.

I have seen similar machines in Guangzhou, and I have heard that they do nothing but spread lies and evil thoughts, and that some people have been arrested for becoming slaves to these devil's devices.

I am worried that this evil-looking thing is draining the life and the laughter out of Chit-wing. She's been avoiding her father. She has turned me away. (I have asked Siu-ming to throw away that black box so Chit-wing can rejoin the living, but your husband only laughed at me.)

Dear daughter, I'm afraid your leaving has made Chit-wing close upon herself, a water-lily weeping over its dying pond.

You left behind such silence and space. I don't even know where to start, where to find the heart of this home. But I promise you: I will be by your side as often as I can. I will keep away the grass and bring forth the flowers. I will look after Chit-wing like I've looked after you — my very own daughter. I will do my best to reach her so she'll know that she is loved. That there's no need to be angry or be alone. I will give her my hands, old and weak as they are, so she can feel you and know that you will always be with her.

With these words I have started to reach out to her. That if the greedy dog of Death snatches me away like it had devoured you, or if I am sent away and the border is again raised between us, Chit-wing may read in here the message from my heart, and find in my words the soul of her pond to help her bloom in time.

With all my love,

Mama

*    *    *    *

Return-Path: solwan@hkglobe.com
Date: Sun, 12 Dec 1999 21:30:58
From: Sol CW Wan <solwan@hkglobe.com>
Subject: Weaving Webs
To: helenyu@canadanet.com

hi helen!

big news! just found a nifty web site with tips on making ur own page. & it has instructions for english & chinese sites! will post my english theme on the site once i've spiffed it up after christmas. the file's in the mac so will be easy transferring to web site. hate editing onscreen so i've been printing them for checking & revisions. gonna be major, la!

by the way (or should it be BTW? ha-ha!) told The Emperor of Ice Cream about The Empress. told him about the space invasion thingy. don't know what got into dad lately but he's been soooo nice to The Empress. (she's probably put something in his food.) dad said to try to understand the old woman & to talk to her. is he mad? what's she doing here anyway? she's no longer needed here. she should go back to her chicken farm & vegetable patch on the mainland. where was she when mom was sick? how come she was nowhere around when mom died?

migod! old people always come crawling back to u when they're about to die & too poor to take care of themselves. hope dad wakes up from his goody-goody spell. wish mom was here to knock some sense into his frozen coconut. actually, wish mom IS here . . .

sorry for lapsing into a hallmark moment. i do miss mom worrying about my eyesight & nagging me to keep my back straight when using the mac & braiding my hair & fixing my lunch box & teasing me about BFs at school & all those corny mother-daughter thingies. The Empress has been doing most of these now. but she's not mom. she's only doing them coz she's staying with us for free. she doesn't really care.

anyway. have to start thinking about my web site now, as they say, i have a web site, therefore i am. how about u? do u exist in cyberland? ha-ha!

cya! (dya think it's good to put my ho-leng pix on the web page? just asking)

sunny sol:-)

*    *    *    *

Hi, sweetheart! How's my lovely wife? I'm writing this letter in my heart where I know you'll find it in a zip. You left us more than a year ago — actually one year, one month and 20 days — so this will be the first Christmas without you here. Of course, I know that you'll always be around. Like this wedding ring. You know, I didn't really understand why you had to go like that. Everything just happened so fast. One moment you're all pink from the vitamin treatments, next thing you're as thin as chopsticks, paler than congee. I was so shocked when you started losing you hair. It seems amusing now, but you did put on a brave face, kiddo. Well, at least you tried. But didn't work on me. No way, baby. After all, I'm your one-and-only so I know you in and out, sweetheart. I saw the pain. I saw the sadness. And the guilt! Why did you have to feel so bloody guilty about being sick like that? It wasn't your fault. Though it was a bit hard juggling things, with you in hospital and Chit-wing having to go to school. But it was okay. We managed somehow. Then it all came crashing down. Just like that. I'm sorry for just going blank, love. You know how it is. Being an orphan and all, probably. I'd had nothing before I met you and then you just slipped away like that. What was I supposed to do? I felt so cold and bone-dead like a mahjong tile. I actually thought of doing that Tarantino thing, you know, killing all the useless doctors at the cancer ward. Scary thought, huh? But, you know what? What's even scarier is that I think I've been a very bad father to Chit-wing, leaving her with her own loss while I just gathered mould like a piece of old tofu. (And I'd been going through my work like a zombie really. But most professors are like that anyway. What a bum.) Lucky thing Mama is here. She's been dragging me to the cemetery almost every week. Oh, you should see us! Ha-ha-ha! Like secret lovers meeting at the cemetery gate. Actually, it took me a month to move from the gate to your grave. Mama has done a good job. There are now bright yellow flowers round your tombstone. Kinda like a golden halo really. Which I think you deserve, my angel. Me and Mama have been talking there, by your grave. I don't exactly know when it happened, but I slowly understood what she was trying to do: Don't think too much about the space you've left behind. It just won't work that way. Instead, try to remember the good and happy things about you. It's very simple, isn't it? It's really strange how stupid I'd been, not to know this. So, being a good father and all that, I'd tried talking to Chit-wing about this. Bad thing is, she's shut me off. Even Mama has been turned away. There's just no way of reaching her now, sweetheart. So, if you don't mind up there, I was thinking that maybe this Christmas, maybe I could ask a small favour from you? It's nothing much, but it would mean a lot: Do you know the way to Chit-wing's heart? That's all I wanna know. The rest will follow.

Miss you much,

Siu-man

*    *    *    *

Return-Path: solwan@hkglobe.com
Date: Sun, 2 Jan 2000 22:20:18
From: Sol CW Wan <solwan@hkglobe.com>
Subject: What a Bug I Am
To: helenyu@canadanet.com

hi helen!

don't know where to start. been a very weird new year. finally finished my english theme last december 29. made inputs of corrections & then trashed printouts. went out for a boring new year's eve cum new millennium party at school. opened my files yesterday & WHAM! they're all gone. everything! kaput! zilch! nada! my baby web site! my calendar! my phone numbers! but worst of all — my english theme! migod! it was so stupid not to have it on a diskette. four months of work down the drain. sleepless nights. a cheekful of pimples. eyebags as droopy as an old watson's shopping bag. all for nothing.

after the screams, came the tears. dad tried everything to retrieve the files. nothing. more tears. more screams. The Empress stood dumbly behind us, looking like a greasy dai pai dong plate washer. she started asking questions & i screamed at her to just shut up coz she didn't know a whit about what was going on anyway.

migod! she probably hadn't even seen a computer till she was 60 years old! & it wasn't her business anyway. she scurried away like a rat. came back a minute later cradling a big pile of papers bound by her old stockings. Dad looked at the pile. then he looked at me with these big open eyes, his cigarette clinging to his lower lip. i looked at The Empress. then at the papers on her arms. then i looked at dad. i looked at the Empress again & all I saw was this tiny old woman— my grandma — forcing a smile over her strange & heavy load.

migod! there they were! the printouts of my address book! my phone numbers! the calendar! & my english theme! from the very first outlines to the final corrected version! all this time, grandma's been collecting them, binding them with her stockings & putting them under her bed, in her tiny closet, under her pillow, every nook & cranny of her little room. dusting them off regularly. guarding them against moths, silverfish & mildew. all this time. & u know what she said? in her funny inland cantonese? "Sorry, Chit-wing. The binding is not very good."

my knees buckled. i had to hold on to the computer desk as i laughed & cried like a mad woman in a canto opera. i was having a short circuit. i needed to upgrade my motherboard . . . WARNING: another hallmark moment coming . . .

i had a talk with grandma until late last night yesterday. dad came into my room to say goodnight to me & to grandma. then, from his breastpocket, he took out this gold necklace that mom wore on their wedding day. dad kissed me on the forehead, and for the first time since mom died, i saw him smile. i had to stop myself from crying when he helped me put on the necklace. dad pinched my nose — my abalone nose, grandma said — & then he walked out the door, humming celine dion's titanic song. (yes, he & mom used to sing it just to drive me mad! aargh!) and then i saw The Emperor of Ice Cream slowly melting on the floor.

as we sorted out the computer printouts, grandma told me why she was held up in guangzhou when mom was sick. we talked about grandpa. what mother was like when she was a little girl growing up in a farming village on the fringes of the city. what they did to survive the Red Book craze & the famine. how grandma hid grandpa from the commies who wanted him dead for planting his own bak-choy. (imagine that!) how she devised ways to grow the damned vegetables herself & search for more food in the hills of guangzhou while grandpa was hiding in the granary behind their house.

migod! her story was far better than anything i've read in english class! it was just so stunning to hear the tale of this tiny woman who held her family together while typhoon signal 8 raged around here. (& i've got her genes, la!) then we talked about mother's favourite flowers & how grandma used to braid my mother's hair. smooth & silky as cornhair, she said. just like mine, she said. i touched the necklace near my heart & took grandma's hand. slowly, i turned my back to her. then i let her braid my hair.

cloyingly urs,

extra sunny sol:-))

*    *    *    *

Return-Path: solwan@hkglobe.com
Date: Tues, 4 Jan 2200 22:20:18
From: Sol CW Wan <solwan@hkglobe.com>
Subject: Message from Grandma
To: helenyu@canadanet.com

hi helen!

i'm sending u a very special letter. it's also on the first page of my web site (http://www. hkglobe.com/members/sunnysol). check it out! it's by granny. i know, i know. she can be corny, but she's ok, la!

it took a while before i could drag her to the computer. she kept muttering some kind of anti-evil-spirit chant before i could put her fingers on the keyboard. i had to tell her it was just like an ordinary typewriter. but she looked at me with such horror & dismay that i had to show her how to use it. i said it was just like going to the market & pointing to the garoupa or the bak choy or whatever it is u want to buy. she still looked hesitant. actually, she looked like she was about to cry.

so i told her the machine could send messages to mom anywhere in the world & beyond. well, that did the trick. & off she went like a hovercraft to macau. ha-ha! hope it brightens ur day . . .

super sunny sol:-()

Attachment Follows:/

JANUARY 4, 2000 SHEUNG WAN

MY DEAR DAUGHTER,

I AM NOW HERE. CAN YOU SEE ME FROM UP THERE?

CHIT-WING SAID SHE WOULD PUT THIS LETTER ON THE TV-LOOKING TYPEWRITER, OR THE MAC AS SHE CALLS IT. THE LETTER WILL BE IN ENGLISH AND CHINESE. SHE SAID THAT PEOPLE ALL OVER THE WORLD WOULD BE ABLE TO READ IT. I DON'T KNOW HOW CAN THAT BE. I BELIEVE HER JUST THE SAME.

BUT SHE JUST LAUGHED WHEN I ASKED HER IF MY MESSAGE COULD INDEED BE READ BY PEOPLE UP IN HEAVEN. I SAID THAT IF GOD AND HEAVENLY BEINGS CAN READ HEARTS, HOW MUCH MORE SIMPLE MESSAGES LIKE THIS?

SORRY. I HAVE TO USE BIG CHARACTERS BECAUSE IT IS VERY HARD FOR ME TO SEE. BUT I AM SURE YOU CAN READ THIS. AND I AM SURE YOU CAN FEEL THE HAPPINESS IN MY HEART.

THE LITTLE BLACK SQUARES WITH LETTERS, NUMBERS AND CHARACTERS MAKE ME FEEL VERY DIZZY. THERE ARE SO MANY OF THEM. AND THEY HAVE FUNNY NAMES. ONE IS CALLED "ESC". ANOTHER IS CALLED "END". AND THERE IS ALSO "DELETE". BUT MY FAVOURITE ONES ARE "HOME" AND "ENTER".

WITH ALL OUR LOVE,

MAMA, SIU-MAN AND CHIT-WING

Hi, sweetheart! How's my lovely wife? Thanks for guiding us back to Chit-wing's heart. Now we're a family once again. But I'm afraid it might not last. So, can I ask for another favour, love? Maybe this one's for an early Valentine's treat? It's about Mama's one-way permit . . .

# Back Street

## 2000

*Nicole Wong Chun Chi*

'Papa, where are we?'

'At the back street, at the end of the street we live in.'

'Why are we here?'

'I'm here to play.'

'Can I play too?'

Papa raised his hand. He was standing against the sun; his face was dark. I drew a deep breath to keep myself from crying. I did not want to be slapped on the cheek.

'We're going up to a flat. I'll take you to desserts later. Don't tell anyone that we have come here today. Did you hear me?'

I nodded. My head was heavy. I kept trying to tear my hand out from his. If I turned around and ran inside the crowd Papa could not probably catch me. It was just one street. It is the 'Women's street' in Mong Kok. The whole street is a fair, where people are always thronging back and forth, grabbing and bargaining over the cheapest goods. Clocks, watches, accessories, bags, clothes — the panties with pink fur. Mama yelled at me when I asked her if she had got any.

It was no use running home. Grandpa and Mama were working. Grandma had gone out. I had a fight with my neighbour XiXi the day before. Maybe I could get lost. Then when Papa found me, he would be crying and would not beat me. But I did not want Mama to cry. The only time I got lost I went to a policeman. The moment I saw Mama again I grinned and thought she would say I was clever, but she just held me and cried.

'My life is hard enough!'

Her tears rolled down to my forehead. I wiped mine away at once. Mama would cry harder if she knew I was crying too.

So we came into this back street. Trash was spilling out from the back plastic bags. Soft drink cans, plastic bottles, paper boxes — red and orange, blue and green — the colors clashed with one another and the smell of rotten food. Next to the trash was a metal gate. The sun shone on the silver but not the rust. Above the gate were the thin black frames, and old posters of movie stars on the windowpane. On the walls pasted advertisements that blew lightly in the wind. They read: second-hand cars for sale. I must have made some of these details up. I have come back from time to time to make sure it is the right back street, and it looks about the same from how I remember it to be.

Papa pushed the gate open. I could hardly see the stairs.

'The stairs are so long! It takes all my strength away. How can I have fun then!'

I had never seen Papa giggle like that. I was panting but I did not want Papa to know. We might be climbing up the stairs and panting in the dark forever. We might never get out from this building. That would be better than lying dead in the Women's Street. I would scare those hawkers to death. Papa and Mama always fell sound asleep before I did. Sitting between them, I could not help looking out from the windows.

The stairs ended. There stood another metal gate, painted in green. The dark brown of the wooden door looked dark red, like blood that had dried. Father strode towards the door and pressed the doorbell, which was covered in dirt and fingerprints.

'Honey, I'm coming!'

'Hurry up!'

So the blood melted. A pair of fake eyelashes was flashing behind the gate. The eyeline and eyeshadow had melted into a thin dark circle. As the woman opened the gate Papa started giggling again.

'How have you been? Busy?'

'Many customers today. Is this your daughter?'

'Her mom has to work today and I have to look after her. So troublesome!'

Papa dragged me into the flat and we sat down on the sofa. The woman closed the door and leant against it. She was wearing a purple, semi-transparent dress and brick red lipstick,

'Why bother to have a family then. You can always have fun here, right?'

'Of course! My wife can never do things that you can.'

Papa held her by her waist and leant forwards to kiss her. She glanced at me.

'Let's deal with your daughter first. Little sweetheart, will you be a good girl? Don't run around or touch anything. If you're bored watch the streets. Papa will take you home soon. How old are you?'

'Four.'

My voice trembled. I often saw Papa with different women. Sometimes it was the same woman. Sometimes it was a new one. They all asked the same question, 'Has your Papa taken you to meet another woman?' I always said 'No' as Papa told me to. I did not want to upset them. Sometimes they told me how I looked and acted when I was a baby. I thought they liked me because of Papa. But this woman had been staring at me so hard till I sat up on the sofa and looked out from the windows. Her voice was so thin that I wanted to cover my ears. I had never imagined seeing Papa with such a woman. I had to clench my fists to stop myself from shivering. I had to look at the sky; the cars on the road; the pedestrians on the zebra crossing — to forget the sound of the shower.

A door opened. I turned around and sat down on the sofa, my ankles on my knees, my hands on my ears. Another door closed. I put my hands down and scratched some plastic off the black sofa with my fingernails. There were lots of scratches on the white walls, some longer ones were filled with dirt. In front of the sofa was a white plastic table. As I stood up I saw a bowl of soaked noodles and a pair of chopsticks. Next to the bowl lay a heap of magazines. Noise was coming out from the room in the dark corridor. It thundered in my ears but I had given up covering them. On the first page of the magazine the woman had her whole body bound with ropes and her legs spread. Papa was growling and the woman screaming. I knew what they were doing, but I could not picture it in my head. The woman on the next page was squeezing her breasts. I stood there and read on. The noise stopped. I jumped up to the sofa and knelt looking out from the windows. The clouds were moving fast in the sky. I heard Papa's footsteps and begged myself to weep, or to at least look shocked.

'Hey, girl. We're going.'

Papa was combing his hair with his fingers. I sat gazing at him though I could stand up at once. The woman appeared, her semi-transparent dress swaying under the fan. Her grin was different from those of other women that Papa went out with. I was waiting for Papa to look at me again, but he was smiling and whispering something in the woman's ears. I had seen Papa doing this to a woman for many times. Maybe a man always does this to a woman other than his wife.

'We're going to have desserts. Don't mention this to anyone, not even Mama. Ok?'

I nodded. I always told Mama that it was only Papa and I when we went out. I did not want her to run away from home again.

The woman hugged Papa, and pinched my cheek as she said 'Goodbye!' to me.

The blood melted again. Papa pushed the green metal gate closed. I was glad that he did not hold my hand as we walked down the stairs.

# The Perfect Day

## 2001

*Iris Eu*

Yeah, I'm okay. *Smile.* Yeah, I'm feeling a lot better today. Guess I slept. My plans? Um . . . go out with George, I guess. Yeah, he knows. What? Yeah . . . I told him. He's coming to pick me up at ten. No, you don't have to call him. He'll be here for sure. We've got today all planned. No, ma, go right ahead. Seriously, mom! *Smile.* It's cool. Don't worry so much! Look, I'm feeling good, okay? Really. Now go. GO! *Smile.* Tell Dad I said hi. I'll be home tonight anyway. *Smile.* Man, I swear I'm gonna scare Taylor so badly when I walk in like this!! He'll bark like mad, but I guess I can scare him off with the light I can reflect off my head! *Laugh with her.* No, no I don't need the hat — I'll just go like this. It's cooler this way anyway . . . Now GO! You're late already! Shoo!! Nurse nurse . . . get my mom out of this room pronto!! Give her a shot! I don't care! Get her out!! She's harassing a patient! *LAUGH. Smile. Keep smiling. Look at the nurse. Smile. Wave. SMILE! Turn the head.* My boyfriend's coming to pick me up at ten, is that okay? Yeah, I'm all packed. Glad to get out of here. Even though I'll miss you! *Smile.* Yeah, I'm okay. The best I can be. Yeah, okay . . . see you later . . .

*Smile. Watch her go. See the door close. Breathe. Look out of the window. See the trees, past the bars and the sterile walls. Past the needles and the treatment and the discomfort. See past Mom and Dad and George and Taylor. See past the head with long hair. Look at the clouds — how beautiful. A perfect day. See grass and sun and trees dropping leaves. See past the suffering and pain that close out the pleasures of the world outside the window; past the bars. No more bars. No more pain. No more waiting. Breathe. Slip the hand into the mattress and reach for the hidden bag. Take it out — pour all of it out. See the small speckles; see the imprints in the specks and the manufactured name. Roll it in the palm. Don't ask, just do. Do, because you know there is no other way. Do because you want to. Count and place each one on the tongue. One by one. Drink. Swallow. Drink. Swallow. Drink, swallow. Drink, swallow, drink swallow, swallow swallow swallow. Count. Look. All gone. Fold the bag, place it neatly in the packed bag. Lie back down. Breathe. Turn the head. Look at the clouds. Feel the sun.*
*Breathe.*
*Relax.*
*Wait.*

*Sleep.*

# To Victoria Park

## 2001

*Chun-kit Fan*

This staircase, made of fine polished pine, with vigor and absolute firmness, leant in the middle of the hall. An unceasing carpet of lamb's wool, red, ran through every step and clothed the stairs with a velvety dress. The pinewood, oozing a carmine complexion, was harmonizing and merging into the redness of the hall. Vermilion light trapped in several scattered, red silky lampshades, radiated onto the railings in a suppressed silence. The railings extended to infinitude, embraced entirely. Everything had grandeur.

A hand, a sweaty young man's hand, held and warmed the railings.

It was Stephen's hand.

He was mounting the stairs.

Two weeks ago when he had stepped out of Ms. Fan's office after that two-hour interview, he instinctively foresaw that he would be here tonight. At the top of the staircase, he knew nothing but concentration.

Stephen followed the waiter. The corridor looked like a gallery. The vista of the wall hung small and large pieces of oil painting. Ex-premier Deng Xiaoping shaking hands with British Prime Minister Margaret Thatcher in the signing of the Joint Declaration Li Peng smiling with his big jaw Premier Zhu Rongji walking in his tight western suit President Jiang Zemin toasting a million spectators. Turn by turn, painting by painting, Stephen followed the waiter, eventually to the Victoria Room. There was a gold-plated stand next to the doorframe:

*The Pre-selection Dinner of*
**The Rhodes Scholarship**
1997–1998

| Hosts | Guests |
|---|---|
| MS SANDY FAN | MR MARCO AU |
| DR MILLER MEAD | MS JEAN RALPH |
| MR WILLIAM WEAR | MR CHRIS SUM |
| | MR STEPHEN TAM |

*At Victoria Room*
*The China Club HK*
*8th December 1997, 7:00 p.m.*

[*A gale of laughter blew from the room.* MS FAN, DR MEAD, CHRIS *and* JEAN *were standing and chatting next to the round table. Each of them was holding a drink.*]

*Enter* STEPHEN

STEPHEN: [*shake hand*] Nice to meet you again, Miss Fan.
MS FAN: Nice to meet you, Stephen. Let me introduce Dr. Mead,
Chris and Jean.

A train of "nice-to-meet-you" ran out of their mouths. Stephen was led to the conversation circle. Dr. Mead is a professor of a design school — names — Chris is a philosophy major in the University of Hong Kong — names — Jean is a comparative literature major in the University of Michigan — names — I am an English major in The Chinese University of Hong Kong — names — Miss Fan is a lawyer in — names — I had to remember.

*Enter* WAITER

WAITER: Want any drink, sir.
STEPHEN: Perrier will be fine.
DR MEAD: See, I told you every one of us is addicted to Perrier!

The waiter twisted off the cap. The pouring sound penetrated into Stephen's ears. Sparkling drink sparkling scene sparkling people.

DR MEAD:     [*pointing to a small picture behind* STEPHEN] It's a nice painting, looks like an old Chinese compass.
STEPHEN:     Yes, it's a compass car, probably invented by King Wang, the legendary king in pre-historic times. He used it in war and he won.
DR MEAD:     Impressive. China was such an inventive and productive state in the past. They invented —
STEPHEN:     The Four Great Inventions.
DR MEAD:     Perfectly. But suddenly they invented nothing.
STEPHEN:     I think China had scientific technology but not science.
DR MEAD:     [*smiling*] But they have now!

Stephen smiled when Dr. Mead smiled. He saw that Ms. Fan, Chris and Jean were talking absorbedly next to the window. Chris straightened up three of his fingers counting something with his lips. Ms. Fan and Jean glared at the three upright fingers. What was he counting? Dr. Mead asked something about Stephen's choice in Oxford. The English Department, M. Phil. in the modernist period. He only left one finger upright, Stephen thought, it must be his last point.

STEPHEN:     [*recollecting*] Yes, I applied to the English Department, M.Phil in the modernist period.
[MS FAN, *accompanied by* CHRIS *and* JEAN, *approached near* DR MEAD *and* STEPHEN]

MS FAN:     It must be a serious congestion that holds them up on the road.
DR MEAD:     Never mind, we've time. Shall we have a nice walk? There is a small library here.
MS FAN:     Oh really? Some books will always be a perfect appetizer. I'm full of thoughts lately. [*smiles at the three candidates*]
CHRIS:     Where is it, Dr. Mead? I'd love to see it.
DR MEAD:     Follow me.

*Exit* DR MEAD, MS FAN, CHRIS, MARCO, JEAN *and* STEPHEN

Picking up his glass of Perrier, Dr. Mead walked out of the room meekly. A line of curious heads, in sequential order, followed him: Chris, Ms. Fan, Jean and Stephen. It was now, being at the end of the row, maneuvering his curiosity to the unknown library in a restaurant, that Stephen started to see Dr. Mead a glowing figure. Moving in that polished slender corridor, Dr. Mead's light khaki suit, as if a piece of tender, silvery tiger fur, roamed in a Siberian forest. It must be a forest at night, Stephen thought, with his intense eyes capturing the silky flutter of those gentle trousers, every leading step was a nailing march of a powerful man. Even that halt was a special —

## *Enter* WAITER

WAITER:    Excuse me, Dr. Mead. The library is reserved for a party tonight.
DR MEAD:    Fabulous! We would want some fresh air after such a walkathon, right?
WAITER:    The balcony is this way, Dr. Mead. Door unlocked.
DR MEAD:    Perfect.

## *Exit* WAITER

Meandering for three more turns Dr. Mead eventually brought his disciples to the balcony. It was a huge rectangular balcony with at least three hundred square feet. Nobody was there.

## *Enter* DR MEAD *and* his followers

They came together instinctively as a circle at the centre of the rectangle, ready to talk about every incident on earth. The Bank of China was on their right, the Hong Kong Bank on their left. Under their feet were the Statue Square, The Queen's Pier and the Legislative Council, what used to be the old Supreme Court five months ago.

DR MEAD:    My wife is a club member here. Every time she comes she brings her friends to this balcony, as if this place is a never-ending discovery.
CHRIS:    Your wife also works as a designer?
DR MEAD:    She says that creativity is a burden of mind. I'm glad that she is not an artist; otherwise she'd possibly get insane someday. [*sips some Perrier leisurely*] She is a lawyer in London.
CHRIS:    [*excitedly*] Ms. Fan is also a lawyer. What a coincidence!
JEAN:     I'm applying to the Law School in Oxford too.
CHRIS:    Same here.
MS FAN:    So we've a balanced number of males and females in the law industry here.
DR MEAD:    You forget counting my wife and you too, Sandy.
MS FAN:    Oh! A bit stronger feminist power. Sorry gentlemen.
STEPHEN:    Then I must consider the Law School, to make a balance. [*people laugh*]

Laughter was a perfect full stop to an excellent dialogue, Stephen thought. Perhaps, instead of being a lawyer, he could change his sex to balance the gender. Male and female. Is "male" the suffix to "female" or "fe" the prefix to "male"? Dr. Mead and Miss Fan: M & F. I —. Stood still. Betwixt and between Dr. Mead and Miss Fan, Stephen looked at the view of Hong Kong. It was a very hazy night. I —. Layers of foggy veil, far from the Victoria Harbour and close to the Hong Kong Bank, blurred everything. I —. Freckles of light, yellow and white, floating and fading here and there, covered this mere Hong Kong Island. I —. Suddenly on, suddenly off, on, off, off, on, the light in mist replaced the hustle and bustle of this palpitating city. I —. Light brush of yellow spots shaped the roads and ports, hills and seas. I —. Stephen gazed at the scene. I —. It was light gala. But I —

DR MEAD:     It was strangely hazy tonight.
STEPHEN:     Yes. I —. [*recollecting*] It was very hazy.

Catching the word "hazy" Chris and Jean started to talk about the air pollution index, Stephen looked up to the sky. The fog gradually moved forward, and the Bank of China emerged floodlit, like a keen sword in the dark. The fog was cut and diverged once it met the blade and merged again afterwards. Stephen felt that the haze passed him and roved towards the windows behind him. He glanced back at dozens of people who dressed extravagantly and held their glasses of champagne, partying inside the warm-lit library.

STEPHEN:     [*to* DR MEAD] It must be the library you've talked about.
DR MEAD:     Yes, quite a scene there, it seems.
CHRIS:       [*facing* DR MEAD] Do you think Mr. Wear and Marco have come already?
MS FAN:      [*rising tone*] Oh! We nearly abandoned them in that cold room.
DR MEAD:     Maybe we should continue to abandon them. They deserve detention.
MS FAN:      Mill, you're charming tonight!
DR MEAD:     Sandy, you must be talking about my tie. It's a gift from my wife and it's
             strangling me.

Miss Fan's radiant grin orchestrated a band of laughter. Chris bugled, Jean oboed, Dr. Mead cymbaled Stephen bassed. The notes of delight were marching, with harmonious undulations of distinctive sound, buoyantly through the meandering corridor and back to the Victoria Room door.

[MR WEAR *and* MARCO *were sitting at the round table and talking about the car crash on Des Voeux Road. The paper cards stood on every delicate white plate. Seats assigned. The dinner was about to be served.*]

*Enter* DR MEAD and the rest

MR WEAR:     [*standing up*] Hello Miller! I heard your voice igniting the air in the corridor.
             What makes you so excited?
MS FAN:      We're excited about your punctuality!
MR WEAR:     Oh! Sandy, I was kept on the road. By the way, I'm not the last one. Somebody
             was later than me.
MARCO:       [*smiles skillfully*] Mr. Wear is alluding to me. I'm terribly sorry, everybody. I
             was kept on the road too.
DR MEAD:     By an elephant?
MARCO:       Something similar to the size of an elephant. A truck actually, a car crash, on
             Des Voeux Road.
MS FAN:      You've been hurt in the crash? Oh! Sorry Marco, I'm kidding. I swallowed too
             much wind on the balcony.
DR MEAD:     Sandy, you're charming tonight!

MR WEAR:　　And discriminating the latecomers too!

CHRIS:　　　[*wittily*] Discriminate all of us then. We just come back from the balcony; so we're all late for the dinner. And Stephen has just stepped into his room. He should be the last one.

STEPHEN:　　[*acting*] Sorry, I was kept in the corridor by an elephant.

JEAN:　　　　[*acting more*] Are you alluding to me, Stephen? I was in front of you!

MS FAN:　　[*playfully*] And me too!

STEPHEN:　　[*with difficulty*] Well . . .

CHRIS:　　　[*competitively*] Oh! We're all charming tonight!

Platitude always ended unendingly, Stephen thought. Ting —. Someone hit a fork against an empty wineglass while sitting. Would the sound of that car crash be so delicate? Somewhere on Des Voeux Road, there must be somebody who was involved in the crash. Somewhere there must be someone, like us, who talked about the crash. What made that difference? Sitting at this round table by accident and talked about the accident as if it was not an accident. Was this an accident too? Why —

Wine and dinner were served. Chinese food, chopsticks, dialogue, chopsticks. Eat, drink, talk and talk. No one was really dining. The round table divided people into three conversational groups. Dr. Mead with Chris, Miss Fan with Jean and Mr. Wear with Marco. Stephen was drinking his white wine. He heard that Chris was saying something about social work.

MS FAN:　　[*considerately*] Stephen, you told me you teach English in a rehabilitation house. [*several 'really?' thrown to the dinner table*]

STEPHEN:　　Yes, I did. I teach some young drug addicts English once a week.

MR WEAR:　　[*concerned*] How did you know them?

STEPHEN:　　By chance. A friend of mine is Christian and it seems like in a music concert that my friend introduces me to the chairman of that Christian group, St. Matthew Society. They help people get rid of drugs. I think I can do something to help. So I teach them English.

MR WEAR:　　I'm very interested in the way you teach. [CHRIS *nods dramatically*]

STEPHEN:　　Starting from ABC, because some of them barely remember alphabet, and I'm introducing some poems to them. William Blake's Songs of Innocence, for example.

MR WEAR:　　Poems! Very interesting! How can they know poetry?

STEPHEN:　　Everyone does. I just guide them to know.

MR WEAR:　　[*murmurs*] Very interesting. [*enquiringly*] Are you a Christian?

STEPHEN:　　[*plainly*] No.

Stephen's definiteness made all wineglasses touch people's lips. No. That unknowably problematic NO carved on everyone's face. No, no, no —

MR WEAR:　　[*to all assuredly*] I'm just wondering about the power of religion. Those drug addicts, no doubt, regain their lives through religion. It heals them and of course many people. But what if there is no religion on earth? Will they never be healed? [*voice strengthened*] Religion, in some sense, creates another reality, which some humans depend on. A reality differs from our reality. A reality of ultimate answer to all obscurities. It is an external ultimate that fits the ignorance of mankind. What if the ultimate is not to us but from us, not external but internal? What if there is only one reality and it is the one in which we reside, regardless of the existence of all religions?

The speech convulsed the gravity of the room. Stephen felt a whirling and sucking force driving him to spin and spin like a current with the dinner table, chairs, napkins, spoons, wine and everything around and round the axis of Mr. Wear. Ultimate truth, skepticism, existentialism, determinism, atheism, monism — ceaseless abstract notions were solidified by the utterances of Mr. Wear, Dr. Mead and Miss Fan, throwing visible, concrete words into the whirl, mixing with the swinging pendulous air. Swaying with the flowing concepts, Stephen, having caught sight of the vagueness on Marco's, Jean's and Chris's face, was digesting every single word in the air. Except Chris who occasionally contributed some blunt response, the other three candidates were possessed by the wordy air.

Marco didn't speak. Jean didn't speak. Stephen couldn't speak.

*Enter* WAITER *and tidy the table*

MS FAN:   The wine is splendid, Will. I'm afraid of getting drunk.
DR MEAD:  I am already. And scared them into silence. [*people laugh*]
MR WEAR:  [*playfully*] Why not to have another bottle? People talk about crazy things when they're drunk! [*people laugh again*]
MS FAN:   You've already talked about crazy things, Will. [*glancing at her watch and concluding*] It's ten thirty and they need rest for the interview tomorrow.

[MS FAN, DR MEAD *and* MR WEAR *stand up, say goodbye and lead the candidates to the door. The leaving people greet them in return.*]

*Exit* CHRIS, JEAN, MARCO *and* STEPHEN

*Door closed*

A blind street.
A dying lamp.
A hollowed tram station.

Stephen, along the spiral stairs of the tram, climbed up to the upper deck and sat near a window on the left side, in the middle of the compartment. Right in front at the head, he was gazing at a discolored bronze tablet:

**Tramline from Kennedy Town to Shau Kei Wan**
Completed in 1904
**Opened by Sir Matthew Nathan**

He had been traveling by trams since he was in his mother's womb and yet he had never recognized there was such a tablet, a birthmark of some history. 1904. What happened in this year? Must be something significant. Ting-ting-ngzz —. The tram wriggled. The winding rails, beaming weak silver, like a pair of twin snakes' shed skins and elongated along the north shore of the island. Ting-ting-ngzz —. The tram wriggled slowly and haltingly, with historic difficulty. The hanging leather handgrips, the leaning window plates, the snoring heads of some passengers, rocked and echoed with the rhythmic movement of the historic compartment. Ting-

ting-ngzz —. Stephen's head occasionally touched the windowpane and he felt some kinetic waves surrounding him and prompting him to move forward. To where? He chewed the question in his mind and the kinetic waves enveloped his entire body, resembling the native swing in his mother's fluid. Hot, he felt hot from his retina, though the December wind rushed through the window-crack. Ting-ting-ngzz —. Where was I? Passed the Statue Square, Bond Centre, Lippo Building already. On Hennessey Road? Yes. [全港市民熱烈歡渡香港回歸！] Handovered. Who would demolish these signs? Government? They put them on and pulled them down. So many signs. They put them on and would pull them down, someday. Ting-ting-ngzz —. So many ads hanging on the sky. [OXFORD DICTIONARY: THE MOST AUTHORITATIVE DICTIONARY IN THE WORLD] Ting-ting-ngzz —. To England. To Oxford. Ting-ting-ngzz —. Why?

11:30 p.m. Great George Street was still trod by the lingering feet of late shoppers. A city's shadow was its people, roaming like some lost unnameable nomadic tribes, from one shop to another, with paper or plastic livestock feeding on their wrists. Stephen saw no shadows from the window since the question mark manacled the nerve of his soul.

No reverie was deep enough to reconcile him. His soul was thrown into a pond without a ripple. His searching mind betrayed him. He wanted to know why he had been in the China Club, dined with the people he barely knew and talked in a tone he found alien. He felt his own voice leaving his mind and his mind leaving him. He wanted to choke and throw up. He wanted to leave, or to fail winning the scholarship. He didn't know why. But what did it matter?

The tram halted. A man climbed to the upper deck and sat beside Stephen. Stephen didn't know until the tram turned left and the man's arm patted him. He felt the man's biceps pressing softly against his biceps. He felt warmth from the warmth of the other.

The tram was crossing Gloucester Road and Stephen leant his head tightly against the windowpane. The man's biceps were still pressing. He wanted to cry suddenly, crying into the windowpane.

Just then he saw the entrance of Victoria Park receding from the window-frame.

The dark Victoria Park resided in the heart of Hong Kong.

Drawing back his crying breath, Stephen recalled that the year was 1997, and the final interview would be held tomorrow morning.

But he was passing Victoria Park.

And now he had passed Victoria Park.

# Addiction

## 2001

*Nancy Tsui Yuk Chun*


### 1

A parched heart encounters a day in spring. Thoughts being trapped in a room of idleness are playing hide-and-seek. Under the sun, flowers dance painfully to welcome sweat. I shade my eyes with my hands. Sunrays peep through the cracks between my fingers. Squinting in the bright sunlight, I see pools of green splash on the linen in the air. It is safe to go across, it says. I know I should go for a walk.

Then, roses have lost their dangerous colour. Red departs from the lips. It drops a strand to the ground. A ribbon of blood. Marijuana. The aroma of delirium. (I have a good excuse for not going out today, I think). Wreaths of smoke filter the curls of clouds, and then go away. Then, the lines on a paper meander along the trails of smoke. The slender beauty of a black snake. Then it splits. I see loads of notes jumping. Straight tights with round heels come in a blink. Sparkles give out warnings. Despair is being burnt in a small roll. Breath after breath. It is burning. Breath after breath. It is still beating.

Didactics hide their faces in the smell of peace. Abandonment cries in the glory of disgrace. Memories in a marsh.

Happiness is floating aloft. Consciousness flies higher and higher, and then falls off. Melancholy stands right at the tip, smiling at me, laughing at me. The betrayed kneels down before the betrayer to beg for mercy. Dogmas are standing there in mask, shooting jelly arrows. Turning and turning is the ceiling with patterns of ecstasy. The phone rang to send a shiver down my spine.

'It's Sunday. Let's hang out,' she says.

'Why should we hang out?' I ask.

'Everyone is going out,' she answers.

Eyelids cover the entrance of light. The warmth of the newly washed quilt captures my sense of smell. My hair flops on my face to tease the heat. The air sends out the voice of palpitation. Innocence runs after wickedness in a clock. If the arms had gone in reverse, which Sunday would I have met?

The burnt-out ashes land on the floor . . .


### 2

I had many weird dreams. I dreamt that several office ladies with faces of a bunch of flowers wandered along the coast of Victoria Harbour. I dreamt that men with skin made up of chocolate were running after the ladies. The chocolate was melting. I dreamt that my hallmate was in a tub filled with roses and forget-me-nots. I dreamt that creatures from a planet came to visit my hallmate by UFO on the 14th February. I dreamt that they examined and recorded the length and duration of her smile. I dreamt that in the dark my cousin was wearing push-up bras.

I dreamt that I was invited to her wedding.

I smelt the fragrance of flowers and perfume of women pervading the wedding hall in which tears filled my Aunt's eyes, and rolled down my cousin's cheeks; and the bridegroom was allowed to shed tears; and everyone ended up with a tear-tainted face with a smile; and everyone said it was a perfect match.

Then after a long time — maybe one day or two, maybe a year, I could not remember — I left my room, and wandered about in the streets.

Then, I went to my Aunt's place, and sat by my cousin.

My cousin was suing for a divorce from her husband.

She pouted a bit, and handed me a newspaper.

Read newspaper, she said.

Then, I took a taxi to a church, and sat by my friend.

My friend was a devoted Christian, they said.

She pouted a bit, and handed me the Bible.

Read the Bible, she said.

Then, I went back to my dorm room, and sat by my computer to go online.

:-

It met me online a few months ago.

It was a good man, a decent man, a decent good man, it said.

It pouted a bit, and sent me a file.

Look at the XXXX picture!!!!, it said.

Then.

Then, I woke up.

A real awakening. A painful headache. Three o'clock in the afternoon. The ceiling is still white. The fan does not move. How long did I sleep? I turn around, and get up by the bedside. My feet touch the floor. The ashes stay on my feet. I must take a shower. Water showers on my head, my neck, my shoulders, my arms, my back . . . Breathless. I like to watch the whirlpool at the very eye of the tub. I like the heat of water. Back to the dorm room, wet, I pass the ashes. The computer is still on. The file is still there.

I work as a part-time translator for a network marketing company. The previous brochure I translated was an introduction of a network marketing company. Deception. To sell herbal drinks and pills to every friend and person you know. Isn't that deception? Last time I called a staff of that company to know if my translation was good. The marketing staff did not let go of me. She kept telling me the advantages of their products.

'You can lose ten pounds in three days! One of our clients did it successfully. Don't think network marketing is something bad. It is very common nowadays.'

Nonsense! I guessed she thought I was a fool. To lose ten pounds in three days . . . This is not a well-paid job. I do it because I do not want to be a private tutor as many of my friends are. What difference does a private tutor make, to herself or to the student? I gave private tuition to a girl years ago. Nothing was made but a few thousands bucks.

Nothing good was done.

Now I am a translator. I translate for a firm which makes money out of deception. The firm is legal, but it cheats people. Housewives and young women are their target customers. In Hong Kong, nine women out of ten think they are too fat; nine women out of ten want to lose weight; nine women out of ten do not want to eat less and work more. They want to buy slim bodies. They want to buy youth. They want to buy health. There is a large market. Smart.

Those companies.

I do not need any healthy drinks or vitamin pills. I hated that staff who hard sold their products to me the other day. That was her job. I have my job too. I have to translate the brochures. I work for them. I work for those who deceive people. But I need money.

'You can quit this job, and work for another firm. You want to become a writer, don't you? You've written a pile of stories and prose. Take those manuscripts out from the shelf, and get them published! Published? Who would publish my stories? Contact a publisher to see.'

I laugh at myself. I laugh at my foolishness. Who would publish my stories? I do not write about the daughter of a banker, living in a villa in the Southern part of Hong Kong Island, who loves a guy she meets at Repulse Bay someday. They amble along the beach wandering about in breezy air, and then, have crazy sex on the beach to the wavy sound of the sea in full moon light. That is what the publishers want. That is what the best selling fiction in the bookstores in Hong Kong is all about. I do not write about that. I cannot.

I guess I should not write. I should not have written . . .

## 3

I need marijuana. Marijuana is my best companion.

Marijuana by the window catches my sight. You little plant looks so good to me . . .

The plant is sticking up quietly under the sun. I cut off a leaf into small bits, and roll them with a paper. I want to light up the roll. No, I should not taste it anymore. I have four pieces of translation to work on. The editor just called yesterday. He said if I could not hand them in today, I would be fired. No payment would be given. I have been doing free-lance translation for almost two years. Herbal supplements, diet pills, network marketing, all sorts of products which cheat people. I do the translation work because it is better to translate all that stuff than sell it as a salesperson does. I guess. I laugh.

I go to light up the marijuana roll.

The afternoon sun in early spring is warm. The campus is taking a nap. Blocks of buildings and the mountain beyond slide on the windowpane. Geometry distorts the harmony of circles. Three buildings. No, two. One is blurred, another also blurred.

Heat is under siege. "1" is becoming shorter and shorter, tilted, spinning in a hot desert. Sahara. Twisters come. "1" becomes "0", and then "8".

Sometimes, it is "8"; sometimes upside down. No difference whatsoever.

"8" and "8" are extremely different. Must be. The former one has two circles; the latter none.

Summer lingers around "8". Smoke encircles it. Jupiter is far away. But smoke encircles "0". Solid ascends. Smoke stays on the floor. Someone is giggling. People are good at being cheated.

The breezes from the ocean have met Hong Kong, but do not touch it. The sun is jealous of the attractive breezes. But it surrenders to the moon. The moon is made up of two "8s". A moon is at the top, and a moon bottom. 2 plus 2 equals 1. There is only one moon.

Decadence and delirium stand side by side with an "=" in between. I inhale ecstasy, and puff out despair. Good is good. "+" and "-" are the same. To be or not to be doesn't make any sense.

Circles gather on the skin. Curve by curve.

A curve moves up to touch another curve. It cuts it. They intersect. On a plain. A white plain. A net.

I must check out the intersection point of Demand Curve and Supply Curve. There comes the equilibrium price. There comes marriages. Marriages happen at the equilibrium point. Divorces are set aside in the shade beyond the point. One ring and one ring equal "8". A man and a woman make up 20. Then, 2 goes to the left, and 0 to the right. One ring and one ring equal 0.

Skin is frozen. Great joy is buried hundreds of miles down. Fossils. The woman is 5 million light years from the man. Peace appears in a place for battles. Paralyzing takes place of writhing. Torsos speak in silence.

'The ceiling paper is so shabby; it's time to change it,' she says.

'. . .'

'Don't forget the condom,' she says.

'. . .'

Crowds of women masked with condoms are holding banners to ask for sexual emancipation on a road paved with contraceptive pills. Girls in Mosuo clothes stand beside, laughing at them.

Have a second go. Yes I would like to. She is waiting for you. Yes I know. Someone is knocking at the door.

'What did you do?' She screams out.

Marijuana, how fascinating . . .

Marijuana dries up all damp memories.

# Colonial Courtship

1997

*David McKirdy*

Tuesday 3rd June, 1997

I wake up at 4.00 in the morning to close all the windows. It's absolutely lashing down outside and the rain bounces off the window ledge next to my bed and into my face. A much more effective alarm call than my 'Wallace and Grommet' clock / radio that says 'Eh up! Grommet, shall we see what's on the wireless.'

I actually love the rain. Hong Kong's air is very polluted, even where I live, in the country-park, over twenty miles from Tsim Sha Tsui. The pollution comes mainly from the unregulated industrial free-for-all over the border and is one of the generous contributions from the glorious motherland to Hong Kong.

The rain has a cooling and purifying effect on the atmosphere, like a parish priest dispensing absolution from the confessional. On the way to town there are trees across the road in several places and I end up water-skiing on more than one occasion. The roads can be quite treacherous when it rains and most people don't modify their driving to compensate. Not surprisingly, during my journey, I come across four accidents.

I stop in Saikung, which is the nearest town, to pick up the newspaper and a McDonald's 'Big Breakfast'. Most people view Saikung as one of the last surviving, quaint, rural, fishing villages, but it's 'the big smoke' compared to Hoi Ha.

My first experience of Saikung was when I was eight years old. My big brother (and my hero) Bob took me on a canoe-camping adventure. We set off from Hebe Haven, which is a bay just round the coast from Saikung, and paddled out to one of three remote beaches, called 'The Three Sisters'. We were sleeping out under the stars, but a storm blew up in the middle of the night and we had ringside seats to the most spectacular lightning storm I've ever seen. The water was alive with phosphorescent algae and as I ran through the surf I left a sparkling, blue-green trail behind, which made me feel like Peter Pan chased by a thousand Tinkerbells. It rained so hard that night that we had to shelter under our canoe and a make-shift tarpaulin that Bob rigged up from some discarded canvas. We spent a very uncomfortable night being bitten by sand mites and getting soaked. But I was elated to have experienced my first real adventure and thought I was one of 'The Hardy Boys'.

I read in the paper that a local political personality, the Chief Secretary, hints that she MAY quit the new government, in which she will occupy the same post, 'If REPEATEDLY asked to enforce decisions that go against her principles or conscience.' What kind of shit is this? Will she accede to one, or two, or a hundred bad decisions before she MAY decide to quit? In my opinion one either sticks to one's principles or not. Ethics are supposed to be absolute and not some flexible yardstick that can be modified to suit the circumstances that prevail. It looks as though Hong Kong's nascent politicians are every bit as slippery as their experienced counterparts in the West.

The next day an editorial in the South China Morning Post refers to her as 'the conscience of Hong Kong'. I'm afraid I remain steadfastly unimpressed. I have great admiration for Burma's Aung San Suu Kyi. That's what I call the conscience of a people. Hong Kong's version is crap, just like the occasional hunger strikers outside the legislative council building who arrive at 11.00, having consumed their morning dim-sum in preparation for the rigors of political life, only to be carted off to hospital at 3.00 suffering from the effects of a hypoglycemic crisis brought on by the absence of their mid-afternoon repast.

I wake up with the alarm clock at 8.30 and promptly knock it off and go back to sleep until 11.00. I feel completely wiped out today. I've forgotten how tiring it is to just listen to music, which I did for about fourteen hours yesterday. I've noticed that when I do fill-in gigs with other bands, if they're really loud and I wear ear protection I feel much less tired at the end of the night.

I drive out to David's house to carry on working on the Aston Martin. I go via Ma On Shan which is a district overlooking the Tolo Channel, across the water from Tai Po. It's full of medium-cost, high-rise housing, all thirty to forty stories high on a plot of land about the size of a basketball court. They all have names like 'Splendid Olympia' and 'Golden Athena' and the architects have tried to lend them a touch of class by the application of fiberglass pilasters on the facade, and fake green corroded bronze metal fitments. They really are wasting their time, all they need to do is leave the buildings up for two years and they'll look antique all on their own, when the chunks of masonry start falling off due to greedy building contractors using illegal and impure beach sand in the concrete.

It's drizzling, and the combination of rain and row upon row of tall soulless buildings evokes images of the Ridley Scott film 'Blade Runner'. The whole area was countryside just ten years ago and now it's a town of over sixty thousand people. As a teenager I used to come here trail-riding on motorbikes with my friends and it was extremely remote and unspoiled. I think the constant encroachment by urban development, into the truly beautiful natural scenery of Hong Kong, is the one thing that is more likely to hasten my eventual departure than any political or social restrictions.

How fortunate I was to grow up here during the 60s and 70s when things were so much less hectic than they are now. I can recall my Dad taking us all into Tsim Sha Tsui when I was a child and just leaving the car on Nathan Road (one of Hong Kong's busiest roads) outside St. Andrews church, which is still there. It's difficult enough to stop on foot now at the same location.

Dad would often use me as his alibi. We were ostensibly going shopping for some necessary purchase or other but we would invariably end up in the 'Ship Inn' for a couple of beers and a chin-wag. There were always big fat sailors, with Popeye-type anchors tattooed on their forearms, and slim, painted, Chinese ladies of indeterminate age and dubious lineage, who teased me good naturedly, but at the same time kept me well stocked with soft drinks and potato crisps. Needless to say, I was always a willing accomplice and Mum never asked why we came back from a trip to buy blue jeans with a glazed look in Dad's eye and a knowing smile on my lips, not to mention a few model cars in my pocket from one of the numerous toy shops in the area (Thanks Dad!).

We lived in the Hong Kong and Whampoa Dock company staff quarters in Hung Hom in those days, because my Dad was a marine-engineer. (Now that he's retired, he refers to himself as a 'Professional Golfer'.) We had a three-story colonial terraced house in a row of eight. They were built in the 1920s and they had high ceilings, a verandah off every room and real fire places. This was wonderful for the eight weeks or so that constitutes a Hong Kong winter, with those accompanying lingering, heady smells of aromatic oils from the carved camphor-wood chest that sat in the hallway, as the sweaters and blankets emerged to elicit excitement amongst us at the prospect of the upcoming celebrations. These blended into one long festive-season, from Christmas to Easter and included Chinese New Year and all the other festivals in between. There were also the birthdays in March on three consecutive days of myself and two of the other dock-boys my own age. We had our own private club house with a badminton court, table tennis, snooker, tennis courts, a play-park, football pitch and a bowling green. The kids had their own lounge in the club house and we could have as much food and drink as we wanted and just sign a chit for it. At home we had three servants and I now realize that we led the life of Riley.

Hong Kong really was a colony in those days, with all that this entailed, good and bad. The staff in the company club house were addressed as 'Boy' by all and sundry, including little kids. These boys were generally old enough to be my grandfather and my Mum warned me that if she ever caught me calling anyone 'Boy' who was not actually a pre-adolescent, she would thrash me to within an inch of my life.

My Mum is only four feet, nine inches tall but she doesn't take shit off anybody and I'm sure she could beat me in a fair fight even now. I don't actually remember my parents hitting me and none of my siblings were ever beaten to death, so I suppose it was a case of her bark being worse than her bite, but oh! what a formidable bark.

My parents come from a Scottish working-class background and my Dad was a staunch trade unionist and rather left wing in his youth. My Mum calls him 'Joe Stalin' when talking about his political leanings, but they inculcated in all three of us kids a sense of egalitarianism and fair play. They took the view that we were guests in a foreign country and should behave accordingly.

This was in stark contrast to most of their contemporaries who held that this was a British colony and 'The natives' could 'bloody well learn English like the rest of the civilized world'. These people wittered on about 'the white man's burden' as they quaffed their gin and tonics, regularly topped up by the dutiful boy, who was often a university graduate from mainland China, working two jobs to give his five kids a good education and a start in life.

I'll never forget that during the 1967 riots, which were a direct result of the Cultural Revolution, there was strike at the dockyard and a great deal of tension and nastiness, but my father was held in such high regard, that his staff risked their lives to escort him home through the picket lines.

My working day has been pretty lacklustre, I'm just too tired. I work until 8.30 then call it a day after not a great deal of progress. The prospect of an early night is very enticing.

\*     \*     \*     \*

Friday 18th July, 1997

I found out where the butterflies go. It's lashing down outside but there's squadrons of them fluttering about in the garden. There is one in particular that I love, that has a velvety British racing green base-colour, with two large aquamarine eyes on the wings. They manage to delicately zig zag their way through the droplets falling from the banana trees as they sample the delicious nectar of the diverse flora, which includes wild bauhinia, buttercups and the frangipani that is used in the making of fragrant tea.

I call Peter Scherr to organize our studio session for tomorrow and then I make my way over to the Immigration Department in Wanchai, where I need to replace my identity card. It's completely wrecked, it's delaminated and the information is unintelligible, from years of being used to open doors and getting left in the wash.

On my way from the car park to Immigration Tower, I notice a woman with her face right up next to the mirrored glass wall siding of one of the grand Wanchai commercial buildings which I use as a short cut. She's squeezing her pimples and the funny thing is that it's one-way glass and she is oblivious to the thirty-five or so spectators in the lift lobby inside the building. It reminds me of those nature documentaries where researchers film termites through a nest bisected by a plate glass viewing screen.

I spend less than an hour in the ID card office, during which time one of the staff asks if I want to apply for 'right of abode'. I have no idea what the benefits are, if any, and I thought I automatically had my right of abode transferred from the last administration. However it appears that I have 'unconditional right to land' which is a different thing. I take the reams of paper that make up the application forms and information package, but I'm not really any the wiser after reading it. It would appear that 'right of abode' confers more rights on the holder than the status I seem to have now, so I'd better get my application in.

I go next to a travel agent in Central and buy a ticket for my holiday. If I leave before the 1st of August I can get a cheap deal, so I opt for the non smoking British Airways flight, leaving on the evening of the 31st of July. It leaves fifteen minutes later than the smoking-flight and I tell the lady at the desk that I hope we don't have to fly all the way to London in their polluted slipstream. Anyway I'm really looking forward to my trip.

The last time I was in Scotland I took a long walk one morning in my own company along the old 'Largs Road', which my parents' bungalow backs onto. I immersed myself in the sensual solitary pleasure of communing with a nature that was at once fascinatingly familiar, yet foreign to me. Along the road on both sides the fields were enclosed by wooden fences, festooned with wool rubbed off by sheep relieving an itch, fences encroached on by tenacious wild hedges, covered in moss and looking like the stunted bonsai trees carefully cultivated over generations by Japanese Paleobotanical perfectionists. The purple pink and lilac flowers shared these hedgerows with thistles and heather; wrens and robin red-breasts kept company with countless cows and sheep, inquisitive and alert in the wet green fields.

Diamond-like dew drops adorned the webs of absent spiders and an occasional bumblebee made its selections and paid court to the chosen blooms in this horticultural heaven. As I strolled along, thirty ruminants, like the crowd in a slow-motion replay of 'set-point' at Wimbledon, turned their heads as one, to follow my languid progress through their bovine domain. The hushed sound of the wind in the mist was punctuated by the bleat of lambs and the haunting cries of the gulls, as well as the irregular crunch of feet on loose gravel that was my own vaguely inappropriate contribution to this restful scene. The smell of pine was more vivid and exhilarating than the strongest scientifically designed air-freshener and the whole experience remains forever fixed in my mind.

The people in Scotland are friendlier and more gregarious than those in England. If you take the train up from London, the moment you cross the border the atmosphere becomes more relaxed and people start talking to each other once they realise that they share the same destination. I got talking to an old gent who was a fighter pilot, in the Polish wing of the Royal Air Force, during the war. He had been evacuated to North Africa for training and then was shipped to England via Glasgow. He met a girl on his 48-hour furlough, fell in love and has lived here since the end of the war. He was just coming back from a trip to Warsaw, his first visit in over fifty years. This is what I love about Britain, it may well have an older population, but what wonderful stories you can hear if you take the time and effort to listen.

It's now back to Admiralty for a meeting with the owner of our record company to see what the future has in store. We have a good meeting, during which we agree that the best thing is for us to have more autonomy and responsibility than that normally conferred on an artiste by a standard agreement. We have to come up with some kind of specific proposal over the weekend and meet again on Monday if possible. Phil and I have a cup of coffee and a discussion in a café downstairs and both express our satisfaction with the way the meeting has gone.

After Phil and I go our separate ways I go to the Fringe and bump into some French girls who I met a few weeks ago at a barbecue at a neighbour's house. I join them and meet Elizabeth who is both interesting and alluring. She loves classic cars and she wants to come and spend a normal working day with me, so we agree to do it next week. Sophie arrives as does Stefano, Sylvester, Bruce Parker and Maria, looking absolutely stunning in a stylish silk dress of Italian design. I feel a bit like a boy caught with his hand in the cookie jar. It's been nearly a year since we split up, but we still have a very strong hold over each other. I sit with her and we talk, but we can both feel the tension and she leaves after about twenty minutes. The band is great and I stay until 2.00, then give Elizabeth a lift back to her place in Sheung Wan and eventually get home in the wee small hours.

# Life's Wonderful

## 2001

*Wong Ho Yin*

There is an old Chinese saying: "When you are alive, never go to a police station; when you are dead, never go to Hell."

In my undergraduate days, I treated a tutor's office like a police station, or Hell. I remember my exhilaration, however, the first time I set foot in my own office when I was appointed as a tutor at the University of Hong Kong. I finally had my own office! And also the key with which to open the door!

Without hesitation, I opened the door as if I was unwrapping a birthday present. I had an office all to myself — and five other tutors. Six small desks for tutors are crammed in a miraculous way into this office, which also manages to fit bookshelves, filing cabinets and two computer desks. Well, small desks are better than none.

Seated at my desk, my back is to the door. With the door open, people talk behind my back. That's a precarious position for me, as I do not have any idea how far a student would go, should his tutor give him a low mark.

The good thing about my desk is that the tutor who previously occupied the place posted in front of it pictures and postcards of Audrey Hepburn, Vivian Leigh, fabulous scenery and artistic monuments. This could give the impression that I am an artistic and refined young man, at least to those who don't know me well.

Nevertheless, I've decided it's better to show my true colours. That's why I've placed a freak-show display on the desk — figurines of Frankenstein, the Mummy, and the Wolfman. It would be too tedious to remove all the elegant pictures and postcards and I like to think the incongruity of Audrey and my exhibits could be understood in light of post-modernism, not just my laziness.

### LITERARY LIFE

Although the room is very crowded horizontally, it is quite spacious vertically. The ceiling is indeed high, so high it could well be used to house a giraffe or Shaquille O'Neal, or any other giant NBA basketball player. I estimate that eight people could sleep one over the other in a multi-layer bunk-bed and still have ample space.

I don't know why, but when I'm in my office I feel drowsy. All I can see are rows and rows of bunk-beds.

I no longer treat my office as Hell. Of course, it does look like Hell every time I finish an essay. My handwritten notes and photocopied references lie all over the place. Sometimes they're not only on my desk, but also on some other tutors' desks or even on the floor. That's why the process of writing an essay consists of three important parts: research, typing the essay, and last but not least, tidying up the place after the ordeal. Every university student should bear in mind this tripartite process.

The office might still be a police station, but now I am the police officer. However, I'm a modern police officer who wants to revolutionise the force. Gone is the mysterious and intimidating tutor's office. I always keep the door open when I'm not using the air-conditioner, and that way, I can see the corridor. I sometimes smile at students who pass. Most smile back, but some dash away.

Is there something wrong with me? Are they afraid? Of what? I wonder. The three plastic figurines on my desk? Of Audrey Hepburn? It can't be me!

## My Probe

### 2000

*Anita Cheung*

My probe
(not unlike that of a clairvoyant's)
dissolves
with that faint curl of the lips
Distant reminder
of that notoriously
ambiguous smile –
You perfected
the art of
equivocation

\*   \*   \*   \*

## Fried Chestnuts

### 2000

*Michelle Fok Ka Ling*

Next to the ditch and rubbish bin,
where flies and cockroaches linger,
I meet a man
who waits for customers
from midnight film shows.

With a rusted metal spade in his hands,
he grins and says,
"Twenty-four dollars for a pound."
He fries
the chestnuts in the wok.

Wounds
on his finger-tips expose
the soft flesh under his wrinkled skin.
You had hands coarser than his,
but I liked the way you patted my face.

Cracks
on the reddish-brown shells
show the golden kernel.
You bought me fried chestnuts
and the yellow mist in your eyes thickened.

Your last days in the white prison,
no snack but glucose.
I won't buy fried chestnuts again,
as soaked with tears,
they are bitter.

\*    \*    \*    \*

# The Kite

2000

*Wong Ho Yin*

The Airport Express
Travels back along the time path
The nearer it gets to its des-
tination, the closer comes the past.

Once the two of us played with kites
You really wanted to be one.
High above the ground you fly
The line would always let you come

Home safe and sound. Now that you're
Leaving Hong Kong for real,
Keep this kite with you,
I will keep the reel.

# Yau Ma Tei, Early 80s

## 2001

*Winnie Cheung Wing Yee*

The fireball hit a wooden cell
which stood in Reclamation Street.
A child moulded "M"s on her copybook.
An infant slept in a thorny cradle.
He struggled, cried in a gloomy cell.
Red spots kept growing on their necks.
Their Mum lit *huo shui** and boiled the water.
The wooden cell became their heater:
their cheeks, their wounds, their spots were reddened.
They gazed at the door. They gazed for the knock.
They longed for a man in uniform
to announce "Move house!"
But such a man never appeared;
they were sweating, in pain, in Yau Ma Tei.

\*    \*    \*    \*

# She asked "Who is Franz Kafka?"

## 2001

*Raslo Layton*

She asked "Who is Franz Kafka?"
I told her
he's a Greek-Argentinian
who runs a small deli and coffee place
down in Lan Kwai Fong
I thought she'd be much happier with that
than with the truth

---

\*    *huo shui* – kerosene.

# Life on a Treadmill

## 2001

*Chloe C. Li*

I live my life as if
I'm running on a treadmill
Destination not revealed
But I just can't stand still

In order to accomplish more
I let my whole body go sore
Going, going nowhere
My sweat congeals
into Despair

\*    \*    \*    \*

# Caterpillar

## 2001

*Li Wai Iu*

On the solid cement ground, a striped caterpillar
In its fastest pace, hastily but steadily
Squirming in sunlight, stopped me

I was on my way home
In a hurry, with things undone
Troubles unsolved and future unknown

With its soft body, long and thin
It crossed a hole and passed a pit
Though I thought it was hard for it

A long way for it, from here to there
To surmount obstacles, to achieve the aim

It was doing something I could never claim

Everything is hard for me
Holes and pits, ups and downs
Problems seemed existing all around

It was greater than I, though small in size
With respect for my tiny insect hero
I stopped my steps and guarded its path

\*    \*    \*    \*

# The Tear Collector

## 2001

*Sharon Sung Sau Fun*

The tear collector,
every tear I shed
he squats and picks.

I tell him mine are too bitter to take.
He smiles,
and says he collects.

"What do you want them for?" I ask.
"To chain them together,
and put them around your neck one day."

# Coming Through

## 2002

*Canti Lui*

I see faces outside the room,
watching as they become clear
at one moment, vague at another. I hear
voices of different people but
I do not understand them.

Below my feet I see a swamp
with many scalpels, stained.
Three o'clock in the morning people are
sweating, breathing under antiseptic masks.
I wander around the room
searching for something to drink.

At four a.m. I am set free,
I see myself lying stiffly on the table.
The swamp has disappeared
and my pain is fading with
the running water through the scalpels.

# Please

*from Hong Kong Nocturne*

## 2002

*Ted Mathys*

*M'goi    M'goi    M'goi    M'goi*

There is a beautiful Cantonese boy
sitting with me, knees bent
into the terrible plastic of this red top
mini bus from Tsim Sha Tsui through holy Kowloon.
And I'm sure he's the one
I saw curled up in the enormous arms of that German man

quaffing rice wine in the stairwell on Elgin street, the boy
clutching the deutsch pectorals beneath double-hung
windows and kissing his shoulders and yes,
he did lick his stubbled chin like an eager pawn,
tossing around, waiting for action. And I'm sure
that later on, when night was pitched upon the city
like a dusty fish net from the South China Sea
and the karaoke bars resumed their ritual halcyon glow,
that he is the one
I saw sifting through the stacks
of porno VCDs on Temple Street.
You should have seen the way the videos in the yellow
jewel cases wiggled out of the pile and into his combing fingers
because here yellow is not cowardice but desire.

*M'goi    M'goi    M'goi    M'goi*

There is a beautiful Cantonese boy
now almost asleep next to me as we careen
up Castle Peak Road, his head stuck to the seat cushion
and my head rattling against the metal handrail
on the window and out the window
the harbor stacked with yachts and diesel-driven junk boats
shouts its triple edict of dimsum, rhythm, and light.
Dimsum, rhythm, and now fingers of light
bounce off the black-eyed water
and I think I begin to understand
as the shimmer catches the face of this big-money boy

and ripples through his cheeks. I am reading
Foucault's history of sexuality, volume 1, and in the wind
my bookmark is a teasing runaway feather that has finally settled
on his folded calf. But even as the bus charges around bends
as sharp as a broken chopstick, Foucault just sits here in my hands
saying absolutely nothing of how to retrieve this paper feather
with tact.

*M'goi     M'goi     M'goi     M'goi*

There is a beautiful Cantonese boy
now inebriated with sleep next to me
and in front of him the girl
with dry skin impetigo is chewing on her hair,
the misspelled English on her t-shirt saying
"taker me strongly" and she
has mastered the mandatory Hong Kong puppy-love pout lip,
yelling at her Nokia for support, digging in her bag

for a toothpick. When she stands and her hand
grabs the seatback before us, delicious knuckles
there but for a second and I'm sure that she too
is the one,
I know I have to get off

*M'goi     M'goi     M'goi     Yao Lok*

because this Hong Kong nocturne has grown
as inevitable as birth, as elastic as gender, as loud as creation.

# Do Not Talk to That Girl

## 2002

*Albert Tan*

Do not talk to that girl anymore,
Or your head will be cut off.
Endure, Endure, Tolerance.

The girl is merely a passer-by,
We'll just meet for half a minute,
So do not talk to that girl anymore.

You are left behind,
An angry look is in front,
Endure, Endure, Tolerance.

It is *your* fault,
No matter how much you apologize,
Do not talk to that girl anymore.

You find no reason to be like that,
But because you are you and it's fate,
Endure, Endure, Tolerance.

The Judge is always correct,
There is no room for misunderstanding,
Do not talk to that girl anymore,
Endure, Endure, Tolerance.

# References for Selections

**PROSE** (in chronological order as per table of contents)

**Novel Excerpts**

Preface, Ch. 3 excerpt 'Rich Man Poor Man', Ch. 6 'Hong Kong Profiles', and Ch. 10 'Amour Profane' from *A Many Splendored Thing* by Han Suyin. Signet Books, New York, 1955, pp. xi–xii, pp. 26–30, pp. 121–3 and pp. 169–71. First published by Jonathan Cape, London, 1952.

Ch. 3 excerpt from *The World of Suzie Wong* by Richard Mason. Pegasus Books, Publishers Associates Ltd., Hong Kong, 1996, pp. 22–27. First published by William Collins Sons & Co., Ltd., 1957.

Epigraph and Ch. 1 from *Kampoon Street* by Lin Tai-Yi. The World Publishing Company, Cleveland and New York, 1964, pp. 14–22.

Ch. 1 from *The Virgin Market* by C. Y. Lee. Alvin Redman, London, 1965, pp. 1–8.

Excerpt from *The Chinese Box* by Christopher New. Asia 2000 Ltd., Hong Kong, 2001, pp. 63–66. First published by W. H. Allen, London, 1975.

Ch. 11 excerpt from *The Monkey King* by Timothy Mo. Paddleless Press, London, 2000, pp. 92–96. First published by André Deutsch Ltd., Great Britain, 1978.

Ch. 1 excerpt from *Running Dog* by Lee Ding Fai. Heinemann Asia, Hong Kong, 1980, pp. 1–6.

Ch. 3 excerpt from *Sour Sweet* by Timothy Mo. An Aventura Original, Random House Inc., New York/Canada, 1985, pp. 41–44. First published by Sphere Books, London, 1982.

Ch. 6 excerpt from *Struggle of a Hong Kong Girl* by Lily Chan, ed. by Anne Wong. Vantage Press, New York, 1986, pp. 169–73.

Ch. 13 from *A Change of Flag* by Christopher New. Asia 2000 Ltd., Hong Kong, 2001, and pp. 227–32. First published by Bantam, New York, 1990.

*The Iron Tree* by Martin Booth. Pocket Books, Great Britain, 1994, pp. 12–19. First published by Simon and Schuster Ltd., Great Britain, 1993.

Part One Ch. 1 excerpt from *A Chinese Wedding* by Simon Elegant. Judy Piatakus Publishers, London, 1994, pp. 3–9.

'4:05 pm' excerpt from *Asian Values* by Nury Vittachi. A Chameleon Hellman & Schoenberg Book, O'Donald Publications Ltd., Hong Kong, 1996, pp. 35–40.

Ch. 1 excerpt from *Hong Kong Rose* by Xu Xi. Asia 2000, Hong Kong, 1997, pp. 17–21.

Ch. 4 and Ch. 5 excerpts from *All The King's Women* by Mimi Chan, Hong Kong University Press, Hong Kong, 2000, pp. 66–69 and pp. 87–89.

Ch. 10 excerpt from *Renegade or Halo²* by Timothy Mo, Paddleless Press, London, 2000, pp. 181–4 and 201–6.

Ch. 5 excerpt from *The Unwalled City* by Xu Xi. Chameleon Press, Hong Kong, 2001, pp. 41–46.

## Short Stories

'The Thrush and the Snail' and 'The Captain' by Rodney Davey. *Imprint* 2, University of Hong Kong, 1980.

'Lost River' and 'Red, Amber, Green' by David T. K. Wong. *Lost River and Other Stories,* Asia 2000 Ltd., Hong Kong, 1990.

'The Cocktail Party' by David T. K. Wong. *Hong Kong Stories,* CDN Publishing, Hong Kong, 1996.

'Valediction' by Xu Xi. *Chinese Walls & Daughters of Hui,* Chameleon Press, Hong Kong, 2002. First published by Asia 2000, Hong Kong, 1996.

'A Final Appeal: Three Weddings at Tuen Mun' by Yang Yi Lung (John D. Young). Unpublished manuscript, Hong Kong, 1996.

'Lau the Tailor' by Charles Philip Martin. *Manoa,* 10:1, University of Hawaii Press, Honolulu, 1998.

'Transcript t/23-098076/89' by Simon Elegant. *dimsum,* 1:1, Chameleon Press, Hong Kong, 1999.

'The One-Legged Rickshaw Boy' by Lawrence Gray. *dimsum,* 1:2, Chameleon Press, Hong Kong, 1999.

'The Catholic All-Star Chess Team' by Alex Kuo. *Lipstick and Other Stories,* Asia 2000 Ltd., Hong Kong, 2001. First published in *dimsum,* 1:4, Chameleon Press, Hong Kong, 2000.

'Mysterious Properties' by Nury Vittachi. *The Feng Shui Detective,* Chameleon Press, Hong Kong, 2000.

'Conversion of a Village Ghost' by Jane Camens. MFA Thesis, Vermont College, Montpelier, VT, 2001, manuscript copy.

'Until the Next Century' by Xu Xi. *History's Fiction,* Chameleon Press, Hong Kong, 2001. First published in *Carve,* 2:1, USA, 2001.

'Walking on the Melting Ice' by Hark Yeung from author's manuscript, forthcoming story collection, Hong Kong, 2001.

## Essays

'Why Compromise? Get Divorced Instead' by Nury Vittachi. *Only in Hong Kong.* South China Morning Post Ltd., Hong Kong, 1993.

'Thanks for the Memories' by Yang Yi Lung (John D. Young). *Asia Magazine,* Hong Kong, 18–20 October 1996, The 'Sting' column.

'Colonial Life and Times' by Charles Philip Martin. *South China Morning Post, Postmagazine,* Hong Kong, 13 July 1997, the 'charlesmartin' column.

'Uneasy Riders' by Jesse Wong. *Lives in Transition*, a collection of articles from *The Asian Wall Street Journal*, Dow Jones & Company, Inc., 1997.

Ch. 7 from *Our Elders* by Hark Yeung and Fong So. Fong & Yeung Studios, Hong Kong, 2000.

Two excerpts of 'Season of Storms' by Nury Vittachi. *North Wind,* Chameleon Press, Hong Kong, 2001, pp. 19–20 and pp. 83–85.

## Memoirs

'The District and the World' from *Myself a Mandarin* by Austin Coates. Heinemann, Hong Kong, Singapore, Kuala Lumpur, 1968, pp. 217–28.

Ch. 18 excerpt 'Learning About People' and Ch. 26 'Transport, Triads and Intrigue' from *Crusade for Justice* by Elsie Elliot (Elsie Tu). Heinemann Asia, Hong Kong, Singapore, Kuala Lumpur, 1981, pp. 176–83 and pp. 238–46.

'Breaking In' and excerpt of 'City View' from *I am Jackie Chan* by Jackie Chan with Jeff Yang. Ballantine Books, New York, 1998, pp. 131–5.

## POETRY (in alphabetical order by poet)

### Ambacher, Brent

'Trying to Find the Name of Love, Again', and 'Learning New Steps' from *Vs,* Big Weather Press, Hong Kong, 1993.

'A Four-Inch Beam Seems Narrower One Hundred Feet from the Ground' from *Tolo Lights: An Evening of English & Chinese Poetry Readings,* The Chinese University of Hong Kong, 10 March 1993.

'One Perfect Kiss' from *Tolo Lights: A Collection of Chinese and English Poems,* compiled by Andrew Parkin and Wu Ningkun, Shaw College, The Chinese University of Hong Kong, 1995.

### Baker, Barbara

'Courtship in Hong Kong' from *Round,* Asia 2000 Ltd., Hong Kong, 1998.

### Barrett, Dean

'At the Cemetery Above Happy Valley Racetrack' from *Hong Kong: Images on Shifting Waters,* an anthology compiled by Joyce Hsia and T. C. Lai, Kelly & Walsh, Hong Kong, 1977.

**Blunden, Edmund**

'A Hong Kong House', 'An Island Tragedy', and 'On Lamma Island' from *Hong Kong: Images on Shifting Waters*, an anthology compiled by Joyce Hsia and T. C. Lai, Kelly & Walsh, Hong Kong, 1977.

**Booth, Martin**

'Those Not Swimming', 'Dead Bones', and 'Martin Booth on a Poet' from *Hong Kong: Images on Shifting Waters,* an anthology compiled by Joyce Hsia and T. C. Lai, Kelly & Walsh, Hong Kong, 1977.

**Chen, Juliette (Tran Ngoc Linh)**

'Face', 'Dinner with an Eligible Bachelor', and 'Night Folk' from *The Bluest Part of the Harbour,* ed. Andrew Parkin, Oxford University Press, Hong Kong, Oxford, New York, 1995.

**Fitzpatrick, Liam**

'The Hot Bus' from *Tolo Lights: An Evening of English & Chinese Poetry Readings,* The Chinese University of Hong Kong, 10 March 1993.

'The Garden', 'The Passing Train', and 'Home' from *Vs,* Big Weather Press, Hong Kong, 1993.

**Ho, Louise**

'Prose Poems I and II' from *Tolo Lights: An Evening of English & Chinese Poetry Readings,* The Chinese University of Hong Kong, 10 March 1993.

'City', 'Pop Song 1: "At Home in Hong Kong" 1964', 'Pop Song 2: "Hong Kong Soul"', 'Home to Hong Kong', and 'Well Spoken Cantonese' from *Local Habitation,* Twilight Books, Hong Kong, 1994.

'New Year's Eve, 1989' from *The Bluest Part of the Harbour,* ed. Andrew Parkin, Oxford University Press, Hong Kong, Oxford, New York, 1995.

'Meeting', 'Island', 'Flags and Flowers', 'Hong Kong Riots, 1967 I', 'Hong Kong Riots, 1967 II', and 'Migratory' from *New Ends Old Beginnings,* Asia 2000 Ltd., Hong Kong, 1997.

**Ismail, Jamila (Jam)**

'from kid inglish', 'translit', 'goon yum', and 'wooway' from *West Coast Line,* Vancouver, 1997.

'ratio quality' from *Dialogue Among Civilizations Through Poetry: Hong Kong Poetry Readings,* The Chinese University of Hong Kong, 28 March 2001.

**Kaiser, Timothy**

'My Father-in-Law at Twenty' from author's manuscript. Earlier version appeared in *Yuan Yang* 1, Department of English, the University of Hong Kong, 2000.

'eradication' and 'Lunch Hour Detention with Little Ming' from *Dialogue Among Civilizations Through Poetry: Hong Kong Poetry Readings,* The Chinese University of Hong Kong, 31 March 2001.

### Kuo, Alex

'The Immigrant', 'The Picture', and 'There are Many Ways to Listen' from *Changing the River,* I. Reed Books, Berkley, California, 1986.

'Coming into Beijing', 'The Day the War Ended', and 'The River' from *This Fierce Geography,* Limberlost Press, Boisie, Idaho, 1999.

### Lam, Agnes

'First Draft', 'Petals', and 'My Mother-in-Law' from *Woman to Woman*, Asia 2000 Ltd., Hong Kong, 1997.

'Apology' from *dimsum* 1:3, Chameleon Press, Hong Kong, 2000.

'White Dust', 'You Say', 'Writing in the Middle of the Road', 'Water Wood Pure Splendour', 'A Song from the Moon', and 'I Have Walked on Air' from *Water Wood Pure Splendour,* Asia 2000 Ltd., Hong Kong, 2001.

### Leung, Ho Hon

'A Commodity in a Pure Competitive Market', 'After the Three Characters' and 'An Old Man in Hong Kong' from *Bridge,* Vol. 8, No. 4, 1983.

### Leung, Ping-kwan (Ye Si)

'At the North Point Car Ferry', 'The Leaf on the Edge', 'An Old Colonial Building', and 'Images of Hong Kong' from *City at the End of Time,* Leung Ping-kwan translated with Gordon T. Osing, Twilight Books in association with the Department of Comparative Literature, the University of Hong Kong, Hong Kong, 1992.

'Leaf of Passage' from *World Englishes* 19:3, Blackwell Publishers, Oxford and Boston, November 2000.

'Still-life' from author's manuscript, 2001.

'Tiger Balm Gardens' and 'Leafing Through Wingo and Holly's Photo Albums' from *Travelling with a Bitter Melon*, Asia 2000 Ltd., Hong Kong, 2002.

### Lim, Shirley Geok-lin

'Passports' from *Yuan Yang* 1, Department of English, the University of Hong Kong, 2000.

### Moss, Peter

'Western Approaches' from *Hong Kong: Images on Shifting Waters*, an anthology compiled by Joyce Hsia and T.C. Lai, Kelly & Walsh, Hong Kong, 1977.

**Parkin, Andrew**

'In the Forum at the Chinese University' from *Tolo Lights: An Evening of English & Chinese Poetry Readings,* The Chinese University of Hong Kong, 10 March 1993.

'Shadows of Morning' from *Tolo Lights: A Collection of Chinese and English Poems,* compiled by Andrew Parkin and Wu Ningkun, Shaw College, The Chinese University of Hong Kong, 1995.

'Hong Kong Tanka', 'Astronaut', 'On a Mountain above Tolo Harbour', and 'Song of an Illegal Immigrant' from *Hong Kong Poems* by Andrew Parkin & Laurence Wong, Ronsdale Press, Vancouver, Canada, 1997.

**Rao, Mani**

'2 14' from *The Last Beach,* Asia 2000 Ltd., Hong Kong, 1999.

'Keep Talking' from *salt,* Asia 2000 Ltd., Hong Kong, 2000.

'Let Us Move from Lonely to Alone' from *Outloud: An Anthology of Contemporary Poetry from Outloud Readings,* Xtraloud Press, Hong Kong, 2002. First published in *Dialogue Among Civilizations Through Poetry: Hong Kong Poetry Readings,* The Chinese University of Hong Kong, 28 March 2001.

**Slavick, Madeleine M.**

'Passage' and 'Mongkok Market' from *Round,* Asia 2000 Ltd., Hong Kong, 1998.

'Looking' from *Dialogue Among Civilizations Through Poetry: Hong Kong Poetry Readings,* The Chinese University of Hong Kong, 28 March 2001.

'Mid-Levels Front Door' from *Outloud: An Anthology of Contemporary Poetry from Outloud Readings,* Xtraloud Press, Hong Kong, 2002. First published in *English New,* ed. Chiu Man Yin and Christopher Kelen, The University of Macau, 2001.

**Sulke, Walter**

'Hong Kong — An Unfinished Symphony for Five Million Instruments' from *Hong Kong: Images on Shifting Waters,* an anthology compiled by Joyce Hsia and T. C. Lai, Kelly & Walsh, Hong Kong, 1977.

**Wong-Chu, Jim**

'fourth uncle', 'the old country', and 'old chinese cemetery kamloops july 1977' from *Chinatown Ghosts,* Vancouver, Canada, 1984.

'how feel I do?' from *Swallowing Clouds: An Anthology of Chinese-Canadian Poetry,* ed. Andy Quan and Jim Wong-Chu, Arsenal Pulp Press, Vancouver, Canada, 1999.

**Wong, Laurence Kwok-pun**

'I Fear I May Grow Old Before Frost Fall', 'The Great Bell of Yongle', and 'Rhapsody on a

Rainy Night' from *Hong Kong Poems* by Andrew Parkin and Laurence Wong, Ronsdale Press, Vancouver, Canada, 1997.

'Dawn in the Mid-Levels' from *First Hong Kong International Poetry Festival — A Collection of Poems: Hong Kong in the Decimal System and HK1997,* ed. Florence Lam, Hong Kong Arts Centre and Provisional Regional Council 1998, Hong Kong, 1998.

**Yuen, Che-hung**

'Unfinished Poems' and 'Grandma Is Dead' from *Tolo Lights: An Evening of English & Chinese Poetry Readings,* The Chinese University of Hong Kong, 10 March 1993.

## NEW VOICES (in chronological order as per table of contents)

### Novel Excerpts

*The Monkey Trap* by Andrew Barker, unpublished manuscript, Hong Kong, 2002.

### Short Stories

'Bid for Carpet Woven with Memories' by Divya Vaze from *South China Morning Post,* short story competition, 26 November 1999.

'Press Enter' by Lex Lao from *dimsum* 1:3, Chameleon Press, Hong Kong, 2000.

'Back Street' by Nicole Wong Chun Chi from *Yuan Yang* 1, Department of English, the University of Hong Kong, 2000.

'The Perfect Day' by Iris Eu from *Yuan Yang* 2, Department of English, the University of Hong Kong, 2001.

'To Victoria Park' by Chun-kit Fan (Keat Fan Chun-kit) from *CU Writing in English,* Vol. 1, Hong Kong, 2001.

'Addiction' by Nancy Tsui Yuk Chun from *CU Writing in English,* Vol. 1, Hong Kong, 2001.

### Essays and Memoirs

'Tuesday 3rd June, 1997' excerpt, 'Thursday 5th June, 1997', 'Friday 18th July, 1997' by David McKirdy from *Colonial Courtship*, unpublished manuscript, Hong Kong, 1997.

'Life's Wonderful' by Wong Ho Yin from *Literary Life, HK I-Mail,* Hong Kong, 3 April 2001, pp. A20.

### Poetry

'My Probe' by Anita Cheung from *World Englishes* 19:3, Blackwell Publishers, Oxford and Boston, November 2000.

'Fried Chestnuts' by Michelle Fok Ka Ling from *Yuan Yang* 1, Department of English, the University of Hong Kong, 2000.

'The Kite' by W. H. Y. Wong Ho Yin from *Yuan Yang* 1, Department of English, the University of Hong Kong, 2000; *World Englishes* 19:3, Blackwell Publishers, Oxford and Boston, November 2000.

'Yau Ma Tei Early 80s' by Winnie Cheung Wing Yee from *Yuan Yang* 2, Department of English, the University of Hong Kong, 2001.

'She asked "Who is Franz Kafka?" ' by Raslo Layton from *English New,* ed. Chiu Man Yin and Christopher Kelen, The University of Macau, 2001.

'Caterpillar' by Li Wai Iu, unpublished poem, 2001.

'Life on a Treadmill' by Chloe C. Li, *The Silence Within,* an anthology by poetry.com, 2001.

'The Tear Collector' by Sharon Sung Sau Fun from *Yuan Yang* 2, Department of English, the University of Hong Kong, 2001.

'Coming Through' by Canti Lui from *Jacuzzi* Volume 1, Department of English, Lingnan University, Hong Kong, 2002.

'Please' excerpted from 'Hong Kong Nocturne' by Ted Mathys from *Outloud: An Anthology of Contemporary Poetry from Outloud Readings,* Xtraloud Press, Hong Kong, 2002.

'Do Not Talk to That Girl' by Albert Tan from *Jacuzzi* Volume 1, Department of English, Lingnan University, Hong Kong, 2002.